Responsible Tourism

Critical Issues for Conservation and Development

Edited by
Anna Spenceley

publishing for a sustainable future

London • Sterling, VA

First published in hardback by Earthscan in the UK and USA in 2008
First published in paperback in 2010

ISBN: 978-1-84971-070-1

Typeset by MapSet Ltd, Gateshead, UK
Cover design by Rob Watts

For a full list of publications please contact:

Earthscan
Dunstan House
14a St Cross Street
London, EC1N 8XA, UK
Tel: +44 (0)20 7841 1930
Fax: +44 (0)20 7242 1474
Email: earthinfo@earthscan.co.uk
Web: **www.earthscan.co.uk**

22883 Quicksilver Drive, Sterling, VA 20166-2012, USA

Earthscan publishes in association with the International Institute for Environment and Development

A catalogue record for this book is available from the British Library

Library of Congress Cataloging-in-Publication Data

Responsible tourism : critical issues for conservation and development / edited by Anna Spenceley
    p. cm.
  ISBN 978-1-84407-639-0 (hardback)
  1. Tourism–Africa, Southern. 2. Biodiversity conservation–Africa, Southern. 3. Economic
development–Africa, Southern. I. Spenceley, Anna.
  G155.A312R47 2008
  338.4'79168–dc22

                                                                            2008016069

This book was printed in the UK by MPG Books,
an ISO 14001 accredited company.
The paper used is FSC certified.

Mixed Sources
Product group from well-managed
forests and other controlled sources
www.fsc.org Cert no. SA-COC-1565
© 1996 Forest Stewardship Council
FSC

Contents

UCB
179204

Part I Policies, Institutional Interventions and Market Forces

Part 2 Responsible Nature-based Tourism

Part 3 Community-based Tourism

Part 4 Conclusions

List of Figures, Tables and Boxes

Figures

Tables

Boxes

List of Contributors

Editor

Dr Anna Spenceley is an independent consultant and researcher based in South Africa who focuses on responsible tourism and sustainable development issues, mainly in emerging economies. Her doctoral research with the International Centre for Responsible Tourism led to the development of a multi-disciplinary Sustainable Nature-Based Tourism Assessment Toolkit, and her post-doctoral research fellowships at the University of the Witwatersrand focused on the economic impacts of the Great Limpopo Transfrontier Conservation Area. Anna is a member of a number of professional associations including two World Conservation Union (IUCN) World Commission on Protected Areas Task Forces, the IUCN's Southern African Sustainable Use Specialist Group (SASUSG), and is a director of the International Centre of Responsible Tourism – South Africa. She consults for a range of international and local agencies, including the World Bank, the International Finance Corporation, the International Trade Centre of the United Nations Conference on Trade and Development and the UN World Tourism Organization. Contact details: annaspenceley@gmail.com. Website: www.anna.spenceley.co.uk.

Authors

Caroline Ashley is a senior research associate of the Overseas Development Institute. Her work for the Department for International Development (DFID) in 1999 coined the phrase 'Pro Poor Tourism' (PPT) and put PPT on the international agenda. She established and ran the Overseas Development Institute's (ODI) Tourism Programme until moving to Tunis in 2005. Her pioneering research into how the impacts of tourism on the poor can be enhanced has focused heavily on the role of the private sector and changing business practice. She is now developing methods for assessing and adapting tourism value chains, to enhance participation of the poor. Her numerous publications include guidelines both for businesses and government. Beyond tourism, she works with the African Development Bank and ODI on how big business can enhance the development of small enterprises. Contact details: c.ashley@odi.org.uk.

Dr Jonathan Barnes is a South African national, and specialist in environmental and resource economics based in Namibia. He is trained in both ecology and economics and has a PhD in economics from the University of London in the UK. His professional experience has embraced economic and policy analysis, land use and development planning, and natural resources assessment, mainly concerning wildlife, fisheries, forestry, rangelands and agriculture. Contact details: jibarnes@iafrica.com.na.

Steve Collins is a rural development facilitator and is currently the managing director of J&J Bioenergy, based in Johannesburg. Prior to this position he worked for GTZ for five years implementing Community-Based Natural Resource Management in South Africa. A part of his portfolio for GTZ involved facilitating the People and Parks process in South Africa, advising communities and government on how to implement progressive community based conservation policies. He is a board member of the African Safari Lodge Foundation and the National Project Coordinator for TRANSFORM from 2001 to 2007. Contact details: steve@jandjgroup.com.

Louise Dixey is a PhD researcher and associate staff member at the International Centre for Responsible Tourism in Leeds Metropolitan University. Her doctoral research focuses on economic informality, collective action and pro-poor tourism development in Africa through an examination of the developmental consequences of a trade association, the Association of Small-Scale Enterprises in Tourism (ASSET), in The Gambia. Louise has ten years' professional experience in tourism, mainly in community-based tourism development in east and southern Africa and the Caribbean. Contact details: L.Dixey@leedsmet.ac.uk.

Nicole Frey holds a Masters degree in Marketing from the University of Cape Town (UCT) School of Management Studies. Nicole is a lecturer, researcher and supervisor in marketing at UCT. She has also contributed to various tourism management books and has consulted on strategic marketing strategies in the public and private sector including Cape Town Tourism, Limpopo Tourism and Parks, Graham Paddock and Associates, the Unilever Institute and Viglietti Motors. Contact details: nicole.frey@uct.ac.za.

Dr Richard George is a senior lecturer in tourism management and services marketing at UCT. He holds a PhD in marketing from UCT. His research interests include safety and security issues in tourism and tourism marketing. He is the author of several academic books and articles related to these topics, in particular, *Marketing South African Tourism*, 3rd Edition, Oxford University Press Southern Africa and *Managing Tourism in South Africa*, Oxford University Press Southern Africa. He has consulted widely for a number of public and private sector tourism organizations in South Africa including Spier Wine Estate, Limpopo Tourism and Parks, Cape Town Tourism and Polokwane Municipality. Contact details: richard.george@uct.ac.za.

Gareth Haysom is employed by the Sustainability Institute as the programme coordinator of the Sustainable Agriculture Programme and is appointed by Stellenbosch University in the School of Public Management and Planning as an extra-ordinary lecturer. He has a Diploma in Hotel Management and spent many years managing various tourism and hotel facilities in various parts of South Africa. In 2007 he graduated cum laude with an MPhil in sustainable development planning and management from Stellenbosch University, with a research project that developed a strategic development planning framework for the Western Cape town of Grabouw. He has extensive experience in management, entrepreneurial development, project facilitation, research and more recently in educational facilitation in the sustainable agriculture field. Contact details: duffhaysom@mweb.co.za.

Peter John Massyn has extensive experience in tourism as a form of rural development. He has worked in the private sector as a tourism entrepreneur and a consultant in the fields of tourism, conservation, development and land reform. He is currently executive director of the African Safari Lodge Foundation, and an independent consultant to various clients including the International Finance Corporation. Contact details: pjm@global.co.za.

Joseph E. Mbaiwa is a senior research fellow in tourism studies at the Harry Oppenheimer Okavango Research Centre, University of Botswana. His research focus is on tourism development, rural livelihoods and conservation in the Okavango Delta, Botswana. He has so far co-authored a book on tourism and the environment in the Okavango Delta, published over 25 journal articles, 10 book chapters and several conference papers on tourism development, livelihoods and conservation in the Okavango Delta. His PhD was awarded by the Department of Recreation, Park and Tourism Sciences, Texas A&M University in April 2008. Contact details: JMbaiwa@orc.ub.bw.

Hitesh Mehta is one of the world's leading authorities, practitioners and researchers on ecotourism physical planning and both the landscape architectural and architectural aspects of ecolodges. He also has vast experience in protected area physical planning and has worked on sustainable tourism plans in 20 countries. After ten years of working with EDSA, (Florida) the world's largest landscape architecture and planning firm, Mr Mehta has re-started (January 2007) his firm HM Design, which began in Kenya in 1991. Mr Mehta is currently working on five ecolodge projects in Belize, Indonesia, Rwanda, Dominica and Uganda, and a Conceptual Tourism Master Plan in Costa Rica. He is the main editor of the *International Ecolodge Guidelines* and the author of the chapters on 'Site Planning' and 'Architectural Design'. Mr Mehta regularly conducts research on international trends in Ecolodges and is currently writing a new book – *Authentic Ecolodges*. He sits on the executive board of The International Ecotourism Society, advisory boards of Adventure Council, *Green Travel Magazine* and BIOSFERA (Brazilian Environmental Society), and is one of the founding members of Ecotourism Kenya. Mr Mehta is the international advisor for the Japan Ecolodge Association and the French Ecotourism Association. Contact details: mehta_h@bellsouth.net.

Fred Nelson has worked on community-based natural resource management, ecotourism and conservation policy in eastern Africa since 1998. From 2000–2005 he served as the first Tanzania programme director for the Sand County Foundation Community Based Conservation Network, working with a number of pastoralist communities in northern Tanzania and helping to establish the Tanzania Natural Resource Forum. In 2007 he founded Maliasili Initiatives, a consulting firm working to address biodiversity conservation and natural resource management challenges using innovative, collaborative and market-based strategies. He is a member of the IUCN Southern Africa Sustainable Use Specialist Group and IUCN Commission on Environmental, Economic, and Social Policy. Contact details: fnelson@habari.co.tz.

Michaela Pawliczek, based in Madagascar, is working as a tourism specialist for the World Bank/International Finance Corporation's ecotourism programme as well as managing the local green portfolio of the Kreditanstalt für Wiederaufbau (KfW). Both positions focus on ecotourism development in Madagascar (e.g. development and implementation of a concessioning policy to improve the viability of Madagascar's National Parks, and facilitation and promotion of opportunities for future ecotourism investors). Previously she was an advisor as a German Government official (CIM) to the National Malagasy Tourism Board (ONTM) on its promotion, marketing and ecotourism activities. She also assisted as a senior project manager on the development of the official Malagasy Tourism Masterplan and supported the tourism programme of the United Nation's Environment Programme (UNEP) as a consultant focusing on work for the Tour Operators' Initiative (TOI). Facilitated by Germany's second largest tour operator, Rewe Touristik GmbH, her PhD thesis was on the 'Development of an internal Environment-Benchmarking-System for tour operators' hotel suppliers'. Contact details: mp@michaela-pawliczek.de.

Piers Relly is an independent consultant specializing in the tourism sector. He has over 20 years experience in the private sector, playing roles in accounting and finance, investment, marketing and property development. He combines his background in these areas, offering services to the tourism sector in developing countries. With an MA in tourism studies, he assists government clients with macroeconomic policy issues through to single enterprises and community-based tourism projects. He is a member of three professional bodies and has held a number of directorships in private enterprises. Contact details: prelly@intekom.co.za.

Andrew Rylance is an independent consultant in local economic development with international experience. Based in South Africa, he specializes in small business development, monitoring and evaluating, strategic assessments and community-based enterprise management. Andrew has received an MA from the

University of KwaZulu-Natal, South Africa. His dissertation identified the constraints that prevent the growth of market sellers and highlights possible opportunities that will strengthen their position within the value chain. He also facilitates workshops and participatory group forums with community groups and small business owners. Contact: andrewrylance@gmail.com. Website: http://andrewrylance.googlepages.com/.

Dr Murray C. Simpson is a senior research associate at Oxford University Centre for the Environment and is principal of Sustainable Solutions Worldwide tourism consultancy. He has extensive experience in sustainable development, responsible tourism, climate change and the environment and has worked at chief executive management level in the tourism industry and in the public sector at board level. Murray has worked with the public and the private sector on a range of tourism initiatives including sustainable tourism development, tourism strategy, tourism analysis and climate change adaptation, and mitigation projects in developed and developing countries, and in small island states; bridging the gap between research, policy and implementation. He has worked in Europe, UK, Australasia, South Africa, the US, Asia, South America and the Caribbean. International organizations he has worked with include the European Development Fund, the Association of Caribbean States, the European Union, UN agencies and the European Travel Commission. Among other committee positions and memberships, Murray is a fellow of the Royal Geographical Society and a member of the United Nations World Tourism Organization Panel of Tourism Experts. Contact details: murray.simpson@ouce.ox.ac.uk.

Herman Snel is an agro-ecologist and rural development anthropologist. He has been working on sustainable rural development, and environmental issues throughout Latin America and Africa as a researcher and development practitioner. His work centres on political ecology, socio-environmental conflict, land reform, migration and colonization, devolution and decentralization, poverty alleviation and local economic development, community-based natural resource management, community forestry and forestry certification, agroforestry, biological agriculture, co-management arrangements, management of biosphere reserves, national parks and buffer zones, organizational development and public–private partnerships related to natural resource management. He coordinates the work on 'Lessons Learned' for the TRANSFORM program. Contact details: herman.snel@gmail.com.

Helen Suich is a development and resource economist. She works on issues relating to poverty alleviation, sustainable economic development, natural resource management and valuation, primarily in southern Africa. Contact details: helensuich@yahoo.co.uk.

Giju Varghese is a trained hotelier and holds a bachelors degree in Hotel Management (Mangalore University, India). After several years of managing hotels and similar establishments in related fields, his expertise, interest and career took a focus on organizational development and turnaround. He then went on to receive an MBA (De Montfort University, UK) and continued his career focus to a broader industry base. His technical understanding of the tourism industry has made him an authority in public–private partnerships in the nature based tourism environment. Giju's career as the head of business development with the South African National Parks ensured the principles of responsible tourism were achieved through public–private partnerships arguably at a higher level than any other organization in the nature-based tourism field. He advises various public and private sector companies on tourism strategy development and execution. He also makes presentations at various forums. Contact details: GijuV@sanparks.org.

Independent reviewers

To enhance the quality of papers presented in this book, a number of academics and practitioners generously provided independent reviews and comments on the contributions, which authors used to strengthen their papers. The reviewers were:

Caroline Ashley, ODI
Sylvie Blangy, Carleton University
Dr Dan Brockington, University of Manchester
Dr Janet Cochrane, International Centre for Responsible Tourism
Richard Davies, Busico cc
Dr Xavier Font, International Centre for Responsible Tourism
Dr Nicole Häusler, Mas Contour
Dr Martha Honey, Center on Ecotourism and Sustainable Development
Brian Jones, Environment and development consultant
Dr David Leslie, Glasgow Caledonian University
Myles Mander, FutureWorks!
Shaun Mann, World Bank
Hitesh Mheta, HM Design
Dr Martin Mowforth, University of Plymouth
Dr Simon Munthali, African Wildlife Foundation
Paula Nimpuno, Ford Foundation
Dr Harry Wells, VU University Amsterdam

Foreword

Once I had the chance to talk with a woman from a poor and remote village, where she ran a small home-stay by renting out a room in her house for tourists. I asked her how many tourists she received last year, and she told me proudly that she had hosted eight people. At first I thought that this was only a few visitors, but then I thought I would find out what this meant in her context. Therefore, I asked her how the visit of eight tourists helped her and her family. She told me that it was very important because with the money received from the tourists she could send her kids to school. I was completely overwhelmed.

Tourism is perhaps the most remarkable socioeconomic phenomenon of modern times. It is an activity that has become an integral part of modern societies, both in developed and developing countries. According to the World Tourism Organization, there were almost 900 million international tourists recorded in 2007, and domestic tourism is similarly booming worldwide. While tourism is now a global activity propelled by technological development in communication, information and transportation, it is ultimately about providing local experiences and supporting local livelihoods in both urban and rural settings, and in developed and poor regions as well. The message to take from the anecdote above is that we should never underestimate the difference that tourism can make to people's lives, even at a very small scale. This shows clearly the importance of tourism in contributing towards development and poverty reduction efforts. Tourism has been formally recognized as a key contributing factor towards the Millennium Development Goals. There are many reasons to support this: tourism is an amalgam of various sectors, and therefore it can provide a wide range of employment and business opportunities – even in remote and poor areas where few other options exist. It is a labour-intensive activity providing jobs for the youth, elderly and women as well. The entry costs for tourism businesses are relatively low, therefore the industry can support many small enterprises.

Nevertheless, tourism can only fulfil its potential if it is developed in a planned and responsible manner, ensuring the long-term sustainability of the sector. Simply put, this means that tourism development needs to ensure the conservation of the natural and cultural environment of destinations, it needs to create viable business and economic benefits to host communities, and it has to provide a high quality tourist experience. To achieve these goals policy makers and managers should apply a range of tools and practices. To adopt an appropriate combination of these techniques, it is essential to learn from past experiences. This publication analyses a range of case studies, and, based on them, provides pragmatic and practical recommendations. It is vital to understand what works and what does not work in order to avoid mistakes made in the past and improve current operations.

There is a rich experience of responsible tourism in Africa, and there is a huge need to transfer this knowledge in order to harness the force of tourism for poverty reduction in a continent that harbours the largest number of Least Developed Countries. The editor and authors contributing to this book have worked extensively in various countries of this region, focusing on a major tourism product of African countries: nature-based tourism linked with community-based and cultural tourism attractions. The complex conditions of tourism development and management are systematically analysed in this publication, drawn from first hand professional experience and based on real evidence. I warmly recommend this book to all professionals who feel committed to embrace tourism as a vector for development, for empowering people, for conserving habitats and wildlife and the integrity of communities living in and around them.

Gabor Vereczi
Chief, Environment and Quality Section
Sustainable Development of Tourism Department
World Tourism Organization (UNWTO)
31 March 2008

Preface

What is this book about?

Tourism is increasingly purported to have an important role to play in poverty alleviation, particularly in developing countries. Tourism is an industry that governments and international development agencies increasingly promote, not as a panacea, but as one of the potential livelihood options for the poor and marginalized members of society.

This book is essentially a tangible response to the questions frequently asked about whether tourism can be used as a development tool – for both biodiversity conservation and poverty alleviation. Increasingly, agencies working in southern Africa endorse tourism as a sustainable livelihood and private sector mechanism to support conservation and alleviate poverty. However, currently there are only fragmented case studies and vague policy papers that exist to justify such an approach. There are large amounts of highly relevant data that explore the linkages between tourism, poverty and conservation hidden in practitioners' consultancy reports, but these are only disseminated within peer-reviewed journals and books in a fragmented manner. Therefore, this book provides systematic and tangible evidence of the successes and failures of tourism to fight poverty, and to enhance conservation, by presenting information directly drawn from the practitioners and researchers across the region.

Therefore, the aim of this book is to help guide the agenda of governments and development agencies in a more focused and output-oriented way. This compendium of contributions systematically demonstrates important new findings which can be applied by stakeholders engaged in tourism interventions to maximize their positive impacts. If governments and development agencies use improved interventions in tourism-oriented programmes, they will ultimately be able to catalyse sustainable long-term opportunities for impoverished people to improve their livelihoods through tourism.

Who will find this book useful?

This book will be useful for academics and students working in the fields of tourism studies (particularly on responsible and sustainable tourism), environmental studies, protected area management, development studies, business studies, geography and political studies.

The papers and syntheses presented here will also be useful for practitioners working in United Nations and development agencies, non-governmental organizations, private-sector tourism enterprises and their associations, protected area authorities and government departments working on tourism and local economic development.

Acknowledgements

The editor would like to thank all of the authors who contributed their time and expertise to the body of work that appears here, and also the reviewers who gave constructive comments that helped strengthen their discussions. Also, I would like to thank the two main institutions that supported the book's compilation: The Transboundary Protected Areas Research Initiative and the IUCN Southern African Sustainable Use Specialist Group.

Transboundary Protected Areas Research Initiative

The Transboundary Protected Areas Research Initiative (TPARI) is a component programme of the International Union for Conservation of Nature (IUCN) in South Africa's Communities and Conservation initiative. It is an interdisciplinary research initiative consisting of a core partnership between the Centre for Integrated Study of the Human Dimensions of Global Change at Carnegie Mellon University (CMU), Pittsburgh, and the South African office of the IUCN. TPARI relies on a network of collaborative relations with researchers and students at universities in Southern Africa, The Netherlands, Germany, the UK and the US. TPARI focuses on the human dimensions of transboundary protected areas and natural resource management. TPARI aims to develop an integrated assessment of the human and environmental dimensions for the Great Limpopo Transfrontier Park and, more broadly, the Great Limpopo Transfrontier Conservation Area (IUCN, 1995–2005).

The process of developing this book was supported by a postdoctoral research fellowship from the National Research Foundation of South Africa, which was institutionally based at the TPARI in the School of Geography, Archaeology and Environment at the University of the Witwatersrand in South Africa.

IUCN Southern African Sustainable Use Specialist Group

The mission of the IUCN is to influence, encourage and assist societies throughout the world to conserve the integrity and diversity of nature and to ensure that any use of natural resources is equitable and ecologically sustainable. The IUCN has six Commissions which are networks of volunteer scientists, experts and practitioners. The role of the IUCN's Species Survival Commission (SSC) is:

> *to provide information to IUCN on biodiversity conservation, the inherent value of species, their role in ecosystem health and functioning, the provision of ecosystem services, and their support to human livelihoods. SSC members also provide scientific advice to conservation organisations, government agencies and other IUCN members, and support the implementation of multilateral environmental agreements.*
>
> (Murphree, 2007)

The Sustainable Use Specialist Group (SUSG) of the SSC was developed to implement the IUCN Sustainable Use Initiative, an interdisciplinary initiative founded in 1995 to enhance and share knowledge of the social and biological factors affecting the sustainable use of wild renewable resources. SUSG's mission is to promote the conservation of biological diversity and alleviation of poverty by:

- *improving the understanding of the social and biological factors that enhance the sustainability of uses of wild living resources;*
- *promoting that understanding to IUCN's members, decision makers and others;*
- *assisting IUCN members, partner organizations, and governments in the application of that understanding.*

(Murphree, 2007)

The Southern African Sustainable Use Specialist Group (SASUSG) was established on 7 April 1995 in Kasane Botswana as a regional sub-group of the global IUCN SUSG. It is a voluntary body of experts, practitioners, policy makers and academics. In southern Africa, SASUSG has led the way in determining how the region would approach and communicate its own perspective on sustainable use, and this has led to various innovative approaches. SASUSG is dedicated to improving the body of knowledge on sustainable use and, through dissemination of information based on valid scientific data, to contribute to the development of natural resource management systems which are ecologically sound, economically viable, financially profitable, satisfying to the users and politically and socially acceptable within the policies and laws of the individual countries of the southern African region (Murphree, 2007).

Support for the publication of this book through Earthscan, and also production of one of the chapters (on the review of wildlife tourism in southern Africa) was generously provided to SASUSG through a grant from NORAD.

Anna Spenceley
1 April 2008

References

IUCN (World Conservation Union) (1995–2005) 'Transboundary protected areas research initiative', accessed from www.iucnsa.org.za/our_work/initiatives/tpari.htm on 12 February 2008

Murphree, M. (2007) 'Southern Africa Sustainable Use Specialist Group: Institutional review: Report of findings and recommendations', Report to the IUCN Southern Africa Sustainable Use Specialist Group, unpublished report, Pietermaritzburg South Africa

Acronyms and Abbreviations

ADMADE	Administrative Management Design for Game Management Areas (Zambia)
AFD	Agence Français de Développement
AITO	Association for Independent Tour Operators
ANGAP	Association Nationale pour la Gestion des Aires Protégées
APETUR	Association of Small Tourism Enterprises on Ilha (Mozambique)
ASSET	Association of Small-Scale Enterprises in Tourism (The Gambia)
B&B	bed and breakfast
BBBEE	Broad Based Black Economic Empowerment
BCEA	Basic Conditions of Employment Act
BDU	business development unit
BEE	Black Economic Empowerment
BIOSFERA	Brazilian Environmental Society
CAMPFIRE	Communal Areas Management Program for Indigenous Resources
CANARI	Caribbean Natural Resources Institute
CBNRM	community based natural resource management
CBOs	community based organisations (Botswana)
CBT	community-based tourism
CBTE	community-based tourism enterprise
CBTI	community benefit tourism initiative
CCA	Conservation Corporation Africa
CHAs	controlled hunting areas (Botswana)
CMU	Carnegie Mellon University
CPA	Communal Property Association
CPPP	Community–Public–Private–Partnership
CRB	Community Resource Board
CSD	Commission on Sustainable Development (UN)
CSI	corporate social investment
CSR	corporate social responsibility
CST	Certification for Sustainable Tourism
CTO	Caribbean Tourism Organization
DEAT	Department of Environmental Affairs and Tourism (South Africa)

DFID	Department for International Development (UK)
DLA	Department of Land Affairs
DMO	destination management organization
DRC	Democratic Republic of the Congo
DWNP	Department of Wildlife and National Parks (Botswana)
EAO	Escola de Artes e Ofícios (Mozambique)
EDBM	Economic Development Board of Madagascar
EMEs	exempt micro enterprises
EPRP	Export-led Poverty Reduction Programme (ITC)
EU	European Union
FTTSA	Fair Trade in Tourism South Africa
GDP	gross domestic product
GMAs	Game Management Areas
GRI	Global Reporting Initiative
GTZ	Deutsche Gesellschaft für Technische Zusammenarbeit (German Technical Co-operation (GmbH))
HDI(s)	historically disadvantaged individual(s)
HWC	human–wildlife conflict
ICRT	International Centre for Responsible Tourism
IDP	Integrated Development Plan
IFC	International Finance Corporation
IIED	International Institute of Environment and Development
IMF	International Monetary Fund
INTH	Institut National de Tourisme et d'Hôtellerie
IPEX	Institute for Export Promotion
IRTA	Imvelo Responsible Tourism Awards
ITC	International Trade Centre (UNCTAD)
IUCN	International Union for Conservation of Nature
KAZA TFCA	Kavango–Zambezi Transfrontier Conservation Area
KDT	Khwai Development Trust (Botswana)
KNP	Kruger National Park
KZN	KwaZulu-Natal
KZNNCS	KwaZulu-Natal Nature Conservation Services
LDCs	least developed countries
LED	local economic development
LOC	lodge operating company
LSA	Luangwa Safari Association (Zambia)
MAP	Madagascar Action Plan
MDGs	Millennium Development Goals (UN)
MGR	Madikwe Game Reserve (South Africa)
MIGA	Multilateral Investment Guarantee Agency
MNRT	Ministry of Natural Resources and Tourism (Tanzania)
MTENR	Ministry of Tourism, Environment and Natural Resources (Zambia)
NACSO	Namibian Association of CBNRM Support Organisations

NBSAP	National Biodiversity Strategy and Action Plan
NDFFC	Nyanga Downs Fly Fishing Club (Zimbabwe)
NEAP	National Ecotourism Accreditation Program (Australia)
NEAP3	Nature and Ecotourism Accreditation Programme
NEPAD	New Partnership for Africa's Development
NGOs	non-governmental organizations
NORAD	North American Aerospace Defense Command
NPWS	National Parks and Wildlife Services (Zambia)
NWPTB	North West Parks and Tourism Board
OAU	Organisation of African Unity
ODI	Overseas Development Institute
OKMCT	Okavango Kopano Mokoro Community Trust (Botswana)
ONE	National Office for the Environment, Madagascar
ONTM	National Malagasy Tourism Board
PARPA	Action Plan for Absolute Poverty Reduction (Mozambique)
PDEs	previously disadvantaged employees
PGRs	private game reserves
PIC	Pôle Intégré de Croissance (Madagascar)
PPP	public–private partnership
PPT	pro-poor tourism
PPT Pilots	pro-poor tourism pilots
PROFIT	Production, Finance and Technology programme (Zambia)
QSE	qualifying small enterprise
RDCs	Rural District Councils (Zimbabwe)
RETOSA	Regional Tourism Organization for Southern Africa
RTM	responsible tourism management
SADC	Southern African Development Community
SAM	social accounting matrix
SASUSG	Southern African Sustainable Use Specialist Group (IUCN)
SMMEs	small, micro and medium-sized enterprises
SNV	Netherlands Development Agency
SPTDM	Strategic Plan for Tourism Development in Mozambique
SRA	Stormsriver Adventures
SSC	Species Survival Commission (IUCN)
ST-EP	Sustainable Tourism – Eliminating Poverty
SUSG	Sustainable Use Specialist Group (SSC)
TANAPA	Tanzania National Parks
TEP	Tourism Enterprise Partnership (South Africa)
TFCA	Transfrontier Conservation Area
TGCSA	Tourism Grading Council of South Africa
THETA	Tourism, Hospitality and Sport Education and Training Authority
TIA	Travel Industry Association of America
TIES	International Ecotourism Society
TOI	Tour Operators' Initiative

TPARI	Transboundary Protected Areas Research Initiative
TRANSFORM	Training and Support for Resource Management
TSA	Tourism Satellite Account
TTCI	Travel and Tourism Competitiveness Report
UCT	University of Cape Town
UN	United Nations
UNCTAD	United Nations Commission on Trade and Development
UNDP	United Nations Development Programme
UNEP	United Nations Environment Programme
UNHCHR	United Nations High Commissioner for Human Rights
UNWTO	UN World Tourism Organization
URT	United Republic of Tanzania
USAID	United States Agency for International Development
USP	unique selling points
VAST	Village Action for Sustainable Tourism
WCS	Wildlife Conservation Society
WMA	Wildlife Management Area
WSRTF	Wildlife Sector Review Task Force
WSSD	World Summit on Sustainable Development
WTTERC	World Travel and Tourism Environment Research Centre

Introduction
Responsible Tourism in Southern Africa

Anna Spenceley

Sustainable and responsible tourism

Sustainable development

Development is a process that improves living conditions (Bartelmus, 1986) by increasing wealth (Dudley, 1993), and also by addressing human and institutional change (Hapgood, 1969). However, development is also associated with a number of environmental problems, such as pollution and climate change (Horobin and Long, 1996). In the 1970s concern for the local and global consequences of development-related degradation led to the evolution of the notion of 'sustainable development' (Basiago, 1995).

An output of the United Nations' (UN) World Commission on Environment and Development was the Brundtland Report, entitled *Our Common Future* (WCED, 1987). This landmark report suggested that intergenerational equity could not be achieved unless the environmental impacts of economic activities were considered. The report defined 'sustainable development' as that which '... *meets the needs of the present generation without compromising the ability of future generations to meet their own needs*' (WCED, 1987, p43). The definition received criticism for being vague, too general, rhetorical and impractical (e.g. Redclift, 1987), but despite this it sparked an important debate between stakeholders within government, academia and industry regarding the characteristics of sustainable development.

A decade after the Bruntland Report was published, the UN stressed the need for a holistic approach, and suggested that *economic* development, *social* development and *environmental* protection were three interdependent and mutually reinforcing components of sustainable development (UN, 1997). Elkington (1997) referred to this simultaneous pursuit of economic prosperity, environmental quality and social equity as the 'triple bottom line' of sustainable development. Elkington's (1997) book supported the view that companies were accountable for their impact on sustainability through the triple bottom line, and that accountants had a role to play in measuring, auditing, reporting rating risks and benchmarking it (rather than simply addressing their finances). The Seventh Session of the UN Commission on Sustainable Development (CSD) reinforced the need to consider the triple bottom line, and stressed that sustainable consumption included, '... *meeting the needs of present and future generations for goods and services in ways that are economically, socially and environmentally sustainable*' (CSD, 1999). Other parties also suggested that sustainable development should be carried out within the context of an open and accountable system of governance (Robins and Roberts, 2000), and that it should address poverty and inequality (Smith, 1992).

Ten years after the 1992 Earth Summit in Rio de Janeiro, the World Summit on Sustainable Development (WSSD) was held in Johannesburg, South Africa. The WSSD reaffirmed that sustainable development was a central element of the international agenda, and its meaning was broadened and strengthened; particularly with regard to important linkages between poverty, the environment and the use of natural resources (UN/DESA, 2002). The Global Reporting Initiative (GRI) released sustainability reporting guidelines and indicators (GRI, 2002b), and there was an increasing emphasis on demonstrating processes and performance by companies that contributed towards sustainable development.

Sustainable tourism

Even before Rio, Krippendorf had argued that the world needed a new, less exploitative form of tourism that could be considered with regard to its capacity to contribute to *gross national happiness*, by measuring '... *higher incomes, more satisfying jobs, social and cultural facilities, and better housing*' (Krippendorf, 1987). The concept of 'sustainable tourism' has evolved since Krippendorf's statement, and Butler (1993) subsequently defined 'sustainable development in the context of tourism' as:

> ... *tourism which is developed and maintained in an area (community environment) in such a manner and at such a scale that it remains viable over an indefinite period and does not degrade or alter the environment (human and physical) in which it exists to such a degree that it prohibits the successful development and wellbeing of other activities and processes.*
> (Butler, 1993, p23)

One of the outcomes of the Rio Earth Summit had been a global action plan called Agenda 21. Approved by 182 countries, Agenda 21 integrated the goals of environmental protection and economic development into an action plan for sustainable development, but based on free market principles (McCormick, 1997). Agenda 21 promoted the '... *formulation of environmentally sound and culturally sensitive tourism programmes as a strategy for sustainable development*' of tourism (United Nations, 1992). In 1999 the Seventh CSD promoted a balanced approach to sustainable tourism by the private sector, widening the debate from an environmental focus, to local economic development and poverty alleviation (CSD, 1999). The commission called on the tourism industry to:

> ... *promote sustainable tourism development in order to increase the benefits from the tourism resources for the population ... and maintain the cultural and environmental integrity of the host community; ... promot[e] linkages within the local economy in order that benefits may be more widely shared; [emphasizing] greater efforts [for] employment of the local workforce, and the use of local products and skills.*
>
> (CSD, 1999)

CSD7 urged governments to maximize the potential of tourism to eradicate poverty by developing appropriate cooperative strategies with major groups, indigenous and local communities (CSD, 1999).

In 2002 UNEP's Tour Operators Initiative (TOI) responded to the launch of Global Reporting Indicators by releasing a series of pilot indicators for the tour operators' sector (GRI, 2002a). These indicators addressed environmental, social and economic indicators of core business processes of project management and development, internal management, supply chain management, customer relations and cooperation with destinations (GRI, 2002a).

This international policy and global focus has provided the context for interventions in Africa and, in particular, in southern Africa.

Responsible tourism: The policy framework in southern Africa

The New Partnership for Africa's Development (NEPAD) strategic framework document arises from a mandate given to the five initiating Heads of State (Algeria, Egypt, Nigeria, Senegal, South Africa) by the Organisation of African Unity (OAU) to develop an integrated socioeconomic development framework for Africa. The 37th Summit of the OAU in July 2001 formally adopted the strategic framework document. NEPAD is designed to address the current challenges facing the African continent, including escalating poverty levels, underdevelopment and the continued marginalization of Africa (NEPAD, 2005). NEPAD's primary objectives are (NEPAD, 2001):

*   to eradicate poverty;
*   to place African countries, both individually and collectively, on a path of sustainable growth and development;
*   to halt the marginalization of Africa in the globalization process and enhance its full and beneficial integration into the global economy; and
*   to accelerate the empowerment of women.

NEPAD identified tourism as an important vehicle to address the current challenges facing the African continent, and its broad objectives are to (NEPAD, 2001):

- identify 'key' anchor projects at national and sub-regional levels which will generate significant spin-offs and assist in promoting interregional integration;
- develop a regional marketing strategy;
- develop research capacity; and
- promote partnerships via sub-regional bodies.

The actions proposed to address these objectives (and which are relevant to the theme of this book) are to (NEPAD, 2001):

- forge cooperative partnerships to capture the benefits of shared knowledge, as well as providing a base for other countries wishing to enter tourist-related activities;
- provide the African people with the capacity to be actively involved in sustainable tourism projects at the community level;
- market African tourism products, especially in adventure tourism, ecotourism and cultural tourism; and
- increase regional coordination of tourism initiatives in Africa for the expansion and increased diversity of products.

Individual countries in southern Africa have taken different approaches to implementing the NEPAD tourism action plan, and towards promoting sustainable tourism growth. Interventions within a range of southern African countries are explored throughout this book. As an introduction, however, South Africa provides a good example of responsible tourism policy development within the continent.

Responsible tourism policy in South Africa

In 1996 the Department of Environmental Affairs and Tourism (DEAT) published its *White Paper on the Development and Promotion of Tourism*, which recognized that tourism had largely been a missed opportunity for South Africa, but which also considered that tourism could provide the nation with an 'engine of growth, capable of dynamizing and rejuvenating other sectors of the economy'. A foresighted part of the paper promoted the development of *responsible and sustainable* tourism growth. The key elements of responsible tourism were to (DEAT, 1996):

- ensure communities are involved in and benefit from tourism;
- market tourism that is responsible, respecting local, natural and cultural environments;
- involve the local community in planning and decision making;

- use local resources sustainably;
- be sensitive to the host culture;
- maintain and encourage natural, economic, social and cultural diversity; and
- undertake assessment of environmental, social and economic impacts as a prerequisite to developing tourism.

Following the White Paper, DEAT produced national *Responsible Tourism Guidelines*, which included targets for the tourism sector and emphasized the need to address the triple bottom line of sustainable development (economic, environmental and social sustainability) (DEAT, 2002). DEAT envisaged that tourism industry groups would take the guidelines and develop sub-sector guidelines that are applicable to their business, and that codes of best practice would be derived. Through such voluntary systems, it was hoped that enterprises would achieve market advantage over their competitors by being demonstrably 'responsible' (Spenceley, 2003).

As a tool to assist the tourism sector, a *Responsible Tourism Manual for South Africa* was published by DEAT in 2002. This aimed to provide 'mainstream' as well as community-based tourism enterprises (CBTEs) with information about responsible tourism and the opportunities that it presented for improving their business performance. Specific to South Africa, and in line with international best practice, the manual provided a range of practical and cost-effective responsible actions available to tourism businesses, and referred to many useful sources of information that could guide their implementation of responsible business activities (Spenceley et al, 2002).

Also in 2002, South Africa hosted the first conference on Responsible Tourism in Destinations, just prior to the Johannesburg World Summit on Sustainable Development. The Cape Town Conference was attended by 280 delegates from 20 countries, and resulted in a declaration that called upon tourism enterprises to '... *adopt a responsible approach, to commit to specific responsible practises, and to report progress in a transparent and auditable way, and where appropriate to use this for market advantage*' (Cape Town, 2002). In particular, the Cape Town Declaration states that responsible tourism (Cape Town, 2002):

- minimizes negative economic, environmental and social impacts;
- generates greater economic benefits for local people and enhances the well-being of host communities, improves working conditions and access to the industry;
- involves local people in decisions that affect their lives and life chances;
- makes positive contributions to the conservation of natural and cultural heritage, to the maintenance of the world's diversity;
- provides more enjoyable experiences for tourists through more meaningful connections with local people, and a greater understanding of local cultural, social and environmental issues;
- provides access for physically challenged people; and

- is culturally sensitive, engenders respect between tourists and hosts, and builds local pride and confidence.

The declaration makes a commitment to '...*work with others to take responsibility for achieving the economic, social and environmental components of responsible and sustainable tourism*'.

In 2008 the second conference on Responsible Tourism in Destinations was held in Kochi, India. Strengthening the principles of responsible tourism outlined in the Cape Town Declaration, the declaration recognized that 'responsible Tourism is not a product; it is an approach which can be used by travellers and holidaymakers, tour operators, accommodation and transport providers, visitor attraction managers, planning authorities, national, regional/provincial and local government. An integrated approach is required, involving many stakeholders in any place or space which attracts tourists' (Kerala, 2008). For example, the Association for Independent Tour Operators (AITO) developed a Responsible Tourism policy (see Box 0.1), and the World Travel Market in London annually hosts a Responsible Tourism Award (see www.responsibletourismawards.com), using the Cape Town Declaration description of tourism to guide them.

Poverty alleviation through responsible tourism in local communities

Economic impacts of tourism

The WTO (2002) reviewed the significance of international tourism to poor countries, and found that tourism was a principal export for 83 per cent of developing countries. Eighty per cent of the world's poor people (living on under US$1 per day) live in 12 countries, and in 11 of those countries tourism is significant or expanding (i.e. over 2 per cent of GDP or 5 per cent of exports) (see Table 0.1). This implies that as a growth sector, international tourism has the potential to provide economic benefits in developing countries where large populations of poor people reside.

Economists consider tourism to be a response to a particular consumer demand, which directly and indirectly creates the need for a wide variety of products and services. The industry stimulates a wide range of economic opportunities that impact on many sectors including transport, communications, infrastructure, education, security, health, immigration, customs and accommodation. Tourism is an attractive industry to developing countries as the start-up costs and barriers to entry are generally low, while income may flow quickly under favourable strategic and marketing conditions. However, economic benefits may not be maximized in developing countries in cases where there are high levels of foreign ownership and deep leakage effects, caused by few local economic linkages (OMT/WTO Secretariat, 2002). A number of potential economic impacts and consequences of tourism that are relevant to this research are outlined in Table 0.2.

Table 0.1 *Significance of international tourism in countries with 80 per cent of the world's poor people*

Country	Is international tourism an important economic sector?[1]	Have international tourist arrivals grown significantly (1990–97)[2]	Percentage of population living on under US$1 a day[3]
Bangladesh		Yes	?
Brazil	Yes	Yes	29%
China	Yes	Yes	22%
Ethiopia	Yes		34%
India	Yes		53%
Indonesia	Yes	Yes	15%
Kenya	Yes	?	50%
Mexico	Yes		15%
Nepal	Yes	Yes	53%
Nigeria		Yes	29%
Pakistan	?		12%
Peru	Yes	Yes	49%
Philippines	Yes	Yes	28%

Notes: 1 International Tourism Receipts of more than 5% exports or 2% of GDP in 1996. Data adapted from WTO, 1998 and World Development Indices 1998.

2 Percentage change between international tourist arrivals for 1990 and 1997, adapted from WTO, 1997 and WTO, 1998.

3 UNICEF, 1999; World Development Indices, 1998.

Source: WTO, 2002

There is debate regarding what forms of tourism optimize economic benefits. For example, Ashley and Roe (1998) compared package tourists and backpackers and found that although the total spend by backpackers was often lower than package tourists, more of their money reached local people. Research in the Philippines indicated that independent travellers spent significantly more per day than backpackers, but there was little difference in reported spending between domestic and international tourists (pers. comm. Goodwin, 2003, cited in Spenceley, 2003).

Poverty

Globally it is estimated that there are 1.2 billion people living in extreme poverty, of which about a quarter live in sub-Saharan Africa and three-quarters work and live in rural areas. More than 800 million people (or 15 per cent of the world's population) suffer from malnutrition, and the life expectancy at birth in the least developed countries is under 50 years (27 years less than in developed countries: UNDP, 2003). The United Nations classifies 49 nations as Least Developed

Table 0.2 *Potential economic effects of tourism*

Area of impact	Range of consequences
Employment	**Number of jobs:** Tourism is a labour intensive industry (de Kadt, 1979; Boo, 1990) where jobs are particularly accessible to women (OMT/WTO Secretariat, 2002). Indirect employment may also be generated from locally re-spent income earned by people through tourism (Opperman and Chon, 1997) **Low wages:** Employment options may be menial, with low wages and low skills, with little opportunity for the advancement and training of local people (Ruf, 1978) **Seasonal job losses:** Variations in vacation times, climate or temporal attractions may lead to job losses during low seasons (Opperman and Chon, 1997)
Local business development	**Supplying the tourism sector:** Demand for a wide range of supporting products and services (e.g. agriculture, laundry, transport, craft, furnishings, construction) entrepreneurial activity and business development to support tourism may be stimulated (Lea, 1998) **Demand from tourists:** Tourists may develop preferences for destination products during holidays that continue when they return home, stimulating international demand for certain products (Cox et al, 1995) **Reducing leakage:** Local ownership of tourism enterprises, and opportunities for those enterprises to purchase supplies locally reduces leakage. Leakage is the effect where a portion of foreign exchange earnings generated is repatriated (e.g. through foreign owners' profits, imports of equipment, materials, capital and consumer goods) (Voss, 1984; Diaz, 2001) **Seasonal business:** May cause difficulties for enterprises to sustain profits during low seasons (Opperman and Chon, 1997)
Diversified economy	**Improved standards of living:** Tourism activity may provide complementary livelihood strategies, especially for poor, rural people – who rarely rely on one activity or income source (Ashley and Roe, 1998) **Opportunity costs:** Tourism may be incompatible with other revenue-generating industries such as agriculture or mining. In addition, it may not be the most appropriate tool for economic development in a particular area (Mathieson and Wall, 1982) **Dependency on tourism:** If the local economy is not diverse, service and product providers are vulnerable, and at risk if there is a downturn in visitation (Krippendorf, 1987) **Patchy distribution of benefits:** Benefits are often accrued by a small elite (Krippendorf, 1987; Saville, 2001) rather than the poorest people
Infrastructure	**Investment:** Attraction of private investment to finance infrastructure and supporting business development in tourism destinations, which may benefit local people **Taxes:** Government taxes accrued from tourism provide funds to increase infrastructure investment in schools, health facilities, roads and services such as education, policing and healthcare

Countries (LDCs), due to their low GDP per capita, weak human assets and high economic vulnerability, and 34 are located in Africa.

The UN states that for ease of reference and coherence in global assessments, development agencies often employ quantitative financial measures of poverty, such as those setting a threshold of US$1 a day. Specific indicators relating to certain economic and social factors (such as infant mortality and literacy rates) are also used, but many aspects of poverty, some of which are crucial to a human rights analysis, are not reflected in the statistical indicators. Economic deprivation (or a lack of income) is a standard feature of most definitions of poverty. However, financial measures alone do not take account of the wide range of social, cultural and political aspects of poverty. Poverty is not only deprivation of economic or material resources but also a violation of human dignity (UNHCHR, 2002)

Therefore, poverty can be defined using both economic and non-economic approaches (Sultana, 2002). The economic approach typically defines poverty in terms of income and consumption. The non-economic approach incorporates concepts such as living standards, basic needs, inequality, subsistence and the human development index. The range of characteristics integrated within the notion of poverty means that definitions of the term may differ both within and between societies, institutions, communities and households.

In the most comprehensive and rights-sensitive definition of poverty to date, the United Nations Committee on Economic, Social and Cultural Rights defined poverty as '*a human condition characterized by the sustained or chronic deprivation of the resources, capabilities, choices, security and power necessary for the enjoyment of an adequate standard of living and other civil, cultural, economic, political and social rights*' (UN, 2001).

In terms of tackling and resolving the problems of global poverty, the 1992 Rio Declaration challenged all people to, '*... cooperate in the essential task of eradicating poverty as an indispensable requirement for sustainable development*' (UN, 1992). A decade later, a key outcome of the WSSD in 2002 was a reaffirmation of the Millennium Development Goal to halve the number of people living in poverty by 2015 (UN/DESA, 2002).

Poverty and tourism

The term 'pro-poor tourism' emerged from a desk-based review of tourism and poverty conducted by Deloitte and Touche, the Overseas Development Initiative (ODI) and the International Institute of Environment and Development (IIED) that was commissioned by the UK's Department for International Development to explore the role of tourism in reducing poverty (DFID, 1999; Sofield et al, 2004). The review identified a number of strategies for developing or supporting poverty alleviation through tourism, but noted that these strategies had not been tried or tested. Subsequent work by the ODI, IIED and International Centre for Responsible Tourism (ICRT) generated a series of reports and case studies that measured the economic impacts of tourism in destinations across the world, and which considered different parts of the tourism industry (see www.propoor-tourism.org.uk). The series of case studies undertaken during 2000 and 2001 evaluated the impacts of tourism on the poor using a common approach, from the Caribbean, Ecuador Nepal, Namibia, South Africa and Uganda (PPT Partnership, undated). Further research followed, with additional working papers, discussion papers, policy briefs, 'How to ...?' workbooks and annual registers of pro-poor tourism interventions which considered the role of different stakeholders (e.g. governments, development agencies, the private sector) and the impacts of tourism on poverty reduction internationally.

Pro-poor tourism (PPT) is defined as tourism that generates net benefits for the poor, and aims to ensure that tourism growth contributes to poverty reduction. It is not a specific tourism product, or sector of the industry, but an approach to developing and implementing tourism activities. PPT strategies aim to facilitate opportunities and break down barriers for the poor to gain in terms of revenue, livelihood or participation in decision making (Ashley et al, 2001). Ashley et al (2002) consider that although agriculture tends to be at the core of most rural people's livelihoods, diversification strategies were critical for poor households in order to decrease risk and increase their rewards. Tourism's 'pro-poor' potential lies in four main areas (DFID, 1999; Ashley et al, 2001):

*   tourism is a *diverse industry*, which increases the scope for wide participation of different stakeholders and businesses, including the involvement of the informal sector;
*   the *customer comes to the product*, which provides considerable opportunities for linkages (e.g. souvenir selling) to emerging entrepreneurs and small, medium and micro-enterprises (SMMEs);
*   tourism is *highly dependent upon natural capital* (e.g. wildlife and culture), which are assets that the poor may have access to – even in the absence of financial resources; and
*   tourism can be more *labour intensive* than other industries such as manufacturing. In comparison to other modern sectors, a higher proportion of tourism benefits (e.g. jobs and informal trade opportunities) go to women.

The Pro-Poor Tourism Partnership is a collaboration between the ODI, IIED and ICRT, which emphasizes the importance of looking at tourism and poverty in a livelihoods perspective; that it can have both positive and negative social, economic and environmental impacts on local communities, and it is essential that a broad view is taken when assessing likely impacts and determining whether or not to proceed with particular initiatives (Spenceley and Goodwin, 2007). A southern African pro-poor tourism pilot project was established in May 2002 by the Pro-Poor Tourism Partnership to promote strategies that could be used by tourism companies to create and enhance linkages with local people or enterprises *that* make business sense to the company. The project worked closely with five 'pilot' tourism enterprises in southern Africa to promote and facilitate local linkages (Ashley et al, 2005). Over three years, the project facilitated a number of initiatives with the pilot enterprises to strengthen local linkages and enhance local economic development. The enterprise activities generated increased local employment, increased use of local contractors and suppliers, upgrading existing product development facilities and stronger local relationships between the private sector and local community (PPT, 2005).

International initiatives for pro-poor tourism

There has been an increasing emphasis among non-governmental organizations (NGOs) and development agencies over the past two decades to use opportunities presented by tourism to diversify livelihood options and alleviate poverty. Although tourism may create problems for the poor, including limited access to markets, displacement, local inflation and loss of access to resources (Roe and Urquhart, 2002; WTO, 2002), agencies have become increasingly focused on the potential for tourism to provide net benefits to the poor. This has been reflected in international initiatives, such as the WTO's *Global Code of Ethics for Tourism* (WTO, 1997). The code argues that local populations should equitably share in the economic, social and cultural benefits generated from tourism, and in particular from employment opportunities (WTO, 1997).

At the WSSD in 2002 a number of agencies promoted tourism interventions and publications that related to poverty alleviation, such as the WTO paper specifically on poverty alleviation and tourism (WTO, 2002). This paper was the first formal response to the issue of poverty from the agency, and reviewed experiences and lessons learned by governments, industry, development agencies and communites. Also during WSSD the WTO and the United Nations Commission on Trade and Development (UNCTAD) launched the 'Sustainable Tourism – Eliminating Poverty' (ST-EP) programme. The programme aims to alleviate poverty through sustainable tourism by financing research and development, and also providing incentives for good practice (WTO undated: see Box 0.1). As a contribution to the WSSD, UNEP brought together a consortium of the World Travel and Tourism Council, International Hotel and Restaurant Association, International Federation of Tour Operators and the International Council of Cruise Lines to develop a paper regarding the role of the tourism industry in sustainable development. The report noted that one of the main barriers to achieving sustainable tourism had been the inherent fragmentation of the industry and the relative fragility of viable operating margins – especially for the small and medium-sized enterprises that made up most of the industry. Although these barriers had indirectly led to a deficiency of accountability in both the private and public sectors, the report stated that the tourism sector was increasingly recognizing the need to protect cultures, heritage and the environment, while allowing developing countries to obtain the full economic potential of tourism (WTTC/IH&RA/IFTO/ICCL, 2002).

Within this context, a number of UN programmes, donor agencies, private sector associations and NGOs have developed initiatives to encourage sustainable tourism development. For example, UNEP is now in the process of developing baseline criteria for sustainable tourism for presentation at the IUCN World Conservation Congress in October 2008. Although agencies have predomina
prioritized environmental issues, some have taken a more holistic sta
address sustainable development. A number of these are summarized i

Box 0.1 Examples of sustainable and responsible tourism initiatives from different stakeholders

United Nations Initiatives

The **United Nations World Tourism Organisation' Sustainable Tourism – Eliminating Poverty programme**. The ST-EP programme includes four main components. The first is a research base to identify linkages, principles and model applications. There is also an operating framework for promoting and developing incentives for good practice among companies, consumers and communities. Forums for sharing and exchanging information, ideas and plans are designed to bring together private, public and non-governmental stakeholders. Finally, there is the ST-EP Foundation which was originally concerned with attracting new, dedicated financing from business, philanthropic and government sources. The Foundation operates under the guidance of the ST-EP Board of Directors, which includes representatives from eight different countries as well as the Netherlands Development Organization, SNV (www.unwtostep.org). One of the programme's initiatives in southern Africa has been the development of an online community-based tourism directory (Spenceley and Rozga, 2006).

The **International Trade Centre of the United Nations Conference on Trade and Development** is a technical cooperation agency whose mission is to support developing and transition economies, and particularly their business sectors, in their efforts to realize their full potential for developing export and import operations with the ultimate goal of achieving sustainable development. ITC's Export-led Poverty Reduction Programme (EPRP) is to contribute to the goal of reducing the proportion of people living in extreme poverty by half by the year 2015 and operates through pilot projects in countries having submitted to ITC a formal request for technical assistance in sectors that offer the best leverage for poverty reduction: Community-based Tourism (CBT) being one of them. The EPRP concept of CBT focuses on the development and promotion of tourism businesses and services in which poor communities can play an entrepreneurial role (ITC, 2005).

Private sector initiatives

The Tour Operators' Initiative (TOI) for Sustainable Tourism Development was launched in 2000 and is hosted by UNEP. TOI is a network of tour operators that have voluntarily joined forces to improve their business practices and raise awareness within the industry. It provides a platform to develop ideas and projects to address the economic, social, cultural and environmental aspects of sustainable development within the tourism sector (WTTC/IH&RA/IFTO/ICCL, 2002). The TOI drafted the Global Reporting Initiative indicators for the tour operators' sector (GRI, 2002a).

The **   n for Independent Tour Operators (AITO)** developed a
                        sm policy in 2001 that prioritizes protection of the environment;
                        ultures; maximizing the benefits to local communities; conserving
                        nd minimizing pollution. It is anticipated that within a few years
                        b endorse AITO's responsible tourism guidelines as a condition of

membership. Members are assisted in formulating their own Responsible Tourism strategy through a database of Responsible Tourism Advice Notes, available to them on the member's only section of the AITO website (www.aito.co.uk).

NGO initiatives in Southern Africa

Fair Trade in Tourism South Africa (FTTSA) is a non-profit organization initiated as part of the World Conservation Union (IUCN), and in 2002 launched a trademark that it would award to enterprises meeting FTTSA's criteria of 'fairly traded'. FTTSA markets the brand so that tour operators and consumers can choose tourism products that have obtained an independent hallmark of 'fairness' (Spenceley et al, 2002). (www.fairtourismsa.org.za).

The International Centre for Responsible Tourism – South Africa (ICRT-SA) has a mission to contribute to economic development, social justice and environmental integrity through the development and promotion of Responsible Tourism by (1) influencing public institutions, the tourism industry, donors and tourists to integrate the principles of responsible tourism into their policies, operations and activities; (2) communicating the principles of responsible tourism through capacity building, education and awareness programmes to the broadest possible constituency; (3) initiating and undertaking research to develop knowledge to support the implementation of responsible tourism; and (4) creating a network of individuals, institutions and tourism enterprises supportive of the objectives of the Cape Town Declaration on Responsible Tourism in Destinations. The ICRT SA is part of a network of organizations in the United Kingdom, The Gambia and India (www.icrtourismsa.org).

Biodiversity conservation and nature-based tourism

The tourism industry and socioeconomic status of people have critical implications for biodiversity conservation, particularly in remote and under-developed areas where many of the poor reside. Biodiversity can be defined as, ' ... *the variability among living organisms from all sources including, inter alia, terrestrial, marine and other aquatic ecosystems and the ecological complexes of which they are part; this includes diversity within species, between species and of ecosystems*' (UNEP, 1994). Threats to biodiversity include poverty, poor planning, market failure, excessive wealth and open-access exploitation (Caldecott et ~~parallel~~ with the globalization debate, van der Duim and Caalders (2 the:

> ... *growing concern for the deterioration of nature is a*
> *the developed world, whereas a large part of this nat*
> *jurisdiction of Third World countries. They generally*

> *many social and economic problems, which are felt to be more urgent than*
> *environmental and ecological ones.*
>
>   (van der Duim and Caalders 2002, p745)

Redclift (1992) warned that the poor often had little choice but to choose immediate economic benefits at the expense of the long-term sustainability of their livelihoods. He noted that under these circumstances it was useless to appeal for altruism and protection of the environment, as individuals were effectively forced to behave 'selfishly' to survive. Since the tourism industry relies on the natural resource base to attract clients, reducing poverty in tourism destinations becomes vital in maintaining the viability of products over time.

Nature-based tourism and ecotourism

Since the term was coined in 1983 (Ceballos-Lascuráin, 1996), 'ecotourism' has been the subject of much debate, with a plethora of different definitions promoted by researchers, NGOs and the tourism industry (Goodwin, 1996; Stewart and Sekartjakarini, 1994). The WTO defines 'ecotourism' as '... *all forms of tourism in which the tourists' main motivation is the observation and appreciation of nature, that contributes to the conservation of, and that generates minimal impacts upon, the natural environment and cultural heritage*' (Frangialli, 2001). However, some enterprises have abused the term, and have marketed nature-based tourism products that have *not* benefited local people, or have damaged the environment as 'ecotourism'. The consequence has been a dilution of the term's value.

A WTO study in seven of the main ecotourism generating markets of Europe and North America highlighted that the use of the term 'ecotourism' in the private sector was actually very limited (Vereczi, 2001). Tour operators were quite reluctant to use the concept in their marketing literature and brochures, and instead preferred to use words like 'sustainable', 'responsible', 'environmental' and 'ethical' (Vereczi, 2001). Perhaps the most damning comments came from the AITO; whose members perceived that ecotourism was a hangover from the past, and a brand name that their clients found meaningless (Goodwin and Townsend, 2002). Despite such perceptions, the WTO and UNEP declared 1992 to be the 'International Year of Ecotourism'. During that year the WTO convened a series of regional conferences on ecotourism, culminating in a World Eco-tourism Summit in Quebec, and production of a report to the UN General Assembly on activities undertaken by governments and international organizations globally (UN, 2003). However, debates surrounding the World Eco-tourism Summit in Quebec, Canada were described as 'acrimonious' (Roe and Urquhart, 2002) and activists used the event to highlight cases of poor and negligent practice by 'ecotourism' operations.

'Nature-based tourism' is a simpler concept than ecotourism, and is ￢tivated by enjoying wildlife or undeveloped natural areas (WTTERC, 1993). ᵌncorporate natural attractions including scenery, topography, waterways, ⁻vildlife and cultural heritage; and activities like hunting or white-water ⁻s-Lascuráin, 1996). Nature-based tourism does not necessarily contribute to the conservation of biodiversity, nor must it benefit host populations, but it includes sub-categories of tourism that may do so (for example, ecotourism). Some tourism researchers have chosen to avoid the confusion and controversy surrounding the term 'ecotourism' by using 'nature-based tourism' as a less contentious concept (e.g. Deng et al, 2002; McKercher, 1998).

'Wildlife tourism' is a form of nature-based tourism that includes the consumptive and non-consumptive use of wild animals in natural areas (Roe et al, 1997). Roe et al (1997) noted that wildlife tourism has frequently been used to link wildlife management with economic incentives to promote conservation in developing countries. Wildlife tourism has the potential to contribute towards the management of protected areas by generating revenue, employment, conservation awareness and stimulating economic activity. Within rural areas, wildlife tourism also provides a mechanism to realize tangible benefits from conservation and wildlife for local communities (Roe et al, 1997). Wildlife tourism may be undertaken through guided or self-drive excursions in vehicles, or through guided walks. During 'safari' excursions in southern Africa tourists learn about, observe and photograph charismatic and dangerous wildlife such as elephant, rhino, buffalo, lion and leopard.

Many of the chapters in this book consider the impacts of nature-based, and, in particular, wildlife, tourism in southern Africa. This form of tourism is particularly important in this region, because of the immense biological diversity and charismatic megafauna of savannah areas of southern Africa; because nature-based tourism often takes place in areas that are marginal for agriculture (e.g. due to soil quality and water availability); and because it can provide a sustainable and commercially viable livelihood opportunity for the private sector and poor people living in remote areas.

Tourism in Southern Africa

The tourism industry in southern Africa is very small, by comparison to the rest of the world, and in 2007 the total demand represented just 1.3 per cent of world market share (WTTC, 2007). However, over the past 20 years tourism development as a whole has been positive in Africa, and during the 1990s tourism grew at an average annual rate of 6.2 per cent in contrast to 4.3 per cent for the world. The continent is heavily endowed with some of the exceptional attractions which can be packaged into tourism products for local and international markets, including natural resources and sites of historical importance. Nature-based tourism is the main component of the African tourism product and the continent boasts a wide range of natural attractions (Mukugo et al, 2004).

The World Travel and Tourism Council (WTTC) estimated that travel and tourism in sub-Saharan Africa in 2007 would generate US$ 90.1 billion of economic activity, and would account for 8.1 per cent of GDP and 10.4 million jobs (5.9 per cent of total employment). The industry is expected to grow by 4.5 per cent per annum (in real terms) between 2008 and 2017 (WTTC, 2007).

Research commissioned by NEPAD and the Southern African Development Community (SADC) assessed tourism growth in southern Africa, and indicates that South Africa and Mauritius had advanced tourism sectors, contributing 2.9 per cent and 4.2 per cent to gross domestic product (GDP) growth respectively in 2005. Tourism markets in Botswana and Namibia are still maturing; Zambia, Mozambique, Tanzania and Madagascar are emerging countries in terms of tourism growth; and Zimbabwe's market has regressed; while the tourism potential of Lesotho and Swaziland are promising. NEPAD has made tourism a priority sector with the potential to diversify economic opportunities and generate income and foreign exchange earnings for African countries. This is in line with the African Union and NEPAD tourism action plan, adopted at the union's third general assembly in Ethiopia in July 2004. However, the report noted that there was inadequate tourism education, training and awareness for the general public, and a lack of protection for the environment (Gadebe, 2005).

This book focuses on 'Responsible Tourism: Critical issues for conservation and development' in southern Africa. Responsible tourism practices are of particular interest in this part of the world: in part because of the context of NEPAD; due to the presence of national responsible tourism and poverty alleviation policies; because of the rich biological diversity and abundant charismatic wildlife, and because of the regional importance of local economic development and devising viable livelihood strategies for the poor.

Outline of the book

Following this introduction, the book is structured into three main sections.

Part 1: Policies, institutional interventions and market forces
Part 2: Responsible nature-based tourism
Part 3: Community-based tourism

An overview of the three parts of the book follows.

Part 1: Policies, institutional interventions and market forces

The implementation of responsible tourism in southern Africa has been shaped by a number of interlinking factors. These include government policy frameworks; programmes and interventions by donor agencies and NGOs; and (because tourism is, of course, a business) by market forces and supply chains. In the first part of this book, practitioners working in Mozambique and South Africa present six chapters that describe the role and activities of governments, development agencies, non-governmental agencies and the private sector in initiatives that promote conservation and poverty alleviation through tourism.

social

In Chapter 1, Andrew Rylance describes tourism and poverty reduction policies and plans in Mozambique, and critically considers how the institutional framework has manifested in responsible tourism planning and local economic development in Nampula Province. The role of policy and planning in developing a sustainable ecotourism industry in Madagascar is the subject of Chapter 2, where the role of government interventions is evaluated by Michaela Pawliczek and Hitesh Mehta. In Chapter 3, Giju Varghese considers the role of public–private partnerships in national parks, and explains the commercialization process and lessons learned in South Africa. In Chapter 4, Steve Collins and Herman Snel describe the role of development agencies in facilitating responsible tourism development, using the example of the German development agency (GtZ) and its activities in South Africa. In Chapter 5 Nicole Frey and Richard George present a suite industry and NGO responses to the South African national policy on responsible tourism, and also consider the market supply and demand for this type of travel. Concluding this part of the book, Chapter 6 presents information on how the private sector can adapt its supply chains to promote local economic development and poverty alleviation. Using data from a joint intervention of a development agency and private sector, Caroline Ashley and Gareth Haysom present evidence of 'win–wins' for both business and local economic development.

Part 2: Responsible nature-based tourism

A series of six chapters describe the implications of responsible nature-based tourism (including ecotourism and wildlife tourism) in southern Africa for conservation and development, and interventions by government and the private sector. In Chapter 7 Anna Spenceley reviews research on the economics of wildlife tourism in southern Africa, and in particular the level of evidence that wildlife tourism reduces poverty. In Chapter 8, Helen Suich considers the role of protected areas, and, in particular, transfrontier conservation areas in delivering financial benefits for people, using the Kavango-Zambezi transfrontier conservation area as an example. Joseph Mbaiwa explores the impacts of wildlife tourism on conservation and development in Botswana in Chapter 9, and then Peter John Massyn provides insights into the participation of Botswanans in the lodge industry of the Okavango Delta in Chapter 10. This section is concluded with two papers from South Africa. In Chapter 11 Murray Simpson demonstrates the impacts of high-value nature-based tourism on rural livelihoods and poverty, and in Chapter 12 Piers Relly evaluates the impacts of the Madikwe Game Reserve on the local economy.

Part 3: Community-based tourism

Four practitioners review the impacts of community-based tourism enterprises (CBTE) on local livelihoods and conservation in southern Africa. In Chapter 13 Anna Spenceley synthesizes the impacts from 215 CBTEs located in Botswana, Lesotho, Mauritius, Madagascar, Malawi, Mozambique, Namibia, South Africa,

Swaziland, Tanzania, Zambia and Zimbabwe. Fred Nelson then considers both macro- and micro-economic issues of wildlife-based CBT in Tanzania in Chapter 14. Louise Dixey provides a critical examination of donor funded CBTE programmes in Zambia in Chapter 15, and Jon Barnes concludes this section with very positive data on the livelihood impacts of communal-land conservancies in Namibia in Chapter 16.

The three sections of the book are followed by a conclusion in Chapter 17. This paper incorporates a discussion of the implications of the papers collated in this volume for policy, interventions by conservation and development stakeholders, and for the implementation of responsible tourism.

References

Ashley, C. (2005) 'Facilitating pro-poor tourism with the private sector. Lessons learned from "Pro-Poor Tourism Pilots in Southern Africa"' Working Paper 257, Overseas Development Institute, London

Ashley, C. and Haysom, G. (2006) 'From philanthropy to a different way of doing business: Strategies and challenges in integrating pro-poor approaches into tourism business', *Development Southern Africa*, vol 23, no 2, pp265–280

Ashley, C. and Haysom, G. (2008) 'The development impacts of tourism supply chains: Increasing impact on poverty and decreasing our ignorance', in Spenceley, A. (ed) *Responsible Tourism: Impacts on Conservation and Poverty Alleviation in Southern Africa*, Earthscan, London

Ashley, A., Haysom, G. and Poultney, C. (2005) 'Pro poor tourism pilots in southern Africa. Practical implementation of pro-poor linkages by tourism companies', Mboza Tourism and Overseas Development Institute, London

Ashley, C. and Roe, D. (1998) 'Enhancing community involvement in wildlife tourism: Issues and challenges', IIED Wildlife and Development Series No. 11, International Institute for Environment and Development, London

Ashley, C., Mdoe. N. and Reynolds, L. (2002) 'Rethinking wildlife for livelihoods and diversification in rural Tanzania: A case study from northern Selous', LADDER Working Paper No. 15, March, Overseas Development Group, University of East Anglia, Norwich

Ashley, C., Roe, D. and Goodwin, H. (2001) 'Pro-poor tourism strategies: Making tourism work for the poor: A review of experience', Pro-poor tourism report No. 1, April, ODI/IIED/CRT, The Russell Press, Nottingham

Bartelmus, P. (1986) *Environment and Development*, Allen and Unwin, Boston

Basiago, A. D. (1995) 'Methods of defining "sustainability"', *Sustainable Development*, vol 3, 109–119

Boo, E. (1990) *Ecotourism: The Potentials and Pitfalls*, vol 1, World Wildlife Fund, Washington DC

Brohman, J. (1996) 'New directions in tourism for Third World development', *Annals of Tourism Research*, vol 23, no 1, 48–70

Butler, R. W. (1993) 'Tourism – an evolutionary perspective,' in Nelson, J. G., Butler, R. and Wall, G. (eds) *Tourism and Sustainable Development: Piloting, Planning, Managing*, Department of Geography Publication Series No. 37, University of Waterloo, Waterloo, Ontario, 27–43

Caldecott, J. O., Jenkins, M. D., Johnson, T. H. and Groombridge, B. (1996) 'Priorities for global species richness and endemism', *Biodiversity and Conservation*, vol 5, 699–727

Cape Town (2002) The Cape Town Declaration of Responsible Tourism in Destinations, August 2002, Cape Town, available from: www.icrtourism.org/Capetown.shtml (accessed 27 June 2008)

Cater, E. (1996) 'Community involvement in third world ecotourism', Discussion Paper No. 64, Geographical Papers: Series B, Department of Geography, University of Reading, Reading, UK

Ceballos-Lascuráin, H. (1996) *Tourism, Ecotourism and Protected Areas: The State of Nature-based Tourism around the World and Guidelines for its Development.* IUCN, Gland, Switzerland, and Cambridge UK

Commission on Sustainable Development (CSD) (1999) *Report on the Seventh Session.* 1 May and 27 July 1998, and 19–30 April 1999, Economic and Social Council Official Records, 199, Supplement No. 9, United Nations, New York, 1999. Copyright © United Nations Division for Sustainable Development 02/09/1999

Cox, L. J., Fox, M. and Bowes, R. L. (1995) 'Does tourism destroy agriculture?' *Annals of Tourism Research*, vol 20, 210–213.

de Kadt, E. (1979) *Tourism: Passport to Development*, Oxford University Press, London

de Kadt, E. (1990) *Making the Alternative Sustainable, Lessons from Development for Tourism,* Oxford University Press, Oxford

Deng, J., King, B., and Bauer, T. (2002) 'Valuing natural attractions for tourism', *Annals of Tourism Research*, vol 29, no 2, 422–438

Department for International Development (DFID) (1999) *Tourism and Poverty Elimination: Untapped Potential*, April, DFID, London

Department for International Development (DFID) (2000) *Halving world poverty by 2015: economic growth, equity and security*, 1/9/2000, Available from: www.dfid.gov.uk/Pubs/files/tsp_cconomic.pdf (accessed 15 January 2002)

Department of Environmental Affairs and Tourism (DEAT) (1996) *The development and promotion of tourism in South Africa,* White Paper, Government of South Africa, Pretoria

Department of Environmental Affairs and Tourism (DEAT) (2002) *Guidelines for Responsible Tourism Development*, Department of Environmental Affairs and Tourism, Pretoria

Diaz, D. (2001) *The Viability and Sustainability of International Tourism in Developing Countries.* Report to the Symposium on Tourism Services, 22–23 February 2001. World Trade Organization, Geneva

Dudley, E. (1993) *The Critical Villager: Beyond Community Participation.* London: Routledge

Elkington, J. (1997) *Cannibals with Forks: The Triple Bottom Line of 21st Century Business*, Capstone Publishing Ltd., Oxford

Frangialli, F. (2001) 'World Tourism organization perspectives on the International Year of Ecotourism', *Industry and Environment*, UNEP, vol 24 nos 3–4, 4

Frey, N. (2007) 'The effect of responsible tourism management practices on business performance in an emerging market', Dissertation presented for a masters in Marketing at the School of Management Studies, University of Cape Town, September 2007

Frey, N. and George, R. (2008) 'Responsible tourism and the tourism industry: a demand and supply perspective', in Spenceley, A. (ed) *Responsible Tourism: Impacts on Conservation and Poverty Alleviation in Southern Africa*, Earthscan, London

Gadebe. T. (2005) 'Huge tourism potential for SADC', 26 October, BuaNews, accessed from www.southafrica.info/doing_business/economy/key_sectors/sadc-tourism-261005.htm (12 February 2008)

Global Reporting Initiative (GRI) (2002a) *Tour Operators' Sector Supplement*, Pilot version 1.0, 6 November 2002, Global Reporting Initiative, Amsterdam, available from: www.globalreporting.org/reportingframework/sectorsupplements/touroperators (accessed on 27 June 2008)

Global Reporting Initiative (GRI) (2002b) *Getting started on GRI Reporting*, Global Reporting Initiative, Amsterdam

Goodwin, H. (1996) 'In pursuit of ecotourism', *Biodiversity and Conservation*, vol 5, 277–292

Goodwin, H. and Francis, J. (2003) 'Ethical and responsible tourism: Consumer trends in the UK', *Journal of Vacation Marketing*, vol 9, no 3, 271–284

Goodwin, H. and Townsend, C. (2002) *The Market for Ecotourism in the United Kingdom*, Draft, A report to the World Tourism Organisation, Centre for Responsible Tourism

Hapgood, D. (ed) (1969) *The Role of Popular Participation in Development Report of a Conference on the Implementation of Title IX of the Foreign Assistance Act, June 24–August 2, 1969*. Cambridge, MA: MIT Press., cited in Tosun, C. 2001. Op. Cit.

Horobin, H. and Long, J. (1996) 'Sustainable tourism: the role of the small firm', *International Journal of Contemporary Hospitality Management*, vol 8, no 5, 15–19

International Trade Centre (ITC) (2005) *Conducting an opportunity study for community-based tourism: Guidelines, Export-Led Poverty reduction programme*, ITC/DTCC/06/2792, ITC, Geneva

Kerala (2008) Kerala declaration on Responsible Tourism in Destinations, Downloaded from www.icrtindia.org/kd.htm on 27 March 2008

Koea, A. (1977) 'Polynesian migration to New Zealand', in Finney, B. R. and Watson, A. (eds) *A New Kind of Sugar: Tourism in the Pacific*, Centre for South Pacific Studies, University of California, Santa Cruz, Cited in Mathieson, A. and Wall, G. (1998) Op. Cit.

Krippendorf, J. (1987) *The Holiday Makers; Understanding the Impact of Leisure and Travel*, Heinemann, Oxford

Lea, J. (1998) *Tourism and Development in the Third World*, Routledge, London

Martin, A. and Stubbs, R. (Undated) *Future Development in Tourism*, MORI – Mori 1995/7 research.

Mathieson, A. and Wall, G. (1982) *Tourism: Economic, Physical and Social Impacts*, Longman, New York

McCormick, J. (1997) *Rio and Beyond*, in McDonagh, P. and Prothero, A. (eds) *Green Management: A Reader*, International Thomson Business Press, London

McKercher, B. (1998) *The Business of Nature-Based Tourism*, Hospitality Press, Melbourne

MINTEL (2001) *Ethical Tourism*, © International Group Limited, October

Mitchella, R. E. and Reidb, D. G. (2001) 'Community integration: island tourism in Peru', *Annals of Tourism Research*, vol 28, 112–139

Mukogo, R., Dieke, P. U. C., Razafy, R. J. and Nyakunu, E. T. (2004) *New Partnership For Africa's Development (NEPAD) Tourism Action Plan: Phase one: Preliminary Report on the Tourism Baseline Study*, Available from: www.satourismproducts.com/downloads/ NEPADTourism.pdf (accessed on 12 February 2008)

Müller, H. R. and Landes, A. (2000) *Tourismus und Umweltverhalten. Befragung zum Reiseverhalten*, Forschungsinstitut für Freizeit und Tourismus (FIF), Hans Imholz-Stiftung, Switzerland Travel Writers & Tourism Journalists Club Zürich (STW), Bern März

New Partnership for Africa's Development (NEPAD) (2001) Buja, Nigeria, October 2001, available from: www.nepad.org/2005/files/inbrief.php (accessed on 14 February 2008)

New Partnership for Africa's Development (NEPAD) (2005) NEPAD in Brief, available from: www.nepad.org/2005/files/inbrief.php (accessed on 14 February 2008)

OMT/WTO Secretariat (2002) *The Least Developed Countries and International Tourism*, World Tourism Organisation, Madrid

Oppermann, M. and Chon, K.-S. (1997) *Tourism in Developing Countries*, ITBP, UK

Poultney, C. and Spenceley, A. (2001) *Practical Strategies for Pro-poor Tourism, Wilderness Safaris South Africa: Rocktail Bay and Ndumu Lodge*, PPT Working paper No. 1, CRT/IIED/ ODI

Pro-Poor Tourism Partnership (PPT) (Undated) 'Background to the project: "Practical strategies for pro-poor tourism"', available from www.propoortourism.org.uk/background.html (accessed on 8 February 2008)

Pro-Poor Tourism (PPT) (2005) Update on Pro-poor tourism pilots, April 2005. Pro-Poor tourism pilots: Southern Africa. PPT in Practice, available from: www.propoortourism.org.uk/archive_newsletter.htm (accessed on 30 June 2006)

Redclift, M. (1987) *Sustainable Development: Exploring the Contradictions*, Routledge, London

Redclift, M. (1992) 'The meaning of sustainable development', *Geoforum*, vol 23, 395–403

Robins, N. and Roberts, S. (eds). (2000) *The Reality of Sustainable Trade*, April 2000, IIED, London

Roe, D. and Urquhart, P. (2002) *Pro-poor Tourism: Harnessing the World's Largest Industry for the World's Poor*, World Summit on Sustainable Development Opinion, International Institute for Environment and Development, London

Roe, D., Leader-Williams, N. and Dalal-Clayton, B. (1997) *Take Only Photographs, Leave Only Footprints: The Environmental Impacts of Wildlife Tourism*, Wildlife and Development Series, No 10, International Institute for Environment and Development, London

Ruf, W. K. (1978) Toourismus and Unterentwicklung, *Zeitschrift fur Kulturaustausch*, vol 28, no 3, 108–114, Cited in Oppermann, M. and Chon, K-S. 1997. *Op. Cit.*

Saville, N. M. (2001) *Practical Strategies for Pro-poor Tourism. Case Study of Pro-poor Tourism and SNV in Humla District, West Nepal*, Pro-Poor Tourism Report, ODI, IIED, CRT, London

Sims-Castley, R., Kerley, G. I. H., Geach, B. and Langholz, J. (2005) 'Socio-economic significance of ecotourism-based private game reserves in South Africa's Eastern Cape Province', *Parks*, vol 15, no 2, 6–18

Smith, R. A. (1992) 'Beach resort evolution', *Annals of Tourism Research*, vol 19, no 2, 304–322

Sofield, T., Bauer, J., Delacy, T., Lipman, G. and Daugherty, S. (2004) *Sustainable tourism-Eliminating poverty (ST-EP): An overview*, CRC for Sustainable Tourism, Queensland, Australia

South African National Parks (SANParks) (2000a) *Preliminary Notice to Investors: Concession opportunities under the SANP commercialisation programme*, 24 May, South African National Parks, Pretoria

South African National Parks (SANParks) (2000b) *Concession Contract for the [ ] Camp in the [ ] National Park, South African National Parks*, Draft of 26 September 2000, South African National Parks, Pretoria

South African National Parks (SANParks) (2001) *Prequalification memorandum for the second phase of the concession programme*, South African National Parks, Pretoria

Spenceley, A. (2003) *Tourism, Local Livelihoods and the Private Sector in South Africa: Case Studies on the Growing Role of the Private Sector in Natural Resources Management*, Sustainable Livelihoods in South Africa Research Paper 8, Sustainable Livelihoods Southern Africa project, Institute of Development Studies, Brighton UK

Spenceley, A. (2007) *Responsible Tourism Practices by South African Tour Operators*. International Centre for Responsible Tourism, South Africa

Spenceley, A. (2008) 'Local impacts of community-based tourism in Southern Africa', In
    Spenceley, A. (ed) *Responsible Tourism: Impacts on Conservation and Poverty Alleviation
    in Southern Africa*, Earthscan, London
Spenceley, A. and Seif, J. (2002) *Sabi Sabi Imvelo Responsible Tourism Assessment*,
    Confidential report to the Federated Hospitality Association of South Africa, cited in
    Spenceley, A. and Seif, J. (2003) *Strategies, Impacts and Costs of Pro-poor Tourism
    Approaches in South Africa*, Pro-Poor Tourism working paper No. 11, January 2003,
    available from: www.propoortourism.org.uk/ppt_pubs_workingpapers.html
Spenceley, A. and Goodwin, H. (2007) 'Nature-based tourism and poverty in South
    Africa', *Current Issues in Tourism*, vol 10, nos 2 and 3, pp255–277
Spenceley, A., Goodwin, H. and Maynard, W. (2002) *Commercialisation of South African
    National Parks and the National Responsible Tourism Guidelines*, Report to
    DfID/SANParks, April 2002, Natural Resources Institute, Greenwich
Spenceley, A., Relly, P., Keyser, H., Warmeant, P., McKenzie, M., Mataboge, A., Norton,
    P., Mahlangu, S. and Seif, J. (2002) *Responsible Tourism Manual for South Africa*, July,
    Department for Environmental Affairs and Tourism, Pretoria
Spenceley, A. and Rozga, Z. (2006) 'Technical Assistance to RETOSA for Update of
    Database and Marketing Support for Community-based Tourism Products in
    Southern Africa', Final report to UNWTO, Madrid, UNWTO/STEP-ESA / RETOSA
    (Regional Tourism Organisation of Southern Africa) / SNV Tourism Practise Areas
    (East and South Africa)
Steele, P. (1995) 'Ecotourism: An economic analysis', *Journal of Sustainable Tourism*, vol 3,
    no 1, 29–44
Stewart, W. P. and Sekartjakarini, S. (1994) 'Disentangling ecotourism', *Annals of Tourism
    Research*, vol 21, 840–841
Sultana, N. (2002) *Conceptualising Livelihoods of the Extreme Poor*, Working paper 1,
    January 2002 Department for International Development, London
Tearfund (2001) *Guide to Tourism: Don't Forget Your Ethics!* 6 August, Tearfund, London
Tearfund (2002) *Worlds Apart: A Call to Responsible Global Tourism*, January, Tearfund,
    London
Tosun, C. (2001) 'Challenges of sustainable tourism development in the developing
    world: The case of Turkey', *Tourism Management*, vol 22, 289–303
UNICEF (1999) cited in WTO (2002) op. cit.
United Nations (1992) *Agenda 21*, Earth Summit, Available from:
    www.un.org/esa/sustdev/documents/agenda21/english/agenda21chapter1.htm12
    (accessed on 15 January 2003)
United Nations (1997) *Agenda for Development*, United Nations, New York
United Nations (2001) 'Substantive issues arising in the implementation of the interna-
    tional Covenant on Economic, Social and Cultural rights: Poverty and the International
    Covenant on Economic, Social and Cultural Rights, Statement Adopted by the
    Committee on Economic, Social and Cultural Rights on 4 May 2001', *Poverty and the
    International Covenant on Economic, Social and Cultural Rights: . 10/05/2001.
    E/C.12/2001/10. (Other Treaty-Related Document)*, United Nations, New York
United Nations (2003) *Report of the Economic and Social Council Assessment of the Results
    Achieved in Realizing Aims and Objectives of the International Year of Ecotourism*, United
    Nations A/58/… Fifty-eighth session, Item 12 of the Provisional Agenda. Available
    from www.world-tourism.org/sustainable/IYE-Main-Menu.htm (accessed on 18
    February 2008)
United Nations/DESA (2002) *Key Outcomes of the Summit, Johannesburg Summit 2002*,
    World Summit on Sustainable Development, Johannesburg South Africa, 26 August–4
    September, United Nations

United Nations Development Programme (UNDP) (2003) *Human Development Report 2003*. UNDP, New York, available from http://hdr.undp.org/en/reports/

United Nations Environment Programme (UNEP) (1994) *Ecotourism in the Wider Caribbean Region: An Assessment*. Technical Report No. 31. Kingston: Caribbean Environment Programme Technical, UNEP, Kingston

United Nations Environment Programme (UNEP) (2001) *Principles for the Implementation of Sustainable Tourism*, UNEP, Paris

United Nations High Commissioner for Human Rights (UNHCHR) (2002) *Poverty, United Nations High Commissioner for Human Rights*, Geneva, Switzerland © Copyright 1996–2002. Available from: www.unhchr.ch/development/poverty-02.html (accessed on 8 February 2008)

van der Duim, R. and Caalders, J. (2002) 'Biodiversity and tourism: impacts and interventions', *Annals of Tourism Research*, vol 29, no 3, 743–761

Van der Merwe, M. and Wöcke, A. (2007) 'An investigation into responsible tourism practices in the South African hotel industry', *South African Journal of Business Management*, vol. 38, no 2, 1–15

van Jaarsveld, A. (2004) *Application in terms of Regulation 16.8 of the Public Finance Management Act ('PFMA'), 1999, Dealing with Public Private Partnerships, for approval of amendment and variation of agreements for the concession contracts*, South African National Parks, Pretoria

Vereczi, G. (2001) *Preliminary Results of the WTO Research Programme on Ecotourism Generating Markets*, Presentation at the Conference on Sustainable Development and Management of Ecotourism in Small Island Developing States (SIDS) and other Islands, Preparatory Conference for the International Year of Ecotourism, 2002, Mahé, Seychelles, 8–10 December 2001

Voss, J. (1984) Die Bedeutung des Tourismus für die wirtschaftliche entwicklung, Ein beitrag zur integration von tourismus forschung und entwicklungspolitik, PhD dissertation, University of Berlin, Cited in Oppermann, M. and Chon, K.-S. 1997. op. cit.

Wilkinson, P. F. (1989) 'Strategies for tourism in island microstates', *Annals of Tourism Research*, vol 16, 153–177

World Commission on Environment and Development (WCED) (1987). *Our Common Future* (Brundtland Report), WCED, Geneva

World Development Indices (1998) cited in WTO (2002) op. cit.

World Tourism Organization (WTO) (1997) *Global Code of Ethics for Tourism*, World Tourism Organisation, Madrid

World Tourism Organization (WTO) (2002) *Tourism and Poverty Alleviation*, World Tourism Organization, Madrid

World Tourism Organization (WTO) (Undated) *(ST-EP) Sustainable Tourism – Eliminating Poverty*, World Tourism Organization, Madrid

World Tourism Organization (WTO) (1998) *Tourism Taxation*, WTO Madrid, cited in WTO (2002) op. cit.

World Travel and Tourism Council, International Hotels and Restaurant Association, International Federation of Tour Operators, International Council of Cruise Lines (WTTC/IH&RA/IFTO/ICCL) (2002) *Industry as a partner for sustainable development: Tourism*, UNEP, London

World Travel and Tourism Council (WTTC) (2007) 'Sub-Saharan Africa: Travel and tourism navigating the path ahead', The 2007 Travel & Tourism Economic Research. WTTC/ Accenture, available from: http://wttc.travel/download.php?file=http://www.wttc.travel/bin/pdf/original_pdf_file/sub-saharanafrica.pdf (accessed on 12 February 2008)

World Travel and Tourism Environment Research Centre (WTTERC) (1993) *World Travel and Tourism Environment Review*, World Travel and Tourism Environment Research Centre, Oxford

Part 1

Policies, Institutional Interventions and Market Forces

1

Local Economic Development in Mozambique:
An Assessment of the Implementation of Tourism Policy as a Means to Promote Local Economies

Andrew Rylance

Introduction

In 2001 the Mozambique Government produced a framework for economic development entitled the 'Action Plan for Absolute Poverty Reduction' (PARPA). PARPA highlighted the importance of poverty reduction and job creation as focal points for economic growth. The policy stresses the importance of local economic development (LED) as one of the most effective ways of contributing to poverty reduction, creating sustainable jobs and building local capacity (Empel et al, 2006). The Government of Mozambique identified tourism as an instrument to promote local economic development. This chapter analyses the PARPA document and the validity of tourism as a proposed solution to achieving PARPA's objectives. It assesses the structure of LED in Mozambique before analysing whether the practical experience reflects the policies and promotion of sustainable growth of local economies.

Helmsing defines LED as 'a process in which partnerships between local governments, community and civic groups and the private sector are established to manage existing resources to create jobs and stimulate the economy of a well defined area. It emphasizes local control, using the potentials of human, institutional, physical and natural resources. LED initiatives mobilize actors, organizations and resources, develop new institutions and local systems through dialogue and strategic actions' (2003, p69). Consequently, LED strategies require engagement with all relevant stakeholders and must promote equitable development and access to resources.

This chapter assesses whether the promotion of tourism has achieved its goals against Vázquez Barquero's (1999) framework that LED strategies ought to focus on three criteria: *hardware, software* and *orgware* (in Rodriguez-Pose, 2001, pp10–11). Hardware is the facilitation of the physical environment by the government to assist the development process (Vázquez Barquero, 1999 in Rodriguez-Pose, 2001). This often includes the development of infrastructure, legislative and tax systems, enabling an efficient environment in which businesses can operate. Software is the construction and implementation of comprehensive and sustainable development strategies. Vázquez Barquero asserts that these strategies ought to be balanced between the competitiveness of local firms, the attraction of investment and the advancing of human capital (Vázquez Barquero, 1999). Orgware goes beyond the structural development of the economy, seeking to involve and empower civil society in the decision-making process and the recipients of the end goal: sustainable development[1] (Vázquez Barquero, 1999). The criteria, recommended by the International Labor Organization (Rodriguez-Pose, 2001), focused on balanced growth, rather than traditional strategies, which were designed to attract foreign investment. It is an appropriate tool for assessment because it satisfies the preceding definition of LED as involving communities, encouraging local control and job creation. Therefore, this chapter assesses the implementation of PARPA upon reflection of these criteria, using practical field data, and whether it has achieved its goals of poverty alleviation, employment creation and local capacity building.

Although Rodriguez-Pose provides an applicable monitoring tool for assessing strategies, the organizational effort involved in developing a strategy that incorporates all relevant stakeholders may be viewed as inefficient and it cannot be guaranteed that the most effective strategy will evolve (Rodriguez-Pose, 2001, p12). There is not one single comprehensive tool for assessing LED strategies but this enables current practice to be compared to the objectives of policy. The criteria allow broad observations and recommendations to be made. In addition, this study is confined by the lack of empirical data on Mozambique. The Strategic Plan for the Development of Tourism in Mozambique confirms that there is 'limited reliable statistical data and satellite accounts to form a base for planning and to measure the actual economic impacts of tourism on the national economy' (Ministério de Turismo, 2004, p46). Consequently, this chapter aims to stimulate debate and highlight issues around the impact of tourism on local economies.

Economic background to Mozambique

The economic development of Mozambique has been variable. Whilst it has maintained strong macroeconomic management, it remains characterized by high levels of corruption, inefficiency and poor infrastructure. In turn, this has discouraged foreign investment in the country. Nevertheless, since 1993, real GDP

Box 1.1 Objectives of PARPA

'The central objective of the Government is a substantial reduction in the levels of absolute poverty in Mozambique through the adoption of measures to improve the capacities of, and the opportunities available to all Mozambicans, especially the poor. The specific objective is to reduce the incidence of absolute poverty from 70% in 1997 to less than 60% by 2005 and less than 50% by the end of this decade' (Republic of Mozambique, 2001, p1).

---

growth was 7.2 per cent in 2004, while GDP per capita grew at an average of 8 per cent per annum over the last decade. Annual inflation decreased from over 54 per cent in 1995 to 13.5 per cent in 2003 and 9.1 per cent in 2004. Socially, literacy rates and school enrolment have all recorded significant increases, which are reflected by an increase in government spending on education (USAID, 2007, p1).

Despite these achievements, Mozambique remains one of the poorest countries in the world and in 2004 per capita income was equal to $320 (UNDP, 2004). The economy remains largely dependent on international donor funding and the lack of capacity of the government means that there is an over-reliance on local economic development agencies to provide social services and local economic projects. Agriculture is the prominent sector of employment accounting for 80 per cent of all jobs in 2003 and contributing to 26 per cent of GDP (SNV Mozambique, 2007, p3).

PARPA

The Government's PARPA is a series of five-year plans that act as the integrated development plan of the country. The 2001–2006 plan aimed to substantially reduce the levels of absolute poverty from 70 per cent of total population (1997) to 50 per cent in 2010 (Republic of Mozambique, 2001, p1), whilst the 2006–2009 plan (PARPA II) is intended to reduce the incidence of poverty from 54 per cent in 2003 to 45 per cent in 2009 (Republic of Mozambique, 2005, p1).[2,3] The main economic policy goal, therefore, links strong and broad-based growth with poverty reduction. It acknowledges that whilst it has achieved economic growth, social development remains unresolved. The PARPA states that *'the country remains one of the poorest in the world, and poverty clearly remains as the key challenge facing the country. Our ability to address this challenge is still limited by a severe scarcity of resources resulting from a serious structural weakness of the economy'* (Republic of Mozambique, 2001, p2). PARPA has identified rapid economic growth as the catalytic force that will assist in addressing these concerns. Therefore, to achieve these objectives, the government has asserted that Mozambique needs to be viewed as a favourable environment for foreign investment and must facilitate the expansion of its private sector (Republic of Mozambique, 2001).

The strategic plan argues that it has developed strategies to ensure that growth is inclusive and benefits the poor, but that primarily there must be a climate that can facilitate this growth. In other words, the large private hotels must first exist before jobs can be created for its staff. The PARPA states that '*pro-poor growth strategy also requires a policy climate which stimulates the private sector to accelerate job creation and increase income generating opportunities through self-employment... The dynamics of human development and broad-based growth are interdependent*' (Republic of Mozambique, 2001, p3).

The collation of evidence by the government was wide-ranging and included Participatory Rural Appraisals, taking into account the views of the poorest communities. PARPA states that '*in the 2001 diagnoses, the need for access to basic social services was emphasized, particularly the shortage of health posts near where people live, lack of transportation for the sick (ambulances), and insufficient personnel. Problems of corruption, lack of a potable water supply – especially the poor maintenance of the existing infrastructures (such as pumps) – were also reported during this diagnosis*' (2006, p20).

Although the strategic plan makes a strong case for promoting pro-poor development, the document produced a strategy without an action plan. It primarily focuses on what Bond (2003) refers to as 'smokestack-chasing' of foreign investment. Bond further asserts that '*orthodox LED strategies that desperately seek foreign investment will only exacerbate their shortcomings*' (2005, p155). In addition, Clarke and Gaile argue that urban policies have often '*favoured investment in amenities, such as hotels*' which tends to benefit the skilled rather than the unskilled (1998, p31). Chasing investment rather than controlling development in a strategic manner hinders its pro-poor impact. PARPA creates a gap between policy and action that should be coordinated by central government.

Tourism as an instrument of development

Tourism was identified by the PARPA (Republic of Mozambique, 2001) as a strategic area that could assist the government to achieve its objectives. PARPA states that '*the travel and tourism industry now ranks first, worldwide, in terms of revenue generation. It is the industry that employs the most people and an industry that has demonstrated an ability to adapt quickly to crises that have battered the world economy*' (Republic of Mozambique, 2001, p135). For these reasons it was highlighted that Mozambique was ideally suited. It has the potential to attract foreign investment into the area and a labour-intensive industry, promoting extensive job creation. It was agreed that Mozambique's natural assets have provided it with a comparative advantage to other holiday destinations.

The Mozambique government has taken a series of actions to promote the tourism sector, including creating a separate Ministry of Tourism in 2001, adopting a Tourism Policy and Implementation Strategy (2003), producing a National

Biodiversity Strategy and Action Plan (NBSAP), and by preparing a Strategic Plan for Tourism Development in Mozambique (SPTDM) (Ministério de Tourismo, 2004).

The SPTDM argues that tourism in many developing countries has been proven to be a significant catalyst for economic growth and job creation. Tourism is labour-intensive and 'pro-poor', with significant opportunities for women and unskilled workers as well as opportunities at the level of small, micro and medium-sized enterprises (SMMEs) and communities (Ministério de Tourismo, 2004). In 2001, tourism accounted for 7.5 per cent of total employment in sub-Saharan Africa (Ministério de Tourismo, 2004, p2). Therefore tourism can play a fundamental role as an instrument in poverty alleviation.

Despite the above, although tourism may have economic benefits for developing countries, it does not come without some negative social impacts. While tourism may be labour intensive, it demands low skills and produces correspondingly low wages. Ashley and Roe maintain that tourism '*brings disadvantages to the poor, by causing displacement, inflation, inequality and social disruption*' (2002, p61). Archer (1978) argues that tourism has reduced the moral standards of developing countries and that they have experienced increases in crime, prostitution and gambling as means of generating incomes (in Mathieson and Wall, 1992). Rothman (1978) found that crime was positively correlated to increases in tourism (in Mathieson and Wall, 1992). The experience of Jangamo District in Mozambique found that '*an increase in thieving ha[d] been mentioned by tourist operators and begging is quite obvious on driving through the villages*' (SLE, 2003, p67). In addition, one may argue that tourism erodes the social culture and local environment to accommodate the demands of tourists.

Impact of tourism on LED

Tourism within Mozambique remains relatively underdeveloped but its '*key strengths lie in the quality of its beach product, the exotic ambience and cultural profile of the country and in its wilderness areas with high bio-diversity. It is one of few countries that can offer this diversity of products*' (Ministério de Tourismo, 2004, piv). Tourist attractions in Mozambique include beautiful sandy beaches and coral reefs; islands; cultural heritage in historic towns; and islands, natural forests and wetlands. Investment is increasing in the area but is concentrated along the coastal and nature reserve areas. However, in terms of being used as an instrument to alleviate poverty and increase employment, tourism has been found wanting. There has been little emphasis on community-based tourism and responsibility has been deferred to foreign organizations, such as The Netherlands Development Agency (SNV) and the NGO TechnoServe, to promote the potential of this market.

Hardware

The development of a physical environment that enables businesses to operate efficiently in Mozambique has been lacking. Mozambique faces some severe structural problems that hinder local economies, beyond the large hotels, from ever exploiting the tourist trade. The poor infrastructure, especially with regards to the state of the roads, means that tourists can only access many communities with four-wheel drive vehicles. Hotels and lodges are predominantly located along the coast, with a small number in game reserves. Tourists are usually transported directly to these areas by the tour companies and have little opportunity to explore the wider communities. As a result, there is little evidence of the 'trickle-down' effect that the Washington Consensus advocates but rather revenue re-circulates around the established firms, foreign owners and middle classes (Stiglitz, 1998).

The issue of locality is central to the development of local economies in Mozambique. The lack of transportation for communities and the poor road system mean that local economies are restricted by the lack of mobility of tourists but also the transfer of knowledge and skills between communities. Therefore, infrastructure seems to be a persistent barrier to development for local economies that exist outside of major cities.

Corruption is also one of the major hindrances to the competitiveness of the tourism trade in Mozambique. A study into the investment climate in the Inhambane province discovered that nearly two-thirds (63.8 per cent) of firms in the province reported being subjected to corrupt actions by public officials. The situation is at its worst in Vilanculo (82.1 per cent) and least prevalent in Maxixe (38.1 per cent). It is calculated that firms spend an average of 9.5 per cent of their gross revenue on corruption (Governo de Provincia de Inhambane, 2004, p2).

Furthermore, land rights are an evident problem in Mozambique as all land is owned by the State. Land delimitation is costly, complex and time-consuming. Some private sector residents on Ilha de Mocambique still do not possess title documents to prove ownership of their property after years of negotiation with local administrators. The informal acquiring of land in prime locations along the coastline is dominated by white-owned private investors and is '*exacerbated by local officials who see the opportunity to cut themselves into any profits from the land*' (McEwan, 2004, p2). Local communities do not have the knowledge or power to negotiate their role in the development of tourism enterprises. Therefore, they either provide the private sector with the rights to develop or lose it as a result of illegal procedures. Corruption could deter investment and in turn thwart the implementation of PARPA. These problems are compounded by the inefficiency of the tax collection as the Inhambane government estimates that it collects only 36 per cent of taxes due from firms (McEwan, 2004, p2).

In summary, although PARPA has identified the need to facilitate an environment conducive for business, it has failed so far to implement its policy recommendations with regards to employment creation and poverty alleviation. Lack of infrastructure, corruption and inefficiency in collecting taxes all have causal affects on software issues such as investment and competitiveness.

Software

Software assesses the inclusive nature of the strategy that aims to attract investment, advance the competitiveness of local firms, and development of human capital (Vázquez Barquero, 1999). As highlighted previously, private investment in tourism is increasing but has been deterred by hardware issues such as corruption, poor infrastructure and the laborious regulatory process. McEwan estimates that tourism investments have involved foreign investment for 70 per cent of the projects in Mozambique (2004, p7). Local borrowing from the banks is exceptionally costly (15 per cent interest in real terms) and makes it very difficult for a local entrepreneur to raise loan capital for investment in a tourism enterprise (McEwan, 2004, p7). Therefore the Mozambique tourism industry remains highly dependent on foreign investment and international aid, and maintains high barriers preventing local businesses from evolving.

Mozambique ranks low in terms of its competitiveness, placed 93rd out of 102 countries in the World Economic Forum's 2004 Competitiveness Index (USAID, 2007, p2). Overall, Mozambique's business environment discourages labour-intensive growth and the establishment of formal sector small and medium-sized enterprises. This situation is worsened by disproportionately high costs of entry and operation in the domestic market. The lack of available finance for small formal business and the time involved in starting a business discourages the majority of society from contributing to the formal sector. As an illustration, according to the World Bank's 'Doing Business in 2004' report, it takes on average 153 days to open a business in Mozambique (World Bank, 2004).

Consequently the formal sector remains extremely small with one of the lowest labour participation rates in the world, at 5 per cent it accounts for 500,000 out of a workforce of 10 million (USAID, 2007, p1). Clarke and Gaile argue that a 'wealth-creating approach entails removing barriers to the creation and expansion of smaller firms and increasing the rate of enterprise development within the community' (1998, p53). Therefore, the development of small formal businesses is both a valuable method of revenue generation for the government through taxation and is a tool for promoting job creation and entrepreneurship in many local economies.

In addition, the tourism trade in Mozambique is uncompetitive when compared to its main competitor, South Africa. Air travel to Mozambique is expensive and the limited number of hotels and lodges predominantly cater for the wealthier clients, which are reflected in their prices. Air travel within Mozambique is limited to the government-owned LAM and Air Corridor, based in Nampula. South African Airways also flies regularly to Maputo. It provides little incentive to price competitively and promote the growth of the airline industry to attract tourists. The average cost of a flight from Maputo to Pemba is US$203.[4] Consequently, this potentially reduces the scope for tourists and also the number of tourists that communities are able to access.

Human capital is recommended by PARPA as a key sector for advancement. However, genuinely local, poor people are still mainly employed in tourism in low level jobs, such as cleaners and bar staff, which hinders their opportunities for wealth advancement (SNV Mozambique, 2006). There have been increases in employment but these are predominantly for low waged jobs where there is little possibility for advancement (Spenceley and Rogza, 2007). This is reflected in Rogerson's analysis of South Africa, he states that '*apart from the job opportunities created for black employees, the prime beneficiaries of this local tourism-led economic development process have been a set of white-owned tourism businesses*' (2002, p161). One private sector organization in Nampula province reported that they were no longer employing members from the local community because they were 'stealing' and instead favoured people from Zambezia province as they were 'more honest'.

Despite the above, there are attempts by NGOs to provide some training for local community members who want to access the tourism market. In Nacala, ADPP, a national association in Mozambique, runs the Escola de Artes e Oficíos (EAO) Nacala, running a one-year professional training in tourism and catering. To date, more than 475 professionals have graduated from the programme.

There is little government involvement in the training of local community members so that they can access the tourist market. Instead responsibility is often deferred to LED Associations working in the area or to apprentice-based learning schemes from the private lodges and reserves (Spenceley and Rozga, 2007). Currently, the IFC Global Business School Network is considering the development of a Tourism Training Network where Mozambicans can learn skills in hospitality and business development (Spenceley and Rozga, 2007). Bendick and Egan (1993) argue that '*community development policies centring on programs for education and training of the smaller, more ethnically diverse future labor force ... will be the preconditions for effective local economic development*' (in Clarke and Gaile, 1998, p202). Therefore, by not providing training or expertise to local communities, the government automatically reduces their long-term economic growth.

Language remains a constraint to local economies accessing the marketplace. Of the total annual arrivals in 2003, only 7.5 per cent were from Portugal, whereas 67 per cent were from South Africa (SPTDM, 2004, pv). Therefore, language constitutes a large barrier to entry for entrepreneurial businesses, as it is extremely difficult to break into the market when one cannot communicate with potential customers. Although Portuguese is the official language, it is rarely spoken in rural areas, further separating communities from the tourism market. The government has identified the need for capacity building and training but there remains little government action. Without policies and investment to reverse this barrier, it essentially excludes the vast majority of the country from participating and benefiting.

Consequently, it is evident that the government has failed to provide a competitive environment for investment and a commitment to pro-poor growth. The constraints on small businesses and communities accessing the tourist industry remain prominent. However, NGOs and associations have begun to address human capital concerns through training and knowledge-sharing, which will assist in lowering the barriers to entry for local economies.

Orgware

Orgware assesses the empowerment of civil society and whether tourism-led LED has led to sustainable development. Including society in the process of sustainable development is important for achieving the government's goals of competitiveness and economic growth (Boddy, 2002, p42). Boddy argues that social exclusion '*goes well-beyond simple notions of poverty, emphasizing broader ideas of "deprivation"*' (Boddy, 2002, p43). Social exclusion is not a separate process but has causal mechanisms, affecting savings and consumption, which are important areas for taxation revenues. Economically, exclusion adversely affects private investment due to higher levels of crime, lower levels of human capital and quality of life (Boddy, 2002). Lower levels of disposable income places a greater burden on the government to provide public services, such as health care, which it is currently unable to sustain through taxation. The creation of Associations such as APETUR (Association of Small Tourism Enterprises on Ilha de Moçambique) and Naherenque-Assopena (an Association of Fishermen in Nacala) are positive steps towards empowering civil society but what influence they exert on the decision-making process is still to be determined.

Nampula province

Nampula province has been relatively undeveloped with regards to tourism and has an opportunity to grow under an integrated plan to promote pro-poor tourism and avoid the negative effects suffered by the south as a result of unregulated tourism development.[5] Dollfus and Laurent (2007) suggest that Nampula province is suffering from a negative image and a poor reputation as a tourist destination. Table 1.1 displays the unpredictable flow of domestic and international tourists into the province. Domestic tourists peaked significantly in 2004 before declining once again. Dollfus and Laurent state that 'the province receives less than 3 per cent of total admissions of foreigners in Mozambique when it represents 10 per cent of the country's land and 19 per cent of the population.[6]

Nevertheless, despite the discrepancies between policy and practice in Mozambique, there are positive examples. The following case studies outline a pro-poor tourism venture by the sector and the informal economy linking into the tourism market.

Table 1.1 *Tourist entries in Nampula province*

	2002	2003	2004	2005	2006
National	12,737	17,132	34,449	11,947	13,245
International	3627	13,563	13,524	8318	10,130
Total	16,364	30,695	47,973	20,265	23,375

Source: Interview: Director of Tourism for Nampula Province, 2007

Case Study: Diverse eco-operation

'Diverse eco-operation' or 'Diverse Cooperation' has established an 800 hectare concession at Memba, north of Nacala. With the permission of the local community, of approximately 1500 people, they are in the process of developing luxury tourist accommodation. The intention is to use tourism to promote local economic development within the community. Fishermen, instead of over-fishing reefs, will be assisted to develop and manage a marine conservation zone where tourists will pay a fee for snorkelling and diving. Furthermore, through language training and accreditation, they will be able to offer boat trips to neighbouring communities, provide deep sea line fishing and act as tour guides promoting the cultural and historical diversity of Mozambique. Indirectly linked to tourism, 50 construction workers have already been trained and will be assisted to find other contracts as a small business. The surpluses of fresh produce cultivated by the community will be sold at the Nacala markets and other tourist destinations, such as Ilha de Mocambqiue.

To date Diverse eco-operation have constructed a borehole for the community and paid women from the community to collect sea urchins. In addition, they have encouraged fishermen not to fish in the bay and, once fish stocks have been replenished, the fishermen will construct a marine conservation area from which they can generate income by charging tourists a fee. This has already been implemented in Nacala by Bay Diving, who have found that fish stocks returned to their original state after six months. Bay Diving are currently engaging with local fishermen to manage the marine site.

Despite the remoteness of the location and poor road access, investors have developed an operation based on the principle of providing opportunities for the community and backed this up with a solid business plan, developed with the assistance of TechnoServe. Two of the investors are tour operators, and one has already made bookings sufficient for 100 per cent occupancy when they open at the end of 2009.[7]

This chapter has criticized both the government for not providing sufficient support to community members wanting to access the tourism market and the private sector for their limited action, limited employment of and limited involvement with community members. However, Diverse eco-operation intends to develop businesses owned by the community and contract their services. As tourist sites grow and demand for their services increases so too will their prices, eliminating the cap on their financial development. Finally, investors have negotiated a land delimitation, which provides the community with ownership of the land and the investors pay rent for its occupation.

Case Study: ASARUNA

ASARUNA is an association of craftsmen in Nampula town, consisting of 50 members who pay US$4 initially for their membership and then US$0.85 in monthly installments.[9] Business support has not come from the government but rather initially from an NGO named 'Aid for Artisans', which provided basic business skills and training to improve the quality of the products. As a result, ASARUNA have linked to the export market and currently sell to the US, China and Europe, as well as participating in trade fairs. The Association are not content with their current size and want to be linked directly to buyers in Europe, removing links in the chain, such as intermediaries that reduce their profit. They have been assisted by the Institute for Export Promotion (IPEX), a non-profit socio-economic unit, to make links with foreign buyers and display their products at international trade fairs. In addition, ASARUNA want to conduct market research to identify what products different markets demand and which of these options are financially viable.

Conclusion

This chapter has addressed the disparities between the intentions of PARPA and the practicalities of its implementation. It finds Nel and Rogerson's conclusion that LED in South Africa is '*pro-poor in policy not practice*' applicable in the case of PARPA and Mozambique (2005, p16). It has assessed the appropriateness of tourism as an instrument to promote local economic development, concluding that it is a valid avenue for stimulating the growth of local economies but, in reality, it has not gone far enough to promote the development of communities. National and local governments lack the financial resources, experience and capacity to construct and implement an LED strategy. Instead, responsibility has been deferred to NGOs and Associations, exposing a gap that links policy to action in a coordinated manner. Development agencies are offering solutions to developmental problems but not in a strategic, structured approach. The question is: if central government cannot perform this role then who will?

Nevertheless, the case studies from Nampula province have provided some encouragement for the future and the assistance that the private sector and NGOs can offer to communities to access the opportunities of tourism.

Vázquez Barquero's criteria have provided a framework from which one can assess whether the PARPA policy has been transferred into practice. It has allowed broad conclusions to be drawn using current empirical data but does not provide a conclusive statistical analysis. The ambiguous nature of the assessment criteria limits their validity but instead, it does highlight the discrepancies between the policy and practice of tourism-led LED in Mozambique and encourages debate around the role of NGOs and pro-poor community development strategies. However, the lack of statistical data and the recent construction of PARPA (2001) mean that it is difficult to draw firm conclusions.

Notes

1   This chapter will elaborate on these criteria in their related sections.
2   This chapter will draw upon evidence from both the 2001–2006 and the 2006–2009 plan.

3   The absolute poverty rating is based on the UN definition of those living on less than
     US$1 a day.
4   www.lam.co.mz (accessed 8 September 2007) and converted www.concierge.com/
     tools/currency.
5   Dollfus and Laurent (2007, p11).
6   Dollfus and Laurent (2007, p10).
7   Dollfus and Laurent (2007, p10).
8   www.concierge.com/tools/currency accessed 4 January 2008.

References

Ashley, C. and Roe, D. (2002) 'Making tourism work for the poor: Strategies and
    challenges in southern Africa', *Development Southern Africa*, vol 19, no 1, 61–82
Boddy, M. (2002) 'Linking competitiveness and cohesion', in Begg, I. (ed), *Urban
    Competitiveness*, Policy Press, Bristol
Bond, P. (2003) 'Debates in local economic development policy and practice', *Urban
    Forum*, vol 14, no 2–3, 1003–1024
Cities Alliance (2007) 'Understanding your local economy: A resource guide for cities',
    Washington. www.citiesalliance.org, accessed 27 November 2007
Clarke, S. and Gaile, G. (1998) *The Work of Cities*, University of Minnesota Press,
    Minneapolis.
Dollfus, A. and Laurent, A. (2007) *Nampula Province: Plan for the Development of Tourism:
    Action Plans 2008–2013*, French Embassy, Maputo
Empel, C., Urbina, W. and Villalobos, E. (2006) *Formulating a National Local Economic
    Development (LED) Policy: The Case of Mozambique*, Local Economic Development
    Program, International Labor Organisation
Governo da Provincia de Inhambane (2004) *Inhambane Investment Climate Report: Results
    and Suggestions*, Government of Mozambique, Maputo
Helmsing, A. H. J. (2003) 'Local economic development: New generations of actors,
    policies and instruments for Africa', *Public Administration and Development*, no 23,
    67–76
Hindson, D. and Vicente, V. (2005) 'Whither LED in South Africa?', An unpublished
    Commentary on the Policy Guidelines for Implementing Local Economic
    Development in South Africa, March 2005
McEwan, D. (2004) *Study of Economic Potential of Tourism in Mozambique: Transfrontier
    Conservation Areas (TFCA) and Tourism Development Project*, Ministry of Tourism,
    Mozambique, February
Mathieson, A. and Wall, G. (1992) *Tourism: Economic, Physical and Social Impacts*, Prentice
    Hall, Harlow
Ministério de Turismo (2004) *Strategic Plan for the Development of Tourism in Mozambique
    (2003–2008)*, Government of Mozambique, Maputo
Nel, E. and Rogerson, C. (2005) 'Pro-poor local economic development in South Africa's
    cities: Policy and practice'. *Africa Insight*, vol 35, no 4
Porter, M. (1998) 'Clusters and the new economics of competition', *Harvard Business
    Review*, November–December, 77–90
Republic of Mozambique, Council of Ministers (2001) 'Action plan for the reduction of
    absolute poverty, PARPA, Strategy document for the reduction of poverty and promo-
    tion of economic growth' (final version, approved April 2001), available from
    http://poverty2.forumone.com/files/Mozambique_PRSP.pdf (accessed on 28
    November 2007)

Republic of Mozambique, Council of Ministers (2005) 'Action plan for the reduction of absolute poverty, PARPA II (2006–2009)', available from www.open.ac.uk/technology/mozambique/pics/d53720.pdf (accessed 29 June 2008)

Rodriguez-Pose, A. (2001) 'The role of the ILO in implementing local economic development strategies in a globalized world', ILO commissioned paper, Geneva, ILO, Local Economic Development Programme, available from www.ilo.org/dyn/empent/empent.Portal?p_prog=L&p_subprog=&p_category=PUB, (accessed on 19 July 2007)

Rogerson, C. M. (2002) 'Tourism and local economic development: The case of the Highlands Meander', *Development Southern Africa*, vol 19, no 1, 143–167

SNV Mozambique (2006) 'Strategy paper – Sustainable pro-poor tourism (SPPT)', SNV Mozambique, 2007–2009

SNV Mozambique (2007) 'Strategic plan 2008–2009', SNV Mozambique

Spenceley, A. (2006) *Sustainable Nature-Based Tourism Assessment of Covane Community Lodge. Transboundary Protected Areas Research Initiative (TPARI)*, University of the Witwatersrand

Spenceley, A. and Rozga, Z. (2007) 'IFC Tourism Training Network market research', *Report to the Global Business School Network*, International Finance Corporation, Washington DC

Stiglitz, J. (1998) 'More instruments and wider goals: Moving towards a post-Washington Consensus', *Annual WIDER lecture*, Helsinki

UNDP (2004) 'Human Development Report 2007/2008, Country Fact Sheet, Mozambique', available from: http://hdrstats.undp.org/countries/country_fact_sheets/cty_fs_MOZ.html (accessed on 29 June 2008)

USAID (2007) *Trade and Investment Programme Tourist Activity: Fiscal Years 2005–2007*, USAID Mozambique

Vázquez Barquero, A. (1999) *Desarrollo, redes y innovación: Lecciones sobre desarrollo endógeno*, Pirámide: Madrid

World Bank (2003) 'Local economic development: Quick reference', www.worldbank.org/urban/led accessed 12 June 2006

World Bank (2004) *Doing Business in 2004, Understanding Regulations*, World Bank/OUP, Oxford, available from www.doingbusiness.org/Documents/DB2004-full-report.pdf

2

Ecotourism in Madagascar:
How a Sleeping Beauty is Finally Awakening

Michaela Pawliczek and Hitesh Mehta

Introduction

Madagascar is located in the Indian Ocean between Mozambique (Africa mainland) and the islands of Mauritius and Reunion. It is the fourth largest island in the world, and is home to 5 per cent of the world's plant and animal species, of which more than 80 per cent are endemic. Most notable are the lemur infraorder of primates, the carnivorous fossa, three endemic bird families and six endemic baobab species (Goodman et al, 2003). However, due to various political, economic, and social factors, Madagascar's tourism and, in particular ecotourism,[1] potentials have been 'asleep' for a long time. The story of Madagascar is similar to that of Walt Disney's 'Sleeping Beauty'. Often called 'divine creation', a 'biodiversity hot spot', a 'Garden of Eden', 'The kingdom of baobabs' or 'Madagascar – La vie en grand', these slogans are increasingly matching the reality. Madagascar is currently awakening to its potential for tourism development and has much to offer to tourists. Some of Madagascar's attractions include:

- 4828km of mostly untouched coastline (CIA World Factbook, 2008);
- the third largest reef in the world and several world renowned spots for diving;
- a unique population, combining African and Asian influences, integrating ancient traditions into modern living;
- a wide variety of options for tourists, including sun and sand tourism, nature and cultural tourism, and adventure tourism; and
- 46 existing protected areas (one of the highest levels in the world for one country) covering 1,700,000ha and hosting 6 natural heritage sites.[2] In and

around these protected areas 85 per cent of flora, 39 per cent of birds, 91 per cent of reptiles, 99 per cent of amphibians and 100 per cent of lemurs are endemic (MAP, 2006, p98ff).

With such a varied diversity of natural and cultural resources, one might think that Madagascar has a very promising base for ecotourism development, especially as the country's political and economic conditions have been stabilized in the recent past. So why has Madagascar not been better recognized as a destination on the tourism map? Why has tourism development not increased living standards for the local population in one of the most underdeveloped countries of the world?[3] Why has a country with such outstanding natural and cultural resources not been able to create a proper ecotourism niche and sustainably manage their resources? These are the questions which this chapter will try to answer by reviewing in detail Madagascar's tourism development history and current ecotourism development.

Background

Before 2002, there was minimal but steadily increasing tourism development in Madagascar. However, this was abruptly stopped in 2002 due to a political crisis surrounding the presidential election. Tourism development came to a halt until 2004 when the few existing tourism operators slowly started to regain their businesses. But they did not receive official recognition from the government and they were therefore left to rebuild their industry alone. Finally, in 2005 when tourism became a prominent foreign currency generator for the country, the government recognized it as a vehicle for the development of the country. At long last, tourism was seen as an instrument to tackle poverty and to increase the living standards and level of education of the local population. To a lesser extent, tourism was also seen as a way to preserve the country's unique biodiversity. During these years the World Bank discerned a need to find ways in which tourism could be used as a tool to improve the lives of local people as poverty worsened during and after the political crisis in 2002. It therefore conducted a major tourism sector study (Christie et al, 2003) which focused on sustainable tourism and ecotourism. One of the main recommendations was to create sustainable tourism physical master plans for key areas as a first stage in a process to improve livelihoods. This study was also the basis of further tourism-related efforts by the World Bank (e.g. The Pôle Intégré de Croissance (PIC) Project).

   In parallel to this the Malagasy Government decided to conduct a thorough plan concerning future Malagasy tourism development supported by the German government. The Malagasy Tourism masterplan (hereafter the masterplan), officially adopted by the government, tourism stakeholders and donors in April 2005, and is available and widely cited (Gato, 2005). Unfortunately, this plan has not been implemented and its recommendations have not been followed up. One reason for the lack of implementation of the plan was a lack of

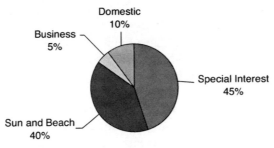

Source: Tourism masterplan (GATO, 2005, p131).

Figure 2.1 *Types of tourism projected for Madagascar until 2012*

knowledge of how to implement it, as well as the lack of capacity of the former Ministry for Culture and Tourism to convince donors to finance the plan's activities. The masterplan reports a mix of tourism types, as illustrated in Figure 2.1.

The special interest category includes ecotourism, culture and landscape tourism, sports and adventure tourism, and cruise trips. These types of tourism are seen as having a high growth potential. It was suggested that ecotourism should remain as a niche in order not to endanger the ecologically sensitive areas visited (GATO, 2005, p129ff.). In Madagascar, this does not seem to interfere with the establishment of the critical mass needed to make it a profit-earning industry, especially for the local population.

Ecotourism development started its upward movement in 2005 with the initiation of PIC Project by the World Bank. The PIC Project focuses on infrastructure development, administrative facilitation and lobbying among international investors. The project also tries to deal with different banks to minimize credit costs for tourism investors, as expensive finance hinders nationals wishing to invest in or enlarge their businesses. This project considered sustainable tourism development for two 'poles': the island of Nosy Be (EDSA et al, Plan D'amenagement Touristique Durable de Nosy Be, 2005a) in the north-west and the region around 'Taolagnaro' (EDSA et al, Plan D'amenagement Touristique Durable de Taolagnaro, 2005b) in the south.

The Nosy Be and Taolagnaro Sustainable Tourism Development Plans addressed the quadruple bottom line of sustainable development: economic, environmental, social and spiritual sustainability. The main philosophy of these plans was that all types of tourism are important to the creation of a successful sustainable destination as long as they adhere to environmental and social guidelines and respect the spiritual beliefs of the local people. In particular, the plans identified specific sustainable tourism and ecotourism projects in both locations which would act as a catalyst for sustained growth. These plans, like the GATO masterplan have unfortunately not been fully implemented, mainly due to a restructuring of the PIC in the direction of more mass tourism development. However, some of the specific projects that were identified in these plans have been taken to the next stage (Nirina Ratsimbazafy, PIC, email 30 June 2008):

- CNRO: a hotel school prioject application is awaiting approval by the Minister of Education;
- Tourism Land Reserve of Sakatia: a request for proposals is being revised by the Economic Development Board of Madagascar; and
- Evatra Lokaro: a part of the land is going through a new delimitation process.

A new national vision to develop tourism with a focus on the environment, 'Madagascar – *naturally*' was publicly announced by the President in February 2006. This was followed by the Madagascar Action Plan (MAP)[4] in November 2006, which sets out the government's political goals until 2012. Looking at the sections on the environment, the MAP outlines two major strategies:

1   Ensure environmental sustainability by adopting strategies for sustainable development and the protection of natural resources.
2   Use resources intelligently and productively: 'We need to minimize the loss and maximize the gain to assure an intelligent and productive use of the nation's resources' (MAP, 2006, p11).

To adopt and implement these two main strategies into practice, eight recommendations were identified, including concrete objectives and indicators. Ecotourism has been included in two of the eight MAP recommendations (see the appendix). These recommendations give a better understanding of changes the government foresees until 2012 (MAP, 2006, 93ff). Some of the important recommendations related to ecotourism are mentioned below:

- Identify and launch new tourist sites and products.
- Promote the destination 'Madagascar' as a superior and unique ecotourism destination.
- Establish a national ecotourism framework and strategy to contribute to the protection and promotion of the environment and to ensure 'eco–eco' harmonization (economic–ecological).
- Establish an Ecotourism policy, charter, code that states the vision, the commitment, the values and the approach for the promotion and implementation of ecotourism throughout the country.
- Establish special zones for ecotourism.

The new national vision presented by the President was followed by further activities at the national, regional and institutional level, including a workshop at the national level entitled 'Assises Nationales sur le Tourisme Durable', in November 2006. Four objectives were given to the participants to discuss and propose actions to improve the situation:

1   improve the management synergies of the acting partners;
2   better integration of the sector into the decentralization programme of the government (strengthen the regional tourism departments to deal with

investors on their own);
3   better repartition of revenues, especially at the community level (better integration of the community into tourism development advantages); and
4   access to finance for projects focusing on sustainable and ecotourism (which is limited today by very high interest rates).

Over three days, around 150 people from the public and private sector as well as donors and NGOs put together a strategy and implementation document to bring to life the MAP's vision. The participants proposed more than 70 concrete actions on how to facilitate and push forward the development of ecotourism and sustainable tourism in Madagascar in the coming years. It became clear that a lot of technical and financial support from the donors would be needed.

Madagascar's National Tourism Board (ONTM) also initiated the platform Ecotod (*eco*tourisme et *to*urisme *d*urable) in early 2006 following demand from its members, including regional tourism boards, tourism associations, Ministry of Transport and Tourism and the private sector to learn more about ecotourism and sustainable tourism. Ecotod's mission is to provide a platform for exchange on these types of tourism between members and different parties (the members include ONTM, NGOs, donors, private and public sector), facilitating discussion of specific topics, the exchange of experiences, expert input and information on current trends, to create synergies between the participants, and also to study and initiate defined and concrete projects with practical and replicable results for the tourism sector. The first year of Ecotod, 2006, showed a remarkable list of practical results:

•   the establishment of codes of conduct for tourists, local population and the private sector;
•   a monthly Ecotourism Newsletter;
•   an implementation plan for eco- and sustainable tourism development in Madagascar for the next five years using the objectives of the Madagascar Action Plan and linking them to activities undertaken in recent years at the national level (such as tourism masterplan, Assises, Ecotod) but also at the international level (e.g. Local Agenda 21);
•   creating synergies between stakeholders and provoking discussions on several topics (e.g. renewable energy); and
•   the development of a Malagasy definition of ecotourism.[5]

With no financial support, this circle of 120 participants, predominantly from the private sector, have demonstrated the interest and will of the Malagasy tourism sector to push forward the necessary actions to develop and broaden this niche industry.

The current status of ecotourism in Madagascar

The current tourism arrival figures for Madagascar are far lower than they could be, considering the country's enormous tourism potential. This is possibly because the Malagasy authorities never really believed in the potential of tourism and its development in their own country. This might appear surprising, but looking deeper into Malagasy culture, the concept of leisure tourism, including travelling for the purposes of a holiday and staying in a hotel, are locally unknown. Similar to African mainland countries, such as Rwanda, the majority of the local population does not have the financial means to travel and if they travel, they stay with family or friends.

Nevertheless, recent tourism development has shown promising results within a very short period: in four years visitor arrivals have more than doubled with over 300,000 in 2006 and the annual growth rate has been between 15 and 20 per cent. Tourism still ranks among the main providers of foreign currency for the Malagasy economy and reached second position in 2006. The average length of time spent in the country is 20 days (Ministry for Culture and Tourism, 2006), which is significant compared to the global average ratio of 12 days (World Tourism Organization, 2006). Europe remains Madagascar's main source market, with the greatest numbers of tourists coming from France and Italy, followed by Switzerland and Germany. In the recent past other countries, such as the US and China, and especially Madagascar's neighbours Reunion, Mauritius and South Africa have discovered the island as a tourism destination (Ministry for Culture and Tourism, 2006). The majority of the tourists are travelling with a tour operator by bus or by car with a local driver.

Current tourism development is concentrated in the North (Nosy Be Island, Diego-Suarez), the north-west (around Morondava), the south road, RN 7, from the capital Antanananarivo to the village of Túlear and to the east including Ste. Marie Island.

As the masterplan has been neglected in the past, the country is unfortunately still lacking an overall understanding of what is needed for tourism development and hindering aspects are the same as 10 years ago. There are insufficient links between the necessary institutions and the private sector; poor accessibility due to limited direct flights from abroad; inconvenient and unreliable infrastructure including road networks, railroad systems and public transport; a lack of tourist facilities such as accommodation and existing products and services do not meet international tourism standards (Gato, 2005). Services are often carried out in the country's own style of 'mora mora' (meaning 'slowly, do not stress!'). The private sector works hard to act more professionally but this is difficult due to a lack of quality training institutions (Spenceley and Rozga, 2007).

From a marketing perspective, Madagascar still lacks an international destination image. Although it is, unfortunately, still an undiscovered location, one could say that it is also one of the best hidden secrets of international tourism today. The push for development, especially ecotourism development, and the lobbying for

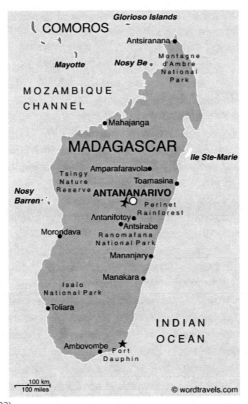

Source: World Bank (2003)

Figure 2.2 *Map of Madagascar showing protected areas and major towns*

international investors is still coming mainly from the private sector and donor institutions. Ecotourism is practised on only a small scale in the country. It is concentrated mainly on visits to the several National Parks and special reserves during tours lasting for a day or two. Many parks and reserves are situated along the well known tourism roads, for example, the National Parks of Montagne d'Ambre, Ankarana, Andasibe-Mantadia, Tsingy de Bermaraha (a World Heritage Site), Ranomafana, Andringitra and Isalo and to some extent Ste. Marie Island and Baie d'Antongil. The training for tourist guides is normally handled by ANGAP (Association Nationale pour la Gestion des Aires Protégées), the national park institution. A three-month training course is given (to be paid by the guide), combined with field work in one of the National Parks. Nevertheless, this is still only a basic level of training and the majority of guides are practising 'learning by doing' or are undertaking self-study courses (e.g. languages). The Chamber of Commerce has established, beginning in 2007, a new one-year dual training course for local guides (50 per cent theory, 50 per cent practice) following a highly successful model from Germany. If this new course is successfully received by students and the private sector, it will be further implemented by Chambers of Commerce in the provinces.

A specific approach for ecotourism development has been initiated from the International Finance Corporation (IFC) together with the concerned Ministries, the National Park Authority (ANGAP) and USAID's MIARO programme in mid 2007. They have put in place a task force for the development of a concession policy for Madagascar's protected areas, namely within the national parks, similar to those existing in South Africa, Tanzania, etc. It is the first time that the Malagasy Government has decided to provide the private sector with concessions to establish their business inside the National Parks. This is a big step for Madagascar, showing once again its desire for ecotourism development, and the government is working with ther IFC and Conservation Corporation Africa (CCAfrica), as an experienced and successful private sector ecotourism player. This step will give Madagascar the potential to promote itself among the globally known ecotourism destinations such as South Africa, Tanzania, Kenya, Botswana, Costa Rica, Belize, Brazil and Australia.

In addition to this programme the national and international private sector is looking forward to setting up or extending their business activities to ecotourism, because it has proved to be profitable in Madagascar, with most tourists (55 per cent in 2007, Ministry of Environment, Water, Forestry and Tourism, 2007) coming for nature experiences. But lacking awareness and training, the majority of the Malagasy tourism private sector do not follow or practise even the basic principles of ecotourism: conservation of nature, benefiting local communities and providing a rich interpretive experience for tourists. Only a very limited number of ecotourism operators (tour operators, agencies and lodges) have made an attempt to specialize in this niche and provide authentic ecotourism tours or projects which satisfy the international criteria for ecotourism:

- Boogie Pilgrim, a notable ecotourism operator, has been working for a number of years with the NGO Fanamby to create a community tourism site in an area of forest near the capital.
- Somacram, another tour operator, is training people in six villages around Antananarivo to develop a tourism product.
- Tsara Guest House has set up an association in Fianarantsoa to support cultural heritage, as well as supporting a number of local NGOs.
- The hotels Princesse Bora Lodge and Spa and Bungalows de Vohilava have established a partnership with the international whale protection association, Megaptera, giving tourists the opportunity to take part in scientific whale observation.

The following paragraphs present two of the above projects in more detail.

Tour operator 'Boogie Pilgrim' and NGO 'Fanamby'

Boogie Pilgrim has been active in ecotourism activities around Madagascar for nearly 10 years (e.g. Mananara Lodge, Anjozorobe, Ecolodge 'Bushhouse', Canal de Pangalanes, 'Tsara Camp', Andringitra) and works together with the NGO Fanamby.

Fanamby, Boogie Pilgrim and 13 local communities came together in their desire to establish an ecotourism project in Anjozorobe, 90km north-east of Madagascar's capital Antananarivo. The forest corridor there (125,000ha including primary forest) has the highest biodiversity level in this region with 11 species of lemurs, 82 species of bird and 423 species of plants. Comprising local communities land and Boogie Pilgrim's managers' privately owned territory 'Domaine de Croix Vallon', the 'SOA Camp' was established in 2002 and extended to the 'Mananara Lodge' in 2007. This ecotourism project tries to conserve the biodiversity around the lodge by providing the local population with sources of income and tries to stop the ongoing deforestation and burning of the forest by creating employment through the lodge's activities (guiding, tourism services, kitchen), establishing educational activities (a training programme for guides, green classes for local schools, tree planting activities) and supporting mini-projects of local inhabitants (agricultural projects, pisciculture, honey production). Tourists' money is spent to support this project. Boogie Pilgrim's partner, Fanamby, ensures holistic integration (vertical: administration–organism–community and horizontal: intercommunal relations) and further economic promotion for the local people by extending the ecotourism project into other surrounding regions. Fanamby emphasizes a scientific approach and has created a biodiversity information system for all stakeholders concerned, including the international donor community. For this project, Boogie Pilgrim was awarded with the 'Sustainable Tourism Award for Tour Operators' of 'Deutsche Reiseveranstalter-Verbund' (German Association of Tour and Travel Agents) in 2005.

Princesse Bora Lodge and Spa, Bungalows de Vohilava and Megaptera, Ste. Marie Island

Each year, between July and September, Ste. Marie Island, situated in the East of Madagascar, provides an important refuge for the humpback whales that come to give birth. The hotels, Princesse Bora Lodge and Spa and Bungalows de Vohilava, have established a partnership with the international whale protection association, Megaptera, giving tourists the opportunity to take part in scientific whale observation. Megaptera's scientific station is installed at Princesse Bora Lodge and tourists leave by boat to see the whales, accompanied by scientists and volunteers. In addition to learning about marine ecology, tourists are integrated into the research activities. They can be involved in locating whales, taking pictures, listening to males with a hydrophone or recording the position of a group of whales. The data collected (sounds, behaviour and descriptions) are added to existing data. These trips, paid for by tourists, help to finance additional scientific expeditions. A part of the revenue from these trips is given to Megaptera as a voluntary donation. In addition to the scientific work undertaken at sea, both hotels hold conferences and present films on behavioural and ecological topics concerning sea mammals (their characteristics, ways of life, threats to their preservation, as well as potential solutions and efforts being made for their protection).

In 2008, after several years of raising awareness and training the local population around the two hotels, the project plans to expand and provide village men
with boats to offer trips to tourists and establish their own micro businesses.
Village women will be trained in making humpback whale handicraft and they will
learn how to establish their own small handicraft stalls.

Ecolodge greenwashing

The misuse of the term 'ecotourism' unfortunately minimizes the reputation and
the activities of proper ecotourism businesses such as those cited above and
undermines their competitive advantage. Lodges calling themselves 'ecolodges'
are mushrooming in Madagascar as a lot of traditional lodge owners use the term
for promotional activities without a proper understanding of the value of the
term. This form of marketing is called 'greenwashing', whereby lodges are claim-
ing to be something they are not. At the present time, there are no regulations and
norms on what can be classified as an 'ecolodge' on administrative level. With this
in mind, the International Ecotourism Society developed an Ecolodge criteria
system in 2002 for determining whether an 'ecolodge' is truly an ecolodge (Mehta
et al, 2002). For an accommodation facility to be called an ecolodge, it needs to
satisfy five of the following criteria, three of which must embody the three main
principles of ecotourism mentioned earlier in this paper:

1   help in the conservation of the surrounding flora and fauna;
2   have minimal impact on the natural surroundings during construction;
3   fit into its specific physical and cultural contexts through careful attention to
    form, landscaping and colour, as well as the use of vernacular architecture;
4   use alternative, sustainable means of water acquisition and reduce water
    consumption;
5   provide for the careful handling and disposal of solid waste and sewage;
6   meet its energy needs through passive design and renewable energy sources;
7   use traditional building technology and materials wherever possible and
    combine these with their modern counterparts for greater sustainability;
8   endeavour to work together with the local community;
9   offer interpretive programmes to educate both its employees and tourists
    about the surrounding natural and cultural environments;
10 contribute to sustainable local development through education programmes
    and research (Mehta et al, 2002).

There is flexibility within this criteria system. For example, an ecolodge does not
need to satisfy the use of local building materials criteria if there are non available.
If this criteria system is implemented and enforced in Madagascar, then greenwashing can be reduced, as has been evidenced in some areas of Australia and
Kenya.

With only a few true ecotourism operators in existence and with the incredible biodiversity Madagascar is able to provide for ecotourism products, it is quite
clear that Madagascar's ecotourism potential is far from being exploited and that

its value to the country's overall economic development has still not been recognized.

It seems that the necessary points for tourism development, especially for sustainable ecotourism development, need to be reinforced or adapted to ensure more successful tourism development in the future. Looking at Madagascar's main competitors cited in the masterplan (GATO, 2005) – Costa Rica, Australia, Brazil, Belize, South Africa, Ecuador, and Mozambique and Kenya – and how they manage and direct their tourism development, a number of elements can be identified that seem to serve as a basis for their successful approach:

- A harmonization of stakeholders' efforts with the creation of synergies between them on a national, regional and local level.
- A clear and practical administrative structure.
- A proper vision and policy for ecotourism development through a realistic development plan, with achievable objectives and concrete activities in a set timeframe; supported by a legal framework that works correctly.
- The development of the countries' unique selling points (USP) with the help of specific products and services, especially at the regional level; increased national and regional promotion and marketing efforts.
- Sufficient education and training systems of a high quality.
- Well-established guiding, tour operator and accommodation certification programmes, such as the Nature and Ecotourism Accreditation Program (NEAP3), International Ecotourism Standard (Green Globe), Eco-rating Scheme (Kenya) and the Certification for Sustainable Tourism (CST) (Mehta, 2007).
- A government that facilitates the tourism development approach for the country by providing and supporting the necessary investment climate and conditions.
- A private sector that wants to produce a profit, but follows a sustainable way as supported by the government and donor institutions.
- The integration of and benefit for the local population from tourism development.

It is clear that one competitor alone is not able to provide all these elements in common but together they provide a framework for long-term ecotourism development focusing on sustainability.

Challenges to address

There are still several hindrances which need to be eliminated or facilitated to finally realize the government's vision as described in the MAP. Some have been already mentioned and will be explained in more detail now. In addition, there are a number of views and suggestions which are currently under discussion by stakeholders that can offer a wider picture to the reader.

Coordination of activities with stakeholders at national, regional and local levels

Increasing efforts from the Malagasy public and private sector and, in recent years, from donor organizations and NGOs have been very intense, especially for ecotourism development. Unfortunately, there is no one body to streamline the different activities of the stakeholders into one common programme, as has been done in some other countries. For a destination that publicly announces that it wants to become one of the main ecotourism destinations worldwide, this is not an encouraging base. Therefore, it is increasingly important that one institution takes the lead in coordinating and streamlining the various efforts of the different stakeholders into one programme. Normally this would be the role of the acting Ministry of Tourism but this has not been the case: neither the former 'Ministry of Culture and Tourism', nor its successor the 'Ministry of Transport and Tourism' have taken up this task. The disorganization of ecotourism development was deepened by the lack of links between the different Ministries responsible for tourism in the past and the Ministry for Environment, Water and Forest. In addition, the links to tourism administration in the provinces are still difficult and hindered by energy supply, technical problems (e.g. internet access) as well as cultural disagreements between the capital and the coast. Therefore people from the provinces often feel excluded from the development process, which creates frustration and tension.

At the time of writing, it seems that the merger of the Ministry of Tourism and the Ministry of Environment, Water and Forest in November 2007, has created the role of a leading institution for ecotourism development for the first time. The necessary decisions are being made more quickly and information is being channelled more effectively to the regional offices for implementation.

Concerning the public–private relationship, the private sector was accustomed to not expecting help from the Ministry when it needed to solve tourism development problems. Business owners grew accustomed to solving those problems that should have been regulated by the responsible institutions at the national and regional level (e.g. ensuring tourists' security, preservation of the environment, establishing training programmes, promoting the country outside). There exists an urgent need for the administration to take over these roles and responsibilities so that the private sector can focus on moving forward with their businesses.

Concerning donors' roles, it was not unusual in the past for two donors to develop the same plan and therefore spend double the amount of money to achieve the same goal. This resulted from a lack of communication. Fortunately, donors have started to communicate and work more intensively together on ecotourism development (e.g. the MIARO programme bringing together USAID, Conservation International and the World Conservation Society, IFC's concession programme linked to the World Conservation Society, Conservation International and Kreditanstaltfür Wiederausbau (KFW). Regarding ecotourism activities from the private sector and local populations and the NGO and donor community there is still a lack of know-how in securing donor and NGO finance, which results in a lot of frustration for all parties wanting to implement ecotourism projects. More technical assistance is needed to meet donors' advanced reporting requirements.

Creation of a clear administrative structure

As a former colony, Madagascar's administrative structure is based on the French system. This has resulted in a top-down rather than bottom-up decision-making process. Ongoing decentralization is being pushed by the President by redistributing manpower: lowering staff numbers in the capital and adding employees in the provinces. Decentralization will strengthen provincial tourism entities and give them greater institutional responsibility.

It was mentioned in the previous section that between 2005 and 2007 the Ministry of Tourism was attached to three different ministries and the minister in charge was exchanged four times. From 2005 until December 2006 it was the Ministry of Culture and Tourism. From December 2006 to November 2007 it became the Ministry of Transport and Tourism. Since November 2007 to the present day, it has been known as the Ministry of Environment, Water and Forest and Tourism. The merge between the ministries of tourism and the environment had been long awaited by tourism businesses and donor institutions focusing on ecotourism. The move supports government statements for ecotourism development in Madagascar. Furthermore, a new department, dedicated to ecotourism development and services, will be launched within this new ministry resulting in a proper base for ecotourism development and activities. The former poor communication and administrative complexity will be hopefully minimized by the merge of these two ministries.

Implementation of an ecotourism development plan that is supported by a legal framework

The masterplan analysed the major obstacles for tourism and ecotourism development in Madagascar and indicated that one big problem is that a certain vision and definition of 'ecotourism' has not been agreed upon in Madagascar. Ecotourism is often confused with nature tourism and the local population has not been sensitized to understand the difference. 'Ecotod' has proposed a definition to the ministry which has been used in the Malagasy tourism law (Code du Tourisme), currently under revision. The revision of this law by the actual Ministry and supported by the IFC can be seen as an enormous step forward, as relevant changes and facilitation were agreed, including those for investment procedures. In addition, ecotourism issues have been integrated into a law for the first time.

Hotel and lodge classification is also under revision. The current indicators are outdated and the classification indicators cannot be checked due to financial constraints. Ministry officials cannot travel to the hotels and lodges to revise their status. As a result, hotel and lodge managers have the ability to list their accommodation in whichever category they like, but not necessarily in the category that matches reality. This is why much accommodation is wrongly classified or not classified at all. It is hoped that the new classification system follows established international criteria and environmental and social issues will be integrated, covering the whole of Madagascar's hotel and lodge business.

Between 2006 and 2007, the President was supported by an 'ecotourism advisor' as a result of the movie 'Madagascar'. In exchange for using the name 'Madagascar', DreamWorks Corporation made a donation to Conservation International and the advisory position was created. Thanks to the advisor's work, ecotourism issues have been largely integrated into the MAP (commitment 7).

The announcement of the MAP as government strategy has resulted in several regional workshops on how to tackle its demands up to 2012. The environmental strategy plan has been reviewed and has been brought in line with this new overall government strategy. The Office National for Environment (ONE) has implemented a green label (Label vert). The indicators used have been largely copied from Australia's National Ecotourism Accreditation Program (NEAP) and are therefore difficult to adopt to Malagasy reality (e.g. the recycling of waste is currently very unusual in Madagascar). This might be the reason why the ONE label is currently not well known or adopted by the hotel industry. Nevertheless, it is a good step towards sensitizing hotel operators and to increasing the competitive environment at the same time. One of the propositions of the Assises Nationales and Ecotod was to implement a so-called 'sustainability label', including not only environmental but also socio-cultural, economic, quality and service aspects, based on the new hotel classification. Seen at the international level, Madagascar would be one of the first countries to group these important aspects for sustainable tourism development into one label.

Ecotod has revised the MAP for ecotourism issues and presented a 'MAP/Ecotod Report' to the Minister. This report presents practical implementation guidelines underlined by a development strategy, action plan, best practice examples, indicators, budget allocation and a time frame. It took into account the already existing plans (e.g. the masterplan) and efforts (e.g. Assises Nationale sur le Tourisme Durable, Ecotod's proper programme), and also used the Local Agenda 21 for the Travel and Tourism Industry as a base for its own framework and as a link to international development efforts for sustainable tourism (Pawliczek, 2006b).

Together with the main Malagasy tourist associations, Ecotod's members have developed the first Malagasy Sustainable Tourism Codes of Conduct for the different stakeholders in tourism. The material for the codes, namely for hotels and restaurants, tour and transport operators, visitors as well as the local population, were based on the experiences and data derived from the earlier development of an ecotourism definition for Madagascar. To keep this definition short, there has been an agreement to explain several aspects further using these codes. The codes are structured using the three aspects of sustainability (environment, socio-cultural and economic) and give practical advice that can be easily followed.

Development of the country's USPs and improvement of marketing efforts

Madagascar has not been promoted aggressively enough by the National Tourism Board (ONTM) in recent years due to financial and institutional constraints. Efficient destination marketing and promotional activities including trade fairs, tour operator familiarization, and press trips are necessary to increase the awareness of potential tourists, tour operators and travel agents. Another problem is that ONTM has had difficulty in finding an all-inclusive slogan for Madagascar. There have been serious discussions about the branding and image of Madagascar. Should there be a single focus on ecotourism or not? Should sun and beach be offered with ecotourism? The country offers a wide variety of holidays for tourists and it was thought that focusing only on ecotourism would not represent the uniqueness of Madagascar and its tourism potential.

In addition, it seemed to be a wise decision of the ONTM to wait to use ecotourism for marketing purposes until it is properly implemented. Instead new promotional material (brochures, a sales manual, website) was developed in line with the presidential vision 'Madagascar – *naturellement*', for activities focusing on the environment. For a marketing campaign in France in 2006/2007 financed by the donor community, the overall slogan, 'Madagascar – La vie en grand' was chosen. Unfortunately this slogan is very much 'French' in the sense that it is difficult to translate its meaning into other languages.

The ONTM has also raised the 'vignette touristique', a tax to be paid by the tourist and the financial base for the ONTM to finance its promotional activities. This decision will hopefully result in increased promotional activities at the international and regional level in the future. Established as recently as 2005, its first three years have seen some promising beginnings for the ONTM. This institution now needs to focus on greater professionalism and higher quality efforts and less of the internal conflicts that hinder it from doing its work properly.

Increasing the availability of education and training for the local population

Training and education in ecotourism matters are unfortunately still nonexistent at the time of writing, which is surprising for a country wanting to become a leader in ecotourism. Sadly, not only for ecotourism but for tourism in general, Madagascar lacks a proper system for education and training. As a result, Madagascar has a large number of unqualified people working in the tourism industry which is preventing it from reaching international standards and demonstrating a more professional approach.

Some training courses do exist (e.g. the national hotel school INTH (Institut National de Tourisme et d'Hôtellerie), the University of Antananarivo and a dual training course from the Chamber of Commerce) but they lack professionalism and international scope (Spenceley and Rozga, 2007). Qualified trainers lack international experience, too, as well as specialization in ecotourism. The major problem is that there has been no decentralization of ecotourism education and training to the different Malagasy districts as currently most of the activities and schools are located in the capital. For many students the costs to cover education and living in the capital or abroad are too high. A starting point would be the establishment of tourism institutions in each of the country's districts and a proper programme to train instructors.

The training of tourism guides is normally handled by the national park authority ANGAP. A three-month training course is given to paying students, combined with field work in one of the National Parks. Nevertheless, this is basic training and the majority of guides are learning on the job or undertaking self-study courses in languages. At the beginning of 2007 the Chamber of Commerce established a one-year dual training course for local guides (50 per cent theory, 50 per cent practice) following a highly respected education pattern in Germany. If this new course is successfully received by the students and the private sector, it will be further implemented in Chambers of Commerce in the provinces.

The recent introduction of English as the third official language, after Malagasy and French, by the Malagasy government is an attempt to open the country up to the international community. The government is also starting green education in primary schools to raise awareness of environmental issues among children and their families.

Government support of the investment climate and conditions for tourism development

Although there has been increasing public demand to improve the investment climate, there has been little active support from the government. Activities have been more or less driven by donor institutions who have tried to facilitate and guarantee investments for the country (e.g. USAID with BAMEX, Agence Français de Développement (AFD), World Bank/IFC). Although the current government has been trying to accelerate tourism development, it is still hampered by a difficult investment climate and investment conditions. Investors are hindered from providing money because of a lack of basic requirements including: land ownership and land issues, investment procedures, the necessary documents being in place, contact people, land speculation in attractive tourism areas, the slow implementation of government decisions, a low level of coordination between the private and public sector and inside governmental bodies, and interest rates which are far too high for national investors to get involved in this business. Special incentives or tax reductions for tourism development and for the construction of proper ecolodges, the recuperation of products and materials and minimizing the use of natural resources, using renewable energies or the implementation of ecotourism products following international standards are not given and it seems that they will not be given until 2009 prior to the demands of the International Monetary Fund (IMF) and its country strategy.

It is no surprise that in the latest Travel and Tourism Competitiveness Report (Blanke and Chiesa, 2008) Madagascar was placed 118 out of the 130 countries that were studied. The Travel and Tourism Competitiveness Report (TTCI) aims to measure *the factors and policies that make it attractive to develop the T&T sector in different countries*. The TTCI is composed of 14 'pillars' of travel and tourism competitiveness. These are:

1　Policy rules and regulations;
2　Environmental sustainability;
3　Safety and security;
4　Health and hygiene;
5　Prioritization of travel and tourism;
6　Air transport infrastructure;
7　Ground transport infrastructure;
8　Tourism infrastructure;
9　ICT infrastructure;
10　Price competitiveness in the travel and tourism industry;
11　Human resources;
12　Affinity for travel and tourism;
13　Natural resources;
14　Cultural resources.

These facts and statistics have a negative impact on potential investors at the national and international levels to finance new projects to boost the Malagasy economy and it lowers their confidence in the country's financial practices. It should not be hidden that in the past international investors for Madagascar were sometimes unlucky and news of their lack of success has spread around the globe, giving Madagascar a less than favourable reputation with investors.

The country is one of the least developed countries in the world and it does not have large amounts to invest in tourism development, therefore it finds itself in the same position as other African countries: it is under pressure to show its credibility to investors as it needs their money to develop the country and move forward. One of the activities showing the country's willingness to give more support to investors today is the creation of the Economic Development Board of Madagascar (EDBM) for investors in 2007 (linked directly to the Presidency), designed to speed up necessary processes for investors (e.g. visa requirements). One current example of this is the improvement of Madagascar's investment climate following the revision of existing laws and procedures (e.g. the above mentioned tourism law with its investment procedures).

Integration of the local population in tourism development

In general, the Malagasy population shows a positive attitude and willingness to participate in tourism development (e.g. intense participation in the development of tourism masterplans). Seen from a tourism perspective, the Malagasy culture is unique: initially coming from Malaysia, today it is a mixture of Asian, African,

Table 2.1 *MAP's tourism development indicators*

	2005	2012
Revenue generated by the tourist sector (millions US$)	184	577
Number of direct jobs created within the sector of tourism	21,167	40,100
Number of tourists visiting Madagascar	150,000	500,000

Source : MAP, 2006

Arabian and European influences. The Malagasy highland tribes (Merina) were colonized by the French who introduced a communist system. Subtle tensions between the Malagasy people from the highland region and those from the coastal region has complicated the development of the country. Malagasy culture is characterized by its great pacifism and is driven by the idea of 'fihavanana', or harmony, which makes it necessary for all stakeholders to discuss and agree on each decision. Decisions take time and much energy with this system. The Malagasy communication style follows the 'fihavanana'-approach which means that overly direct or loud discussions are avoided (Dahl, 1999).

A greater awareness of tavy culture and the integration of the local population into tourism development is desperately needed. Currently only a small proportion of the Malagasy people profit from tourism development and this tends to be those who are already wealthy. The majority of the population have seen no advantages from tourism development. Instead of destroying their natural resource base in the medium term, it should be used for sustainable exploitation such as ecotourism development.

In order to integrate the Malagasy people in tourism development, it is important to be aware of the traditional belief systems, which have been augmented by imported organized religions. A firm belief in the existence of close ties between the living and the dead constitutes the most basic of all traditional beliefs and the foundation for Malagasy religious and social values.

Everyday life in rural Madagascar is regulated by numerous *fady* (taboos) which vary from one region to another. *Fady* can forbid foods (pork, lemur, turtle, etc.), wearing clothes of a particular colour, and bathing in a river or a lake. There are also some sacred places or sites on the island that are *fady* because people believe that some spirits of the ancestors are living there and they offer sacrifices such as zebu and red chicken. Whether as investors, developers, consultants or tourists, it is important to respect these prohibitions so as not to offend local people, even if the foundation of the belief is sometimes debatable. Visitors should inform themselves about local *fady* before travelling to a new place.

Summary and outlook

As a unique biodiversity hotspot and cultural destination, Madagascar has great resources to offer the crowded tourism market. The illustrated indicators defined by the MAP show that developing ecotourism as a niche market has enormous potential.

If only half of these indicators are achieved by 2012, Madagascar's ecotourism development will have made a great step forward. What has not been indicated in the MAP are the necessary actions to meet these indicators.

This chapter has tried to explain in detail the state of tourism and ecotourism development in Madagascar, and we return now to the three questions asked at the beginning.

Why has Madagascar not been better recognized as a destination on the international tourism map?

For a long time, tourism was not even seen as a proper industry sector and efforts for tourism development came from the private sector and donor institutions (especially for ecotourism development). This situation changed in 2005, when tourism became the leading foreign currency provider of the country and the government finally accepted tourism as an industry, appreciating its importance to the Malagasy economy and it ability to increase local living standards. Since this time, tourism development has been pushed continually forward, at the present time having its own chapter in the government's strategy programme, the MAP. As the MAP is a vision, it does not give concrete or practical guidelines on how its indicators could be reached. Activities that could help to achieve these indicators are:

- a proper vision and policy for ecotourism development through a realistic development plan with achievable objectives and concrete activities in a set timeframe; supported by a practised legal framework that works correctly;
- an update and implementation of the Malagasy tourism masterplan (adopted already in 2005);
- widespread awareness raising of the main principles of ecotourism;
- an update of the tourism law to the current reality of the tourism sector to facilitate investment processes by making them more financially attractive;
- urgent revision of hotel classifications to international standards;
- taking account of environmental and social issues and ensuring consistent implementation around the country; and
- the official adaptation of the 'Malagasy Sustainable Tourism Codes of Conduct' from the Ministry.

This needs to be indicated and followed-up by a clear and practical administrative structure, which can be achieved by:

- integrating management thinking into administration as well as providing more training and motivation for ministerial staff;
- redistributing manpower (decentralization) and strengthening the provincial tourism entities;

- implementing a new department especially for ecotourism development inside the new Ministry; and
- minimizing administrative complexity and improving communication channels.

Of especial importance is supporting and strengthening the Ministry of Environment, Water and Forest and Tourism for its new requirements and tasks by all stakeholders. It is vital that this institution takes the lead in ecotourism development and that it coordinates and streamlines the various efforts of the public–private–donor sector into one programme, following one action plan to bring the MAP's vision into effect (harmonization efforts on national, regional and local level). The necessary activities should be implemented as soon as possible and well communicated to the administrative institutions at the regional level. The latter should be better trained and forced finally to take over their roles and responsibilities to the extent that the private sector can concentrate and push their businesses forward.

As financial means for destination marketing and promotion are very limited, and the competition on the international tourism market is high, Madagascar does not get the attention it should, taking into account the variety of activities and the nearly pristine destination it offers. This is mainly due to a lack of proper branding and image creation for Madagascar as a tourism destination and the virtually nonexistent marketing and promotional activities. As the tourism tax, the financial resource of the tourism board, is followed up more closely now by the Malagasy Tourism Board, it will provide more income, resulting in improved and more professional efforts on the international, regional and local levels (e.g. trade fairs). The country's USPs must now be developed, especially at the regional level, along with enhanced promotion of the regions by their Regional Tourism Boards.

Why has tourism development not increased living standards for the local population in one of the most underdeveloped countries in the world?

In addition to the points already mentioned, there has not been enough government effort yet to improve the investment climate and conditions for investors to make tourism a lead sector and convince international investors in particular to set up business in Madagascar. One can see that with the push coming from the MAP launch, the activities of the government will start to bring results, but it is not yet enough to draw investors away from other countries where there are better conditions and greater investment security. This situation could be improved by:

- giving special incentives for tourism development (e.g. reduced taxes for the construction of proper ecolodges, recuperation of products/materials minimizing the use of natural resources (e.g. renewable energies) or the implementation of ecotourism products following international standards;

- speeding up the necessary processes for interested investors to encourage them to convince other investors to come to Madagascar;
- supporting the ongoing concession process for the establishment of high class ecolodges of international quality in some of the National Parks;
- facilitating interest in building similar structures around the parks, with special focus on supporting local SME development;
- further lobbying of three to four star brands from around the world that specialize in classic sun and beach tourism as well as smaller specialized operators (e.g. diving, kyte surf, hiking & trekking, climbing, etc.);
- government statements followed up by actions pushing ecotourism development forward; and
- private sector support of the recent launch of concrete measures taken by the government to increase the Malagasy investment climate (e.g. the creation of the EDBM for investors in 2007) to ensure that more of them will follow.

Until today, the local population has unfortunately not been integrated as much as it should be in tourism activities. There is little channelling of the income and benefits from tourism development directly to them due to missing regulations and lack of planning. The private tourism sector is characterized mainly by foreign hotel owners (French, in Nosy Be Italians, few Malagasy citizens) with international brands still missing. In terms of the employment structure, it remains the same: management positions in hotels as well as in tour operator businesses are filled by foreign people. This is due to a lack of indigenous high quality education in this sector. Increased training and education systems complying with international standards as well as management and training programmes for the local population are of the utmost importance if the local population are to keep up to date with and profit from this new development. As most of the very few existing tourism schools and university courses are based in the capital, people from the regions have often no chance to attend as travel and living costs would be too high for them. For a lot of families, the cost of their children's education is already hard to finance. The solution may be in more decentralization of tourism education to the provinces, preferably in each of the regions. This should avoid the local population being displaced by foreigners and tourism development being destroyed by jealousy – which ultimately might result in poor treatment for tourists. What has not been valued yet is the ability of Malagasy people to learn languages very quickly. The native language is composed of a mixture of languages which makes it easy for the locals to pick up other languages. In addition, donors' financial support programmes need to be accessed more easily and supported by technical assistance as interested people can often not follow or satisfy the difficult procedures or reporting requirements. Better awareness raising and start-up measures (e.g. infrastructure development, micro-credits especially for tourism) are often helpful to show to the locals that tourism developments can have positive results.

Why has a country with such outstanding natural/cultural resources not been able to create a proper ecotourism niche and sustainably manage its resources?

The situation for this niche sector of tourism and its value chain is still somewhat unstable; one could also say that, with few exceptions, Madagascar is not yet an authentic ecotourism destination but has incredible potential to be one in the future. The sleeping beauty has been recently awakened by the government's MAP and major activities as, for example, by the PIC project for tourism development and the IFC's concession programme for national parks. The stated willingness of the government to develop this niche has been indicated by several actions taken in the recent past and the signs for future development are promising. Viewing the outstandingly rich but fragile biodiversity of this country, the focus on high class ecotourism seems to be a promising idea for preserving this uniqueness. To make the wish come true to be the premier ecotourism destination in the Indian Ocean and being able to compete with well known countries already specializing in this area, Madagascar might want to re-direct itself using the following five steps:

1   To establish a proper conservation mechanism to preserve its natural resources, which are very much under pressure: by the countries ongoing deforestation[7] through the local populations' tavy culture[8] and their current poor agricultural practices as well as the actual desire of the government to grow stronger in the mining and oil industries. Instead of appreciating and exploiting the country sustainably by installing a proper ecotourism niche, this given base has to be continuously defended today. One way to protect these important biodiverse areas might be to meet with local community religious and spiritual leaders and agree to place *fadys* on pristine areas for both locals and foreigners. This practice of protecting areas through religious and spiritual beliefs is being used successfully in several places in the world.

2   To have a proper vision for what ecotourism stands for in Madagascar (the majority of the people still confuse it with nature tourism).

3   To develop and manage ecotourism development correctly (establish the necessary policy, implementation, strategy and activity by the creation of a new department for sustainable tourism and ecotourism inside the Ministry of Tourism).

4   To follow this up by managing it in a very professional way, supported by appropriate instruments and mechanisms and the integration of the local population (e.g. by awareness-raising measures to preserve their environment and let them personally participate by improved training and education measures that conform to international standards (e.g. for guides), creating jobs or their own businesses or finding ways to channel the benefits through to them).

5   To speak and lobby about its ongoing development and efforts to the world; especially to investors known for their responsible ecotourism activities thereby attracting them to come to Madagascar as well as the well known international organizations for ecotourism.

It is obvious that today, Madagascar stands at a cross-roads between:

*   Unstrategic tourism development for a few with exploitation of natural resources and pursuing non-sustainable and rapid results to boost the country's development.

Or

*   A harmonized mix of different types of tourism (of which ecotourism is an important one) to develop the economy of the country by integrating the local population and improving their living standards, targeting a responsible and long-term vision in which nature resources will be exploited in a sustainable way.

Malagasy tourism development seems to be heading in the second direction and the ongoing activities of the current government are supported by their first positive results. If the country continues like this and develops ecotourism as a means to boost the Malagasy economy and to increase the living standards of the local population, it will hopefully help to improve the country's development. Although donors' help is still needed to provide financial as well as technical assistance for the topics discussed above, it seems that Madagascar has finally started to address the MAP and its vision.

We wish Madagascar, the Sleeping Beauty in the Indian Ocean, recently kissed awake, success in becoming the leading ecotourism destination in the Indian Ocean and for the President's slogan to become true and respected worldwide:

Madagascar – Naturellement!

Notes

1   The International Ecotourism Society (TIES) defines ecotourism as 'responsible travel to natural areas that conserves the environment and improves the well-being of local people.'
2   The Malagasy President has emphasized his willingness to increase protected areas to 6,000,000ha as well as to increase the surface of marine protected areas to 10 per cent of national territory.
3   According to the Madagascar National Institute of Statistics, 68.7 per cent of the island's inhabitants live below the poverty threshold (INSTAT, 2005).

4   'To accelerate and better coordinate the development process and to make a quantum leap, we have created the Madagascar Action Plan, the MAP. The MAP is a bold, five-year plan which establishes direction and priorities for the nation from 2007 to 2012. It states the commitments, strategies and actions that will ignite rapid growth, lead to the reduction of poverty, and ensure that the country develops in response to the challenges of globalization and in accordance with the national vision "Madagascar – Naturally" and the UN Millennium Development Goals' (Marc Ravalomanana, President of the Republic of Madagascar).

5   Ecotod's ecotourism definition reads 'Un tourisme responsable et durable basé sur la conservation du patrimoine naturel et socio-culturel de Madagascar.' [A responsible and sustainable tourism which is based on the preservation of the natural and socio-cultural heritage of Madagascar].

6   'An ecolodge is a 5–75 room low-impact, nature–based, financially sustainable accommodation facility that helps protect sensitive neighbouring areas; involves and benefits local communities; offers tourists an interpretative and interactive participatory experience; provides a spiritual communion with nature and culture and is planned, designed, constructed and operated in an environmentally and socially sensitive manner' (Mehta, 2007).

7   With the average rate of clearance of 111,000ha of forest (1.5 per cent) per year between 1950 and 1985, in this time one half of Madagascar's forests disappeared (Green and Sussman, 1990).

8   Tavy culture is the practice of burning down tropical forest for rice planting and other agricultural purposes.

References

Blanke, J. and Chiase, T. (2008) *The Travel and Tourism Competitiveness Report 2008*, World Economic Forum, Geneva

Christie, I., Crompton, E., Sharma, A., Rajeriarison, P., Ralijaona, A. and Mandinga, N. (2003) *Madagascar: Tourism Sector Study*, World Bank, Washington DC

CIA World Factbook (2008) Madagascar country page, www.indexmundi.com/madagascar/coastline.html, accessed 25 March 2008

Dahl, O. (1999) *Meanings in Madagascar: Cases of Intercultural Communication*, Bergin and Garvey, Westport, CT

EDSA, Détente., GLW Conseil and Spenceley, A. (2005a) *Plan D'amenagement Touristique Durable de Nosy Be*, World Bank and Ministere des Transports, des Travaux, De L'Amenagement du Territoire, EDSA, Ft. Lauderdale US

EDSA, Détente, GLW Conseil and Spenceley, A. (2005b) *Plan D'amenagement Touristique Durable de Taolagnaro*, World Bank and Ministere des Transports, des Travaux, De L'Amenagement du Territoire, EDSA, Ft. Lauderdale US

GATO AG (2005) *Tourism Master-plan for Madagascar*, vol I-III. Unpublished

Green, G. M. and Sussman, R. W. (1990) 'Deforestation history of the eastern rain forests of Madagascar from satellite images', *Science*, vol 248, no 4952, pp212–215

INSTAT (2005) www.instat.mg/, accessed 25 March 2008

MAP (2006) *Madagascar Action Plan*, Presidency of Madagascar

Mehta, H. (2007) 'Towards an internationally recognized ecolodge certification', in R. Black and A. Crabtree (eds) *Quality Assurance and Certification in Ecotourism*, CAB International, Oxfordshire, UK

Mehta, H., Baez, A. and O'Loughlin, P. (eds) (2002) *International Ecolodge Guidelines*, The International Ecotourism Society, Burlington, Vermont

Ministère de la Culture et du Tourisme (1995) *Code du Tourisme. LOI No95-017*

Pawliczek, M. (2006a) Ebauche d'une vision et stratégie pour un département écotourisme et tourisme durable à l'Office National du Tourisme, Madagascar, Ecotod internal document

Pawliczek, M. (2006b) Présentation d'un essai pour le développement d'un cadre pour l'écotourisme et le tourisme durable à Madagascar, Assises Nationales pour le Tourisme Durable, 21–21 November 2006, Antananarivo, Madagascar

Spenceley, A. and Rozga, Z. (2007) *IFC Tourism Training Network – Market Research Report*, Global Business School Network, IFC, Washington DC

Wikipedia (2008) http://en.wikipedia.org/wiki/Madagascar, accessed 25 March 2008

Appendix

Recommendation 6.8 : Intensively promote and develop the tourism sector

Objectives

Madagascar will be a privileged destination for all categories of tourism, with a primary focus given to ecotourism. International hotel chains will be encouraged to invest in Madagascar, so as to solve the problem linked to the lack of infrastructure and suitable accommodation. Local domestic operators will be encouraged to develop further the breadth and standard of their facilities and programmes. Madagascar will be amongst the leading countries in sub-Saharan Africa and the Indian Ocean in the promotion of a high-quality ecotourism experience.

Strategies

1   Attract high quality investors by the provision of incentives, access to land, and general support.
2   Promote the destination 'Madagascar' as a superior and unique ecotourism destination.
3   Support management development and professionalism of the tourist sector.
4   Improve the range of tourism products and services.

Projects and priority actions

- Identify and launch new tourist sites and products.
- Set up a tourist database.
- Broaden the network of tourism agencies.
- Develop e-tourism (online purchase, electronic payment terminal, credit cards, etc.).
- Identify priority tourist sites which are favourable to investment; speed up and facilitate the procedures for the setting up and exploitation of investment projects (EDBM).
- Rationalize the management of hotel assets with public participation.
- Support training activities in the tourism sector.

Recommendation 7: Cherish The Environment (*selection*)

Madagascar will be a world leader in the development and implementation of environmental best practice. After many decades of exploitation and neglect, we have begun to turn the tide. We will become a 'green island' again. Our commitment is to care for, cherish and protect our extraordinary environment. The world looks to us to manage our biodiversity wisely and responsibly and we will. Local communities will be active participants in environmental conservation under the guidance of bold national policies. Given the Government's vision 'Madagascar – *Naturally*' – we will develop industries around the environment such as ecotourism, agri-business, sustainable farming practices, and industries based on organic and natural products. These industries and activities will minimize biodiversity damage and maximize benefits for the nation and the people.

Challenge 1: Increase the protected areas for the conservation of land, lake, marine and coastal biodiversity

Objective: ... Madagascar will become a green nation which contributes not only at its national health but also at the global one.

Strategies
...
5   Establish a national eco-tourism framework and strategy to contribute to the protection and promotion of the environment and to ensure 'eco–eco' harmonization (economic–ecological).

Projects and priority actions
1   Inform and raise awareness with all stakeholders.
2   Carry out Surveys / Inventories.
3   Conduct national, regional and communal consultations.
...
8   ... Provide for the ecological monitoring and the implementation of measures for the conservation of land and watery ecosystems.

Challenge 2: Reduce the natural resource degradation process

Objectives: Madagascar commits to keep its 9 m hectare forest and wetland area for the conservation of its natural richness and the sustainable use of its forest, lake, marine and coastal resources.

Strategies
...
•   Promote the development and use of alternative energy resources such as biofuels that include palm oil, jatropha, soy and sugar cane.
...
•   Promote reforestation and restore degraded habitats.
•   Promote private sector financing to assist in environmental management.

Projects and priority actions
•   Support the use of improved charcoal making techniques.

Challenge 3: Develop the environmental reflex at all levels

Objectives: We will mainstream the environment into all sectoral plans and develop a strong and effective environmental reflex.

Strategies
1   Explore ways that the government (national, regional and local) with the help of the private sector can assist in environmental protection and ensure that the highest global standards are met.
2   Strengthen the framework for preventing environmental damage (including pollution) caused by businesses, miners, farmers, fishermen and tourism.
3   Contribute to the protection of sensitive zones through comprehensive environmental assessment.
4   Internalize the environmental stake into sectoral, regional and communal policies.
5   Implement the Education Policy Relative to the Environment (Politique de l'Education Relative à l'Environnement (PERE)).

Projects and priority actions
*   Assure the ratification and implementation of the international conventions as for example the Kyoto Protocol.
*   Develop the Code of the Environment.
*   Reduce pollution in industrial zones located in urban, rural and port areas.
*   Develop the value chains in potential business sectors to ensure that biodiversity is linked to the economy.
*   Establish an Eco-tourism policy, charter, code that states the vision, the commitment, the values and the approach for the promotion and implementation of ecotourism throughout the country.
*   Establish special zones for ecotourism.
*   Promote and create investment standards to maintain quality
*   Develop, coordinate, share and promote important environmental information.
...
*   Promote the compatibility of investment with the environment.
*   Promote strategic environmental assessment (EAS) in the sectors of ..., tourism, ...

3

Public–Private Partnerships in South African National Parks: The Rationale, Benefits and Lessons Learned

Giju Varghese

Background and introduction

The conservation of nature and heritage provides benefits to societies and this is recognized by all countries. Some of the benefits of nature conservation include the slowing or even elimination of the threat of climate change; having good water supplies and preserving species that can contribute to research for the prevention and control of existing and future diseases. The conservation and preservation of heritage promotes local cultures, creates employment and results in mutual respect and exchange in a positive way. This can lead to the positive co-existence of communities and regions (the peoples of the world) and can positively contribute to global peace. Both nature and heritage conservation in South Africa are government or non-governmental organization (NGO) led: they cannot be led by the private sector as these are areas that do not provide returns on investments. Therefore, certain companies may contribute a very small proportion of their profit towards corporate social investment. Conservation is very expensive and its planning needs to be very much long term: millions of years in the case of nature-based projects. The benefits are often realized after the tenure of government leaders and for this reason conservation may not get the focus it requires. Therefore, conservation funding is frequently unavailable at the desired level.

The conservation of nature and heritage provides an opportunity for tourism, which is already a large and growing industry that contributes significantly to GDP in many countries. The developing world offers various biodiversity hotspots, usually in remote areas where poverty is prevalent. Tourism, as a large scale industry, can be an opposing force for conservation as it could lead to the over-consumption of natural resources that need to be preserved. Tourism developed by large industry players can lead to the prevalence of financially dominant investors and market forces taking precedence over any other socioeconomic or biodiversity needs. Whilst there are various forms of tourism, from largly consuming and commercial to small–medium and micro enterprise (SMME) based, if the context of tourism is responsibly conducted, it can provide a conduit through which to communicate conservation and heritage imperatives.

South African National Parks (SANParks) is a state run conservation body that runs a system of 23 national parks. With its focus on nature conservation, the organization manages over 4 million hectares of pristine wilderness and protects six biomes of flora including the Cape Floral Kingdom, which is unique to South Africa. The organization was an early entrant into nature-based tourism and has a large state run tourism base, with over 6000 beds and 6000 camping sites available. Initially these were exclusively for the use of the minority white population (about 4 million people of European origin) and run on a not-for-profit basis. The democratization of South Africa in 1994 changed the dynamics of the financial model for nature-based tourism in SANParks: the government is now answerable to a larger population of 44 million people and the prioritization of conservation was replaced by more pressing national needs. In addition to an increased need to look after the interests of often poor neighbouring communities adjacent to the remotely located National Parks, SANParks also embarked on a programme to increase the amount of nature conservation land. Thus the organization was faced with increased funding requirements to satisfy both conservation and community needs, and was forced to look for smarter and more effective sources of funding. This chapter looks at SANParks' commercialization initiative as achieved through public–private partnerships (PPPs).

South African National Parks' vision and mission

South African National Parks (SANParks), hitherto known as the National Parks Board, was established as a parastatal through an Act of Parliament in 1927. As per the Public Finance Management Act, Act 1 of 1999 (as amended by Act 29 of 1999), SANParks is a Schedule 3(a) 'public entity' that functions under the ambit of the NEMA: Protected Areas Act, 2003 (Act 57 of 2003) read concurrently with the Biodiversity Act of 2004. The core mandate of SANParks is the conservation and management of biodiversity and associated cultural heritage through a system of National Parks. SANParks is also involved in the promotion and management of nature-based tourism, and delivers both conservation management and tourism services through an authentic people-centred approach in all its programmes.

The organization's operations are totally guided by its vision and mission. The vision is that national parks will be the pride and joy of all South Africans and of the world. SANParks' mission is to develop and manage a system of national parks that represents the biodiversity, landscapes and associated heritage assets of South Africa for the sustainable use and benefit of all. As a public entity, the organization is committed to act in pursuance of the transformation of South Africa's society in support of entrenching South Africa's democracy. In this regard the organization has adopted a transformation mission to guide its efforts accordingly. The transformation mission is designed to ensure an effective transformation both within SANParks and in the broader society and economy, through the implementation of Broad-Based Black Economic Empowerment (BBBEE) in support of the Constitution of South Africa.

To put the transformation objective in perspective, it is important to understand the context of South Africa. For over 400 years the country was ruled by a white minority and for 50 years prior to 1994, the government had structured Apartheid laws that prevented the participation of the black majority of South Africa from the economy. Black people were also stripped of their land and the majority of 40 million black people were relocated from their homes to land that covered less than 20 per cent of the country, and to areas that were often arid and barren. The social injustices that took place over the years need to be reversed, and the current government has introduced a BBBEE policy through the country's constitution. Any people from the black population (i.e. people of African, Asian and mixed race), who did not have voting rights until 1994, are described as historically disadvantaged individuals (HDIs).

From a funding perpective, SANParks receives an annual subsidy from Government which funds 20 per cent of its operational requirements (about R600 million [≈US$80 million]), and the balance of its funding requirements are self-generated through its tourism industry. All revenues generated in national parks are retained and applied to the execution of its mandate, as determined by the Board of Trustees.

SANParks' key strategic objectives

The primary mandate of the organization is the conservation of South Africa's biodiversity, landscapes and associated heritage assets through a system of National Parks. In addition, the organization has a significant role to play in the promotion of South Africa's nature-based tourism, or ecotourism business, targeted at both international and domestic tourism markets. The ecotourism pillar of the business architecture provides for the organization's self-generated revenues from commercial operations that is necessary to supplement government seed funding of conservation management. A significant element of the ecotourism pillar is the Commercialization Strategy, which has as its objective reducing the cost of delivery, improving service levels by focusing on core business and leveraging private capital and expertise in addition to the expansion of tourism products and the generation of additional revenue for the funding of conservation and constituency building.

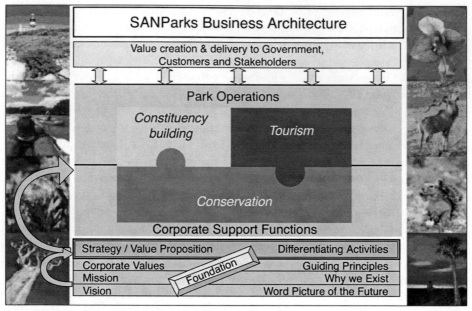

Source: SANParks Corporate Strategy Business Plan V4 (2)

Figure 3.1 *Business architecture of SANParks*

Under the Commercialization Strategy, PPPs allow state institutions to lease assets to the private sector for a period of time, after which the assets revert back to the state. This is different to the privatization of state property where the assets are transferred to the private sector (the state does not have the assets any longer). PPPs are thus a good vehicle for state institutions to utilize to increase a country's global positioning. In SANParks' case, they allow South Africa to increase the tourism infrastructure to allow it to compete with countries like Brazil, India and Thailand in the global market. In addition to attracting capital, PPPs allow state institutions to leverage private sector business skills, transfer business risks to the private sector, create employment and also enhance the state institution's image by putting its resources to good use.

SANParks is required to build constituencies at international, national and local levels, in support of the conservation of the natural and cultural heritage of South Africa. It has to ensure that a broad base of South Africans participate in biodiversity initiatives, and, further, that all its operations have a synergistic existence with neighbouring or surrounding communities for their socioeconomic benefit. Figure 3.1 depicts the organization's business architecture.

Articulation of SANParks' commercialization policy, objectives and strategy

The motivation for commercialization

The IUCN states that:

> *Global conventions and programmes alone are not enough to ensure the continued existence of, and sufficient funding for, protected areas. In times of fiscal austerity and tightening government budgets – especially in developing countries which are home to much of the world's biodiversity – traditional funding sources are increasingly under threat. Innovative alternatives to these traditional sources are needed in order to secure the long-term viability of protected areas.*
>
> (Vorhies, 1998, p6)

In order to encourage greater efficiency in the delivery of public services, in April 1997 the Cabinet approved the establishment of an interdepartmental task team chaired by the Department of Finance, to explore how PPPs could improve infrastructure and service delivery efficiency, and make more efficient use of under-utilized state assets. The key objective of this programme was to develop a package of cross-sectoral and inter-institutional policies and legislative and regulatory reform.

In September 1998, the Department of Environmental Affairs and Tourism articulated the need for SANParks to prepare for less dependence on state funding, which would increasingly be aimed at funding the essential conservation requirements. This formed the basis of the Commercialization Strategy adopted by SANParks in 2000, with its foundation in the economic theory which defines the State's responsibility as one of performing a regulatory function and intervening in the marketplace only where there is market failure. The objective was to reduce the dependence on state funding and improve existing operational efficiencies. This does not imply that SANParks has to be independent of the State but rather that the collective funding sources (i.e. state funding, private donations, NGO and international donations, SANParks' tourism activities and commercialization) must be able to 'sustain' the total business of SANParks. Sustainable tourism development depends on a partnership and a balance between the social, technological, economic, environmental and political values and benefits. Hence, should one source of funding be threatened, SANParks must be able to absorb such withdrawal without compromising its sustainability.

The implementation of the Commercialization Strategy 2000 resulted in the awarding of eleven concession sites to private operators, seven of which are in Kruger National Park, two in Addo Elephant National Park, and two in Table Mountain National Park. A typical concession entails allowing private operators to build and operate tourism facilities within the National Parks, on the basis of a 20-year concession contract. Investors either took over and upgraded specified existing lodge facilities or built new ones. The contractual mechanism is in the form of a concession contract, which enables the concessionaire to use a defined area of land, plus any buildings that may already exist on that land, over a specific time period in return for the payment of concession fees. Against these rights of occupation and commercial use of facilities, there is a set of obligations on the part of the concessionaire regarding financial terms, environmental management, social objectives, empowerment and other factors. Infringement of these requirements carries specified penalties, underpinned by performance bonds, and finally termination of the contract, with the assets reverting to SANParks. In addition to the accommodation concessions, the Commercialization Strategy 2000 also resulted in the awarding of 21 shops and 17 restaurants across all national parks to private operators. Facilities were upgraded at the operator's expense whilst SANParks receives a guaranteed monthly annuity income from these operators.

Tender processes in PPP processes are as prescribed by Regulation 16 of the Public Finance Management Act of South Africa. Once bids are received, they are evaluated for their technical, empowerment and financial credentials. The technical specifications are usually developed with the assistance of industry experts for the specific product being put out to tender. Empowerment (or Black Economic Empowerment, BEE), is a combination of Equity (or ownership), SMME development, and Training and Affirmative Action. BEE requirements are guided by the Tourism Charter (a code of good practice developed for the tourism industry that is currently in the process of being legislated). The financial bid would allow an evaluation of quantifiable investments and a percentage of turnover as committed by the bidder.

Benefits of the Commercialization Strategy 2000

The Commercialization Strategy 2000 yielded benefits to SANParks in terms of strategic value, monetary value, increased infrastructure and socioeconomic value, environmental value and risk transfer.

Strategic value

Implementation of the Commercialization Strategy 2000 has resulted in increased market segmentation and product and price differentiation with 380 additional guest beds in the five-star segment, resulting in increased economic activity and the generation of foreign exchange. SANParks did not previously operate any facilities in the five-star market, as its existing beds and camp sites were in the budget two- to three-star market. In addition, implementation of the Strategy has resulted in improved efficiencies in restaurant and retail facilities, contributing to an enhanced visitor experience for the guests of SANParks.

The Strategy has also resulted in an increased contribution to the broader economy through the tourism multiplier effect and SANParks' image has improved as it is more widely perceived that the national parks are being put to responsible and sustainable use for the economic development of the country.

Monetary value

The Commercialization Strategy 2000 has, since 2002, yielded the net income shown in Table 3.1 to SANParks for the funding of SANParks' operational mandate.

Table 3.1 *Income from commercialization to SANParks*

Product	Total income	US$ Equivalent (R7.50 = US$1)
Concessions	R54,954,278	$7,327,237
Other	R30,299,941	$4,039,992
Restaurant and retail facility rentals	R37,002,267	$4,933,636
Total	R122,256,506	$2,967,534
Commercialization expenses to date	−R15,254,346	$2,033,913
Net income commercialization	R110,002,160	$14,666,955

Note: Figures as at 31 March 2007.

Source: Adapted from SANParks' Annual Report 2006–7

The financial returns depicted in Table 3.1 represent a net benefit/profit to SANParks constituting 11.63 per cent of total tourism revenue (before expenditure).

Increased infrastructure and socioeconomic value

The Commercialization Strategy roll out has resulted in increased infrastructure with the concessions to the value of R270 million (in 2001 terms: US$36 million) with the assets ultimately reverting to SANParks. In addition, it has resulted in the refurbishment of the ageing infrastructure of both the restaurant and retail facilities, to the value of R15 million (≈US$2 million).

The strategy resulted in broadening the participation of BEE partners in the tourism industry, thereby contributing to the demographic restructuring of the industry and poverty alleviation. Private Party agreements included the following contractual commitments:

- increased employment in the tourism industry with 620 new jobs excluding construction;
- BEE Equity in excess of the national Tourism BEE Charter and Scorecard requirements;
- a total of 79 per cent of employees recruited from HDI communities adjacent to the Parks;
- a guaranteed spend of R14 million (≈US$1.6 million) per annum with local community SMMEs;
- considerable continuous skills transfer and training; and
- the tourism multiplier effect to the broader economy.

Environmental value

As a conservation body, stringent Environmental Impact Assessment (EIA) requirements are required before any tourism project is embarked upon. Expert consultants are sourced for tourism development processes to conduct EIAs and the process can take a few months, thus ensuring environmental aspects are covered thoroughly. As a state conservation body, SANParks has also developed benchmarks that are often more stringent than the requirements of the EIA and other government specifications. The environmental regulations that apply to commercial operators are in many instances superior, creating a benchmark in SANParks own nature-based tourism operations and, over time, SANParks will be obliged to comply with these standards. This can only be to the long-term benefit of South Africa's national parks.

Risk transfer

The Strategy has resulted in significant commercial risk transfer to the private sector, including construction risk, availability risk, insolvency risk, market demand or volume risk and operating risk. However, SANParks is still exposed to the risks experienced by the private party and hence effective contract management is essential.

Lessons learnt from the Commercialization Strategy 2000

As such projects typically yield high returns, and thus associated high risks are expected, the need for SANParks to effectively learn and adapt from all the lessons learnt is of the utmost importance.

Fundamental shift towards 'Responsible Tourism and Commercialization'

The Commercialization Strategy 2000 was developed during a period when SANParks was particularly short of cash and experiencing financial challenges and constraints. The Strategy was hence developed as a commercial alternative to state funding in order to ensure survival. The emphasis was placed on the need for SANParks to become financially self-sufficient or self-supporting. However, SANParks subsequently underwent a fundamental shift in its thinking to a more responsible approach to tourism and commercialization.

In developed countries the cost of managing protected areas is mostly borne in full by the state, whereas in developing countries such as South Africa, there is a mix of donor-dependency and heavy reliance on tourism development. SANParks generates approximately 80 per cent of its operational revenue from tourism and commercialization contributes to 12 per cent of tourism revenue. However, there are limitations to tourism performance, particularly if the biodiversity mandate is not to be compromised.

At SANParks the phenomenal national park expansion of 140,000 hectares since 1994 has not been matched by an increase in the state operational grant.

Such under-funding manifests itself in infrastructural disrepair, insufficient resources, an inability to retain competent staff, etc. Only five out of the total of 20 parks generate a surplus or break even. Faced with such statistics, 'financial self-sufficiency' is unrealistic. The Kumleben commission of inquiry into the state of conservation in 1988 concluded that nature conservation could never be self-supporting, and therefore it is short-sighted and fallacious to expect a protected area to become economically self-sufficient (Kumleben et al, 1998).

Thus the State cannot abdicate its primary obligation to fund environmental protection and with the development of the tourism and Commercialization Strategy, cognizance is taken of the ecological integrity of the protected areas.

SANParks' success should be measured in terms of the 'triple bottom line': economic prosperity, environmental quality and social equity (Elkington 1997).

Adopt an increased institutional consultative approach

Whilst the process understanding was high, the maturity level of SANParks and the private party engaged with may not have been ready for a large paradigm shift in park management. Change management and personnel issues require considerable focus: many parks hold the view that the process of project identification and strategy adoption have not been consultative, in many cases the private sector and SANParks showed a lack of understanding of the importance of working as partners. This has resulted in park managers and members of SANParks' executive committee perceiving commercialization, wrongly or rightly, as a process for personal agendas and not for the benefit of SANParks.

Selecting the wrong vendor – the relative weighting of financial model with bid evaluation

The management of outsourced facilities exposes the operations/technical ability of the private sector to a greater extent than that of lodge operators, as the outsourced operations are integrated and serve the same SANParks guests. As a result, there has been more scrutiny of product delivery and thus more replacement of various private, outsourced service providers, such as the restaurant operators in the Eastern Cape and the Kruger National Park.

These lessons led SANParks to critically analyse the vendor selection process. While the financial criteria in PPPs are a fundamental part of the bid evaluation, it has become clear that the emphasis on financial forecasting is taking inappropriate priority relative to other key indicators such as proven operational ability, proven marketing capability and existing client bases, all of which are more accurate indicators of long-term sustainability than financial forecasts that can be manipulated by bidders to win bids.

The argument that bidders are held to their forecasts has limited value when, and if, bidders subsequently end up in technical liquidation, as this will undermine the perceived investment value of the destination, result in reduced development momentum, reduced broader socioeconomic impacts (including employment, BEE and SMME development) and may even compromise environmental management in the project area.

An increased relative weighting and the associated scoring of the technical ability of the bidder will avert the appointment of unsuitable operators. The selection of inexperienced operators – sometimes unable to execute the project whilst being subjected to the limited contract term and PPP fees payable regardless of whether income is generated from the project or not – should be avoided. Technical capacity is essential for quick and responsible delivery, thereby enabling the achievement of financial and BEE objectives.

Likely causes for wrong vendor selection Tourism products should be primarily an 'operations' function, hence the operational strategy and capability of the operator is cardinal. In South Africa, tourism education is largely based on skills education, whilst it is individuals with financial and legal expertise who often submit the bids. The Commercialization process was also run by process managers and their experience in hospitality management was limited. Hence, SANParks could possibly have a high number of operators lacking technical and operational experience. Successful tourism companies have a customer driven operations strategy that drives the financial and legal strategies (i.e. product over process). After all, products are designed to serve the tourist need, which is an operations function. A lesser degree of tourism management understanding as opposed to that of process could have led to wrong vendor selection. Having said that, to engage in such projects requires a thorough understanding of the processes.

Outsourcing activities that should not have been outsourced
A strategic management process has three components: analysis, choice recommendation and implementation (Scholes, 1999). Often projects like the outsourcing of the KNP Wilderness Trails did not follow a transparent and collective strategic management process, and hence are seen as products or activities that should not have been outsourced. There are certain activities that fell under the Commercialization Strategy 2000 that may not necessarily have been outsourced. For example, the hotel at Golden Gate national park and certain restaurant operations are said to have delivered better service outputs before outsourcing. The probable cause of outsourcing such activities may be attributed to a process driven strategy as opposed to a product driven strategy and it is arguable that these products should not have been outsourced at all.

Building and maintaining a corporate culture that promotes good strategy execution
SANParks adaptive management style has enabled the organization to embrace new ways of thinking and hence the execution of the Commercialization Strategy 2000, the approval of an extended scope of commercialization, and the re-introduction of PPPs as a key strategic objective of SANParks.

The lesson learnt is that several governance mechanisms change, while various projects are of a long-term nature and the term is a constant. As a large organization with various stakeholders, it could be difficult to remain focused on the commercialization goals over an extended period. Ministers change,

SANParks' Boards and EXCOs change and the responsible personnel for strategy execution and maintenance change. However, the only constants are the contracts that are entered into, which are, in many cases, for a period of 20 years. While SANParks' leadership encourages an adaptive culture, it is necessary to maintain the view that the Commercialization Strategy is consistent with the core values and business principles at all levels and with all stakeholders.

Losing control of activities

All of the functions that are performed by the private sector are as a result of SANParks' mandate to provide access to pristine conservation areas. These functions are contracted out for a period of time and such a structure, in principle, allows for SANParks to resume these functions subsequent to the term. However, the execution of the strategy did not make provision for SANParks to take over functions at an earlier stage. Post-contract awards highlighted poor service delivery in all restaurant contracts, however, SANParks had lost the competencies to resume this function. In order to effectively manage and not lose control of any activity that is contracted to a private party, it is important to have sufficient understanding of the activity.

Creation of oligopolies and contract management

While there are various restaurant and retail operators in South Africa, the accommodation sector, and particularly the luxury ecotourism game lodge market is very limited and often managed and controlled by a few companies, or an oligopoly, which is not ideal for free market participation or new player entry into that industry. It is important to understand the dynamics of such a situation: often oligopolies, especially in the case of South Africa, previously enabled a few companies access to large areas of land at a low cost, and, with this advantage, they have established relatively strong brands in that limited market. Typically, it becomes difficult for new entrants to enter the market and these companies compete amongst themselves. There may be a few further awards and recognition mechanisms and most of the same companies are recipients of these. As SANParks' private lodge operations are not intrinsically linked with SANParks – in a similar way to the retail and restaurant operations, output is often determined by their ability to pay the rent owed to SANParks. A revision of the financial model provided some form of rent relief to all lodge operators; however, because of limited control of that activity, SANParks is often forced to assume the technical capability of the lodge operator as they are significant players in a limited industry whilst requirements for rent relief and an extension of the term is frequently requested. The negative impacts of an oligopoly was evident during the revision of the financial model for the lodge operators where one or two of the 'leaders' of the lodge industry mobilized all other KNP lodge operators and took the lead in presenting a collective case to SANParks. The spirit of partnership by the lodge operators may be questioned, as contracts awarded are specific and not collective. This poses the question of whether such actions are typical to oligopolies. It is therefore intended that the focus on accelerating private participation in the lodge sector will be less in future projects.

Over optimistic demand

For a competitive bidding system to be effective, it does require that the demand for sites exceed supply. In a situation where there are a number of opportunities but there is an unsophisticated market, a different approach should be adopted. SANParks experienced a unique situation with the concessioning process (in 2000) where National Park land was offered to private lodge developers for the first time. With the limited supply of concession areas, high demand and an overestimated expectation of the anticipated performance of the lodges, unrealistic financial bids were offered to SANParks. As this was the first time such opportunities had been made available, operators did not have similar operations to benchmark their forecasts against. Bidding processes are also by nature competitive, and these two factors can encourage a situation where higher bids secure the awarding of a contract and overinflated demand translates into a higher percentage of turnovers being committed.

In 2004 SANParks were forced to re-evaluate the financial obligations of the concessionaires to avoid overall failure and its associated negative impacts. The optimal bids made it difficult for the Lodge PPPs to operate. After contracts were awarded, there were changes in market conditions: the South African currency appreciated against major international currencies, and the increase in global terror in 2001 reduced international travel to a significant extent. Collectively, the private sector lodge operators approached SANParks to renegotiate the terms of the contracts. SANParks engaged in intensive analysis and found a solution where the financial model could be adjusted and private sector lodge operators could be more flexible on pricing. SANParks could thus ensure the sustainability of the lodges without making material changes to the contracts.

The need for centralized effective contract management

It is clear that ongoing 'balanced' and efficient contract management is essential to the continued success of the process. Sound communications are not only essential for the commercial objectives of the partnership, ongoing monitoring, review and communication are also vital to ensuring continuing progress and commitment to the attainment of agreed BBBEE and SMME development programmes, as well as in support of long-term environmental management. This will provide some confidence to investors, who see opportunities in some places but are deterred by government and its ability to manage the process during its life cycle.

Functionary level institutional capacity and buy-in

The competency of functionary staff in terms of tourism and/or commercial developments should be strengthened. Furthermore, the attitude of functionary level staff in the parks often appears to be in conflict with the Commercialization Strategy and this, in turn, will impact on investor confidence and interest as it translates into an increased business risk. In dealing with such strategically important assets, the need to attract and secure the best investors is just as critical for long-term sustainability. As such their investment and development process should be treated as a priority whereby they are able to interact with the most competent staff who are fully aware of and support the strategic objectives of the organization.

It appears that, within the parks, there is still a large amount of scepticism among managers at all levels as to the virtue of the PPP process. Many see it as a threat to the parks and the ecosystems these parks are designed to support. If real value is to be captured by SANParks in this process, everyone involved in the organization must understand the process and how it is structured. This would, in fact, secure the long-term effective management of the biodiversity.

BBBEE lessons learnt

An important lesson is to be learnt in terms of BBBEE. Whilst there is no disagreement about the strategic importance of BBBEE and the need to trans-form ownership structures in the tourism industry, the reality is that current development support programmes are not well matched to the reality that BBBEE partners face at the project level.

Taking into account South Africa's history, the matching of investors to a typically white luxury lodge industry can be challenging. This calls for a sincere empathy and understanding of the value of diversity in terms of the changes in demographics and relationship of those changes to the buying behaviour of South Africans and the world at large. For example, the social re-engineering of South African society in the last 14 years has seen an increased affordability of luxury products such as high-end cars and thus the benefits to the South African car retail market can be seen. The same could probably not be said for the tourism market because of the limited diversity of ownership within the luxury lodge industry. The global tourist profile is also likely to change from the traditional German and British traveller to accommodate increasing visitors from the Indian and Chinese markets.

In order to ensure sincere empathy, it is important that there is sufficient HDI representation in the initiation of each and every PPP entered into. The HDI representation should not be limited to SANParks' internal PPP capacity, but also include, for example, external legal expertise, which plays a key role in contractual engagements. Some of the disadvantages that could occur if diversity and specifi-cally BEE is not sincerely embraced are listed below, and not embracing such values can put SANParks and South African Tourism at a disadvantage:

1   Product design: Operators may design products to serve only the traditional markets they are accustomed to and can relate to.
2   Target markets and interests: Accordingly, operators may target and under-stand certain markets and consumer behaviour that have limited market profiles.
3   If private partners are from a homogeneous group, there is a risk that they will only approach the members of SANParks that they are comfortable with in order to address critical issues. Diverse views may not be seen as value-added participation.

There are various attempts at all levels to address the issues regarding the increased participation of BEE and specific consideration needs to be given to mitigating such problems as those identified below:

- the capacity of BBBEE participants during the bidding and negotiation stages;
- BBBEE procurement capacity during operations;
- BBBEE interest in participating in tourism PPPs; and
- BBBEE finance.

Conclusion

The Commercialization Strategy has contributed to the implementation of SANParks organizational policy and objectives. An integral component of the Commercialization Strategy is the organizational capacity and ability not only to conclude the procurement of private entities acquiring the use of state property, but also to manage and monitor the agreements and accordingly to recognize market failure and have the ability to mitigate that failure to achieve its organizational objectives.

The Commercialization Strategy in South African National Parks has thus allowed SANParks to:

- increase and capture more of the net economic benefits attributable to parks;
- contribute more to BBBEE and local economic development;
- mitigate environmental impacts; and
- help finance biodiversity conservation, recognizing that only a small fraction of ecologically-important areas have the potential to attract significant tourism.

PPPs are a useful tool in various conservation agencies, as in the United States where such contracts were entered into. In many cases, after contracts were entered into, the contract management was not as effective and PPPs have not yielded its full benefits. The SANParks model is a success case where the organization's procurement process and contract management were equally effective. While commercialization through PPPs is a useful funding model for nature conservation, probably the most significant beneficial result is its ability to reduce poverty in remote areas through the creation of sustainable employment in areas where it is most needed.

References

Elkington, J. (1997) *Cannibals with Forks: The Triple Bottom Line of 21st Century Business*, Capstone Publishing Ltd., Oxford

Johnson, G. and Johnson, S. (1999) *Exploring Corporate Strategy*, 5th edn, Prentice Hall, England

Kumleben, M. E., Sangweni, S. S. and Ledger, J. A. (1998) *Board of Investigation into the Institutional Arrangements for Nature Conservation in South Africa*, Department of Environmental Affairs and Tourism, Pretoria

Mabunda, D. (2004) 'The begging bowl', *Earthyear: The Essential Environmental Guide*, vol 4, August, pp46–48

SANParks Annual Report (2006–2007) South African National Parks, Pretoria

SANParks Corporate Strategy Business Plan V4 (2) – 9 September 2005

Van Jaarsveld, A. and Varghese, G. (2006) *Strategic Plan for Commercialisation 2006*, South African National Parks, Pretoria

Vorhies, F. (1998) *Economic Values of Protected Areas: Guidelines for Protected Area Managers*, IUCN World Commission on Protected Areas, Gland, Switzerland

4

A Perspective on Community Based Tourism from South Africa: The TRANSFORM Programme, 1996–2007

Steve Collins and Herman Snel[1]

Introduction and outline

This chapter gives a perspective on sustainable tourism projects in South Africa from the point of view of an external assistance agency that was involved in a bilateral programme between the South African government and the Deutsche Gesellschaft für Technische Zusammenarbeit (German Agency for Development Cooperation, GTZ). Within this programme GTZ played an advisory role as well as a managing and implementing role. It must be noted that the view portrayed in this chapter is not necessarily an official view of GTZ but rather reflects perspectives of the authors who both worked in the TRANSFORM programme.

The chapter starts with an outline of development approaches that link sustainable tourism to conservation and poverty reduction in the South African context. It then proceeds to give a brief overview on how the GTZ became involved in managing and implementing tourism projects in a joint venture programme with the South African Department of Environmental Affairs and Tourism (DEAT), through the Training and Support for Resource Management programme (TRANSFORM).

TRANSFORM's approach was to work with selected communities chosen by the South African Government and to learn lessons from the field and inform the policy-making process. Subsequently, the second part of the chapter will provide an overview of lessons learned by TRANSFORM during the process of implementing two different kinds of tourism in the Richtersveld and Makuleke, being community-based tourism and private-sector led tourism respectively. The general areas of concern will be the national policy context, tenure and usufruct rights; local institutional building and development; social facilitation; capacity building; and enabling partnerships within the private tourism sector. The chapter concludes with a perspective on the way forward for sustainable community-based tourism in South Africa.

History and context

Following the South African transition to democracy in 1994, policy and programmes were set up to eliminate the legacy of inequitable governance (Reid, 2001, p138; Spenceley, 2003, pp1–2; Spenceley and Seif, 2003, p8). One strategy of the new government was to amend the skewed land tenure patterns inherited from the past and focus on historically disadvantaged groups that claimed rights to land and natural resources (Everingham and Jannecke, 2006; Spenceley, 2003, pp1–2). Poverty alleviation was attempted by linking land claims to an integrated and sustainable rural development strategy. As such, one approach of government to eradicate poverty in rural areas has relied on integrating the growth of the tourist sector within approaches targeting sound environmental management and local economic development (Matlou, 2001). Social and political pressure regarding human rights issues and changing paradigms in managing protected areas severely shaped the approaches taken by government to address the above mentioned issues (Spenceley, 2003, p2). New policy suggested concepts of local level governance, which included devolving the decision-making authority over natural resources to local users. The creation of South Africa's Communal Property Association Act of 1996 allows communities to establish legal common property institutions through which they can claim and own communal property. At the same time, the 1996 White Paper on the Development and Promotion of Tourism emphasized the development of tourism as a potential economic catalyst benefiting rural communities, whilst at the same time enabling and promoting sustainable linkages between the private sector, government and local communities (DEAT, 1997; Spenceley, 2003, p2).

GTZ's involvement with Community Based Natural Resource Management (CBNRM) in South Africa came about as a request from the South African government for assistance on policy related to land claims and community ownership of land in protected areas. TRANSFORM's role was to help design and implement some initial policy guidelines and try out intervention approaches that could become models for success combining tourism, conservation and rural development. Three specific pilot sites were chosen in 1998 for TRANSFORM's assistance: the Kosi bay, Makuleke and Richtersveld communities. The selection of pilot sites was made on a general basis of the valuable contribution that these cases could offer to the transformation of policy and practice in relation to protected areas and communal management agreements. It must be understood that in such partnership programmes GTZ does not work in the traditional donor way of only giving grants and donations, GTZ focuses on giving technical advice and capacity building to development stakeholders.

Tourism has been identified as one of the fastest growing economic sectors in South Africa contributing approximately 7 per cent of the GDP (Shakleton et al, 2007, p568). It is one of the country's top five economic sectors (DEAT, 2002). A 'new and emerging' type of tourism referred to as responsible, fair tourism was envisioned as a potential driver that can enable local communities to enjoy a better quality of life, through increased socioeconomic benefits and an improved environment (DEAT, 2002). The cooperation between GTZ and the South African government that eventually set up the TRANSFORM project was, in essence, a result of this particular context and time, and played a role in creating a 'responsible' tourism framework.

In its first phase (1996–1998), the TRANSFORM programme was working in direct partnership with the Department of Land Affairs, the Department that was directly involved with land reform. TRANSFORM's area of work within land reform was aimed specifically at supporting communities that had a stake in nature conservation areas through ownership, or a claim to ownership. The overall objective was to improve income at the grass roots level – to be generated from tourism and hunting activities related to conservation, as all other land use options were ruled out.

When assessing Phase one, it was felt that TRANSFORM's projects were focusing on tourism and environmental issues and as a result, the collaboration with government shifted to the Department of Environmental Affairs and Tourism (DEAT). This had both advantages and disadvantages. It allowed the projects to gain access to resources that were related to conservation and tourism but had the weakness of getting little support for village-based development outside the protected areas, in the villages where the Department of Land Affairs (DLA) and local government had a bigger role to play.

TRANSFORM's pilot projects represented some of the first experiences within South Africa that shifted the conservation paradigm towards a strategy of projects that integrated conservation and sustainable natural resource management within a new democratic and human rights framework. South Africa had been experimenting with a contractual park model as a way of involving local communities, the state and the private sector in the planning and management of natural areas and reserves. South Africa's old National Parks Act (1976) section 2(b) provides for the establishment of contractual national parks. 'Contractual parks are established on land owned either by the state or by a group of private individuals but managed by South African National Parks (SANP) according to the terms of a joint management agreement drawn up by a joint management committee consisting of representatives from SANP and the landowners' (Reid, 2001, p140). Central to this framework is the fact that no change in ownership takes place and no purchase fees are paid for the area in question. The commercial and land use rights can be maintained by the legitimate owners of the land, if agreed in the contract between the park agency and the owner. The co-management model of managing a conservation area, emerged as a tool to share the rights and responsibilities over natural resources management between a conservation authority and a collective group of landowners or private landowner (Fay, 2007; Reid and Turner, 2004, p225). TRANSFORM tried to take things further by combining the contractual park model with a rural developmental perspective aimed at creating synergies between conservation and rural development.

TRANSFORM's experiences with these types of interventions and approaches range from assisting in policy level design to the on-site implementation of community-based projects. The programme's practices have been centred on integrating CBNRM initiatives within broader planning, advising on rural development decisions, clarifying frameworks for a clearer understanding about resource rights, facilitating and assisting interactions between communities, parastatal conservation agencies and government agencies, as well as assisting with internal community dynamics, particularly with regard to benefit sharing arrangements.

Building consultant capacity and popularizing alternative models
The Africa Safari Lodge programme was a strategic move to try to spread a 'community rights for equity' development model into the rest of Southern Africa. The first ideas for this network emerged from an association between GTZ, the Ford Foundation and Mafisa development consultants. Its mandate has been to facilitate the integration between tourism, conservation and rural development. It was to combine and coordinate efforts from communities, the state and private partners. Within the proposed framework the private partner can be seen as a springboard that can create equity by allowing part ownership, employment and social development within the business venture. Using a process of outside funded interventions, the ASL programme is documenting these experiences and spreading them to their Southern African countries. See www.asl-foundation.org for case studies and information.

Case studies
For the sake of this chapter, two of TRANSFORM's pilot sites have been chosen for in-depth analysis. The subjective choice for these two particular cases was made on the basis that they offer interesting and contrasting perspectives towards community-based tourism. Even if the country context and the rural development objectives were the same, the Richtersveld and Makuleke examples had very clear distinctions in their approach to tourism.

1   In the Richtersveld the community chose an approach based on small community-based tourism operations with no linkages to the private sector.
2   At Makuleke the community and TRANSFORM used a Community–Public–Private–Partnership (CPPP) approach which relied on private sector partners to engage in building, operating and transferring tourism lodges in transparent concession processes.

Case 1: Community-based tourism and conservation in the Richtersveld

Background

The Richtersveld is located in the extreme north west of South Africa in the arid mountainous desert of the Northern Cape province. Situated in the northern Karoo, the area is characterized as a succulent Karoo biome and comprises one of South Africa's most diverse ecosystems, hosting a variety of unique biodiversity. The Orange river which flows into the Atlantic Ocean to the north of the Richtersveld has deposited rich layers of alluvial diamonds on its bed and in the sea and attracted diamond prospectors to the area (Reid and Turner, 2004, p226).

The Richtersveld's extreme remoteness caused this area and the communities inhabiting it to be neglected. Nonetheless, since 1994 the South African government and international donors have begun to pay more attention to the area by putting resources into developing more sustainable land uses such as tourism (Kepe et al, 2003). Besides the diamonds in the land and under the sea, the area has many potential attractions for tourists: the unpolluted skies allow star viewing, the majestic mountain desert gorges along the Orange river and the town of Port Nolloth, which even in summer has a misty English seaside feel to it.

Source: Extracted from the Richtersveld Integrated Development Plan 2001

Figure 4.1 *Location of Richtersveld National Park and other existing or potential multi-use conservation areas*

In 1996 TRANSFORM was asked to support an integrated programme that focused on how the Richtersveld National Park could benefit the residents of the area. The Richtersveld National Park is the first national protected area that is wholly owned by a local rural community and managed by South African National Parks through a joint management committee. In 1991 the Richtersveld leadership signed a lease agreement with SANParks for a period of 24 years, wherein SANParks committed itself to paying a yearly lease fee to a community trust which, in turn, uses the revenue for social and educational purposes. The community did not have much to lose from the agreement, given that they could continue grazing and that diamond mining continued unabated. The national park covers 160,000 hectares of biodiversity rich landscape. It has been identified as one of the world's biodiversity hotspots with extraordinary rates of plant endemism as a result of the mountain desert receiving a cold mist from the sea which deposits water on the succulent flora (Reid and Turner, 2004, p226). Recently the Ai-Ais Richtersveld transfrontier national park was launched and the area has been nominated for world heritage site status. One of the main tourism highlights of the region is the Namaqualand flower season, during which the apparently dormant desert landscape transforms into a colourful blanket of flowers extending to the horizon, attracting large numbers of visitors.

The vision of the Richtersveld National Park as described in its management plan is 'to manage a world-class park where the landscape diversity and biodiversity are maintained in combination with the cultural and traditional practices of the local population. Furthermore mining activities are to be allowed within the framework of sustainable resource utilisation' (Richtersveld National Park Management Plan, 2006). However, to date, there is fairly little tourism in the park partly due to its remoteness and also due to they fact that up to 2004 there was no tourism infrastructure to speak of, not even toilets at the campsites.

The Richtersveld 'community' is far from being homogeneous. However, when facing outside threats, the community is able to create a unified front, nonetheless internally many dynamics and politics divide the community (see also discussions on what comprises a 'community' in, for example, Argwal and Gibson, 1999 and Kumar, 2005). The smallness of the population and the intricate family relations made the Richtersveld an interesting and exciting place to work. As mentioned by Reid and Turner:

> *The nature of Richtersveld society and geography has influenced the Richtersveld experience with co-management and contractual parks ...villages are small and far apart... The Richtersveld is not the simple sort of 'community' that outsiders often take for granted in constructing models of CBNRM and co-management'.*
>
> (Reid and Turner, 2004, p227)

From the land claims process to an integrated development plan

When TRANSFORM started working in the Richtersveld the community was already organizing itself into a Community Property Association (CPA) in the anticipation of their land claim against Alexcor (a diamond mining company) being successful. The CPA has proven itself to be a functional representative institution of the inhabitants of four different villages that are scattered throughout the area at about one hour's distance from one another. The CPA worked well with the Municipality and TRANSFORM spent time working out the different roles and responsibilities of each structure.

Ownership of the communal areas of the Richtersveld needs to be understood as a legacy of South Africa's fractured past. The inhabitants were classified as 'coloured' under apartheid and as a result their communal land fell under the control of the tri-cameral parliament's House of Representatives. The communal land was one of the several coloured reserves that post-1994 has been held in Trust by the national Department of Land Affairs. The ANC government, in an effort to devolve ownership of these communal areas, launched the Transformation Process (Everingham and Jannecke, 2006). This involved allowing residents to chose how their land should be owned and managed. In popular referendums the communities could chose between giving title to the local municipality, individuals or to a legal community entity such as a CPA or Trust. In 2004 the Richtersveld residents overwhelmingly chose the CPA as their communal land owner. This includes the National Park land; however, up to mid 2007 the land had not formally been transferred from Land Affairs to the CPA.

This process was running separately to the Land Claim on Alexcor which ultimately was successfully lodged and was finalized in October 2007.

The Richtersveld has proven a good example of how to integrate CBNRM projects into broader rural development plans, specifically the municipal Integrated Development Plan (IDP). In this particular case good collaboration between the CPA, local municipality and TRANSFORM resulted in perhaps the best example of how CBNRM and conservation projects fit into the municipality's IDPs. TRANSFORM gave financial and technical support for the drafting of the first IDP to integrate tourism and conservation into rural development and local economic development (LED). The aim of this support was to ensure that the Richtersveld became a sustainable tourism destination with infrastructure and tourism facilities by means of involving local government. The overall objective was to assist in changing the nature of the economy of the area from one dependent on minerals to a more diverse, multifunctional economy integrating tourism and conservation as major elements.

Implementing CBNRM in the Richtersveld

In 2001, 10 years after having signed the agreement, no management plan for the National Park had yet been drafted due to continued strife between the community and SANParks. TRANSFORM pushed the involved actors to set up such a management plan and paid for the drafting of the integrated management plan which was signed in 2003. The management plan created a joint management committee but in retrospect, given that the park representatives did not directly come from the CPA, there were divisions between the CPA and the elected community representatives.

It is important to note that adjacent to the national park there is another 150,000ha of land that the community claimed successfully and has set aside as a conservancy. TRANSFORM's initial idea was that the community would lease out a section of this area to a private tourism investor for a period of about 50 years under specific conditions. It was felt by TRANSFORM that it was time that tourism in the area moved beyond community-based tourism, which had not proven itself to be a great employment generator. TRANSFORM urged the community to apply for R6 million of expanded public works money managed by DEAT. The underlying idea was that R3 million could be used to improve the infrastructure of the conservancy and the other R3 million could have been used to purchase community equity in a private sector tourism operation. The community rejected this idea and asked that all the money went into infrastructure and management of the community conservation area. As a result no substantial effort went into marketing the community-based tourism facilities.

From the very outset of this programme the community's decision was that they wanted to improve the already existing community-based tourism facilities including the small bed and breakfast that was in place. TRANSFORM got involved in the capacity building, training and improving some infrastructure but mainly on capacity issues. A lot of resources were spent at the institutional and committee level with limited success. TRANSFORM argued against the idea put forward by SANParks that they use 22 million South African Rand on improving the community-based tourism products. Without the required marketing, these facilities have remained underused and begun to deteriorate. In many ways it would have been better to only improve the park facilities and get tourists to begin using the park more. If this took place the community-based tourism facilities might have seen some traffic. It is clear that at the outset of this venture the community and SANParks and TRANSFORM did not all agree on the same objectives. Nonetheless, TRANSFORM tried to assist the community in following their vision. TRANSFORM gave the communities aspirations a chance but the real intention was to start getting some real financial benefits for the CPA out of their land. Throughout TRANSFORM's activities a total of 14 permanent and 67 temporary jobs were created for the Richtersveld community.

The community had a persistent idea that they would get lots of money from the claim on Alexcor and that they did not need outside private tourism investment. In some ways one got the sense that the community perceived a partnership with a private partner as something dangerous; they felt distrustful of outsiders and considered themselves to have enough knowledge to think they could manage a tourism enterprise themselves. On 12 October 2007 after 10 years of legal negotiations, the Richtersveld communities finally heard the court settlement granting their claim for 84,000ha of diamond rich soils and a compensation payment of R190 million from Alexcor.

At the regional level TRANSFORM supported the setting up of a tourist association that could link the community-based operations and gave them a voice. They became part of the South–North tourism routes marketing efforts. These efforts proved relatively unsuccessful. In essence the cause of this was not on a social or institutional level. The Richtersveld had everything in place, infrastructure, a working CPA, etc. However, the most crucial bottleneck proved to be that there were simply not enough tourists attracted to the area by the lack of an appropriate marketing approach to make the projects viable.

In 2004 after realizing that TRANSFORM's ideas were persistently different from the Richtersveld communities and that the facilitation efforts had not reached their desired impact, it was decided to cease work in the area. It has been interesting to see that the community have continued pursuing the tourism and conservation economy and it will be interesting to see how they will invest the compensation payment. The recognition of the community conservation area by the provincial government is a wonderful step forward. This could become one of the biggest lessons to other areas relating to how one can establish a conservation area using the IDP and in-depth community consultation.

Rumours that the community might want to get out of the National Park contract continue to raise their head, but we think that the community realize that at this stage they are being subsidized by SANParks and that the park will probably always make a loss unless there is a radical change in tourism patterns.

Given the biodiversity in the area and the small population that makes outsiders think they can make a big difference will mean that it is likely that donors will continue to work with the community. However, the key will be to see how sustainable these interventions are. In an economic assessment one could argue that TRANSFORM's efforts in the Richtersveld could have created more employment, economic revenue and capacity building opportunities had the community agreed with the vision of involving a private partner (compared to the revenues and employment opportunities derived from the community tourism facilities). From one perspective, the experience with the Richtersveld case illustrates that for the implementation of CBNRM projects one must reach a point where the practice of raising a common awareness among a community is linked to an implementing perspective which allows the community to grasp the underlying technicalities of implementing and managing their assets. One could perhaps argue that TRANSFORM could have played a stronger role in uniting the community's perception and aspirations to a realistic comprehension of the tourism industry which highlights the necessity of obtaining guidance and support from a sector that is experienced with developing tourism lodges and marketing the business lucratively. Experiences from TRANSFORM show that it is essential to work with up-market tourism ventures to ensure financial return rates to the communities. Two- and three-star lodges often do not provide sufficient economic returns for the community to be financially attractive.

General lessons learned in the Richtersveld

Collective property and community decision making

One of the lessons learned from this experience is that it is definitely very hard to get a good functioning tourist system, including administration, management and marketing system when you work with a community committee. The main reason for this is that: decisions take a long time to be made, the community and its representative committee is too indecisive, nobody is prepared to take a risk. Unless they are really legally responsible and representative they will avoid making a decision on the most basic issues, especially to spend money on marketing outside of the community.

Private investors, on the other hand, think about their investment and know they need to make money to be sustainable. They will not be bailed out by a donor who is prepared to spend money on community projects. If a private owner sees that his enterprise is not working or not correctly working he will do something to fix it and make it better. But in the case of a community they have not invested in the infrastructure and hence they do not feel the pressure personally in their pocket if it does not work.

Realistic tourism development

The expectations created in South Africa about the potential of the tourism industry to assist rural development have had an impact on policy and practice. TRANSFORM indirectly became one of the proponents of these approaches and as such has learned valuable lessons. One of the main factors limiting tourism development is that not every place and location can actually be developed for tourism purposes (Spenceley and Seif, 2003).

The geographical location of the Richtersveld makes it very difficult to set up an income generating tourist industry. In geographical terms the Richtersveld is simply too far away for most people to visit. You need a 4-wheel drive vehicle to see the park. A private investor who is prepared to fly people into the area and has access to vehicles, might be able to deal with this. However self-drive tourists were always going to be scarce. Initially we supported the Trans-Frontier Conservation Area in the hope that a route which allowed tourists to travel through the Richtersveld on their way to Namibia could be attractive. It does not seem like this flow of tourists has materialized.

Advisory roles of implementing agencies

A key lesson for any implementing agency coming out of this project is to clarify where you agree with the community and where you differ early on in the process. As can be seen, while we agreed on the biodiversity conservation and IDP issues, the parties involved differed on the best strategy to promote sustainable tourism. In hindsight one lesson learnt is that TRANSFORM could have played a stronger advisory role in illustrating how an association with a private partner could bring more economic benefits to the community than a community-based tourism venture. TRANSFORM could have started looking for private partners who would be interested in getting involved in the area, but the Richtersveld community was not convinced of such a partnership. On the other hand some people can believe that perhaps, at the end of the day, the lack of tourists will mean less pressure on the biodiversity and if the promised community development takes place perhaps the community will put less goats into the fields and the area will be maintained and conserved nonetheless.

Unclear tenure and land rights
The lagging behind of legal tenure rights in the Richtersveld has complicated and hampered the implementation of sustainable tourism initiatives. It would have been difficult to find private sector partners willing to get involved in setting up lodges in the area without clear tenure arrangements.

Grazing rights
The Richtersveld community has throughout history practised nomadic pastoralism allowing their livestock to follow the availability of fresh pastures. People hold large numbers of animals and can be considered fairly wealthy in terms of livestock. The management agreements within the National Park have stipulated that the community is allowed to continue grazing in the Park. However, as the park is not completely felt as their land to use for their own purposes, overgrazing is taking place. In the community conservancy, similar grazing rights are upheld. As that area is directly managed by the community, there is much more control and care taken in that area than in the National Park. In retrospect one can assume that it is dangerous to establish stable grazing rights in nomadic systems, particularly when the governance and ownership of some areas is relatively unclear and based on joint management. These situations are often prone to falling into open access common property regimes and stereotypically falling into situations of uncontrolled overgrazing.

Poverty relief funds
Poverty relief funds have typically emphasized building and improving infrastructure as well as short-term employment creation. Nonetheless local capacity building and entrepreneurial training should become a part of the package in order to allow for local communities to take effective and lucrative ownership over their acquired assets. Hence government should try to take on a more equilibrated strategy towards development of rural areas. Both infrastructure and effective communal governance are needed, and capacity building together with skills development and adequate governance structures are crucial in the process of enabling such an environment.

Case 2: A community Public–Private Partnership model with the Makuleke Community

Background

In 1969 about 3000 people were forced at gunpoint to burn their homes in an area now known as the Pafuri section of the Kruger National Park (Spenceley, 2003, p85; referring to Elliffe, 1999; Steenkamp and Uhr, 2000, p2). They were forcibly relocated by the department of Bantu affairs to an area some 60km south west of the park known as Ntlaveni, and became part of the former Gazankulu homeland (Reid, 2001, p140; Steenkamp and Uhr, 2000, p2). The displacement of the Makuleke people from this area is characteristic of a period in the history of South Africa where many forced removals occurred throughout the country. The land they were removed from got integrated into the Kruger National Park and became part of a military buffer zone along the Zimbabwean border (Steenkamp and Uhr, 2000, p2).

The most northern Pafuri tip of the Kruger borders upon Zimbabwe and Mozambique and is a core area of the Greater Limpopo transfrontier park. The area is characterized by a rich combination of wild plants, animals and landscapes and as such contains a large bulk of the Kruger National Parks biodiversity (Reid, 2001, p140; referring to Pienaar, 1996). At the same time it contains the richest cultural, historical and anthropological sites of the park. The Makuleke Region of the Kruger National Park compromises 24,000ha of pristine and remote nature experience. DEAT's application to have the area declared as a Ramsar site, a wetland of international importance, has recently successfully been granted.

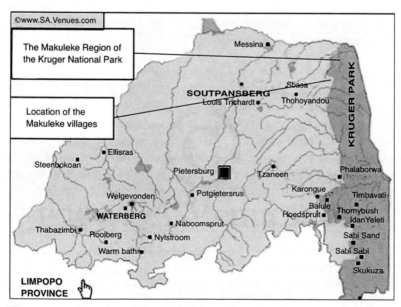

Figure 4.2 *Location of the Makuleke region of the Kruger National Park and the Makuleke Settlements*

The Makuleke were among the first claimants to win back their land under the post apartheid dispensation (Steenkamp and Uhr, 2000, p2). Their case has become one of the success stories of land restitution in South Africa and TRANS-FORM has been privileged to be part of it. For both parties the relationships have brought good mutual learning curves on how to deal with similar issues. TRANS-FORM has helped the Makuleke people engage in negotiations, planning, institutional and capacity building after they acquired the rights over their land, developed a co-management arrangement with SANParks, secured a range of donor and private sector funding and designed and launched a variety of ecotourism enterprises (Turner et al, 2001).

The settlement agreement sets out the framework within which TRANS-FORM worked. The essence of this project was to try to make the agreement work through capacity building, funding consultants and making strategic interventions. The Makuleke CPA Executive committee, its implementation office and the grouping of consultants known as the Friends of Makuleke have been the key partners in this process.

It must be mentioned that one of the success factors for the Makuleke community has been their ability to work closely with outside advisors. There has been a constant commitment of a variety of organizations and civil society sectors towards the Makuleke's cause (Spenceley, 2003, p86; Steenkamp and Uhr, 2000, pp5–9). A variety of institutions have assisted the Makuleke during the initial stages of their land claim and have invested heavily in capacity building in the community. This has certainly allowed for a stronger empowering and enabling environment for the community as a whole as they have been given the capacity to enable them to deal with the private sector, with natural resource management and with business and administration in general.

The CPPP model

When the settlement agreement was discussed, it became clear that the way the Makuleke CPA would exercise their commercial rights was to enter into contractual partnerships with private sector partners. Currently there are a number of tourism businesses operating in the Makuleke Region of the KNP. Commercial hunting took place while the tourism businesses were being set up and has now ceased (Grossman and Holden, 2007, state that the first hunt of two elephants and two buffalo generated some US$33,072 for the community).

The contracts between the CPA and the private partners created a Build–Operate–Transfer agreement where the private tourism company invest the capital to build the lodge, operate it for an agreed period of time and then transfer the tourism business and facility to the CPA at the end of the contract period. It has proven crucial to have correct agreements in place with the private partners in order to ensure that they do not exploit their partner communities.

By 2004 over R60 million had been mobilized and invested by top of the range tourism lodge companies: Matswani safaris, Eco villages and Wilderness safaris. The private sector partners lease concessions for their tourism operations in the communities' land. The agreements stipulate that they can lease the land from the community for a period of 45 years and furthermore should engage in capacity building partnerships with the community as they assist them financially, through training, skills development, job creation and community development. The projected income to the Makuleke CPA from the concession contracts and related job creation has been estimated at US$4,837,260 for the first four years of operation (Adams et al, 2004). By 2003 a total of 39 permanent and 146 temporary jobs had been created for the Makuleke community.

While these tourism businesses seem to be sustainable, the real challenge for the Makuleke has proven to be in meeting the objective of having the community at large benefit from their land. The communities' distance from their land in the park means that, in effect, many community members have little to do with their land. Most of them do not feel the benefit of land ownership until they feel a change in their lives in the villages. Once the private partners have built the lodges with community labourers and trained Makuleke staff to do the full-time jobs, the operators get on with doing business and making money, some of which goes towards community development. Critical in this is the ability of the lodges to get 'bums into beds' because the lease fees are linked to a percentage of turnover.

Community-based development

Up to now the money from the hunting, restitution grant and lease fees has been spent on numerous community developments. These include electrifying two villages, building school classrooms, building a cultural centre and tourist facility, sponsoring community celebrations as well as a new house and car for the Chief.

A key challenge has been to try to stimulate community-based jobs and economic activity. While it is clear that there is more money flowing into the community from the tourism jobs and social welfare schemes, it seems like most of the money is quickly spent outside the villages due to the lack of small businesses. In an attempt to assist small businesses identify markets and get started, TRANSFORM helped the CPA and Wilderness Safaris set up a Small Business Support Company. The small business support company's objective is to support and assist small emerging entrepreneurs to set up businesses that are linked to the emerging tourism and other markets. A total of ZAR369,112 was invested in the small business support company.

The small business support company has focused on building and operating hydroponics fresh produce tunnels, a packaging station and purchasing a vehicle to transport the products (total of ZAR715,557 invested) and finishing the cultural centre and community tourism facilities (ZAR154,989 invested). It has six traditional style rondavels which can house two tourists each. Furthermore the area has a collective dining area, an area for arts and crafts and an area for traditional dance and play performances. The objective is for the community to run this tourist enterprise with help from Wilderness Safaris who will market the facility and organize for tourists to spend nights in the village. The venue and trained staff will allow tourists to experience the Makuleke culture and understand their history. Additionally ZAR,206,695 was invested in the ranger facility which allows the Makuleke community to engage in anti-poaching patrols and general ranger activities.

Lessons learned at Makuleke

Fame and fortune?

While it was a pleasure to be associated with a success story, it was also a curse. Once the Makuleke became famous and started travelling the world it put additional pressure on them and their donors. It also took leadership away from the community and shone a light on the project as many communities, local and foreign government officials, NGOs and academics come to see Makuleke for themselves. It is the kind of pressure that destroys community organization by creating infighting. It is testimony to the few consistent executive members and the full-time staff that the Makuleke continue to make progress.

Traditional and democratic institutions

One of the most difficult tensions to deal with in many communities is the tension between the role of traditional structures and new democratic CPAs/trust and the local councils. Makuleke has not been an exception and conflicts between the aspirations of the chief, who played a vital role in lodging the land claim and asserting Makuleke culture, and the CPA leadership has been an ongoing problem. In essence this tension is a result of easily confused roles between the CPA, which is the new democratic structure that is the formal land owner of the restored land, and the traditional authority which is the land manager of the communal land excluding the restored land. On top of this you have the local municipality which has a duty to deliver services to the communal land and villages. Unfortunately the different family and political differences play themselves out by using these 'overlapping' development roles to suit different individual agendas.

As project implementer and manager, one has to be careful about assuming that democratic systems and institutions will reject the traditional authority and it was tempting to condemn the amount of money and benefits going to the royal family. It was clear, however, that the leadership and community supported the royal family getting a disproportionate amount of the benefit flows. The CPA executive committee decided to hand over a legal proportion of the hunting fees to the royal family. These were used to build a new house for the royal family, buy a car and as a bursary for the education of the chief's son. In the end after TRANSFORM's projects started becoming affected by the tensions between the chief and CPA leadership, we asked the Department of Land Affairs to run a workshop and clarify the different roles and responsibilities. They asserted that the chief could not be the chairperson of the CPA executive because at times there will be a conflict of interests, for example, when the Traditional authority applies for money from the CPA. There is now a process being monitored by the DLA which will replace him with an elected chairperson.

Broad-based support and a broad level of community leadership

The professional support given to the Makuleke community has most definitely empowered the community positively. The strong effort that has been put into developing a broad-based leadership has also reaped its fruits as there were always strong leaders and figures in place to follow up on the process and take the developments further. Experiences from other cases have shown that often the falling out of one key leader has meant the end or slacking off of the whole process.

Institutional development for good governance and benefit sharing

One of the key advisory services given to the Makuleke Community has been to design a set of institutions that create a transparent, democratic and effective way of accounting for and distributing income from the land. A broad based institutional set up was created by the Makuleke community in order to allow for an equitable representation of the community at large and to strive for a broad consensus on prioritizing how and where to distribute the generated income. At the overarching level, the Makuleke CPA represents around 18,000 members of the community. Nine elected CPA members constitute the CPA executive committee that is responsible for the day to day running of the CPA. The executive committee is re-elected every two years. The CPA executive committee has, in the past, received donor grants to cover the honorarium costs for the nine members, but in due time the generated income should cover these internal costs. About half of the executive committee are village representatives and the other half are elected by the general meeting of the CPA. There are an additional two full-time staff members who work with the executive committee, an administrator/receptionist and a facilitator whose function is to interact with donors, government and the private sector as well as community-based organizations. The constitution calls for regular feedback meetings between the executive committee and the full CPA membership, but in practice this seems difficult to effectuate. The Makuleke have devised two approaches to bridge this gap and involve a larger representation of the community leadership to interact with the executive committee, share information and build consensus on decision making. First a Development Forum was created which allows community leadership from civic organizations such as women's and youth groups, churches, sports clubs, farmers' associations and policing forums to give input into where money should be spent in the villages. Unfortunately plans for additional communication between the CPA executive and the CPA did not work out, as it was not seen as a priority by the Executive who now use the Development Forum and the Annual General Meetings as their main feedback mechanisms. These extra forms of communication included local youth who were trained as journalists for a newsletter, notice boards and community radio transmissions.

In terms of financial integrity and accountability, the Makuleke Development Trust is the repository of all lease fees and income from hunting. The Makuleke Development Trust is constituted by four elected community members and three members from outside the community. The outsiders are the Makuleke CPA's legal advisor, a professional trust administrator and a representative from the

Department of Land Affairs. The CPA executive, with the help of their legal and trust advisors, make decisions about which projects in the community to support. The Trust has proven to be an effective way in which community leadership can take tough decisions, for example, cutting back the money going to the Chief, with the backing of advisors.

Comparing the Makuleke and the Richtersveld

Throughout the process of implementing different approaches to sustainable tourism development in both case studies many valuable lessons were learned. Even though the two cases are socially and geographically incomparable, there are some overarching principles which emerge in light of the communities' vision of developing the area. The Richtersveld community chose a community-based lodge, for their own reasons. In the end the lack of capacity and funds within the community to set up a proper, top-range tourism industry limited their potential to obtain economic benefits from their claimed land.

On the other hand, the Makuleke community has proven highly resilient and capable of entering into successful agreements with the private sector. With the support of a variety of agencies, they were able to succeed in doing so for their tourism concessions within their claimed land. It has proven very successful to have a broad and deep base of strong, committed and representative community leaders in Makuleke. Aside from the fact of having a strong common history, the availability of a variety of key figures has ensured the success of the Makuleke community. From a sustainability perspective, the CPPP model seems to be the most appropriate model for sustainable tourism ventures. It allows for a broad base of involvement from different sectors such as government, community, civil society, private sector, etc. Furthermore the CPPP model allows for the effective handover of infrastructure and, more importantly, of an effective long-term handover and mentoring of community members with the necessary skills and capacities related to running a lucrative tourism venture.

Interacting with local municipalities

The Richtersveld and Makuleke cases set out two different models for interaction with local municipalities. In the case of the Richtersveld community, consultation and involvement has brought about one of the most successful cases of involving the municipality in the communities' projects and integrating the project into the municipality's IDP. In the case of the Makuleke community, the community chose not to deal too closely with the municipality but they had a variety of other partners collaborating with them. The variety of experiences shows that irrespective of the commitment of the municipality or the relationship to the municipality, community-based conservation projects can thrive. At the core of their success lies the imperative need for solid, stable and good partners. These do not necessarily have to include municipal partners as long as other strong and committed partners are in place. However this has proven to be a weakness in terms of village-based service delivery, where the municipality see the Makuleke as a rich community that are not a priority for development.

Geographical location

In terms of geographical location the case studies illustrate clearly that some areas have better opportunities to develop a good tourism attraction than others. The Makuleke case has a variety of clear advantages over the Richtersveld. Besides its location, its private tourist operators have also made an airstrip available for tourists to fly into the area.

Clear tenure rights

The Makuleke have been lucky in their land claim procedures. The uncertainties and delays encountered by the Richtersveld Land Claim and the corresponding tedious legal battle undoubtedly has affected and will continue to affect the community's development possibilities in many ways.

General lessons learned

In terms of dealing with institutional arrangements and benefit-sharing arrangements, we have experienced a variety of possible scenarios, and the lesson is that for each case a particular strategy and approach must be created. No blue print solution exists. In the end the implementing agency is also helpless to a certain extent.

CBO's without financial capacity will implode

From some perspectives common property arrangements seem to be incompatible with nature conservation and rural development. TRANSFORM's cases show that there are at least potential lessons to be extracted out of its experiences. Community issues seem to intrinsically collide with western ideas of business and financial management. Hence effective businesses run by communities seem to be contradictions in terms, but best practices from cases implemented should be extracted and evaluated. The fact is that if the community does not manage its financial resources well it will fail. In many cases if it were not for a few constant individuals with good leadership capacities fuelling the CPAs, everything might just fall apart.

Private partners must see the community and their culture as an asset

Experiences with private sector investors have shown that unless the private partner sees and integrates rural development and community empowerment into the product and approach, all the efforts towards benefit sharing and joint management will simply be felt as an added burden that slows down the business.

Hence it is crucial to find the appropriate investors with the required experience in that field. It is crucial to keep in mind that tourism operators are not rural development people, they might have noble ideas and good intentions but there are actually only a few that work well and that are able to create something sustainable. Institutional building and business building are crucial aspects to ensure the success of CBNRM projects. Even in the best cases of collaboration that we have experience of, we have seen problems arising.

Policy level

National policy on rural tourism and tourism operators has had very little impact. After the passing of the responsible tourism guidelines, DEAT seems to have withdrawn attention from the issue. Some operators are involved but merely from a personal choice. Policies like affirmative procurement are set up and have good intentions but conservation agencies do not have the capacity to monitor and enforce them.

In terms of responsible tourism, it has been Fair Trade in Tourism (www.fairtourismsa.org.za) which has set the agenda and continues to use voluntary certification as a method to improve relations between communities and tourism operators.

At TRANSFORM, the method of working on pilots to inform policy from bottom up experiences, turned out to be less effective the longer we worked. A degree of cynicism, jealousy or just indifference by certain government officials meant that lessons that were learnt did not become part of the way government works. The impression is that the first round of public servants seemed more willing to learn than the current ones who feel that they know all the answers. It was strange to find TRANSFORM differing from DEAT, the joint venture partner, during the parliamentary portfolio hearing on the Protected Areas Act, where TRANSFORM became the 'voice of the community' and argued for a more progressive approach.

Government capacity and lack of real will

Even though the Makuleke might have achieved a lot without the assistance of external funds and the facilitators TRANSFORM paid for, it is likely that without external help they would not have gone as far and the project might have died due to infighting caused by lack of progress. The problem is that TRANSFORM has partially failed to develop the interest and capacity of government officials who need to be facilitating development. Without a national partner prepared to drive pro-poverty tourism in reality as well as policy, TRANSFORM has felt its limitations as outsiders. As an example of TRANSFORM as a managing and implementing agency needing to push the South African partner, this has been felt most clearly during the People and Parks programme where suddenly, when it suits government, they are happy to show the world the progress being made. The default position of key officials, however, is a conservative conservationist approach to rights and equity.

It is ironic that, nearing the end of the programme, TRANSFORM finds itself working closer with land claims officials than DEAT or park officials. This is probably because TRANSFORM's models and insight are more valued by people trying to implement projects on the ground, rather than national level policy officials. However, as enthusiastic as land claims staff are, government needs more professional people to implement projects and do the social facilitation.

Conclusion

One central issue that has come to the foreground from the implementation of TRANSFORM's projects is that rural people and communities do not understand the business of tourism in the same way as a private tourism operator understands it. That is to say their cultural and material situations do not facilitate a disposition in which rural communities can superimpose their logic or rationalities into understanding why national or overseas tourists come to their areas and what these people expect to get and see. For rural people it is often more comprehensible to understand that people go to the city, to shop and acquire goods. So the desire of wealthy urban dwellers to go to undeveloped rural areas remains culturally intangible. Understanding the market of tourism is a crucial element that is needed if community-based tourism is to be a success. We have yet to see government produce good educational material to develop rural populations' understanding of tourism. Good support networks should be created and developed in order to assist communities in this difficult task. Imperative to a notion of business orientation is the central notion of strengthening administrative capacities and a commercial business orientation in general, including managerial capacities and an awareness of the need to market your product.

Within government there is a lack of coordination throughout and within departments which has hampered rural tourism development. At a strategic level it is of crucial importance for government to get together with a variety of donors and work closely with tourist enterprises. It is only if this discussion takes place regularly that South Africa will be able to deal with the problems of communities' high expectations not being met by their community-based tourism projects or by the lack of serious engagement by major tourism operators and conservation agencies in rural development efforts.

Government must see it as an obligation to establish adequate infrastructure in communities enabling an environment which allows for the development of community institutions and a capacity to deal with the outside world on equitable terms. Up to now government approaches towards integrated conservation and development are still partially contained within the old conservation paradigm and have not found an operational way out in order to integrate community involvement and decision making within the development approach. An inclusive strategy on how to deal with communities and functionally devolve governance to a community level must still develop further.

TRANSFORM has been developing a community–private–public–partnership model in which it emphasizes the interaction of government, communities and the private sector. The approach includes the setting up and strengthening of multi-stakeholder forums, local and regional development frameworks, municipal involvement and assistance in setting up adequate benefit sharing systems with the private sector. At a community level, the PPP approach aims at building up strong local institutions and leadership skills, building up local capacity in a broad spectrum of themes including business management, administration and marketing.

TRANSFORM's experiences highlight the fact that CBNRM cannot be used as a panacea and fitted into blue print solutions for alleviating poverty in rural areas. Each specific site needs to be evaluated in terms of its socioeconomic context, including the community's capacities to run and operate a tourism enterprise, be it on their own or in a partnership with the private sector and the institutional strength of the CPA. The area's environmental conditions, present livelihoods and occupations, the potentials and risks of establishing tourism in the area and each project all need long standing support. Hence partnerships and a broad base of assistance are required to establish equitable benefit sharing mechanisms. Several examples illustrate that in most cases a partnership with the private sector is most beneficial for the community in economic terms but also in terms of establishing strong arrangements which ensure the transfer of skills and capacity from the private sector to the community.

Notes

1   The authors would like to thank Johannes Baumgart, Michelle Terblache and Harry Wells for their comments on earlier drafts of this chapter.
2   See annex: Map 1, for a detailed map of the area.
3   See annex: Map 2, for a detailed map of the area.

References

Adams, M., Steyn, L., Tanner, C., Turner, S. and White, R. (2004) 'Case studies on investment on community land in Southern Africa', Foreign Investment Advisory Services (FIAS), World Bank Group

Argwal, A. and Gibson, C. C. (1999) 'Enchantment and disenchantment: The role of community in natural resource conservation', *World Development*, vol 27, no 4, 629–649

DEAT (1997) 'White paper on the conservation and sustainable use of South Africa's biological diversity', Government Gazette No. 18163, Government Printer, Pretoria, South Africa

DEAT (2002) *National Responsible Tourism Guidelines for South Africa*, Department of Environmental Affairs and Tourism, Pretoria, May

Elliffe, S. (1999) 'Guidelines for the release/development of dormant state or community assets for ecotourism development in the context of community involvement, land issues and environmental requirements'. Unpublished paper presented at the Community Public Private Partnerships Conference 16–18 November, Johannesburg

Everingham, M. and Jannecke, J. (2006) 'Land restitution and democratic citizenship in South Africa', *Journal of Southern African Studies*, vol 32, no 3, 545–562

Fabricius, C. (2004) 'The fundamentals of community-based natural resource management', in Fabricius, C., Koch, E., Magome, H. and Turner, S. (eds) *Rights, Resources and Rural Development: Community-based Natural Resource Management in Southern Africa*, Earthscan, London, pp3–43

Fay, D. A. (2007) 'Mutual gains and distributive ideologies in South Africa: Theorizing negotiations between communities and protected areas', *Human Ecology*, vol 38, 81–95

Grossman, D. and Holden, P. (2007) 'Case studies on successful Southern African NRM initiatives and their impacts on poverty and governance: South Africa'. Paper created for USAID-Frame

Kepe, T., Wynberg, R. and Ellis, W. (2003) 'Land reform and biodiversity conservation in South Africa: Complimentary or in conflict?' Programme for Land and Agrarian Studies, PLAAS, University of the Western Cape, Cape Town

Kumar, C. (2005) 'Revisiting "community" in community-based natural resource management', *Community Development Journal*, vol 40, no. 3, 275–285

Matlou, P. (2001) 'The potential of ecotourism development and its partnership with spatial development initiatives (SDI)'. Presentation at the seminar on Planning, Development and Management of Ecotourism in Africa, Regional Preparatory Meeting for the International Year of Ecotourism, Maputo, Mozambique, 5–6 March

Pienaar, D. (1996) 'The Ecological Significance of the Pafuri area between the Luvuvhu and Limpopo rivers in the northern Kruger National Park'. Unpublished paper. Nature conservation and the department of research and development, Kruger National Park

Reid, H. (2001) 'Contractual National Parks and the Makuleke Community', *Human Ecology*, vol 29, no 2, 135–155

Reid, H. and Turner, S. (2004). 'The Richtersveld and Makuleke contractual parks in South Africa win–win for communities and conservation?' in Fabricius, C., Koch, E., Magome, H. and Turner, S. (eds) *Rights, Resources and Rural Development. Community-Based Natural Resource Management in Southern Africa*, Earthscan, London, ch 16

Richtersveld Nasionale Park Bestuurs- en Ontwikkelings Plan, 31 October 2006

Shackleton, C., Shackleton, S., Buiten, E. and Bird, N. (2007) 'The importance of dry woodlands and forests in rural livelihoods and poverty alleviation in South Africa', *Forest Policy and Economics*, vol 9, 558–577

Spenceley, A. (2003) *Tourism, Local Livelihoods, and the Private Sector in South Africa: Case Studies on the Growing Role of the Private Sector in Natural Resources Management*, Research Paper no 8, Sustainable Livelihoods in Southern Africa: Institutions, Governance and Policy Processes, Institute of Development Studies, Brighton UK

Spenceley, A., and Seif, J. (2003) 'Strategies, impacts and costs of Pro-Poor Tourism approaches in South Africa', PPT Working paper No. 11

Steenkamp, C. and Uhr, J. (2000) *The Makuleke Land Claim Power Relations and Community Based Natural Resource Management*, Evaluating Eden Series Discussion Paper no 18, IIED, South Africa

Turner, S. and Meer, S. (2001) 'Conservation by the people in South Africa: Findings from TRANSFORM monitoring and evaluation, 1999', *Research Report No 7*, PLASS, University of the Western Cape, Capetown

Turner, S,. Collins, S. and Baumgart, J. (2001) *Community Based Natural Resource Management, Experiences and lessons linking communities to sustainable resource use in different social, economic and ecological conditions in South Africa*, TRANSFORM Publications, Pretoria, South Africa

5

Responsible Tourism and the Tourism Industry: A Demand and Supply Perspective

Nicole Frey and Richard George

Introduction

Responsible tourism has been a buzz word in the tourism industry for a number of years. Its popularity has been fuelled by increasing international pressure on the tourism sector to address issues of global warming, social inequality and diminishing natural resources. As a result numerous policies and initiatives have been developed around the world to build a more responsible, more sustainable, more ethical and greener tourism industry. Evidence of responsible tourism management in South Africa, however, is still relatively limited. Questions that need to be raised are: (1) to what extent has responsible tourism been adopted by South African tourism businesses? and (2) what kind of intervention is necessary to facilitate the adoption of more responsible tourism management (RTM) practices?

This chapter aims to juxtapose global developments in responsible and sustainable tourism with the actual situation in southern African. The arguments are based on findings from a recent empirical study into the responsible tourism management practices of Cape Town tourism businesses.

At the 1992 United Nations Conference on Environment and Development it was recognized that tourism could be an important tool for community development. The Department of Environmental Affairs and Tourism (DEAT) subsequently published the White Paper on Development and Promotion of Tourism in South Africa in 1996, which formed the basis for the 2002

Responsible Tourism Guidelines (DEAT, 2002). The guidelines provided a framework for the tourism industry to adopt more sustainable and responsible management practices by safeguarding the social, natural and economic environments in which they operate. Recently the United Nations Millennium Development Goals (MDGs) have provided a common platform for countries all over the world to address key issues of poverty and inequality. The primary goal of the MDGs is to halve the number of people living on less than one US$ by 2015. The tourism industry, being highly labour-intensive and a primary source of income in many developing and emerging countries, has been identified as a key sector in meeting the MDGs. However, in order for the tourism industry to achieve such positive outcomes, a responsible and sustainable tourism approach is necessary.

The amount of attention that responsible, sustainable and related topics have received has led to a host of definitions in the field. Whereas responsible, eco- and sustainable tourism should not be used interchangeably, the approaches all have a common objective of minimizing negative social, economic and environmental impacts, whilst maximizing the positive effects of tourism development. Table 5.1 provides several definitions in this subject area, as well as highlighting the specific focus each one of them has. For the purpose of this chapter the term *responsible tourism management* (RTM) has been used to describe a certain management approach, rather than a specific type of tourism. In investigating what is causing the low levels of responsible tourism management in the industry, it was more important to analyse general attitudes and challenges of managers, rather than differentiating between the definitions. Thus:

> *Responsible tourism management (RTM) is defined as managing the business in a way that benefits its local community, natural and business environment and itself.*

Corporate social responsibility in tourism

It is important to discuss responsible management practices in the context of the broader Corporate Social Responsibility (CSR) debate. RTM can be seen as a form of CSR contextualized in a specific industry sector. CSR can be defined as *'actions that appear to further some social good, beyond the interests of the company and that which is required by law'* (McWilliams and Siegal, 2001, p117). The CSR trend in both large and smaller corporations has risen dramatically in recent years. Internationally, companies, to varying degrees, are being mandated by their customers or legislation to operate in a transparent fashion, serve not only shareholders' but stakeholders' needs and play a far more active role in addressing the social ills around them. The tourism sector, despite being highly dependent on natural and human capital, has been slow to react to this trend. Only 2 per cent of tourism businesses globally are participating in responsible tourism or CSR initiatives such as the Global Compact and South African studies into the hotel and

Table 5.1 *Definitions of sustainable tourism terms*

Term	Definition	By	Emphasis
Responsible Tourism	Responsible tourism is about providing better holiday experiences for guests and good business opportunities to enjoy better quality of life through increased socio-economic benefits and improved natural resource management.	Spenceley et al, 2002	1 Develop a competitive advantage; 2 Assess, monitor and disclose impacts of tourism development; 3 Ensure involvement of communities and the establishment of meaningful economic linkages; 4 Encourage natural, economic, social and cultural diversity; 5 Promote the sustainable use of local resources.
Sustainable Tourism	Sustainable tourism means achieving a particular combination of numbers and types of visitors, the cumulative effect of whose activities at a given destination, together with the actions of the servicing businesses, can continue into the foreseeable future without damaging the quality of the environment on which the activities are based.	Middelton, 1998, pix	The responsible management of resources for the use and enjoyment of present and future generations.
Ethical Tourism	Ethical tourism is a concept that goes beyond the three principles of sustainability. It recognizes that tourists and tourism providers must take some responsibility for their behaviour and attitudes, with each stakeholder group gaining equity in the tourism decision-making process.	Weeden, 2001	Tourists and tourism providers have a moral responsibility for their actions.
Ecotourism	Travelling to relatively undisturbed or uncontaminated natural areas with the specific objective of studying, admiring and enjoying the scenery and its wild plants and animals, as well as any existing cultural manifestations (both past and present) found in these areas.	Ceballos – Lascurainin, 1983, (as cited in Fennell, 2001)	1 Provides for environmental conservation; 2 Includes meaningful community participation; 3 Is profitable and can sustain itself.

Table 5.1 *continued*

Term	Definition	By	Emphasis
Cultural/ Heritage Tourism	Tourism that respects natural and built environments... the heritage of people and place.	www.planeta.com	Respect for the local natural environment and local heritage is emphasized.
Pro-poor tourism	Pro-poor tourism is not a specific tourism product; it is an approach to tourism development and management which ensures that local poor people are able to secure economic benefits from tourism in a fair and sustainable manner.	Goodwin and Francis, 2003	Pro-poor tourism may improve the livelihoods of poor people in three main ways: 1 Economic gain through employment and micro-enterprise development; 2 Infrastructure gains: roads, water, electricity, telecommunications, waste treatment; 3 Empowerment through engagement in decision making.
Alternative Tourism	Alternative tourism aim to put as much distance as possible between themselves and mass tourism.	Krippendorf, 1987, p37	Alternative tourism focuses on individualism and having a unique and authentic experience through interaction with the local community and environment.

tour operator sub-sectors show low levels of transformation (Spenceley, 2007; Wijk and Persoon, 2006; Frey, 2007a; van der Merwe and Wöcke, 2007).

The pressure on companies to manage responsibly does not only emanate from government; customers are also increasingly looking for products and services that reflect their own values and provide a 'feel good' emotion by indirect support of the environment and society. This trend is particularly evident in tourism. International tourists are beginning to factor responsible management practices into their decision making. A MINTEL study in 2001 indicated that even though tourists are influenced most by the standard of accommodation (64 per cent), weather (60 per cent), un-crowded beaches (34 per cent) and price (30 per cent), the ethical stance of a company is starting to enter the consumer purchasing decision. Whilst it is clear that not all tourists seek out green or responsible tourism businesses, this management approach is becoming a differentiating factor and a competitive advantage in the marketplace. Research suggests that tourists, as indeed other consumers, are willing to support companies who respect the local culture and are committed to safeguarding the social and natural environments they operate in. Several research studies propose that a significant shift is taking place in modern tourism (Meyer, 2003; Trauer and Ryan, 2005). Goodwin and Francis (2003) note that wider consumer market trends towards lifestyle marketing and ethical consumption are now spreading to tourism. The global demand for traditional 3Ss holidays (sun, sea and sand) is declining in favour of 'real', authentic and 'experiential vacations' (Bachleitner and Zins, 1999; King 2002; Cohen, 2004, p66; Pérez and Nadal, 2005). Consumers are seeking a '*different type of experience and a much deeper connection to nature and/or the local community*' (Mills, 2006). The implication for the tourism sector is that if the industry wants to remain competitive and reactive to changing consumer needs, then a shift towards RTM and effective marketing and communication thereof is imperative.

The modern day consumer has become more sceptical, discerning and informed. Technological development has been a key driver in making consumers more independent. Potential travellers are no longer reliant on travel intermediaries such as tour operators or travel agents to organize their holiday plans but make use of the internet to gather information on different destinations, compare offerings and independently book their travel arrangements such as flights, accommodation and attractions online (Salazar, 2005; George, 2007, p127). This has led to far more freedom and scope for tourists as well as increased competition amongst destinations and tourism businesses. One way that destinations and organizations can differentiate themselves in this highly competitive industry is through the promotion of local culture and heritage as well as their management style (Allen and Brennan, 2004, p24; Ashley, 2005; Frey, 2007b, p326).

Justification for responsible tourism management

The argument for RTM is built on three main premises. First, tourism is an important sector in terms of job creation and contribution to a country's gross domestic product (GDP). Tourism and general travel are estimated to contribute approximately 11 per cent to global GDP, account for 6–7 per cent of total exports of goods and services and provide employment for an estimated 231 million people (8.3 per cent of total employment) (UN-WTO, 2007; WTTC, 2007). Tourism in South Africa, as one of the largest industries, contributes 8.3 per cent to the country's GDP and was estimated to have created 969,000 jobs in 2007 (7.5 per cent of total employment) (WTTC, 2006). Secondly, international tourism trends indicate that tourists are demanding a unique travel experience and that businesses adopting RTM are better able to meet this demand. Thirdly, RTM is a strategic business decision. In South Africa, CSR, and by implication, RTM is increasingly being seen as an integral part of conducting business and has been shown to lead to increased brand and company reputation, improved staff morale and retention and a higher return on investment (Frey, 2007a; van der Merwe and Wöcke, 2007).

CSR and RTM also have their fair share of sceptics. Some of the key criticisms are that RTM can become a pure public relations exercise, with companies merely promoting their public image (also called 'greenwashing') without committing resources into uplifting communities or the environment. The call for action, rather than more responsible tourism policies is increasingly becoming stronger. Whilst a lot of valuable work has been conducted in devising practical documents to promote responsible tourism, changing management practices are limited. There is a need to move from policy development to implementation and control. There is also some doubt as to the actual size and degree of consumer demand for responsible tourism products. Unfortunately, research in this area is limited but some evidence does suggest that demand is increasing. Other counter arguments that are presented highlight that the only responsibility of business is towards its shareholders and that using company or shareholders' resources on non-profit maximizing objectives is unethical. Friedman (1970 as cited by Windsor, 2006) argued for a 'free market system' where the responsibility of business is to maximize returns for shareholders, based on private ownership, competition and economic freedom. Whilst this line of argument holds in highly industrialized nations where poverty and extreme inequality are relatively limited, this is not the case in developing nations. A pure market system in these countries has often failed to address a host of socioeconomic challenges and can lead to an even greater divide between the rich and the poor. It is therefore the responsibility of the public and private sectors to work together to ensure healthy social and natural environments, and by implication, a healthy economy.

The next section draws on findings from both the CSR and tourism academic literature to support the demand for RTM. However, there is a paucity of research into tourists' preferences and attitudes towards RTM in southern Africa.

Demand for responsible tourism

The Roman philosopher Seneca alluded to the deeper meaning of a holiday when he said that 'you need a change of soul rather than a change of climate. You must lay aside the burdens of the mind; until you do this, no place will satisfy you' (Seneca, as cited in Krippendorf, 1987, pxv). As the tourism industry matures, there is an increasing demand for unique, authentic and meaningful holidays. Tourists are expressing a desire to learn about the visited destination and themselves whilst travelling. Many tourists want to interact with the local culture and actively engage with the tourism product-offering, rather than just passively consuming it (Institute of Directors in Southern Africa, 2002; Pérez and Nadal, 2005). Travelling for some has, thus, become as much an emotional and philosophical journey, as a physical one.

Research indicates, that besides seeking a more meaningful experience at the destination, tourists are beginning to take note of the impacts that their visit has on the host destination (Bachleitner and Zins, 1999). Tearfund's 2001 study found that 30 per cent of tourists are asking about social, environmental and economic issues. The Association of British Travel Agents' (ABTA) research cited that 87 per cent of holidaymakers felt it to be important that their holiday did not damage the environment, whilst 76 per cent of respondents said that tourism should benefit those in the destination through jobs and business opportunities (ABTA, 2002). The Travel Industry Association of America (TIA) and National Geographic Traveller's study of the travel patterns of 3300 US adults found that more than 75 per cent of travellers believed it is important not to damage the environment, and that over 17 million US travellers consider environmental factors when deciding which travel companies to patronize (TIA/NGT, 2003). Whilst these figures do not represent the entire tourism consumer base, and might be inflated due to respondents answering in a manner that is socially acceptable, they do indicate a significant shift and trend towards more ethical and responsible consumption.

Goodwin and Francis (2003) argued that unlike commodities, fair trade and responsible tourism practices can have a positive impact on the product offered. Coffee that has been traded fairly will not differ significantly from regular coffee. Increased community involvement, participation and fair trade initiatives, however, have been shown to add a unique dimension to the tourist's experience. Participation and understanding of tourism by communities often leads to goodwill, resulting in a friendly atmosphere and lower crime rates (Ashley and Haysom, 2006; George, 2007; Tearfund, 2000, 2002; UN-WTO, 2007).

Research on responsible tourism has mostly been based on studies conducted in developed countries such as the UK and the US where wider consumer market trends towards lifestyle marketing and ethical consumption are spreading to tourism. (Goodwin and Francis, 2003). However, consumer trends are not as robust in South Africa as they are in the UK. Research carried out by Frey (2007), van der Merwe and Wöcke (2007), as well as Spenceley (2007) indicates that the hotel, tour operator and greater tourism business sectors are still finding

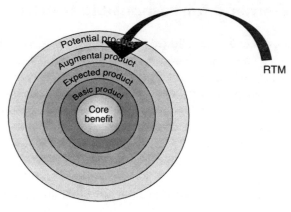

Source: Kotler and Keller, 2006, p372

Figure 5.1 *Product levels*

consumer demand for responsible tourism products to be low (75 per cent of tour operators stated that they had not been asked by tourists about their CSR practices). Whereas tourists are unlikely to demand responsible tourism explicitly, satisfaction levels tend to increase if consumers know that their visit is not harming the host destination but contributing positively. A 'feel good factor results, adding to the value of the product-offering. RTM should thus not be seen as the core product-offering. Rather, as depicted in Figure 5.1, specific company values and reputation constitute an extra layer of benefit for the tourist (Frey, 2007a).

Supply of responsible tourism: Research findings

In 2006, Spenceley replicated the Tearfund study of 2001 in order to evaluate to what extent South African tour operators were engaging in responsible management practices. Spenceley's study involved a sample of 20 predominantly small-sized tour operators attending the 2006 Tourism Indaba (an annual travel trade show in Durban). Each operator completed a self-administered questionnaire which included questions relating to issues such as partnerships, local benefits, training, policies and demand for responsible tourism. The findings revealed that almost all tour operators claimed to have a positive impact on local communities – in areas such as employment, using local service providers and purchasing local products (Spenceley, 2007, p3). However, several tour operators pointed out that they faced numerous barriers in bringing benefits to local people. These included concerns about safety and crime, access and problems relating to capacity – such as skills, language and inconsistent quality. The majority of tour operators indicated that partnerships and relationships with suppliers were very important to them; however, only half of respondents claimed to have responsible tourism policies in place (Spenceley, 2007, p8). A majority of the sampled tour operators did indicate that they were engaging in positive interventions in local communities. These benefits ranged from economic upliftment through employment opportunities, to improved local infrastructure and support for education and health and conservation initiatives (Spenceley, 2007). The perceived costs, as well as benefits, of RTM were further confirmed by Frey (2007a) who examined the CSR practices of 244 tourism businesses in Cape Town.

Van der Merwe and Wöcke (2007) conducted research into the level of responsible tourism practices in the South African hotel industry. The focus of the study was to uncover the level of understanding regarding CSR and what practices from the Responsible Tourism Guidelines (DEAT, 2002) were being implemented. Van der Merwe and Wöcke's findings revealed that, on average, hotels were implementing 47 per cent of the economic guidelines, 45 per cent of the social elements and 40 per cent of the guidelines encouraging general responsible behaviour. A high percentage of the sample did not use CSR in their marketing campaigns and had not set any measurable targets. It should also be noted that the sample included a relatively high number of hotels that belonged to associations promoting responsible tourism such as the Fair Trade in Tourism South Africa (FTTSA) or had participated in the Imvelo Responsible Tourism Awards (IRTA). As a result there was a bias towards businesses that were already more aware and positively inclined towards CSR practices. Despite the potentially elevated figures, results from both studies indicate a low and insufficient level of transformation and RTM practices.

Frey (2007a) conducted a study into Cape Town tourism businesses to find out what was causing the low levels of RTM practices. A conceptual model (Figure 5.2) was developed to test the statistical relationships between management attitude and its effect on business performance indicators (both financial and non-financial). Expert interviews with various tourism stakeholders and focus group discussions with tourism business managers from the accommodation, visitor attractions and hospitality sectors were carried out to deepen the hypotheses and guide instrument design. In order to statistically test the model and quantify results, a questionnaire was sent out to a database of 1,700 tourism businesses in the Greater Cape Town region. A response rate of 14 per cent (244) was achieved.

Frey found that the majority of the study sample (62 per cent) had 1 to 4 employees, with 70 per cent having been in business for 6 years or less (2007b, p139). The sample profile was representative of the local tourism industry which is dominated by young small, medium and micro enterprises (SMMEs). Several authors (for example, Ashley, 2006; Ashley and Haysom, 2006; BEE Tourism Charter and Scorecard, DEAT, 2005) have noted that non-compliance with the transformation agenda may lead to stricter government legislation. For the many SMMEs in the tourism sector, prescriptive legislation will prove to be a significant burden, forcing many out of business, as has been shown in the financial services sector (Ashley and Haysom, 2006). It is far more effective if the industry is left to self-regulate. To communicate and substantiate the strategic business case for RTM thus becomes imperative.

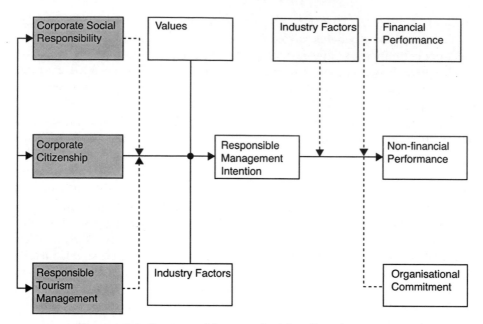

Figure 5.2 *Conceptual framework of the effect of management attitude on performance*

Frey's (2007a) analysis of the data showed that despite the positive attitudes and perceptions of tourism managers towards RTM, evidence of employee training, local procurement and HIV/Aids policies is limited. The six categories from the 2005 BEE Tourism Charter and Scorecard: ownership, strategic representation, employment equity, skills development, preferential procurement, enterprise development and corporate social investment (CSI) were used to determine what the actual level of RTM in the tourism industry is and were measured, weighted and grouped into five categories: very low (3 per cent), low (44 per cent), medium (25 per cent), high (19 per cent) and very high (9 per cent) (see Figure 5.3). Of the sample, 47 per cent show limited evidence of RTM practices. This finding highlights the fact that, despite managers holding and communicating positive attitudes towards RTM, these attitudes are not translating into the desired management changes required to reach the greater objectives of responsible tourism.

The traditional view of attitudes leading to behaviour thus does not hold. Numerous studies have investigated the relationship between environmental values and environmental behaviour and whilst several authors (for example, Meinhold and Malkus, 2005; Schultz et al, 2005; Stern et al, 1999) found a positive association between the two constructs, a more global environmental perspective shows inconsistencies between attitude and behaviour. A German panel-study found that respondents who had a high ecological orientation travelled longer distances and had a significant carbon footprint (Böhler et al, 2006). Frey (2007a) noted that the factors that are disrupting the linear relation-

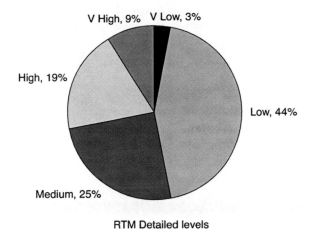

RTM Detailed levels

Figure 5.3 *Levels of actual responsible tourism management behaviour*

ship between attitude and behaviour, from a tourism business's perspective, include the level of competitiveness in the business environment, the industry sub-sector the business belongs to and the perceived costs of implementing RTM. Tourism businesses, being usually quite small and lacking experience, perceive implementing RTM to be difficult and expensive (for example, recycling or procuring from smaller suppliers) and transfer the responsibility for social and environmental change to 'large' corporations or government.

On a positive front, a majority of tourism businesses agreed to the potential benefits of RTM including enhanced brand equity, customer loyalty, improved employee morale and license to operate by surrounding communities. Table 5.2 shows the levels of agreement with scale items measuring the perceived cost and the benefit of implementing RTM. The data show that attitudes agreement with the benefits of RTM is high. The low levels of RTM practices highlights that the perceived costs are outweighing perceived benefits. Tourism businesses are not committing time and resources to addressing their management practices, resulting in a significant divide between attitude and behaviour. This is partly due to a level of lethargy, resistance to change and lack of resources in the industry, but can also be attributed to the channels for change not being in place. Businesses, for example, expressed frustration at not knowing how and where they could procure responsibly. Government policies and responsible tourism guidelines, aimed at addressing transformation in the industry are therefore often ineffective, as the challenge is not only one of awareness and education, but also of the will to implement change (Frey, 2007a).

The findings from the research do suggest that businesses that are employing RTM practices enjoy tangible business benefits ranging from increased employee morale to bottom-line profits (Frey, 2007b). The implication is that it pays to manage responsibly. This confirms other international research in CSR and provides a strong argument for the adoption of RTM.

Table 5.2 *Respondents' level of agreement with costs and benefits of RTM*

Scale Item	Perceived cost or benefit of RTM	% Strongly Agree & Agree
Being ethical and responsible is the most important thing a business can do		94
Business planning and goal setting should include discussions of responsible management		92
Responsible management is essential to long-term profitability		94
Good (responsible) management is often good for business		92
Businesses will have to ignore responsible management in order to remain competitive in a global environment		78
You must forget about responsible management if the survival of the business is at stake		64
Business has a social responsibility beyond making a profit		62
It is too expensive for our business to use smaller suppliers	costs	61
We do not use smaller community suppliers because of safety and security issues	costs	60
Our customers want international standards that smaller local businesses cannot offer	costs	58
Community support helps us run our business better	benefits	47
We think responsible tourism management improves our staff performance	benefits	67
Our employees are proud to work for a socially responsible business	benefits	73
We think responsible tourism management is a useful marketing tool	benefits	81
Our brand, image and reputation benefits from responsible tourism management	benefits	77

Tourism agency initiatives to facilitate RTM adoption

The lack of RTM practices in the South African tourism industry is clear. A host of governmental and non-governmental agencies have emerged in the last ten years to accelerate transformation, provide information on best practices and give practical advice to tourism industry role-players. Despite these positive efforts, van der Merwe and Wöcke's (2007) and Frey's (2007a) research found that an understanding of government policies, such as the Responsible Tourism Manual for South Africa (RTMSA) (Spenceley et al, 2002) and the BEE Tourism Charter and Scorecard (DEAT, 2005) is low. Frey (2007a) found that 44 per cent of respondents understand the RTMSA (Spenceley et al, 2002) badly or not at all (Figure 5.4). The Responsible Tourism Guidelines (DEAT, 2002), which along with the 1996 White Paper on Tourism Development and Promotion (DEAT, 1996) were the national policy precursor to the RTMSA (Spenceley et al, 2002),

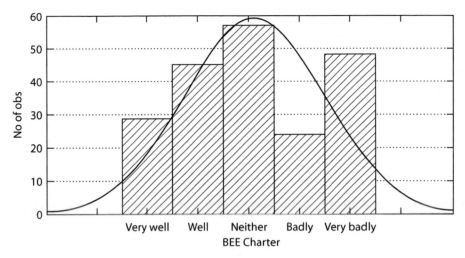

Figure 5.4 *Level of understanding of the Tourism BEE Charter and Scorecard*

are the formal framework on which the transformation agenda and sustainable tourism development in South Africa is founded. The low level of understanding on the part of tourism business managers who are tasked to put in place the recommendations of these policies is disconcerting and would explain the lack of transformation and CSR initiatives in the SA tourism sector. Managers must understand what RTM is before they are able to successfully adapt their business operations and manage them in a more responsible manner.

A further reason inhibiting the adoption of RTM is the scepticism of the tourism industry towards the efficiency and support of government. Figure 5.5 shows that only 17 per cent of respondents perceived government as being helpful in advancing RTM practices. These negative perceptions influence to what extent individuals believe it to be worthwhile to change. Social marketing campaigns aimed at encouraging recycling, for example, are only effective if people believe that their collected waste will be recycled and that this action will benefit the environment (Kotler et al, 2002, p53). Gilg et al (2005) and Yaman and Gurel (2006) demonstrated that for RTM to be effective and transformation to take place, it is imperative that businesses believe that government is supporting them.

Van der Merwe and Wöcke's (2007) research suggests that hotels belonging to an industry association such as the FTTSA have a far better understanding of CSR and responsible tourism. Frey (2007a), however, found that whilst this was true, the general percentage of tourism businesses belonging to the FTTSA or entering the Imvelo Responsible Tourism Awards (IRTA) is relatively low. Indeed, Frey (2007a) noted that only 14 per cent (29 businesses) indicated that they have been able to meet the FTTSA's stringent criteria. FTTSA currently has a total of 30 companies carrying their accreditation. Whilst this is a step in the right direction, qualitative research highlighted that tourism businesses considered the FTTSA criteria too difficult to attain or unnecessary (Table 5.2).

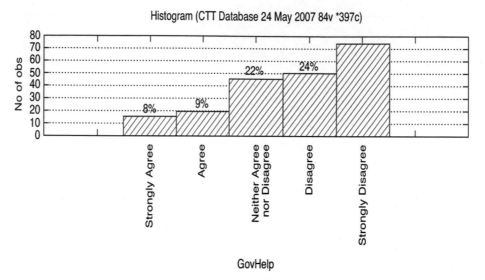

Figure 5.5 *Government is helping us put in place*
responsible management processes

In addition, Frey's (2007a) study found that only 17 per cent of tourism businesses have an HIV/Aids policy in place. This number is disconcertingly low given the high level of awareness and urgency regarding the current HIV/Aids pandemic in South Africa. The tourism industry, which is highly labour-intensive and people-orientated, should be at the forefront of ensuring that employees and tourists have the necessary information and protection with regards to a social health problem that is at the centre of public debate. Once more, the South African tourism industry seems to be slow in reacting to a rapidly changing marketplace.

Figure 5.6 *The FTTSA trademark*

Tourism BEE Charter Council baseline study

A survey commissioned by the Tourism BEE Charter Council in 2007 investigated the state of transformation in the South African tourism industry in more detail. The study noted that larger tourism businesses, with an average annual turnover of R14 billion are, in general, meeting 2006 transformation targets, although often falling short of 2009 goals. The study found that companies are underperforming in the areas of strategic representation (60 per cent below target), especially of black women and preferential procurement (25 per cent below target) (Yarona Management Consulting, 2007). Small and medium-sized companies, which comprise more than half of the sector, however, are struggling to meet both the 2006 and 2009 targets in nearly all measurement areas and, on average, 80 per cent of businesses have not managed to meet 2006 targets. Transformation in the small business tourism sector is thus extremely limited. Reasons for this include: the difficulty small businesses have in reaching the BEE scores, a perception that government tenders do not apply to small businesses and therefore are of little use to them, and a lack of understanding of the seemingly complicated and expensive accreditation process (Frey, 2007a; Yarona Management Consulting, 2007).

Despite these current short-comings, the policies for responsible tourism implementation, support and education for responsible tourism are in place. To facilitate transformation, government and other tourism agencies have to support businesses in the implementation phase of RTM. Frey's (2007a) research shows clearly that responsible management intention – in other words the will and ability to commit resources into bringing about change – is negative. Adopting RTM has to become easy, cheap and fast.

Some of the government agencies that are involved in fostering responsible tourism in southern Africa are listed in Table 5.3.

Marketing implications

In terms of achieving the wider socioeconomic mandate of tourism in South Africa, adopting RTM practices will contribute significantly to bringing about transformation and addressing the inequalities of the past. Globally, RTM is in line with reaching the objectives of poverty reduction and unemployment as outlined in the MDGs, as well as addressing issues around climate change and scarce resource management. Finally, RTM is a tool for the local tourism industry to develop a strategic competitive advantage, diversify the product offering and provide a unique and authentic experience. This chapter has identified various factors, which are negatively affecting management attitude, intention and behaviour. The following section recommends how some of these challenges can be addressed.

The perceived costs of using small suppliers are too high. These costs include insufficient quality standards and quantity capacity, as well as ordering and deliv-

Table 5.3 *Initiatives by various tourism industry associations*

Responsible Tourism Manual for South Africa (RTMSA)	www.icrtourism.org/ sa/tourismhandbook.pdf	Responsible tourism guidelines were developed in 2001 to meet the objectives set out in DEAT's 1996 White Paper 'Development and Promotion of Tourism in South Africa'. The Paper identified the significant potential tourism in South Africa has to address its socioeconomic challenges. The first conference on Responsible Tourism was hosted in Cape Town in 2002 prior to the World Summit on Sustainable Development (WSSD) held in Johannesburg. The conference led to the Cape Town Declaration, which provided a concrete definition of responsible tourism. The RTMSA states that tourism development should be 'government-led, private sector-driven, community-based and labour conscious' (Spenceley et al, 2002). The approach implies that a broad spectrum of people must collaborate to ensure a sustainable tourism industry, ensuring that social, environmental and economic impacts are managed. The guidelines recommend how tourism businesses can manage their operations more responsibly. Consequently the recommendations show how management practices can be adapted so that a company's operations remain profitable, whilst taking social and environmental considerations into account.
Heritage Programme	www.eco-web.com	The Heritage Environmental Ratings Programme launched a responsible tourism guide in 2002. Members are recognized and encouraged for their environmentally conscious business practices.
Fair Trade in Tourism South Africa (FTTSA)	www.fairtourismsa.org.za	Fair Trade in Tourism South Africa (FTTSA) is a non-profit marketing initiative that attempts to promote and publicize fair and responsible business practices by South African tourism establishments. FTTSA has developed a set of stringent criteria to measure the responsible management of tourism companies. If companies meet these benchmarks they are awarded the FTTSA trademark. This independent symbol of fairness in the tourism industry serves as a signal to potential tourists and investors regarding the fair operations of the business. The FTTSA trademark has led to positive publicity, product differentiation and improved consumer attitude for the respective organizations.

Table 5.3 *continued*

BEE Tourism Charter and Scorecard	www.tourismbee charter.co.za	To encourage the transformation of the tourism industry, DEAT together with the Tourism Business Council of South Africa (TBCSA) drafted the Tourism BEE Charter and Scorecard in 2005 to advance the overall objectives of the Broad-based Black Economic Empowerment Act of 2003. This policy outlines the actions tourism organizations need to take in order to become BEE compliant. The Charter looks at seven areas where organizations can 'score' BEE points: ownership, strategic representation, employment equity, skills development, preferential procurement, enterprise development and social development and industry specific indicators.
Tourism Enterprise Programme (TEP)	www.tep.co.za	TEP is a joint DEAT and Business Trust (BT) initiative to encourage the growth and development of SMMEs within the South African tourism sector. It is a government policy vehicle designed to bring about the Tourism Action Plan (TAP). TEP provides marketing support for events, helps SMMEs in business plan development, supports training, facilitates in licensing and certification procedures and assists in the tendering process for these businesses to become suppliers.
Tourism, Hospitality & Sport Education Training Authority (THETA)	www.theta.org.za	Tourism, Hospitality and Sport Education Authority (THETA) is the Sector Education and Training Authority for the tourism, hospitality and sports sectors. THETA aims to raise the standards of skills in these sectors and provide guidelines to ensure quality and appropriateness by providing training for skills that are most required by employers in the tourism sector.
Pro-Poor Tourism (PPT) Pilots	www.pptpilot.org.za/	The aim of this project was to assist southern African tourism enterprises to expand their understanding and use of Pro-Poor Tourism (PPT) strategies. The project focused on identifying and implementing strategies that benefit local people or enterprises and make business sense to the company. This pilot programme ran from May 2002 to May 2005. Its impacts have been felt both in the companies and the communities involved.

ery ease. Many of the tourism businesses indicated that they would use smaller community suppliers if these factors could be addressed. CTT has commissioned an audit of its membership base to address this problem and compile a database of RTM suppliers to facilitate business between members. Long-term capacity building, mentoring and skills transfer to small, medium and macro enterprises (SMMEs) will be essential for economic growth and social improvement.

The lack of safety and security when using small suppliers is a key deterrent for many tourism businesses. Attacks on tourists in informal settlements, corruption and overcharging tourists are making tour operators and other tourism service providers weary of using community suppliers. DEAT is currently developing a strategy to address the safety of visitors and put in place safety and security measures for tourism service providers. Besides the actual problems of crime and violence; there is also a challenge around the perceptions of high crime rates. In many instances local community tourism service providers have a safe and secure product offering. However, an isolated incident can tarnish the image and reputation of the entire industry and has significant negative spin-off effects. It is imperative that the initiatives that have been developed by government to deal with the negative effects of crime are communicated to the tourism industry and that success stories are widely publicized. Factors that are contributing to crime are the high inequality and unemployment levels that currently exist in South Africa. Past research has shown that where communities become involved and benefit from the economic impacts of tourism, support of tourism development increases, licence to operate is gained and crime levels decrease. Increasing the involvement in tourism development, participation and sharing benefits is therefore an important aspect in addressing the safety and security challenges.

The level of competition in tourism is high. One way of addressing international competition is to create a uniquely South African experience. There is often a misconceived perception that overseas travellers demand the same products and services as they receive at home. Whilst there is no doubt that quality standards have to be high, research clearly indicates that tourists are looking for new, authentic and different cultural experiences. Employing RTM practices makes use of local heritage and community knowledge. By engaging with different people and cultures a richer and more competitive product-offering is developed. Clearly, the question of superior customer service and quality cannot be ignored and it is imperative that local community service providers are trained and skilled. Education in the tourism industry, as is the case in most of South African business sectors, needs to be placed continuously at the centre of development.

The perception by tourism businesses of a lack of government support has to be changed. It is imperative that the private sector believes in the competence and will of the public sector to bring about change. True transformation and the achievement of the goals set out by the BEE Tourism Charter and Scorecard (DEAT, 2005), as well as the much wider objectives of poverty alleviation, job creation and environmentally sustainable management, will be achieved only through public–private engagement. Government support needs to be carefully communicated and the effects monitored. By clearly showing tourism businesses what is being done practically to support them, goodwill results and consequently improved buy-in to adopt RTM practices. Along with the scepticism towards government support, comes a lack of understanding in the industry of policy documents concerned with the implementation of RTM. The limited understanding of the RTMSA (Spenceley et al, 2002) and the BEE Tourism Charter and Scorecard (DEAT, 2005) show a level of apathy towards adopting the transformation agenda. It is important that these documents continue to be communicated and disseminated via workshops. It might be necessary, in the face of a continued lack of change, for government to regulate certain minimum requirements for the industry (for example, HIV/Aids policy, waste management and corporate social investment).

Employees prefer to work for a company that reflects their own values and that is seen to be a good corporate citizen. Improved staff morale, in turn, increases staff performance. Communicating the ethical values both to potential employees and existing staff is an important exercise in terms of improving performance. Involving employees actively in community programmes is another way of encouraging CSR and reinforcing the values of the company.

The modern age consumer is increasingly critical of the activities of businesses and their impacts. Adhering to ethical management practices and adopting a triple bottom line accounting approach ensures that businesses safeguard against potential risks with regard to their reputation and image. In a highly competitive environment where product and price parity reigns, purchasing decisions are often made based on brand reputation, recognition or emotional connection. RTM ensures transparency and a balance between financial, social and environmental objectives. Such sensitivity will contribute towards safeguarding the business against activism groups and negative publicity.

In conclusion, this chapter has argued that responsible tourism management is fast becoming a vital objective of tourism business operations rather than an ethical consideration. International research shows that CSR leads to a competitive advantage, increased product differentiation and higher staff morale. Global and local pressure on the tourism industry to transform and take its environmental and social impacts into account is at the same time mounting. In southern Africa, the tourism industry plays a crucial role in addressing poverty reduction, inequality and high unemployment rates. RTM aims to align the business objective of profit-maximization with social and environmental goals. Developing local partnerships, managing scarce resources and working actively with local communities will ensure that the benefits of tourism are spread to more stakeholders. It is imperative that the industry move from policy formulation and awareness campaigns to implementing and committing to transforming management practices. A positive attitude towards responsible tourism will not on its own lead to the changes needed to ensure a sustainable tourism offering for present and future success.

References

ABTA (2002) 'Why corporate social responsibility makes sense for tour operators: responding to consumer demand'. www.tourismconcern.org.uk (accessed July 2006)

ABTA and Tour Operators Initiative for Sustainable Tourism Development and Tearfund (2002) 'Improving tour operator performance: The role of corporate social responsibility and reporting'. www.tourismconcern.org.uk (accessed July 2006)

Allen, G. and Brennan, F. (2004) *Tourism in the New South Africa – Social Responsibility and the Tourist Experience*, I. B. Tauris, New York

Ashley, C. (2005) *Facilitating Pro-poor Tourism with the Private Sector. Lessons Learned from Pro-poor Tourism pilots in southern Africa.* ODI working paper 257. October. Overseas Development Institute, London

Ashley, C. (2006) *How can Governments Boost the Local Economic Impacts of Tourism?*: Tourism Programme: Overseas Development Institute (ODI) and SNV, London

Ashley, C. and Haysom, G. (2006) 'From philanthropy to a different way of doing business: Strategies and challenges in integrating pro-poor approaches into tourism business', *Development Southern Africa*, vol 23, no 2, 265–280

Bachleitner, R. and Zins, A. (1999) 'Cultural tourism in rural communities: The resident's perspective', *Journal of Business Research*, vol 44, no 3, 199–209

Böhler, S., Grischkat, S., Haustein, S. and Hunecke, M. (2006) 'Encouraging environmentally sustainable holiday travel', *Transportation Research Part A.* vol 40, 652–670

Cohen, E. (2004) *Contemporary Tourism: Diversity and Change.* Elsevier, Amsterdam

Department of Environmental Affairs and Tourism (DEAT) (1996) *The development and promotion of tourism in South Africa,* White Paper, Government of South Africa, Pretoria

DEAT (2002) *National Responsible Tourism Guidelines for South Africa,* Department of Environmental Affairs and Tourism, Pretoria, May

DEAT (2005) *Tourism BEE Charter and Scorecard.* DEAT, Pretoria

Fair Trade in Tourism South Africa (FTTSA) (2005) www.fairtourismsa.org.za (accessed July 2005).

Fennell, D. (2001) 'A content analysis of ecotourism definitions', *Current Issues in Tourism,* vol 4, no 5, 403–421

Frey, N. (2007a) 'The effect of responsible tourism management practices on business performance in an emerging market'. Unpublished MA thesis. The University of Cape Town, Cape Town, South Africa

Frey, N. (2007b) 'Managing tourism responsibly', in George, R. (ed) *Managing Tourism in South Africa.* Oxford University Press, Cape Town, 316–333

George, R. (ed.) (2007) *Managing Tourism in South Africa.* Oxford University Press, Cape Town

Gilg, A., Barr, S. and Ford, N. (2005) 'Green consumption or sustainable lifestyles? Identifying the sustainable consumer', *Futures*, vol 37, no 6, 481–504

Goodwin, H. and Francis, J. (2003) 'Ethical and responsible tourism: Consumer trends in the UK', *Journal of Vacation Marketing*, vol 9, no 3, 271–284

Institute of Directors in Southern Africa (2002) Executive summary of King Report on corporate governance for South Africa. www.ecseonline.com (accessed August 2006)

King, J. (2002) 'Destination marketing organisations – connecting the experience rather than promoting the place', *Journal for Vacation Marketing*, vol. 8, no 2, 105–108

Kotler, P. and Keller, K. (2006) *Marketing Management* 12th edn. Prentice-Hall, New Jersey

Kotler, P., Roberto, N. and Lee, N. (2002) *Social Marketing: Improving the Quality of Life* 2nd edn. Sage Publications, California

Krippendorf, J. (1987) *The Holiday Makers: Understanding the Impact of Leisure and Travel*, Butterworth-Heinemann, Oxford

McWilliams, A. and Siegal, D. (2001) 'Corporate social responsibility: A theory of the firm perspective', *The Academy of Management Review*, vol. 26, no 1, 117–127

Meinhold, J. and Malkus, A. (2005) 'Adolescent environmental behaviors: Can knowledge, attitudes, and self-efficacy make a difference?', *Environment and Behavior*, vol 37, no 4, 511–532

Meyer, D. (2003) 'The UK outbound tourism industry and implications for pro poor tourism', Overseas Development Institute (pro-poor tourism working papers Series). www.theinternationalcentreforresponsibletourism.org (accessed October 2005)

Middelton, V. (1998). *Sustainable Tourism – A Marketing Perspective*. Butterworth-Heinemann, Oxford

Mills, S. (2006) 'Shades of green', *Mail & Guardian*, 3–9 March

Pérez, E. and Nadal, J. (2005) 'Host community perceptions a cluster analysis', *Annals of Tourism Research*, vol 32, no 4, 925–941

Salazar, N. (2005) 'Tourism and glocalisation "local" tour guiding', *Annals of Tourism Research*, vol. 32, no 3, 628–646

Schultz, P., Gouveia, V., Cameron, L., Tankha, G., Schmuck, P. and Franek, M. (2005) 'Values and their relationship to environmental concern and conservation behaviour', *Journal of Cross-Cultural Psychology*, vol. 36, 457–475

Spenceley, A. (2007) *Responsible Tourism Practices by South African Tour Operators*. International Centre for Responsible Tourism – South Africa

Spenceley, A., Relly, P., Keyser, H., Warmeant, P., McKenzie, M., Mataboge, A. Norton, P., Mahlangu, S. and Seif, J. (2002) *Responsible Tourism Manual for South Africa*. Department of Environmental Affairs and Tourism, Pretoria

Stern, P., Dietz, T., Abel, T., Guagnano, G. A. and Kalof, L. (1999) 'A value–belief–norm theory of support for social movements: The case of environmentalism', *Research in Human Ecology*, vol. 6, no 2, 81–97

Tearfund (2000) *Guide to Tourism: Don't Forget Your Ethics!* Tearfund, London

Tearfund (2001) *Tourism: Putting Ethics into Practice – A Report on the Responsible Business Practices of 65 UK-based Tour Operators*. www.tearfund.org (accessed May 2006), London

Tearfund (2002) *Worlds Apart: A Call to Responsible Global Tourism*. Tearfund, London.

Tourism Enterprise Partnership (TEP) (2006) www.tep.co.za (accessed September 2006)

Tourism, Hospitality and Sport Education and Training Authority (THETA) (2006) www.theta.org.za (accessed August 2006)

Trauer, B. and Ryan, C. (2005) 'Destination image, romance and place experience – an application of intimacy theory in tourism', *Tourism Management*, vol 26, no 4, 481–491

Travel Industry Association of America (TIA) and National Geographic Traveller (2003) *Geotourism: the New Trend in Travel. Overview of American Travellers*, available from http://news.nationalgeographic.com (accessed August 2007)

United Nations World Tourism Organisation (UN-WTO) (2007) www.world-tourism.org (accessed July 2007)

Van der Merwe, M. and Wöcke, A. (2007) 'An investigation into responsible tourism practices in the South African hotel industry', *South African Journal of Business Management*, vol 38, no 2, 1–15

Weeden, C. (2001) 'Ethical tourism: an opportunity for competitive advantage', *Journal of Vacation Marketing*, vol 8, no 8, pp141–153

Wijk, J. and Persoon, W. (2006) 'A long-haul destination: sustainability reporting among tour operators', *European Management Journal*, vol 24, no 6, 381–339

Windsor, D. (2006) 'Corporate social responsibility: Three key approaches', *Journal of Management Studies*, vol 43, no 1, 93–114

World Travel and Tourism Council (WTTC) (2006) 'South Africa: the 2007 travel and tourism economic research', www.wttc.org (accessed August 2006)

World Travel and Tourism Council (WTTC) (2007) 'Tourism satellite accounting', www.wttc.org (accessed July 2007)

Yaman, H. and Gurel, E. (2006) 'Ethical ideologies of tourism marketers', *Annals of Tourism Research*, vol 33, no 2, 470–489

Yarona Management Consulting (2007) 'Baseline Study to Determine the State of Transformation in the Tourism Industry', Tourism BEE Charter Council. www.tourismbeecharter.co.za (accessed September 2007)

6

The Development Impacts of Tourism Supply Chains: Increasing Impact on Poverty and Decreasing Our Ignorance

Caroline Ashley and Gareth Haysom

Purpose and scope of the chapter

Poor people may earn as much income by supplying goods and services to the tourism sector as they do from working directly in tourism itself. But supply chains are less visible, participation by the poor less understood, and there has been less attention paid to making procurement pro-poor than to other forms of pro-poor tourism action. The purpose of this chapter is to explore the operation of tourism supply chains, and the potential for pro-poor impact.

This chapter starts by presenting data on the importance of supply chains to the poor based on the limited evidence that is currently available. It briefly outlines some of the types of initiatives that have been taken internationally to make supply chains more pro poor. In this context, the core of the chapter is an exploration of a case study from Spier Leisure (Western Cape of South Africa) of the company's intensive three-year investment in assessing and reforming procurement from a sustainable development and pro-poor perspective. Spier's approach to, and results from, a survey of their supply chains are presented. Although it is just one case study, it illustrates the importance of understanding how supply chains are constructed and operate, if efforts at reform are to be effective. Lessons from Spier's process of assessing and reforming the supply chain are drawn out.

Background to tourism supply chains and poverty alleviation

What is known about the scale of income to the poor from supply chains?

Poor people earn incomes from direct participation in tourism as hotel workers, guides, craft sellers or transport operators. But they also earn indirectly through the supply chain – by selling the goods and services that the tourism sector needs. Key supply chain sectors are food, beverage, construction, furnishings and a range of services such as gardening, floristry and laundry. Poor people may operate as micro entrepreneurs, selling direct to hotels, restaurants and operators, or they may have unskilled jobs in larger companies in those supply sectors.

A recent overview of emerging international evidence suggest that – in some destinations – the poor may be earning as much from the tourism supply chain as from direct participation in tourism business (Mitchell and Ashley, 2007). What is more, there may also be scope to *increase* incomes of the poor (or 'pro-poor income') from supply chains. Clearly then, these indirect pro-poor flows are important to assess, and, where possible, to boost.

However, the data are partial, and understanding of good practice interventions on supply chains is weak. On one hand, there is a vast economics literature assessing the indirect economic impacts of tourism due to inter-sectoral linkages ('inter-sectoral linkages' are virtually synonymous with supply chains). However, this literature, while confirming the size of supply chains, does not focus on the distribution of income or relevance to the poor. On the other hand, there is a range of pro-poor tourism research and action.[1] However, researchers have typically paid more attention to assessing direct participation of the poor in accommodation, craft and cultural services, rather than supply chains. Practitioners and companies have focused more on stimulating micro and community businesses in the tourism sector, or on broad community development, rather than on small suppliers. An important exception is the small but growing focus on the food supply chain to tourism.

We consider first what the economics literature tells us about the scale of tourism supply chains. A range of economic analyses suggest that in many developing countries, each unit of economic activity in the tourism sector generates about 0.6–1.2 units of activity in other sectors which supply tourism. Such research uses input–output models, sometimes as part of Social Accounting Matrices, Computable General Equilibrium (CGE) Models or cross-country regression analysis, and comes from a range of countries: Tanzania (Kweka et al, 2003), Hong Kong (Lin and Sung, 1984), Seychelles (Archer and Fletcher, 1996), Singapore (Heng and Low, 1990), Kenya (Summary, 1987), China (Fan and Oosterhaven, 2003), and Egypt (Tohamy et al, 2000).

Generalizing from the detail, these studies suggest that tourism's indirect contribution to the economy through non-tourism sectors can be equivalent to around 60–120 per cent of direct effects, thus roughly or nearly doubling the first

Table 6.1 *Earnings of the poor from supply chains and inter-sectoral linkages*

Destination	Earnings of the poor from tourism supply chains, expressed as a percentage of all poor earnings from tourism		
	Food supply to restaurants	Raw material for craft	Total supply chain income
Luang Prabang	50	13	63
The Gambia	20	–	–
	Unskilled labour in supply sectors	Raw material for craft from communal agriculture	
Namibia	31	6	37

Sources: Analyses of tourism value chains in Luang Prabang (Ashley, 2006) and The Gambia (Mitchell and Faal, 2007), and of economic impacts of tourism in Namibia (Turpie et al, 2004)

round impacts of tourism.[2] A World Bank cross-country regression analysis of data from the World Travel and Tourism Council's (WTTC) Tourism Satellite Accounts provides aggregates for developing countries. Lejarajja and Walkenhorst (2006) find that the ratio of inter-sectoral impacts to direct impact of tourism averages 66 per cent in low income countries and 77 per cent in lower middle income countries. Of course such results confirm the scale of supply chains, but not the participation of the poor.

There are very few studies which have assessed whether the poor earn more, in absolute terms, from supply chains or from work directly in tourism. A few exist indicating that in some destinations such as Luang Prabang (Lao PDR) and Namibia, the poor earn a third or even more than half of their aggregate tourism income from supply chains (Table 6.1).

Of course, whether the poor earn more from working directly in tourism or in supply chains varies enormously by destination. An important factor is the proportion of food that is sourced domestically, because food and beverage are major components of procurement,[3] and at least a considerable share of domestic food spending should reach poor farmers. In Luang Prabang, the estimated share of pro-poor income from supply chains is so high because 50 per cent of fruit and vegetables are estimated to be domestic, and most of the spending at the local market is estimated to reach 'poorish people' whether producers, transporters or market traders.

In other situations, employment in the accommodation sector may far outweigh the supply chain as a source of pro-poor income. This is more likely to be true where wages are relatively high (relative to the availability of unskilled labour) and where the economy is unable to supply food and other inputs, or the scale of analysis is only the immediate vicinity. For example, analysis of incomes to the poor from wildlife lodges in Madikwe (South Africa) found that lodge wages accounted for 68 per cent of income accruing to local households. Small enterprise earnings were small, although increasing a little over time with a programme of supplier support. Non-wage earnings were generally only considerable where there was a community joint venture in place, or a substantial corporate social responsibility programme (Relly, 2004: see Chapter 12 for more details).

Another question is whether the supply chain is proportionately more or less pro-poor than core tourism activities. That is, is the percentage of total economic activity that benefits the poor the same? It is clear that there is no single answer to this question either. Assessments in The Gambia (Mitchell and Faal, 2007) and Luang Prabang (Ashley, 2006) provide examples where indirect impacts appear to be more pro-poor, at least compared to the narrowly defined accommodation and transport tourism sector. The share of accommodation revenue that reaches the poor is low (often around 6–7 per cent of hotel or lodge turnover), and accrues mainly through direct employment of unskilled and semi-skilled staff by hotels and lodges. The share of the income from the food chain that reaches the poor is higher (around 20–45 per cent accruing mainly through the supply of fresh food. However, the reverse can also be true. An innovative CGE analysis in Brazil concluded that the poor mainly benefit from the direct jobs in tourism – rather than the indirect impacts (Blake et al, 2008). Blake et al (2008) found that low income households earn more than other households from direct earnings, whereas indirect earnings are highly significant for high income households.

What approaches exist to boost incomes of the poor from supply chains?

South Africa seems to be the only country where a standardized and formalized approach to encouraging tourism companies to adjust their procurement exists – in this context it is, of course, part of the wider commitment to Broad Based Black Economic Empowerment (BBBEE). BBBEE is based on addressing racial inequalities, rather than focusing specifically on the poor, and is a specific response to the apartheid legacy which largely excluded black businesses and entrepreneurs from the mainstream economy.

The Tourism Black Economic Empowerment (BEE) Charter (DEAT, 2005) provides the overall framework and principles for Broad Based BEE within tourism. Its primary objective is to empower black South Africans within the tourism industry and to make the tourism sector more accessible, relevant and beneficial to black South Africans. Despite the fact that South Africa experienced its first democratic elections in 1994, there has been only a marginal change in control at both the economic level and the management level. The tourism industry remains predominantly white controlled. This can also be said for most other industries. It is for this reason that the government has facilitated the process of Industry Transformation Charters. These Charters are driven by the Department of Trade and Industry (DTI) Codes of Good Practice. The Tourism Charter and Scorecard are currently being revised in order to align with the DTI Codes of Good Practice (DTI, 2007) which were laid out in early 2007. All sector charters have to comply with, or be more stringent than, the basic requirements of the Codes. Business has been an active partner in this process, although many, particularly labour, feel that the final outcome and content of the Codes is slightly less stringent than they should be.

The Code of Good Practice (and by necessity the emerging revised Tourism Scorecard) pays considerable attention to supply chain issues. 'Procurement' accounts for 20 per cent of a company's total score (25 per cent for small companies).[4] A high score on procurement is achieved by procuring from other BBBEE-rated enterprises that score highly. A further 15 per cent of the score is based on a company's performance on 'enterprise development' which involves mentoring and supporting emerging business, which may of course be suppliers. Thus from the South African perspective, these specific categories within the BBBEE process provide considerable incentives to alter supply chain and enterprise development activities.

There are a number of South African companies that are known to have already adopted initiatives to help small black local businesses get established as regular suppliers of food or of services such as guiding, babysitting and laundry (as outlined in Ashley et al, 2005). Umngazi River Bungalows (Eastern Cape) buys all its fruit, vegetables and chicken from local farmers, while also recruiting tourist guides from the local community. This was achieved by investing in communication, training and practical help at the start (such as showing farmers how to cultivate seedlings on site). Sun City has also assisted a local farmers' group to establish a hydroponics project, to supply the resort with lettuce and fresh herbs. In this example, donations for capital investment plus the guarantee of a ready and massive market up the road enabled the local farmers to get established. Stormsriver Adventures (SRA) assisted local women to establish an independent catering company to supply all meals for guests. This involved intensive input from SRA at first, in terms of training, mentoring, equipment, premises and administration. Examples such as these illustrate that a tourism company, large or small, can invest in stimulating small local suppliers, but do need up-front commitment and investment.

Internationally, the main examples of pro-poor supply chain intervention are on the agricultural side. In the Caribbean, tourism is often criticized for relying on imports, even of fruits that are produced locally. Torres (2003) analysed several initiatives that failed in Cancun, Mexico. A major problem was that initiatives focused either on supply, by working with farmers, or on demand, by working with chefs, but not on both together (Torres 2003, 2004). Chefs were suspicious or ignorant of the potential of local farmers, and found it easier to buy bulk food supplies from the capital city (Torres, 2004). Similar messages of the need to combine demand, supply and market intervention come from more successful examples supported by Oxfam in St Lucia (Wilde, 2007). The explicit strategy is to work on enhancing the quality and quantity of farmers' supply, encourage demand by engaging chefs and hotels in a 'buy local' programme, and to improve how the market links producers and buyers, in terms of pricing, ordering, insurance and transport. In these examples, there are some private companies, such as

Sandals resorts, which have taken the initiative and committed considerable staff time, but another necessary ingredient is the involvement of government and non-government actors, from both tourism and agriculture.

The Sandals initiative in Jamaica is one of the very few to generate hard data on how much the poor benefit from a supply chain initiative. The Sandals Resort Farmers Programme began in 1996 with ten farmers supplying two hotels (Lengefeld and Stewart, 2004). By 2004, there were 80 farmers supplying hotels across the island. Farmers' sales increased over 55 times in 3 years, from US$60,000 to $3.3 million. Purchases of watermelon and cantaloupe by just *one* Sandals resort of US$7,200 per month translates into a monthly income of US$100 for 70 families, taking them above the poverty line. This example shows the considerable returns that may be possible from enhancing supply chain linkages.

Compared with the dearth of data on the scale of pro-poor benefits from supply chains, there is considerably more knowledge of the factors that influence or impede participation of the poor and that could be amenable to influence. Areas for intervention are first of all on the supply side – such as the business environment and support for small and micro enterprises, secondly on the demand side – such as attitudes of chefs and hotels, and thirdly in the functioning of the market that enables suppliers and purchasers to engage more efficiently in transactions (Ashley et al, 2005; Meyer, 2006).

It is clear that there is much more to learn about how the poor benefit from supply chains and how these incomes can be enhanced and obstacles tackled. Thus the importance of learning from experience such as that at Spier, to which we now turn.

Supply chain assessment and pro-poor procurement at Spier

The overall approach

Spier Leisure operates a mid-range 155-bed hotel with conference centre just outside Stellenbosch (Western Cape, South Africa). Spier facilities comprise accommodation, restaurants, a picnic area and delicatessen, providing a base for leisure tourists enjoying the winelands, or for conference visitors. The other main businesses are the Spier wine business, Winecorp, and a Spier golf operation, privately owned but managed by Spier, the De Zalze Golf Course. Spier is a family owned company with a strong record on a range of social and environmental initiatives, thus it is not a 'typical' hotel company. In 2004 Spier Leisure embarked on a review and overhaul of its procurement, from a sustainable development perspective. The process from 2004 to 2005 was supported by facilitation from the Pro Poor Tourism Pilots (PPT Pilots) project, and some elements of the reform have been reported by that project (McNab et al, 2005; Ashley, 2005; Ashley et al, 2005). The reform continued after PPT Pilots and was broadened to include Winecorp, and the De Zalze Golf Course.

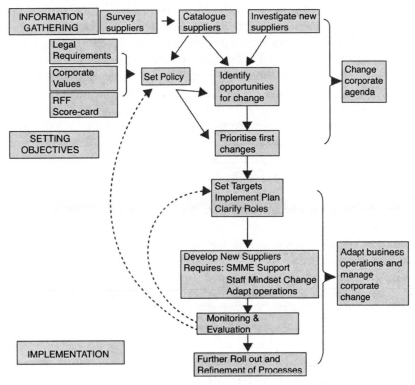

Source: Extracted from Ashley et al, 2005

Figure 6.1 *Strategic approach to procurement reform at Spier*

In 2004, Spier Leisure was going through a strategic shift, realigning the business to a more proactive approach to sustainability and pro-poor impact. In terms of the typology presented by Locke and Siteman (2003), Spier could be said to be grappling with the challenge of moving from a philanthropic state to one of a more encompassing approach to its responsibilities as a corporate citizen. In practical terms, this has meant shifting from a range of ad-hoc donations and small scale interventions towards the integration of both a pro-poor agenda and proactive sustainable development interventions at strategic level within the organization. It meant embedding sustainable development in policy and procedure, then managing performance according to these policies.

Unlike many other companies, Spier chose not to take an opportunistic approach to pro-poor procurement, by simply finding some local procurement opportunities and getting going. It chose instead (in a process similar to that outlined by Font and Cochrane (2005) for supply chain sustainability) to measure current supply chain performance, set priorities and establish performance indicators. The process is depicted in Figure 6.1, in which the initial work to set policy and gather information led to setting specific targets and plans, then to implementation and ongoing adaptation.

There were two somewhat different reasons to analyse the supply chain in detail. First, Spier was presenting itself as a business committed to a sustainable future, keen to 'build innovative models of how business and development can succeed in harmony with our ecology and society' (Spier, 2007). In order to do this, it would be hypocritical should Spier present an image of what it is achieving without understanding its supply chain, an area receiving as much as 40 per cent of all revenues (second only to spending on employment). Understanding the sustainability practices of the supply chain was therefore of critical importance.

Secondly, Spier needed to identify where in the supply chain significant development and pro-poor impact could be achieved, and needed a tangible basis for planning and measuring change. At the time Spier was disbursing ZAR5.7 million (US$0.54 million)[5] in philanthropy. In the same year, total procurement spend for the Spier group amounted to ZAR272 million (US$25.83 million). Thus it was realized that if just 10 per cent of procurement spend could be channelled to local, small and emerging suppliers, the financial impact would far outweigh philanthropy and would be a substantial boost to the local economy. A review of the Spier supplier list provided little information that could be used to inform proactive procurement shifts. So Spier Leisure embarked on an investigation of its supply chain so as to understand where impacts could be achieved, and provide a benchmark against which management would be required to make improvements.

Implementation of a supplier assessment

Starting in early 2004, a Spier-designed supplier survey questionnaire was sent to all Spier Leisure suppliers. The topics integrated conventional criteria against which any business would evaluate its suppliers (such as quality) and specific criteria such as employment practice and environmental action. The 60 questions were broadly categorized into 9 areas ranging from the degree of black ownership, to treatment of staff, to environmental practices. The nine categories and examples of what was scrutinized are shown in Table 6.2.

In addition to these questions, additional questions were asked pertaining to location, revenue, business type, date registered, products and services offered, whether the business operated under a franchise agreement and if the business was certified by any industry or quality specific codes. It was particularly important to establish the size, location and BEE status of the company, as Spier's new procurement policy was to prioritize suppliers that were local, small and black-owned (as outlined in Table 6.2).

Upon receipt of the initial replies from the suppliers, the first challenge became immediately apparent: how could the answers to 60 questions be processed so that suppliers would be uniformly scored and subsequently rated against Spier priorities. Some information was merely statistical (such as size of company), but much was needing to be scored and balanced against other elements of sustainable development performance. As a practical example the supplier needed to be rated on the level of compliance to broad based black

Table 6.2 *Supplier characteristics investigated by the survey*

Nine scoring categories	For example,[a] scores were based on:
Broad-based black economic empowerment	The level of ownership and strategic involvement by black people.[b]
Employment equity	Roles played by women, black and disabled people at different levels of the organization.
Procurement practice	Whether a procurement strategy or manual is in place, extent of procurement from black businesses, and enterprise development support for suppliers.
Human resource practice	Resources or time spent on skill development, conformity with ILO labour standards such as written contracts, grievance and disciplinary procedures and transparent record keeping.
Basic conditions of employment	Leave entitlement of employees, maternity and paternity leave, contributions to unemployment funds.
Labour law compliance	Compliance with labour law requirements such as hours of work, days worked, overtime policies, etc.
Corporate social investment	Whether the business has any policies or approaches for CSI, how funds are spent and beneficiaries are identified.
Health and safety compliance	Whether a health and safety audit has been done, a health and safety representative exists within company, plus staff access to toilets, drinking water, first aid facilities, fire fighting facilities.
Environmental action	What and how much is recycled, any water or energy saving practices, uses of renewable energy, any past fines for non-compliance with industry specific environmental codes.

Additional areas investigated

Size (number of employees)
Location
Legal type of business
Primary business activity
Vat and Company registration details
Turnover
Date started trading
Member of industry associations

Spier procurement priorities:
a combination of
• price, quality, quantity and reliability
• score
• belonging to a preferential category: SMME, local and BEE or PDI[c]

Note: a These are examples of what is included and are not comprehensive.

b In Spier's terms, 'black' means all Black, Coloured, or Indian South African citizens.

c In terms of the Spier Procurement policy, an SMME means a business with less than 50 employees and/or a turnover of less than R5 million. BEE means a business that has more than 25.1% black ownership and PDI means other suppliers defined as being previously disadvantaged (suppliers with disabilities and white women). Spier established a ranking within these preferential categories such that a BEE, local SMME company ranks first, a local BEE company ranks second, a BEE Regional SMME company ranks third, and so on. BEE companies are ranked ahead of PDI companies.

Categories	Company Score	Target Score (out of 5)	Max Score available	Overall score %
Employment Equity	1.55	3.50		
Black Economic Empowerment	3.00	2.50		
Procurement	0.00	2.50		
Human Resource Practices	4.29	4.00		
Labour Law Compliance	4.29	4.00		
Basic Conditions of Employment	3.33	3.00		
Corporate Social Investment	2.50	3.50		
Health & Safety Compliance	4.00	4.00		
Environmental	0.53	3.00		
Total	23.48	30.00	45.00	52.18%

Supplier Scoring Total

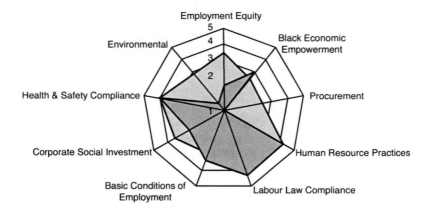

Figure 6.2 *Example for one company: calculating and representing scores*

economic empowerment activities while at the same time scored for their spending on payroll as well as the level of recycling carried out by the business. Capturing and scoring this required two things: a technical tool for data analysis, and decisions on the relative weighting of Spier's values.

An input tool was developed which recorded all the data for statistical purposes, and applied a balanced scorecard approach. Suppliers' answers were scored in each of the nine categories. In each category, the maximum score was 5, and the target score set by Spier ranged from 2.5 to 4. In most cases, 2.5 would represent compliance with legal requirements.

For each supplier the category scores were totalled and converted to an overall percentage which gives the supplier's score. For example, the company shown in Figure 6.2 scored 23.48 out of a total available of 45, thus getting a percentage score of 52 per cent. This company fell short of the target score of 30.

The upper half of Figure 6.2 shows how category scores and the overall score were calculated. The bottom half shows how this was visually represented on a spider diagram which compares achieved scores relative to a pre-determined target score set for all suppliers. Light grey represents the scores achieved; dark grey represents targets set by Spier.

For Spier as a whole, averages for each category across suppliers could also be aggregated, or disaggregated by type of enterprise.

The aim of the capture tool was to allow 'apples for apples' comparisons to be made. But it became clear that in terms of very small suppliers, this was not possible. Small suppliers (judged by Spier to be those with less than 20 employees), did not have the resources to contribute in a significant manner to BBBEE agreements and activities, were generally not able to contribute significantly to Corporate Social Investment programmes and, by law, were not expected to comply with employment equity legislation. So as not to penalize these suppliers, percentage scores were adjusted so that the score achieved was assessed out of 38 not 45.

The first 27 replies were entered into a database and the capture tool tested. The results were debated within Spier with buyers and management, and fine tuning was made so that scores would most accurately reflect the actual performance of suppliers. The process was then initiated in full.

The next challenge was getting a sufficient number of replies with usable data. Spier needed responses from a large percentage of suppliers, in order to get a true picture of its own supply chain. However, this took longer than expected. Some suppliers were intimidated by the questions. Other national South African BEE processes were running at the time, and the Spier process was often confused with this process. A factor causing considerable delay was that surveys were returned with data that was not in the form that Spier required. Some were rejected because information reported was inadequate, not in the format of the questionnaire, or only the positive information about the organization was reported. Some larger organizations returned information only in accordance with their own standard categories or within their own documents, such as Annual Reports. This information was generally reporting only on compliance with legal requirements (such as the Employment Equity Act, the Basic Conditions of Employment Act or the Labour Relations Act) or some voluntary commitment such as Corporate Social Investment, but ignored other parts of the survey. These were rejected as incomplete and suppliers were asked to revise their replies.

There were a number of suspicions about the process which had to be allayed, such as that it would:

- test only the black ownership of Spier suppliers;[6]
- seek ways, through the survey process, to eliminate existing suppliers;
- test only environmental/green actions of the suppliers;
- be simply an academic exercise requiring input time and then not be used as a strategic tool by management;
- be a foil behind which Spier could hide due to its own management and ownership structures.[7]

Table 6.3 *Response rates and average scores to Leisure, Wine and Golf supplier surveys*

	Leisure	Wine	Golf
Total questionnaires returned	265	152	136
Respondents as % of total suppliers	84.38	91.94	83.23
Percentage of questionnaires completed	68.77	83.04	79.49
Average score for suppliers[a]	44.72%	40.23%	46.58%

Note: the 'target' score set by Spier as desirable for suppliers was 66%.
a The average of all the questionnaires processed from suppliers to the specific Spier business unit.

Internal and external resistance or acceptance were linked. The process of running the survey had been given to the PPT facilitator, precisely so as not to place additional pressure on key line staff in the company. However, it was the buyer, not the PPT facilitator, who had the relationship with the suppliers and who was being questioned by the suppliers about the questionnaire. This meant that within Spier more communication and staff buy-in were essential. Internal work sessions were organized to encourage buy-in and respond to internal and external negativity. Once suppliers and staff were comfortable that the survey would not be used in a punitive manner, responses to the questionnaire increased. Internal acceptance grew more rapidly once enough information had been received and processed to start generating findings, illustrating trends and assisting staff. External acceptance increased as the internal perceptions became more positive, although pressure needed to be placed on some suppliers to complete the questionnaires. In 2005, other parts of the Spier Group began using a similar questionnaire. Between 2004 and 2007, questionnaires were distributed to over 500 suppliers of the Leisure, Wine and Golf businesses, with 417 correctly completed questionnaires returned. The response rate varies from 83 per cent for the golf business and 92 per cent for wine, as shown in Table 6.3.

Findings and implication of the supply chain assessment

The first use of the aggregated data was to generate a picture of the Spier supply chain, its breakdown by size, location and black ownership, and inform Spier how it could strategically alter its supply chain.

Analysis of actual spending on different suppliers from Spier Village Hotel (a business unit within Spier Leisure) showed that a fraction of all the suppliers account for the bulk of procurement spend. The same picture trend is also seen in supply chains of lodges within the Timbavati reserve in Mpumulanga South Africa, using a similar approach (unpublished author research, 2007). In the case of the Spier Hotel, the 'largest' 20 suppliers, in terms of their Spier procurement spend, account for more procurement spending than all the other companies combined, as shown in Figure 6.3.

Some findings immediately challenged existing assumptions. For example, the average size and age of most suppliers was much lower than expected. While

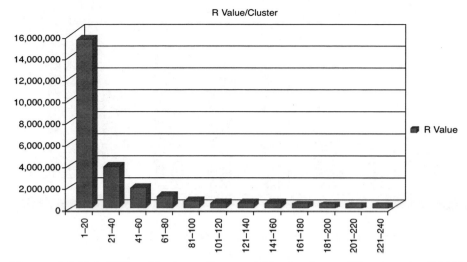

Figure 6.3 *Spier Village Hotel supplier spend, Rand value per 20 companies (2005)*

the average size for all supplying companies appeared to be around 200, this was skewed by a few large companies employing thousands. Once companies of over 1000 employees or less than five were excluded, the average company size was around 50 employees. The buyer in the leisure business had objected to shifting to small suppliers because of the increased workload that this was expected to create, but the survey demonstrated that Spier was already procuring from small and medium companies (as shown in Table 6.4). In fact, 78 per cent of Spier suppliers actually had less than 50 employees. Indeed, 56 per cent of all suppliers reviewed had less than 20 employees.

Table 6.4 *Size of Spier suppliers by number of employees*

Company employee profile	Leisure (%)	Wine (%)	Golf (%)	Average (%)	<20 employees (%)	<50 employees (%)
0–5 employees	19.69	11.83	18.26	16.59	56.33	78.32
6–10 employees	18.49	21.51	19.37	19.79		
11–20 Employees	18.98	23.66	17.22	19.95		
21–50 Employees	22.74	19.35	23.89	21.99		
51–100 Employees	9.24	10.75	9.31	9.76		
101–1000 employees	7.34	10.75	8.43	8.84		
>1000 employees	3.52	2.15	3.52	3.06		
Average company size	180	199	265			
Average company size (> 5 and < 1000)	47	57	65			
Companies formed after 1994[a]	75.88%	59.14%	68.75%			

Note: a Of relevance to this survey to ascertain the levels of transformation subsequent to the first democratic elections in South Africa.

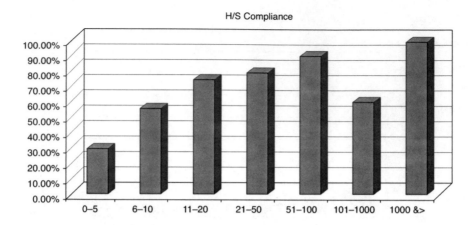

Figure 6.4 *Health and safety compliance by size of company*

While Spier has prioritized small businesses, the data showed that scores increased (in some categories more than others) as the organization increased in size. This is illustrated for health and safety in Figure 6.4. While this could stimulate a valid debate about Spier's preference to procure from small companies, such scores reflect little about the amount remaining in, or leaking from, the local economy and the poverty impact of the business, as discussed further below.

The figures show the degree of compliance with Health and Safety requirements (from 0 to 100 per cent) according to the size of company defined by the number of employees (from 0 to 5, up to over 1000 employees).

Another priority for Spier was to shift procurement to as many local suppliers as possible. The initial survey found that only 16 per cent of procurement spend was on purchases from local suppliers, and the vast bulk (78 per cent) was spent on regional suppliers. From a poverty and BEE perspective this needed to change because 'regional' included many in the business centre of Cape Town, whereas 'local' (within 30km) included a number of poor settlements sprawling between Cape Town and Stellenbosch. These are viewed as stakeholders of Spier, and are where a number of Spier staff reside. The survey enabled management to set objectives for localizing procurement and to evaluate performance for operational staff, with marked results, discussed further below.

Another priority for Spier was to procure from black owned enterprises and particularly local black businesses. The survey analysis revealed that Spier Leisure had only 34 (12.8 per cent) 'black economically empowered' suppliers (meaning more than a 25.1 per cent black shareholding) and of these, only 4 were local. This prompted the establishment of an enterprise development programme to develop new black local suppliers as outlined below, and an increase in the share of procurement from both black and local suppliers, as outlined below.

The second use of the data was to indicate how suppliers were performing on sustainable development indicators valued by Spier. Here again some misconceptions were found.

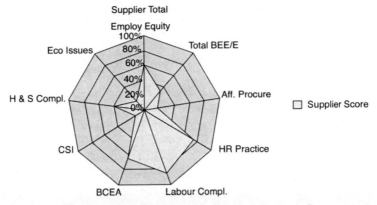

Supplier Total
Employ Equity

Note: Abbreviations (from the top): employment equity, total Black Economic Empowerment; affirmative procurement; human resources practice; labour compliance; Basic Conditions of Employment Act; corporate social investment; health and safety compliance; ecological issues.

Figure 6.5 *Final scores on sustainable development categories for suppliers to Spier Leisure*

Spider graphs were used to illustrate how suppliers scored on each of the nine areas of socioeconomic and environmental performance. The final scores from Spier Leisure (Figure 6.5) show the extent to which suppliers were focusing almost exclusively on legal compliance in areas of human resources, employment equity and labour law, with very little attention given to areas such as corporate social investment, affirmative procurement or ecological issues. Thus suppliers were adhering to law and policy, but where voluntary initiatives or other actions to support transformation were reviewed, the lack of motivation and action was evident.

These results for Spier Leisure suppliers were broadly similar to those in the other Spier businesses, as shown in Table 6.5. Wine business suppliers scored somewhat better on ecological issues, but even worse on employment equity, black economic empowerment and affirmative procurement. This suggests an even slower rate of transformation in the wine industry, perhaps exacerbated by the delays and redrafting of the Wine BEE charter.

The lack of supplier attention to environmental issues, despite the increasing 'environmental literacy levels' was striking: 61 per cent of respondents either did not complete or deleted the environmental section of the questionnaire; 78 per cent were taking no environmental action. Performance on corporate social investment was even worse, with 81 per cent taking no action.

Before the survey, Spier had no way of judging what the scores would be. When they came in, they were disappointing but Spier accepted these as being reflective of the state of the supply chain. It was clear that suppliers were performing well below Spier's own record, as evaluated using the same questionnaire and scoring process. As shown in Table 6.5, Spier's own business units scored from 62 to 72 per cent. On the positive side, it showed there was plenty of scope for encouraging improvements in the supply chain.

Table 6.5 *Average supplier scores by category, by Spier business unit*

Category	Spier Leisure	Winecorp	De Zalze	Average
Labour law compliance	86.07	77.98	80.14	81.40
HR practice	74.17	75.20	82.18	77.18
BCEA	65.43	70.83	65.78	67.35
H&S compliance	44.31	58.17	46.53	49.67
Employment equity	59.91	34.77	48.20	47.63
BEE & empowerment	33.82	17.02	28.08	26.31
Affirmative procurement	19.61	8.33	29.42	19.12
CSI	13.58	15.00	28.06	18.88
Ecological issues	15.99	23.03	10.83	16.62
Average score	**45.88**	**42.26**	**46.58**	**44.91**
Spier Business Score	72.24	62.56	67.53	67.44

Note: HR = human resources, BCEA =Basic Conditions of Employment Act, H&S = health and safety, BEE = black economic empowerment; CSI = corporate social investment

Taking action to reform the supply chain

The process of reviewing the supply chain led to a number of changes at strategic and operational level in Spier, and ultimately in the supply chain.

The first change was that the supply chain analysis enabled Spier to adapt its overall strategy for sustainability, focus heavily on procurement and set rigorous criteria and targets for shifting procurement. The survey results created a broad understanding of the supply chain within the company. The supply chain tool is now a fundamental part of the procurement process and is used to evaluate every new supplier. Old suppliers have not been dropped, but new suppliers all need to achieve a certain, predetermined score. In the past, price and quality were the only factors considered in the decision-making process. A number of suppliers have been selected recently, not due to price, but rather due to the fact that their values, reflected in the supply chain survey, better reflect the values of Spier. In a number of instances, these suppliers were more expensive than alternatives.

Significant results are already evident in the shift from regional to local procurement over four years, as shown in Figure 6.6. The percentage of procurement spend going to local suppliers has more than doubled.

In addition to this, the percentage of suppliers that are BEE (more than 25 per cent black ownership) businesses has also more than doubled, as reflected in Figure 6.7. The trend for PDI suppliers is even steeper, though starting from a lower base.

Secondly, Spier has invested time and effort in stimulating some new small black and local suppliers, and further adapted its procurement approach to assist them. The Spier input here goes beyond simply changing the selection criteria, and involves mentoring, innovative financing and pro-active searching for small black suppliers.

% Leisure Procurement spend going to
Local, Regional and National Suppliers

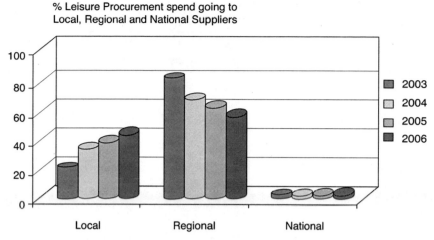

Figure 6.6 *Shift in local and regional procurement spend, 2003–2006*

The focus on shifting supply to emerging suppliers, or those suppliers disadvantaged as a result of the pre-1994 apartheid structures soon encountered
challenges. Due to the structure of the economy, it was often difficult to find
emerging black suppliers that would facilitate the attainment of the set procurement targets. This resulted in Spier management having to seek out and actively
work to develop emerging entrepreneurs. This process has run parallel to the
supply chain survey, initially carried out as a separate project by the PPT facilitator (funded by Business Linkages Challenge Fund, UK), although the two
processes are mutually reinforcing. The supply chain survey helped to identify
supply areas where potential existed to engage in enterprise development initiatives. The enterprise development process quickly showed that a small black

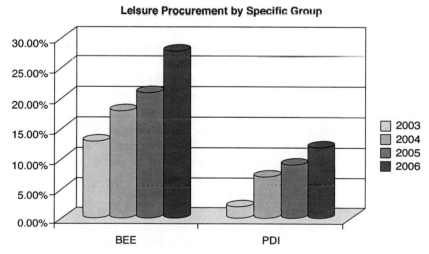

Figure 6.7 *Shift in percentage of suppliers that are BEE or PDI, 2003–2006*

Table 6.6 *Comparison of net benefits of the Enterprise Development laundry compared to an existing contract*

	Laundry I	Enterprise development laundry	Saving to Spier in year I ZAR	US$
Costs and savings to Spier in Year I				
Annual spend by				
Spier (ZAR)[a]	472,000	270,000	202,000	26,933
Set-up cost	–	75,000	–	–
Sundry costs	–	10,000	–	–
Total year I cost	472,000	355,000	117,000	15,600
Earnings into the community per year			Net community gain ZAR	US$
Jobs[b]	2	7	–	–
Salary avg per person				
per month[c]	1700	2000	–	–
Months	12	12	–	–
Local earnings				
ZAR	40,800	168,000	121,200	2400
Local earnings, US$	5,440	22,400		16,960

Notes: a The cost to Spier for the ED laundry is based on actual payments made over 12 months for the financial year ending 2006. Costs to Spier for Laundry I are what Spier would have spent for a year if it had continued with Laundry I, based on the per item costs at which Laundry I was contracted during the first 4 months of the restaurant, when Spier was using Laundry I, multiplied by the volume of items laundered by the ED laundry over the following year.
b Number of employees includes 2 part-time, 4 full-time employees and I owner.
c Salary per month is an average for all staff: full-time, part-time and owner (owner is a black male).

business could also adhere to other Spier standards and criteria, thus dispelling some myths and resistance.

Although no supplier was eliminated in the process, Spier was able to identify areas where the supply of a specific service could be divided between a number of 'enterprise development' suppliers, as was the case with the laundry project (see Ashley et al, 2005). A new black owned enterprise, employing formerly unemployed women, was able to take up a new laundry contract for a new restaurant on the Spier site. Spier assisted with capital costs and premises at the start, and assisted the operator to meet the service standards required.

Table 6.6 compares the benefit to Spier and to the local economy of the enterprise development laundry compared to the benefits of giving the new restaurant contract to existing Cape Town-based laundry suppliers. It shows very clearly the financial gain to both Spier and local incomes.

Benefits to the community from the Enterprise Development laundry are more than four times the benefits from a traditional laundry, because of a higher number of local employees. The fact that the owner is also a member of the community contributes to the high total wage flow. This reflects a very different

Table 6.7 *Impacts of Spier's new procurement from small black and local suppliers, August 2004–August 2005*

Product and supplier	Contract value, ZAR		Job creation			Existing jobs sustained
Suppliers commenced 2004–2005	Up to Aug 2005	Ongoing value P.A.	New jobs	Of whom women	Of whom previously unemployed	
Laundry: Klein Begin	149,890	270,000	11	9	10	None Lost
LPG Gas: Harare Energy Centre	57,000	114,000	0	–	–	3
Cards: Siyazama Paper making	2,000	As needed	0	–	–	8
Deck Construction: Appolus Construction	120,000	As needed	4*	1	–	3
Building Work: Pillay Construction	190,000	As needed	7ª	2	–	–
Fuelwood: Alfred Anthony	10,000	25,000	2ª	–	2	–
Alien Vegetation Clearing: A. Anthony	35,000	180,000	9	–	8	–
Total	**562,000**	**589,000**	**33**	**12**	**20**	**14**
New projects as of 2007	*From start to Aug 2007*	*Ongoing value P.A*				
Staff Restaurant	705,250	380,000	5	4	3	2
Turn Down Gifts	161,798	125,428	12	12	12	All New
Adobe Brick Making	260,000	260,000	21	6	18	All New
Paper Making Initiativeb	0	220,000	8	6	6	All New
2007 total	**1,127,048**	**765,428**	**46**	**28**	**39**	**2**
Plus 2005 data	**1,689,048**	**1,354,428**	**79**	**40**	**59**	**16**

Notes: a Temporary jobs, only for the duration of the contract.
b Paper making is a new project but has a first year contract value as above. Amounts have not been paid to communities as yet.

Source: Ashley (2006a) updated with 2007 information from author interviews with local stakeholders

cost structure in the business compared to the conventional Cape Town laundry, in which profits to the owner, capital equipment and rent would account for a much higher share of financial flows.[8]

From Spier's perspective, the enterprise development approach involved ZAR85,000 (US$11,300) to get going (mainly structure and equipment), but nevertheless saves money overall. Over the first year, the saving of R117,000 (US$15,600) is equivalent to 25 per cent of what Spier would have spent on a conventional laundry. Thus, in this instance, there is a clear commercial business case for shifting procurement, as well as clear returns in terms of Spier's non-financial values.

The laundry was established in August 2004. Since then a number of other contracts have been established with emerging suppliers using a similar approach to helping them get set up, as shown in Table 6.7. These include an alien vegetation clearing business, the staff restaurant business, a brick making business, construction and contracts for specific capital investment. As Table 6.7 shows, just one year later, by August 2005, 33 new jobs had already been created, and 14 existing, if somewhat precarious jobs, were sustained through new contracts. No jobs were lost by switching away from suppliers.[9] As many as 22 of the 33 new jobs have been sustained by on-going Spier contracts, which still continue, and all but 2 of these are held by people who were formerly unemployed (the other new jobs are temporary, according to when Spier needs inputs). A total of 12 are held by women.

By 2007, a further 4 new suppliers were in place, meaning that, in total, 79 new jobs have been created through new supply contracts, of which 59 are held by previously unemployed people, and 40 are held by women.

Most of the enterprise development businesses have shown similar levels of success. One business did get into financial difficulty, not because of the system but due to poor business practices. Here Spier worked with the supplier to develop a more robust and responsible business approach. One of the other successful businesses was the alien vegetation clearing business, as outlined in Box 6.1.

The third and final area of change is that some existing suppliers to Spier have sought to enhance their own performance. A number were interested in their scores after submission of their completed questionnaires, and several approached Spier with a request to be re-evaluated. This was because they had made changes in their company, often in the area of ownership, and sometimes in areas such as affirmative procurement, employment equity and corporate social investment. All those re-evaluated have improved on their previous individual scores.

Box 6.1 Tri-partite win–win–win from alien vegetation-clearing procurement approach

South Africa has a number of tree species declared as Alien Vegetation and landowners are required by law to remove these trees. Spier budgeted for the removal programme and called for tenders for the work but with a specific enterprise development clause inserted in the tender. A small black owned business comprising retrenched forestry workers submitted a tender. Their quote was ZAR200,000 (US$26,650) less than the next best bid. This tender was scrutinized and found to be reasonable. What was evident, however, was that there were certain skill and legal shortfalls within the small business that could have disqualified it from winning the tender. The second tender organization, a white owned business (at the time, one that is now BEE), was approached and asked if they would play a mentor role, for a fee, to support this business in the contract. This they agreed and the resultant 'tri party' approach meant that Spier could reduce the potential risks involved in this particular enterprise development project, the mentor organization could themselves play a role in enterprise development (and get paid to do so) and the emerging business got the best possible advice and mentorship from one of the best businesses in that specific field. This was a win–win–win situation.

The alien clearing contractor completed the contract on time and by the end of the contract was suitably skilled and legally compliant to take on the second Spier contract without mentorship.

Lessons learned at Spier

Spier chose to take a strategic, in-depth approach to procurement reform, and invested considerable management effort into it. The supplier assessment became a large and prolonged piece of work, taking longer than was anticipated, but also delivering more results. Looking back, it is clear that the supplier assessment served multiple functions, by:

- creating an overall picture of Spier's supply chain, and areas of good and weak performance;
- providing information against which specific suppliers could be assessed and, where necessary, informed of the need to improve in order to keep Spier contracts;
- focusing attention inside Spier on the supply chain and its potential pro-poor impact;
- focusing attention of suppliers on sustainability, BEE and other issues, and in some cases leading to action simply by asking questions;
- providing a baseline on the SD performance of the overall supply chain, and specific suppliers, against which improved performance can be assessed and for which managers are accountable; and

- busting a number of myths, for example, by showing that Spier was already procuring from a large number of small enterprises and helping build momentum for the pro-poor procurement approach which was adopted.

Several lessons were learned about how to conduct such an analysis effectively, particularly the need to bring staff on board, and to develop a capture tool that treated data objectively and was finely tuned to the priorities of the company. Perhaps the most important step of all was to translate Spier's broad values and the detailed information supplied into specific targets for managers, with associated monitoring of key performance indicators.

The process of bringing emerging small suppliers into the supply chain proved challenging at first, but has become smoother over time. A number of lessons were learned concerning critical factors that need to be in place to localize the supply chain:

- someone (in this case the PPT facilitator) with enough time to facilitate the process, working intensively at first with the new supplier and staff;
- a champion at senior management level to push the process forward;
- structuring contracts into smaller chunks manageable for an emerging company with limited capital; providing capital where necessary;
- spending as much time changing how operational staff within the hotel work with a supplier as time spent assisting the supplier;
- a non-negotiable insistence on quality standards, combined with advice to the supplier on how to achieve them, or where to source specialist technical input;
- working to unblock small but potentially fatal logistical problems to the new contract, such as on hours of delivery or access, storage, or transport access; and
- maximizing communication, and ensuring that management of the new contract is handed over to operational staff as part of their daily work, rather than remaining outside the mainstream.

Conclusion and implications

It is clear from the experience of Spier, that change in the supply chain can happen in three different ways, and is not just a matter of adding on one or two new local suppliers. Reform can be via a number of routes.

1   Shifts in the overall procurement approach so that operational staff select not only on price and quality but also on other pro-poor or environmental values. The shift in the sustainability profile of suppliers may not be enormous, but over a few years this approach can influence a substantial proportion of the supply chain.

2   The incorporation of a number of small emerging suppliers into the supply chain. The number will be limited by lack of supply capacity and the need for

more intensive mentoring or other support at the start. But the development impact per enterprise can be substantial.

3   Shifts in the behaviour of existing suppliers when they respond to the questions and expressed values of the company to which they supply.

In terms of the poverty impact of supply chain reform, Spier's experience provides some specific, though still incomplete, evidence. The approaches adopted by Spier were focused on broad transformation issues and not specifically on poverty relief – although this was certainly one of the desired outcomes of the process. The poverty impacts range from the very tangible, to the dynamic and less tangible. First there are the flows of income to local enterprise via new contracts, and the new employment created. As Table 6.7 noted, in just over 1 year, localization created 33 new jobs with on-going contract values of US$78,500 flowing into local enterprises. In 3 years it created 79 jobs. It is particularly notable that 59 jobs are held by previously unemployed people, as bringing them back into the labour-market has dynamic benefits, whereas it is often assumed that most benefits of enterprise initiatives are captured amongst those who are already economically active. This high proportion is probably attributable to Spier's specifically attaching value to the involvement of unemployed people when screening new suppliers, based on its understanding of supply chain conditions.

The contracts with Spier will have catalysed further enterprise development among the suppliers, but beyond some anecdotal examples, this is not currently measured. For example, one of the new suppliers gained profile through his work with Spier and was able to become a BEE partner with a larger company. Major constraints for micro businesses are lack of access to the market networks, to credit and to economies of scale. Where contracts with an established business like Spier can help them overcome these, there are likely to be dynamic benefits that go well beyond the specific work commissioned.

Another area of impact is via the mainstream suppliers who were scored by Spier and some of whom have started responding to Spier's criteria. One of the key aims of Spier was to address the challenges of South Africa's inequality by exploring the levels of transformation (BEE), employment equity and equitable labour practices within their suppliers. This is not so much targeted specifically at generating income for 'the poor' but at tackling deep inequality and changing the structure of the economy in the long term. The exact extent of supplier reform to date is unknown, as are the impacts on their employers, but even if they were known, the more substantive impact in changing attitudes and management attention would be hard to measure. In this sense, the impact of Spier's supply chain reform needs to be assessed not only in terms of direct financial flows to poor people (which are significant to those involved but not compared to the scale of economic need in the region), but also as part of a longer-term process of shaping how business is done, for greater equality and impact on poverty.

The Spier experience indicated the enormous potential for pro-poor intervention in the supply chain and the need for this to receive greater attention in tourism. The fact that around 40 per cent of spending goes on procurement and yet there was so little understanding of the profile of the chain is unlikely to be unique to Spier. In Spier's case, suppliers were paying very little attention to sustainability issues apart from those requiring compliance. This again is likely to be common. Spier was able to achieve a relatively rapid increase in procurement from local, black owned and PDI suppliers between 2002 and 2006, albeit from a low base. This is partly due to context. First the peculiarities of the post-apartheid economy in South Africa might mean that there are greater market failures preventing pro-poor procurement than in other countries. This means there are more 'low hanging fruit' available to make a relatively rapid improvement when a conscious effort is made. Secondly, Spier as a company was able to devote substantial management time and commitment to change, probably beyond what 'typical' companies would do. Nevertheless, the shift does show how feasible increases can be achieved with corporate commitment. Thus the tourism sector more widely should be able to use its purchasing power to encourage behavioural shifts within the supply chain.

A further reason for paying greater attention to supply chains comes from a survey finding that the supply chain to Spier was less casualized than the operational side of the business. Given that quality employment is one of the oft-noted development impacts of tourism, it is important for practitioners to note that this may be better attained within the supply chain of the tourism industry as opposed to the operational side of the industry. This contradicts a number of industry related initiatives in South Africa seeking to enhance the impact of tourism by setting up small tourism operators. These operators are often operating in marginal markets, and are subject to the downsides of tourism, particularly the seasonality of the tourism economy, the operational risks and levels of capital needed for many services. These constraints limit the entry and success of small and emerging entrepreneurs. The potential presented by the supply chain raises questions about this focus, given the lack of focus on the supply chain side of the tourism industry. The indications are that supply chain reform may have greater potential for a more equitable distribution of tourism revenues.

The case of Spier also shows how important it is for a company that aspires to be value-driven, or prides itself on integrating sustainability into its operation, to actually understand its supplier profile. In all three cases (leisure, golf and wine), the average sustainable development performance of suppliers fell below that of the Spier company itself. And yet with procurement constituting such a large part of the operation, it inevitably also constitutes a large part of the total societal impact of the business.

It can be argued that Spier is not a typical company, in that it combines a commercial pursuit of profit with strong societal values, and has been able to run over the bottom line while investing in sustainability in a way that other companies could not. Nevertheless, Spier's experience demonstrates a range of commercial benefits that come from procurement reform, in which cost-saving is just one. Spier has also gained in terms of reputation and local social licence, while internally benefiting from improved staff morale. Precisely because Spier has spent time and resources innovating a procurement reform process, the adoption of similar techniques by others can be easier. Of course the data capture tool needs to be adapted on a company-by-company basis to reflect specific priorities, but there are lessons and tools that other companies can gain from Spier.

Our knowledge of the development impact of this procurement shift is still limited to some micro cases, such as the laundry. The need for a better understanding of the pro-poor flows from supply chains, and from changes in supply chains, was highlighted in the international overview at the start, and the case remains. Nevertheless, the laundry example illustrates just how considerable the development impact can be, when one contract of around US$20,000 leads to a fourfold increase in financial flows to poor households. The case for both further action and further assessment of local economic impacts of the tourism supply chain remains strong.

Notes

1   These two sets of literature are outlined in more detail in Mitchell and Ashley, 2007, as are the examples below which are briefly mentioned here.

2   This impact is also expressed as the ratio multiplier being around 1.6–2.2. However, ratio multipliers are readily confused with the quite different Keynesian or output multiplier (Lejarajja and Walkenhorst, 2006), which are invariably less than one. Thus the multiplier shorthand is confusing rather than convenient.

3   A number of sources indicate that food and beverage purchases constitute about one-third of hotel expenditure and the great majority of this supply chain is supplied by domestic resources (Christie, 2006; SRI, 1997; Torres, 2003). Economic assessment based on 1992 data in Tanzania, estimates that half of the total employment impact of tourism is in the staple foods sector (Kweka et al, 2003). In Senegal, 35% of local inputs used by tourism are agricultural and food products (Christie and Crompton, 2003).

4   Application of the code depends on the size of the organization; although the size related delineation is still under debate within the tourism industry. The Codes of Good practice define a qualifying Small Enterprise (QSE) as a business that has a turnover of less than R35 million but more than R5 million. A QSE has to complete only four of the seven categories, each of which account for 25% of the score. Thus if a QSE chooses to be scored on procurement, this would account for 25% of its score, and the same applies to enterprise development. Businesses with a turnover of less than R5 million are termed Exempt Micro Enterprises (EMEs) and do not need to participate in BBBEE.

5   At the average 2002 exchange rate of ZAR10.53 to S$1. Other US$ amounts below are based on the exchange rate of ZAR7.226 to US$1, the current rate on 5 September 2007, unless otherwise noted.

6   Black Economic Empowerment and Broad Based Black Economic Empowerment initiatives were, at the time of the survey, of particular importance, with many suppliers uncertain as to how to proceed and how the market in general would respond to this. It must be stated that there was resistance to this. By 2007 most of the scepticism had been resolved, particularly with the publishing of the Codes of Good Practice by the DTI.

7   Spier is a white-owned family business that has no black shareholding and as such is sometimes challenged to transfer a portion of its ownership. Spier's main focus remains that of broad sustainability which includes an alternative view of transformation and a broader level of black economic empowerment not focused on ownership.

8   The ED laundry pays a low rent of ZAR1000 per month to Spier. While this could be seen as an on-going subsidy by Spier, there is no direct opportunity cost to Spier of the land, thus no cost to Spier is included in Table 6.6. Profits in the ED laundry are estimated to be variable (some low season months are likely to be in the red) and have been mainly reinvested in the business, thus do not count as benefit flow. The owner's income comes from his regular wage, which is somewhat higher than that of other staff.

9   In many cases the contract with an emerging supplier was with a relatively new or expanding service so was not 'taken' away from others. In several cases the traditional service provider is a large firm, for whom a change in Spier contract values is not significant enough to affect employment rates.

References

Archer, B. and Fletcher, J. (1996) 'The economic impact of tourism in the Seychelles', *Annals of Tourism Research*, vol 4, no 1, 32–47

Ashley, C. (2005) *Facilitating pro-poor tourism with the private sector: Lessons learned from 'Pro-Poor Tourism Pilots in Southern Africa'*, Working Paper 257 Overseas Development Institute, London

Ashley, C. (2006) *Participation by the Poor in Luang Prabang Tourism Economy: Current Earnings and Opportunities for Expansion*, ODI-SNV paper, Overseas Development Institute, London

Ashley, C. and Haysom, G. (2006) 'From philanthropy to a different way of doing business: Strategies and challenges in integrating pro-poor approaches into tourism business', *Development Southern Africa*, vol 23, no 2, 265–280

Ashley, C., Haysom, G., Poultney, C., McNab, D. and Harris, A. (2005) *The How To Guides: Producing Tips and Tools for Tourism Companies on Local Procurement, Products and Partnerships. Volume 1: Boosting Procurement from Local Businesses*, London and Johannesburg

Ashley, C., Goodwin, H., McNab, D., Scott, M. and Chavos, L. (2006) *Making Tourism Count for the Local Economy in the Caribbean: Guidelines for Good Practice*, Pro Poor Tourism Partnership, Caribbean Tourism Organization, and the Travel Foundation, London and Barbados

Ashley, C., de Brine, P., Lehr, A. and Wilde, H. (2007) *The Role of the Tourism Sector in Expanding Economic Opportunity*, Economic Opportunity Series. Harvard University, Cambridge

Blake, A., Arbache, J. S., Sinclair, M. T. and Teles, V. (2008) 'Tourism and poverty relief', *Annals of Tourism Research*, vol 35, no 1, pp107–126

Christie, I. T. (2006) *Institutions for Managing Tourism Growth: An Overview*, World Bank, Washington, DC

Christie, I. and Crompton, E. (2003) 'Republic of Madagascar. Tourism Sector Study', Africa Region Working Paper Series no 63

Department of Environmental Affairs and Tourism (DEAT) (2005) *Tourism BEE Charter and Scorecard*. DEAT, Pretoria

Department of Trade and Industry (DTI) (2007) 'Broad Based Black Economic Empowerment Codes of Good Practice 2007', DTI, Pretoria, www.thedti.gov.za/bee/CODESOFGOODPRACTICE.htm, accessed 13 July 2008

Fan, T. and Oosterhaven, J. (2005) 'The impact of international tourism on the Chinese economy', Paper for the 15th International Input–Output Conference, Beijing

Font, X. and Cochrane, J. (2005) 'Integrating Sustainability into Business. A Management Guide for Responsible Tour Operations', United Nations Environment Programme Division of Technology, Industry and Economics (UNEP/DTIE)

Heng, M. T. and Low, L. (1990) 'Economic impact of tourism in Singapore', *Annals of Tourism Research*, vol 17, 246–269

Kweka, J., Morrissey, O. and Blake, A. (2001) 'Is tourism a key sector in Tanzania?: input–output analysis of income, output, employment and tax revenue', TTRI discussion paper 2001/1, www.nottingham.ac.uk/ttri/pdf/2001–1.pdf, accessed 13 July 2008

Kweka, J., Morrissey, O. and Blake, A. (2003) 'The economic potential of tourism in Tanzania', *Journal of International Development*, vol 15, no 3, 335–351

Lejarraja, I. and Walkenhorst, P. (2006) *Of Linkages and Leakages: How Tourism Can Foster Economic Diversification* (draft). World Bank, Washington, DC

Lengefeld, K. and Stewart, R. (2004) 'All-inclusive Resorts and Local Development, Sandals, World Travel Market', www.propoortourism.org.uk/WTM%20Presentations/WTM%20Sandals%20presentation.pdf, accessed 13 July 2008

Lin, T. and Sung, Y. (1984) 'Tourism and economic diversification in Hong Kong', *Annals of Tourism Research*, vol 11, 231–247

Locke, R. and Siteman, A. (2003) 'Note on corporate citizenship in a global economy', Sloan School of Management and Department of Political Science, MIT, http://mitsloan.mit.edu/50th/pdf/corpcitizenship.pdf, accessed 13 July 2008

McNab, D. with contributions from Ashley, C., Haysom, G., Poultney, C. and Nyathi, Z. (2005) 'Impacts of pro-poor tourism facilitation with South African corporates', PPT Working Paper, September, Pro Poor Tourism Partnership, UK

Meyer, D. (2006) 'Caribbean tourism, local sourcing and enterprise development: Review of the literature', PPT working paper no. 18, Pro-poor tourism partnership, UK, www.propoortourism.org.uk/ppt_pubs.html. accessed 13 July 2008

Mitchell, J. and Ashley, C. (2007) *Can Tourism Offer Pro-poor Pathways to Prosperity?* ODI Briefing Paper 32, ODI, London

Mitchell, J. and Ashley, C. (forthcoming) *Pathways to Prosperity? How Can Tourism Reduce Poverty? A Review of the Pathways, Evidence and Methods*, World Bank and Overseas Development Institute, London and Washington DC

Mitchell, J. and Faal, J. (2007) 'Package holiday tourism in The Gambia', *Development Southern Africa*, Special Edition on Tourism (September)

Relly, P. (2004) 'Madikwe Game Reserve: The Local Impacts of Wildlife Tourism', in Rogerson, C. and Visser, G. (eds), *Tourism and Development Issues in Contemporary South Africa*, Africa Institute of South Africa, Pretoria

Rogerson, C. (2000) 'Subcontracting in the tourism industry: The nature of subcontracting between large hotel establishments and small businesses in South Africa', DBSA report, DBSA and Ntsika, Johannesburg

RSA (2003) Department of Trade and Industry, Broad-Based Black Economic Empowerment Act, No. 53 of 2003: Research online at URL: www.thedti.gov.za/bee/BEEAct-2003-2004.pdf, accessed 13 July 2008

RSA (2005) Department of Environmental Affairs and Tourism, Tourism BEE Charter and Scorecard, 8 May 2005. Research online at URL: www.naci.org.za/Innovation_gateway/downloads/tourism_bee_charter_scorecard.pdf, accessed 13 July 2008

Spier (2007) Spier Holdings Annual Report 2006. Spier – In Search of a Sustainable Future. www.spier.co.za/spier.htm, accessed 13 July 2008

SRI International (1997) Tourism Development and Backward Linkages in the Dominican Republic, Prepared for USAID/Dominican Republic, Economic Policy and Practices Project

Summary, R. M. (1987) 'Tourism's contribution to the economy of Kenya', *Annals of Tourism Research*, vol 14, no 4, 532–540

Tohamy, S. and Swinscoe, A. (2000) 'The economic impact of tourism in Egypt', Working Paper 40, June, The Egyptian Centre for Economic Studies, Egypt

Torres, R. (2003) 'Linkages between tourism and agriculture in Mexico', *Annals of Tourism Research*, vol 30, no 3, 546–566

Torres, R. (2004) 'Challenges and potential for linking tourism and agriculture to achieve Pro-poor Tourism Objectives', *Progress in Development Studies*, vol 4, no 4, 294–318

Turpie, J., Lange, G.-M., Martin, R., Davies, R. and Barnes, J. (2004) *Strengthening Namibia's System of National Protected Areas*. Economic Analysis and Feasibility Study for Financing Namibia's Protected Areas, Anchor Environmental Consultants, Windhoek

Wilde, H. (2007) 'Case study of Sandals Farmers' Programme', paper for Harvard conference on Corporate Social Responsibility, Cambridge, MA

Part 2

Responsible Nature-based Tourism

7

Impacts of Wildlife Tourism on Rural Livelihoods in Southern Africa

Anna Spenceley

Introduction

Background to the paper

'Wildlife tourism' is defined as a form of nature-based tourism that includes the consumptive and non-consumptive use of wild animals in natural areas (Roe et al, 1997). Non-consumptive wildlife tourism may be undertaken through guided or self-drive excursions in vehicles, or through guided walks, where wildlife is not physically killed. Wildlife tourism becomes consumptive when wildlife is killed, which usually takes place during hunting tourism.

Table 7.1 summarizes the national statistics for nature-tourism in five southern African countries: Botswana, Namibia, South Africa, Zambia and Zimbabwe. The data indicate that in 2000–2001 South Africa had the greatest number of nature-based tourists, and highest income from nature-tourism in southern Africa. The data also illustrate that Namibia generates the highest average income, per nature-tourist in the region (~US$688 per arrival) (Scholes and Biggs, 2004).

Tourism can have many different types of impact on poor people's livelihoods, and the relative importance of these varies enormously from place to place. Broadly, impacts can be categorized as follows (Ashley and Elliott, 2003):

- financial, where the poor may earn cash from (i) waged jobs, (ii) sales of goods and services by entrepreneurs or informal sector traders, (iii) shares of collective community income;

Table 7.1 *Nature tourism arrivals and income in southern Africa*

Country	Nature-tourism arrivals (000s) (Domestic and International)	Income from nature tourism (million US$)
Botswana	472.9	131.3
Namibia	360.0	247.6
South Africa	4634.5	2298.8
Zambia	459.2	72.8
Zimbabwe	1494.4	143.5

Source: Adapted from Scholes and Biggs (2004). Tourism figures from the period 2000–2001

- non-financial livelihood impacts such as improved or decreased access to infrastructure, communications, water supplies, health, education, security services; and
- empowerment impacts, including opportunities for institutional development and participation in local economic decision making.

Within rural areas, wildlife tourism can provide a mechanism to realize tangible benefits from conservation and wildlife for local communities (Roe et al, 1997), particularly those whose land and interests are affected by wildlife (Barnes et al, 1992). In part, employment and other direct financial benefits can be generated by wildlife tourism and associated activities, which can also promote conservation and prescribe value to wildlife in developing countries (Roe et al, 1997).

This chapter presents and reviews research across southern Africa on the livelihood impacts of wildlife tourism, considering data from Botswana, Namibia, South Africa, Zambia and Zimbabwe. The financial analyses incorporate both direct, overhead and capital costs and can be used to address questions relating to the optimal allocation of resources from a landowner's perspective (Jansen et al, 1992). Data from 2000 onwards have been used wherever possible with information drawn from consultancy reports, institutional publications and journal papers. For each country, and depending on the level of information available, details are provided of the involvement of local community members in wildlife tourism: as employees and as beneficiaries of community dividends or resources.

Sustainable livelihoods and local benefits from wildlife tourism

Botswana

Policy
Botswana's government supports a policy of 'low volume–high value' wildlife tourism, with high entry fees to protected areas (of BWP150 per person, per day [US$ 25][1]) and a limitation on the number of visitors to any lodge in a national park or game reserve. Photographic wildlife tourism and hunting emerged on

communal lands as part of a Community Based Natural Resource Management (CBNRM) programme funded by USAID, which used policies allowing local communities to gain economic benefits from wildlife, natural resources and tourism in Wildlife Management Areas. Communities could apply for a wildlife quota and form registered community trusts. They could then sublease land, sell wildlife quotas or form joint ventures with private tourism operators (Zeppel, 2006). In 2000 there were 14 registered trusts, which operated activities such as hunting and photographic tourism, campsites, bird watching and mokoro safaris (Rozmeijer, 2000).

The trophy hunting joint ventures can generate substantial income. Safari outfitters competitively bid for the rights to hunt in a concession area, and communities sell their wildlife quotas for valuable species such as lion, leopard and elephant. The quotas are paid in advance to community trusts, and refunds are not provided if animals are not killed (Gujadhur and Motshubi, 2000). In addition to revenue, the hunts also provide meat from game animals, and some employment for men tracking, skinning and tanning. Photographic tours are offered in non-hunting seasons (October to March), while community campsites with tours cater to self-drive visitors and mobile safari companies (Zeppel, 2006).

Communal and household benefits

A summary of the benefits received from tourism activities based in communal areas of Botswana are indicated in Table 7.2. In 2001 tourism activities operating in 11 community trusts had generated economic benefits of US$1.25 million,[2] which Zeppel (2006) calculates provided an average of $325 per person, or $82 per hectare.

In the case of partnership arrangements, Arntzen (2003) reports that the poverty reduction potential of CBNRM projects from joint-venture agreements is often similar or much higher to the monthly income accrued by households from wages. Taking a specific community based organization as an example, the Khwai Development Trust is a local institution that the people of Khwai formed to enable them to benefit from wildlife resources through consumptive and non-

Table 7.2 *Summary of benefits from community trusts and tourism ventures in Botswana*

	Area (km²) (n = 10)	Population (n = 10)	Economic benefits (BWP) (n = 11)	Jobs (n = 9)	US$ per person (n = 9)	US$ per ha (n = 9)
Total	27,012	21,030	7,073,337	678	—	—
Average	2701	2103	643,031	75	325	82
Min	589	75	100,000	5	16	4
Max	12,225	10,000	1,500,000	145	1648	218

Note: Originals were in BWP, and converted using exchange rate of 0.16977 on 1 June 2006.

Source: Adapted from Rozemeijer, (2000) and Mbaiwa (2005b) cited in Zeppel (2006)

consumptive tourism purposes. They sell their annual wildlife quota from Department of Wildlife and National Parks through an auction sale to individual safari hunters and safari companies. The Khwai Development Trust generated substantial income (US$510,843) from the sale of their wildlife quotas through auction sales to various hunting companies and individuals between 2000 and 2002 (Mbaiwa, 2005a). In 2000 the Khwai Development Trust accrued $181,062 revenue from community-based tourism enterprises (Mbaiwa, 2000) and $488 per capita from joint-venture income (Arntzen et al, 2003): higher than the average calculated by Zeppel (2006).

Employment

A review of 50 tourist camps and lodges in the Okavango Delta found that there were 1658 people employed in 2001 (Mbaiwa, 2003). Suich et al (2005) found that of 29 enterprises in northern Botswana (19 accommodation and 10 tour operators), 523 of the 902 staff were local people (58 per cent). However, the local people generally hold poor-quality and low-paying jobs that mostly involve manual work. Most local people work as cleaners, kitchen hands, drivers, cooks, watchmen, groundsmen with a few employed as professional guides and assistant managers. For example, Mbaiwa (1999) found that Sankuyo residents generally provided manual labour for tasks such as the skinning of wild animals during the hunting seasons and housekeeping at Crocodile Camp Safaris. In Khwai, local people employed at Tsaro Game Lodge and Khwai River Lodge work as cooks, housekeepers and drivers. On the other hand, expatriate staff occupy senior and management positions such as managers, accountants, professional guides and chefs. These findings are also similar to those by Ndubano (2000) who states that in Maun, accommodation facilities are largely foreign owned and only 6 (14.2 per cent) of management positions are filled by Botswanans (Mbaiwa, 2003).

Mbaiwa (2003) found a disparity in wages earned by local staff and expatriate staff, even when they occupied the same position. On average, Mbaiwa found that local staff earned salaries between US$816 and $2316 per year, while expatriate staff earned US$10,428–$41,736 annually. In Maun, Ndubano (2000) found that of a sample of 50 local people employed in the tourism sector 33 (66 per cent) earned between US$924 and $2292 per year. However, Suich et al (2005) found a far more positive salary level among local staff in northern Botswana. Salaries from 19 accommodation enterprises and 10 tour operators generated US$3.5 million in wages for 823 local staff in 2004. This provided an average of $4295 per employee during that year, or $11.76 per day (Suich et al, 2005). These estimates significantly exceed the figures from Mbaiwa and Ndubano (on Botswana, also more recent research in Chapter 9 by Mbaiwa and Chapter 10 by Massyn).

Namibia

Policy

In Namibia, wildlife-based tourism takes place in protected areas and in communal conservancies. Conservancies in Namibia are areas of communal land that are unfenced, are registered as multiple use areas and are managed by elected committees of community members. Once registered, a conservancy acquires rights and responsibilities for the consumptive and non-consumptive use and management of wildlife, on behalf of the community it represents. The main requirements for registering conservancies are that they must have a defined membership and a committee that is representative of community members. Conservancies must also be legally constituted with clearly defined boundaries that are not disputed with neighbouring communities. The government formally owns conservancy land but communities have rights of occupation (NACSO, 2004). There were 42 registered communal conservancies in Namibia by 2005 (MET, 2005). In addition, 24 private wildlife conservancies have been established by commercial farmers since 1968 (Zeppel, 2006). Areas within conservancies can be zoned for different uses, including wildlife use, hunting and wildlife viewing, and agriculture. Wildlife quotas can be recommended by conservancies, and they can enter agreements with private tourism operators and develop tourism facilities. Members elect committees that manage the natural resources, and then distribute incomes from hunting and tourism (Jones, 1998).

Communal and household benefits

The impacts on employment of tourism in protected areas in Namibia were estimated in 2003 using a Social Accounting Matrix. The analysis found that approximately US$44.3 million was distributed to rural and urban households in Namibia, through wages and salaries, businesses, pensions and gifts, and traditional agriculture (Turpie et al, 2004).

Most of the income from Namibian communal conservancies comes from community-based tourism and campsites (35 per cent), followed by joint tourism ventures (27 per cent) and trophy hunting (21 per cent) (Novelli and Humavindu, 2005, cited in Zeppel, 2006). In 2000 community-based tourism generated US$216,135 out of the total $504,315 accrued from all CBNRM activities on conservancies.[3] Joint-venture tourism operations generate the largest source of income for conservancies – paying bed night levies, rental fees, annual flat-rate fees and percentages of their business income, game for hunting, training and employment (Ashley and Garland, 1994).

Financial benefits generated by rural communities within the conservancy programme have increased dramatically, from around US$188,019 in 1998 to US$1.2 million in 2004.[4] The Namibian economy earned about US$16 million,[5] either directly or indirectly from CBNRM in 2003. Money earned by conservancies is generally used for conservation and land management, salaries/wages or benefits (dividends) for member households. Wildlife populations have also increased substantially in association with the programme (NACSO, 2004).

Barnes et al (2002) calculated the values of five wildlife conservancies on communal land in Namibia (see Table 7.3). The conservancies were found to be economically efficient and able to contribute positively to national income and the development process. They also found that the financial returns for communities from wildlife use initiatives were very attractive and exceeded their investments. The generally highly positive returns come from two sources: (1) direct use

Table 7.3 *Physical characteristics and base case financial values for five Namibian conservancies in 2000 (US$)*

	Torra	≠Khoadi //Hoas	Conservancy Nyae Nyae	Mayuni	Salambala
Characteristics					
Land area (ha)	352,200	386,000	900,095	28,400	93,000
Core[a] wildlife area (ha)	108,586	177,650	900,095	13,300	11,000
Households (no.)	120	700	700	450	1,200
Starting wildlife density[b]					
(ha per LSU equivalent)	427	160	464	43	3,875
Values					
Project financial values					
Initial capital investment ('000s)	$171	$125	$506	$111	$204
Capital investment per ha	$0.49	$0.33	$0.56	$3.88	$2.16
Capital investment per household	$1,400	$178	$723	$246	$170
Annual net cash income ('000s)	$13.7	$10.0	$38.4	$47.9	$19.2
Community financial values					
Annual community cash income[c] ('000s)	$58	$60	$29	$105	$61
Cash income per household	$487	$86	$42	$234	$51
Cash income per ha	$0.17	$0.16	$0.03	$3.74	$0.66
Annual community dividends[d] ('000s)	$33	$30	$16	$32	$24
Dividends per household	$273	$43	$23	$72	$20

Notes: Exchange rate used from 1 June 2000 of N$1 = US$ 0.14368. Original paper in N$
a Core areas, allocated primarily to wildlife (rest of land shared between wildlife and livestock).
b Density calculated for the total land area.
c Includes salaries and wages for conservancy employment, net cash income, and dividends.
d Annual surplus extracted for distribution to households.

Source: Barnes et al (2002)

benefits from the utilization of wildlife – mainly through joint-venture agreements in tourism activities; and (2) non-use values (i.e. willingness to pay for conservation of the wildlife resources) through grants from donors, investing in the CBNRM programme. Barnes et al (2002) concluded that non-consumptive and safari-hunting tourism are particularly important income generators for all conservancies. Also, the existence of natural wildlife populations on conservancies (i.e. reducing the need for investments in stock) is a very significant factor affecting the economic efficiency and financial viability of conservancies (also see Chapter 16 by Barnes in this volume, for a detailed account of this research, and more recent data).

One of the conservancies reviewed by Barnes et al (2002), the Torra conservancy, is located in the Kunene region. In 2003 Torra conservancy earned income

Table 7.4 *Income and disbursements in the Torra Conservancy 1999–2004, in US$*

	1999	2000	2001	2002	2003	2004
Total financial benefit						
Joint ventures	$61,057	$52,982	$56,706	$55,930	$90,580	$168,978
Trophy hunting	$16,319	$25,600	$7250	$18,873	$15,326	$19,329
Non-tourism income	$81,435	$86,999	$76,178	$133,061	$306,436	$284,618
Total	$158,810	$165,581	$140,134	$207,865	$412,342	$472,925
Household income						
Benefit to households	$66,264	$63,435	$57,552	$51,905	$121,327	$269,628
% of total financial benefit	41.7%	38.3%	41.1%	25.0%	29.4%	57.0%
Income from joint ventures	$33,012	$29,454	$27,902	$25,285	$58,007	$126,949
Income from hunting	0	$1185	$749	$668	$1593	$2035

Note: N$ to US$ exchange rates for 1 June each year: 1999 = 0.16038; 2000 = 0.1468; 2001 = 0.12484; 2002 = 0.10114; 2003 = 0.11819; 2004 = 0.15104.

Source: Data from WWF-LIFE on behalf of the CBNRM programme (2005)

from wildlife tourism through a joint venture (the Damaraland Camp operated by Wilderness Safaris) and trophy hunting (NACSO, 2004). Table 7.4 shows that households received quite variable proportions of the total financial benefit through wages and salaries between 1999 and 2004, (25–57 per cent), but that the actual value of the benefit generated by tourism increased by over 250 per cent over the 5-year period from US$77,375 in 1999 to $188,307 in 2004.[6] On average, the proportion of the trust income generated by tourism joint ventures was significant at 48.1 per cent, while the proportion from hunting was minor at only 1.1 per cent. Other forms of income were not wildlife tourism related (e.g. live game sales, meat distribution, use of game, etc).

According to Long (2004), the dividends of US$74 to each member of the Torra Conservancy in 2003 was adequate to support basic grocery costs for a local household for three months. To put this in context, it was almost equivalent to the average amount raised annually from the sale of live goats; equivalent to 14 per cent of the average annual income (US$532) for individuals in the region; and 8 per cent of the average annual income of households (US$946). Interestingly, the most common use of the income reported was to pay for school fees (Long, 2004b).[7]

Another conservancy created by the Ju/'hoansi San of Nyae Nyae in north-eastern Namibia in 1998, covers 9030km². The Nyae Nyae Conservancy and Khaudom National Park (3842km²) jointly span approximately13,000km² of wilderness wildlife habitat. This area is populated by one of the country's most poverty-stricken and marginalized communities. Largely as a result of the game reintroduction effort made since 1999, game numbers increased, which contributed significantly to the livelihoods of the members. The Conservancy provided 28 per cent of all jobs from hunting operations (n = 97), a hunting concession cash payment of US$99,953, wages (US$4267), handicraft sales (US$31,242), game meat (valued at $14,708) in 2002–2003.[8] The per capita benefit in 2002 was estimated at US$75 (Weaver and Skyer, 2003, cited in Skyer, 2004).

South Africa

Policy

The overarching vision of South Africa's Department of Environmental Affairs and Tourism (DEAT) is to ensure a better life for all South Africans through the growth of tourism and the sound management and protection of the country's environment (DEAT, 2004). In 1996 the White Paper on the Development and Promotion of Tourism was published. A foresighted part of the paper promoted the development of responsible and sustainable tourism growth. The key elements of responsible tourism include that communities should be involved in and benefit from tourism, that local resources should be used sustainably, and should respect local, natural and cultural environments (DEAT, 1996). Wildlife tourism in South Africa includes consumptive and non-consumptive activities. (See the Introduction chapter for more details on the South African responsible tourism policy.)

Local spend

In 2002 a social accounting matrix was used by Conningarth Consultants to evaluate the economic effects of nature tourism in Zululand. The analysis found that nature tourism provided better opportunities for impoverished people than did other industries. These advantages included more labour for unskilled and semi-skilled workers, and higher returns on capital to local communities and small businesses than the economy as a whole. For nature tourism 26 per cent of expenditure was spent at small, micro and medium-sized enterprises (SMMEs), and 14 per cent was spent in local communities, while total spending by the economy as a whole was only 15 per cent of expenditure at SMMEs and 11 per cent in local communities (Conningarth Consultants 2002, Aylward, 2003). When luxury and budget accommodation were compared in Zululand, it was found that wildlife tourism operations in lower price ranges (i.e. of US$7[9]) generated more non-management employment, in fact twice the number, of those priced at US$22 or above (Aylward, 2003).

Employment

Also in Zululand, Porter et al (2003) found that higher proportions of employees per hectare, and per bed, were employed at more expensive wildlife tourism enterprises (see Table 7.5). Higher prices are an indication of higher quality, and therefore generate higher requirements for support services, from a hospitality and game management perspective. As property size increases, more staff are also required for conservation management activities, and as the number of beds increase, more employees are needed to provide hospitality to tourists.

Table 7.5 *Average employment on private game reserves in
Zululand in 2000, South Africa*

Price category[a]	Average no. employees	Employees per hectare	Average number employees per bed	Average price per bed (Rands)	Average price per bed (US$)[a]
Low (n = 5)	11	0.012	0.50	120	$17
Medium (n = 3)	18	0.009	0.61	319	$46
High (n = 5)	25	0.058	1.42	885	$127

Note: Low: <R200 per bed, per night; medium: R200–500; high: >R500.

a Exchange rate was 0.14355 on 1 June 2000.

Source: Adapted from Porter et al, 2003, p298

In the Eastern Cape of South Africa, a survey of 7 private game reserves (PGRs) found that the number of employees increased by a factor of 3.5 when properties converted their use to wildlife-based tourism (from 175 people to 623). The average wage bill also increased by a factor of 20, from US$20,848 to $416,000 per year, increasing the average annual salary from $715 to $4064 (a 5.7-fold increase). Employees also received additional benefits that were not normally received by farm labourers, including accommodation, food and training, medical insurance and pension contributions. Despite these benefits, anti-poaching units still monitor the PGRs, with the form of poaching observed being mainly small wire snares (Sims-Castley et al, 2005).

Madikwe is a state-owned game reserve located in the north-west province, on the border with Botswana. The reserve was formed by the former Bophuthatswana Parks in the 1990s (now the North-West Parks and Tourism Board) by purchasing and consolidating farmlands, with the aim of stimulating local employment. In 1999, there were an estimated 85 local people employed in Madikwe, but unemployment in three local villages was very high, and ranged from 58 to 86 per cent (Rutec, 1999, cited by Relly, 2004) (more information on Madikwe can be found in Chapter 12 by Relly). In 2003 there were 12 commercial and 12 corporate lodges in Madikwe, by which time 320 local people were employed (an increase of 276 per cent) (Relly, 2004). Comparing data from Relly (2004) and Porter et al (2003) it can be seen that the number of employees per bed is much higher for luxury lodges (1.34–1.42 employees per bed) in South Africa than it is for the budget lodges (0.48–0.61 employees per bed). Therefore luxury products have the potential to generate more employment and salaries for local people.

Impacts on poverty

Surprisingly few studies have extrapolated information on local salaries to establish the impact on poverty from tourism, but there are data available for Sabi Sabi, a luxury private game reserve neighbouring Kruger National Park. The level of local earnings from this tourism enterprise was estimated, and then related to the proportion of local people living above the international poverty line (US$1 per day), which was determined through surveys within local communities. Approximately 70 per cent of the monthly wage bill was paid to 140 people living within 20km of the enterprise, and the average monthly wage was R2500 (~$357). Local employees effectively earned $12 per day and therefore had the capacity to support their estimated 7–8 dependants to a level just above the poverty line, on $1.5 per person, per day. Cumulatively, local employment from Sabi Sabi was estimated to have lifted between 980 and 1120 dependants in the local area above the poverty line: or approximately 4.1 per cent of the local population (Spenceley and Seif, 2002).

Joint ventures

Joint ventures between the private sector and communities who hold title to wildlife land are also a mechanism for revenue generation in impoverished rural communities. The Makuleke experience is one that illustrates how the land restitution process that followed the end of apartheid has empowered people who were disadvantaged during apartheid to generate sustainable livelihood benefits through wildlife tourism (see also Chapter 4 by Collins and Snel). In 1969 the Makuleke people were forcibly removed by the state from a 24,000ha area that they inhabited in the north of Kruger National Park (KNP). They were compensated for their relocation in 1998, with the restitution of their land and the creation of a contractual park (Elliffe, 1999). A 25-year agreement was forged between the Makuleke and SANParks to return the ownership and title of the land to the people, although the title specifies that the land may only be used for wildlife conservation (Steenkamp, 1998; Steenkamp and Grossman, 2001). The contract that governs the incorporation of the Makuleke land in KNP enables them to make sustainable use of specified natural resources (Spenceley, 2005).

The Makuleke initially operated trophy hunting between 2000 and 2003 for variable quotas of elephant, buffalo, kudu, zebra and impala on their land, earning approximately $590,000 during that time (reaching $200,000 in 2003). Subsequently they made a transition to non-consumptive wildlife tourism. This was due to the perception that photographic tourism would not work together with hunting in their small area given a limited road network (Maluleke, 2003; Collins, 2003). This transition has been implemented through joint-venture agreements (build, operate and transfer) with two private operators: Matswari Safaris and Wilderness Safaris. Matswari invested up to $1.5 million in The Outpost's infrastructure, while Wilderness Safaris invested $3.96 million in Pafuri Lodge. Wilderness Safaris has annually invested more money in wages, concession fees and anti-poaching in the Makuleke concession between 2004 and 2006 than was generated during the hunting periods. However, the revenue directly accrued by the Makuleke people (i.e. in concession fees and wages) have amounted to $54,326 in 2005 and $138,607 in 2006. Although the community earned more money directly from trophy hunting, the total level of investment in the Makuleke's land by the Outpost and Pafuri Lodge (e.g. anti-poaching, capital investment, etc.) is far greater.

Zambia

Policy

Tourism is one of the three main 'legs' of the Zambian economy, alongside mining and agriculture (Hamilton et al, 2007). Tourism is highlighted in the 2001 Poverty Reduction Strategy Paper, and also within the Fifth National Development plan; where targets for tourist arrivals, employment and earnings are specified. The Administrative Management Design for Game Management Areas (ADMADE) programme was established in 1987 in order to decentralize wildlife management and divide the responsibilities and benefits from wildlife more evenly between government, the private sector and local communities. Administrative units operate from participating Game Management Areas (GMAs), which include representatives from traditional authorities, district government, the trophy hunting industry and National Parks and Wildlife Services (NPWS) (Lewis and Alpert, 1997). In the mid-1990s Zambia devised a Medium Term Tourism Strategy and Action Plan, which included strategies to brand national parks as a central focus of marketing tourism in the country (Hamilton et al, 2007).

Employment

Suich et al (2005) found that accommodation in the Upper Zambezi area paid US$809,000 (15 per cent of turnover) to employ 391 staff, of whom 3 were part-time. Suich et al (2005) also found that guesthouses in Livingstone spent an estimated US$237,000 on wages and salaries in 2004 (23 per cent of turnover) paid to 352 employees (of whom 4 were employed part-time).[10] The non-guesthouses paid US$6.1 million (25 per cent of turnover) to employ 1792 staff, of whom 680 were part-time. In all, US$6.3 million was spent in the region on salaries and wages for all 2144 workers in this area. Tour operators in Livingstone spent US$743,000 on wages and salaries (or 19 per cent of turnover) to 412 employees.

Pope (2005) reported that in 2005 there were 14 photographic and two hunting tourism operators in the Luangwa Valley area. The Luangwa Safari Association (LSA) member operators offer approximately 600 tourist beds (400 in camps and lodges and another 200 in campsites), representing nearly 65,000 annual tourist bed nights. Total permanent employment in LSA camps and lodges increased by over 1000 per cent between 1990 and 2003, from a total of 51 in 1990 to 504 in 2003. While the magnitude of LSA employment is insignificant on a national scale, the trend and the tourism-related opportunities elsewhere in the country as a whole are significant. Employment growth among LSA operators is in Zambian nationals – increased tenfold from 40 in 1990 to 471 in 2003. The gross number of expatriates employed increased from 11 in 1990 to 33 in 2003, but the average number of expatriates per company has declined from 6 to 4 over the same period. By 2005 there were just over 500 full-time employees with LSA companies. In gross terms this represents an employee–client ratio of 1.98. This ratio has remained unchanged since 1990 (Pope, 2005).

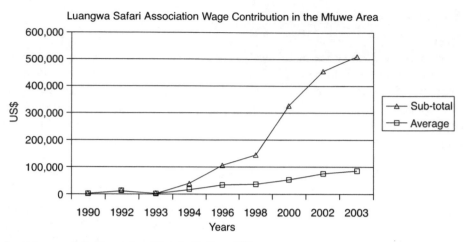

Source: Luangwa Safari Association, 2004 cited in Pope, 2005

Figure 7.1 *Luangwa Safari Association personal employment contributions to the Mfuwe economy, 1990–2003*

Overall, LSA members employed 700 permanent and temporary staff in 2005 in the Mfuwe area, which reflects a significant growth from about 80 people employed in 1990. In terms of the dependants of employees, Pope (2005) estimates that their wages supported around 4200 individuals. Pope (2005) reports that approximately 90 people were formally employed by the 5 safari outfitters operating in the immediate vicinity of the core South Luangwa National Park tourism area and about 30 in the Lupande. Pope (2005) also estimated that the majority of companies also employed another 20 casual employees during camp building and closure (about two months of the year). The salary and wage contributions to the local economy grew from US$2800 in 1990 to US$510,000 in 2003 (see Figure 7.1).

The contribution from purchases and other business items has shown a similar pattern of exponential growth, particularly between 2000 and 2003. Total non-wage contributions now amount to close to US$240,000 per annum (see Figure 7.2). Combined with salary and wage contributions, the LSA tourism group places nearly US$750,000 per annum into the economy in Mambwe District (Pope, 2005).

Adding the probable figure for labour payments for safari hunting outfitters in the Lupande GMA (say US$17,000), and the retained hunting fees (about US$60,000), this would indicate a total contribution into the local economy in the Lupande hunting blocks of approximately US$90,000. The contributions to the local economy from all tourism operations in 2005 were estimated at approximately US$850,000, with the non-consumptive tourist sector contributing nearly 90 per cent (excluding ancillary non-consumptive services and enterprises producing tourism-related goods (Pope, 2005)).

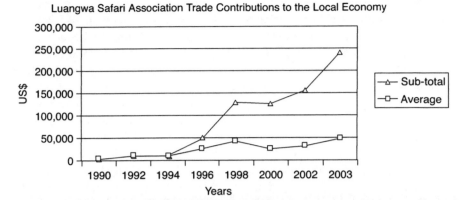

Source: Luangwa Safari Association, 2004 cited in Pope, 2005

Figure 7.2 *Luangwa Safari Association business contributions
to the local economy, 1990–2003*

Zimbabwe

Policy

The Communal Areas Management Program for Indigenous Resources
(CAMPFIRE) was established in 1988 as a mechanism to allow local communities to manage natural resources (including wildlife) on communal lands, and sell
quotas to hunting operators. Rural District Councils (RDCs) were devolved the
legal authority to manage wildlife from the government (Jonga, 2003). However,
in the run up to the 2000 general election, various coalitions of actors, gathered
under the banner of 'war veterans', stepped up a previously low-level campaign of
occupying commercial farms and some state-owned land. ZANU(PF), the ruling
party, fought the election under the slogan 'Land is the economy and the
economy is land' (Wolmer, 2003). In February 2000, a national referendum was
held regarding a draft new Constitution for Zimbabwe, and was followed in June
by a nationwide parliamentary election. These two processes dramatically
changed the country's political environment. Unfortunately, the changes were
traumatic and reported as such, resulting in a poor international image for
Zimbabwe, which had adverse implications for the whole economy, and most
particularly the tourism industry (de la Harpe, 2001). Farm occupations and a
'fast-track' land reform process picked up momentum after the election, underpinned by a policy emphasis on the importance of small-scale peasant agriculture
at the expense of white-dominated commercial agriculture in general, and the
wildlife industry in particular (Wolmer, 2003). Wildlife tourism in Zimbabwe is
considered within this political and historical context.

Communal and household benefits

Wildlife conservation was linked to community benefits from safari hunting and
wildlife tourism, and by 1993, 23 CAMPFIRE districts were earning revenue

from wildlife tourism (Crawford, 2000). This revenue provided rural infrastructure and increased household incomes by 15–25 per cent in rural areas – and led to reduced poaching and improved attitudes to wildlife (Weaver, 1998, Scheyvens, 2002). Between 1989 and 2001, US$10 million was paid in dividends to local communities (46 per cent of revenue earned) (Jonga, 2003). Ninety-three per cent of this was from sport hunting leases, and 2 per cent from tourism leases (Maveneke et al, 1998). Not surprisingly, the hunting options were more popular than photographic tourism due to their higher returns, and lower infrastructure requirements (Baker, 1997, Buckley, 2003, Murphree, 2003). However, some of the conflicts that arose included the uneven distribution of benefits, disagreements between parties about the control of income by RDCs and local elites, and the lack of compensation for crop damage or livestock lost to wildlife (Alexander and McGregor, 2000; Manwa, 2003; Virtane, 2003). Political turmoil since 2000, inflation and unemployment and the resettlement of people in protected and wildlife areas affected CAMPFIRE. Over the years, the RDCs have harvested their natural resources and earned income in the following ways: leasing trophy hunting concessions, utilizing forestry and forest products, leasing ecotourism sites and from live animal sales (Muchapondwa, 2003).

From 1989, the income from safari hunting increased rapidly to US$2 million annually. In terms of Zimbabwe's economy, the multiplier on trophy fees is approximately 3, suggesting that CAMPFIRE areas generated for Zimbabwe a direct annual income from hunting of US$6.0 million. During the period under review, CAMPFIRE areas earned US$20.3 million, and Muir-Leresche et al (2003) estimate that this earned over US$100 million for Zimbabwe. In addition to direct fees to communities, a proportion of safari operating expenses is paid locally as wages and salaries (some US$0.5 million annually), and for the purchase of materials, but this is not captured in CAMPFIRE monitoring records; neither are peripheral economic benefits such as taxidermy, travel, extended tourism activities, food, etc. (Child et al, 2003). The extremely rapid growth up to 1994 can be attributed to two factors (see Figure 7.3): (1) a steady increase in quotas as, initially, more areas were designated for CAMPFIRE and, later, as wildlife populations began to grow; and (2) a significant improvement in marketing activities.[11]

While the data indicate that CAMPFIRE continued to market its hunting well, in the last three years the parallel exchange rate has disrupted the levels of community incomes and is a serious threat to the programme. In 2001 and 2002, safari operators generally paid for hunting at the official exchange rate of 55, compared to the parallel rate of Z$500 and Z$1500. The communities' incomes were therefore less than 10 per cent of what they should have been. In many areas, this situation continued into 2003. Some RDCs have begun to adjust, but are still getting less than a third of the real value of their hunting (Child et al, 2003).

An overview of the benefits, including those from wildlife tourism and hunting are indicated in Table 7.6, in addition to the number of households in the wards and districts concerned. Most revenues from tourism in Zimbabwe's

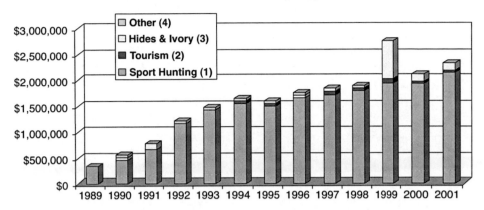

CAMPFIRE: Sources of Direct Revenue (US$)

Legend:
- ☐ Other (4)
- ☐ Hides & Ivory (3)
- ■ Tourism (2)
- ▨ Sport Hunting (1)

Source: WWF database, cited in Child et al, 2003

Figure 7.3 *Income directly attributable to CAMPFIRE*

Communal Areas are generated through the leasing of sites for nature tourism, although in some cases local residents run basic tourist facilities and act as guides (Muchapondwa, 2003). Table 7.6 shows that CAMPFIRE has been calculated to have delivered US$20.3 million in direct income for RDCs and communities between 1989 and 2001. This derives from wildlife in some 90–110 wards, and consistently benefits over 80,000 households (560,000 people) (Child et al, 2003).

CAMPFIRE revenues are allocated to RDCs in levies, management and other activities, and also to communities. The allocation to communities fluctuated between 37 per cent and 59 per cent between 1989 and 2001. Figure 7.4 illustrates the average household benefits from CAMPFIRE between 1989 and 2001. The average remained below $10 per year for the entire period.

Jones (2004) reports that income to communities from CAMPFIRE in recent years in particular has suffered a double blow. Although trophy hunting has continued despite political and economic instability, and CAMPFIRE has tried to diversify away from a reliance on trophy hunting into photographic tourism which, while generating less income, has an important economic multiplier effect and generates more jobs and wages, tourism to Zimbabwe has collapsed (see policy section). To some extent the real value of tourism to CAMPFIRE is not clear because much of this revenue, including direct fees to RDCs, is not recorded directly as CAMPFIRE income, partly because RDCs do not want to be obliged to share it with communities. Booth (pers. com. 2007) comments that RDCs have never regarded non-consumptive tourism income as being part of CAMPFIRE revenues.

Jones (2004) states that data on economic benefits generated by CAMPFIRE show that early in the programme RDCs appeared willing to reduce the amount

Table 7.6 *Rural District Councils' annual income from CAMPFIRE activities (US$)*

Year	Sport hunting	Tourism	PAC Hides & Ivory	Other	TOTAL	Exchange rate	Number of districts (and wards)	Number of households
1989	326,798	28	5,294	17,690	349,811	2.126	3 (15)	7,861
1990	453,424	2,865	42,847	57,297	556,433	2.472	9 (41)	22,084
1991	638,153	15,904	20,859	101,105	776,021	3.751	11 (57)	52,456
1992	1,154,082	18,951	9,429	34,216	1,216,678	5.112	12 (74)	70,311
1993	1,394,060	21,095	14,988	53,730	1,483,873	6.529	12 (98)	90,475
1994	1,553,543	39,985	2,770	46,373	1,642,671	8.212	14 (101)	96,437
1995	1,476,812	54,866	11,685	48,204	1,591,567	8.724	14 (111)	98,964
1996	1,656,338	23,275	39,869	36,429	1,755,912	10.07	19 (96)	85,543
1997	1,708,234	71,258	44,331	13,615	1,837,438	12.444	17 (98)	93,605
1998	1,787,977	40,871	25,205	37,713	1,891,766	24.374	15 (92)	80,498
1999	1,940,366	78,709	720,440	14,442	2,753,958	38.338	16 (112)	95,726
2000	1,919,980	55,668	116,075	13,482	2,105,204	44.616	14 (108)	88,072
2001	2,142,306	41,439	111,914	32,793	2,328,452	55.066	14 (94)	76,683
TOTAL	18,152,074	464,915	1,165,706	507,090	20,289,784			

Notes:

1 Sport hunting – income earned from lease and trophy fees paid by safari operators.

2 Tourism – income earned from the lease of wild areas for non-consumptive tourism.

3 PAC Hides & Ivory – income from the sale of animal products primarily from problem animal control.

4 Other – income from the sale of live animals, collection of ostrich eggs and crocodile eggs, etc.

5 Mean annual exchange rate based on RBZ end of month exchange.

Source: WWF SARPO, Harare, cited in Muchapondwa, 2003; Child et al, 2003

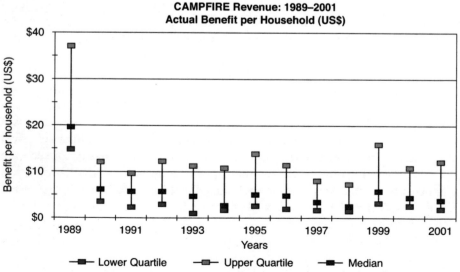

Source: WWF database, cited in Child et al, 2003

Figure 7.4 *Summary of average household benefits from CAMPFIRE*

of revenue they retained and increase the amount going directly to sub-district levels. By 1996 the proportion of income going to communities for use at their own discretion was 62 per cent, with an additional 5 per cent reaching communities but being managed by the RDC. By the year 2001, community benefits fell to only 38 per cent, although there are exceptions such as Binga, which allows communities to receive between 70 and 80 per cent of the wildlife income. The reluctance of RDCs to devolve income generation to lower-level institutions severely reduced the amount of income reaching households.

A review of the Gairezi Resettlement Area in the Eastern Highlands of Zimbabwe in 2006 conducted by Taylor and Murphree (2007) considered the impacts of fly fishing on the Gairezi river. The Gairezi Community Eco-tourism Project seeks to alleviate poverty and improve rural livelihoods amongst households living in the Gairezi Resettlement Area, which was established after 1980. The CAMPFIRE Association provided a series of grants from USAID until 2003, while the community contributed locally available materials, such as stone for building and the provision of labour to construct infrastructure.

The project employs seven full-time staff and a number of occasional staff, and certain households have benefited financially. A small local market for vegetables and other produce is also provided for the Project's visitors. Overall financial returns to the community have been modest by comparison with wildlife income from sport hunting in other areas. Before the Trust came into existence a club of 200 sport anglers, the Nyanga Downs Fly Fishing Club (NDFFC) had made annual cash payments to the community in the range of Z$4000–5000 per annum, or about Z$20/25 per member. In 2004 the payment was raised to Z$10,000,000, which at that time was a substantial improvement (see Table 7.7). In 2005 an innovation in payments was introduced by the Trust. Offered a cash payment by the NDFFC, the Trust suggested that members would prefer to receive payment in fertilizer, something that was difficult for Gairezians to obtain and transport. The NDFFC agreed, and as a result 200 50kg bags of fertilizer[12] were purchased and delivered for distribution. This highly ostensible and practical mode of revenue distribution clearly made a great impact (Taylor and Murphree, 2007).

Taylor and Murphree (2007) state that it would be misleading to suggest that the project could make a vast impact on household incomes or livelihoods, nor to our knowledge has this ever been claimed at either community or district levels. However, Taylor and Murphree (2007) conclude that the project has indeed made a favourable contribution to livelihood improvement in Gairezi through its fertilizer pay-outs at a time of national shortages. Moreover, an average annual return of US$14.8 per household over the past three years compares more than favourably with the equivalent national statistic for CAMPFIRE of US$4.6 per household (Bond, 2001). In the long run, it is also contributing on a more subjective level, for example, by stimulating people to think of other ways in which their environment can be used sustainably. Within an area with few economic alternatives, Taylor and Murphree (2007) suggest ecotourism generally, and fly fishing specifically, can be an extremely competitive land use option.

Table 7.7 *Gairezi Community Eco-Tourism Project income from NDFFC 2004–2006*

Year	Income (ZW$)	Income (US$)	Mean exchange rate
2004	10,000,000	2227	4490
2005	60,000,000	2787	21,351
2006	1,131,925,000	6991	161,909

Source: Taylor and Murphree, 2007

Discussion

This review of the impacts of wildlife tourism on rural livelihoods in southern Africa has identified some detailed research findings from Botswana, Namibia, South Africa, Tanzania and Zimbabwe. However, the range of research techniques used, the timing of evaluations and the scope of the appraisals varies extensively, which makes comparison in terms of similar themes (e.g. ownership, employment, household benefits) very difficult. However, some interesting conclusions can be drawn from the analysis.

Private sector, joint ventures and community-based enterprises

Table 7.8 summarizes the relative benefits of different types of tourism business and different forms of nature-based tourism drawn from the literature reviewed. The overview shows that each type of enterprise has different benefits and limitations for host communities.

Acknowledgement of these different benefits of tourism enterprise structures in southern Africa may help the private sector, government, NGOs, donors and communities to decide which model they wish to adopt, depending on their priorities. If they are motivated by profit, a private sector or a joint venture development may be preferable. If they are motivated by local economic benefits and empowerment, they may be more interested in a joint-venture or community-based enterprise. This analysis indicates that joint ventures tend to generate the best all-round benefits, but they may be more difficult and involve higher transaction costs to get established when compared to simple private sector enterprises.

Employment

The studies reviewed tended to concentrate on the amount of income generated by wages, and the distribution of concession fees within communities through trusts and joint ventures. In general, higher quality, higher priced accommodation in wildlife areas employs more people, at higher salaries than lower value accommodation products, and other forms of agriculture (e.g. Sims-Castley et al, 2005). However, wildlife tourism often takes place in rural areas where levels of unemployment and poverty are very high, and therefore the overall impacts on

Table 7.8 *Benefits to local communities in southern Africa from different forms of tourism*

Issue	Private sector	Type of business structure Joint venture (Community Trust and private sector)	Community based
Relative size of market	Majority of tourism enterprises.	Minority of tourism enterprises.	Minority of tourism enterprises.
Ownership/ Equity	None.	Sometimes partial (e.g. land ownership) but limited responsibilities of community. Dividends to community.	Community owned. Dividends to community.
Commercial viability	Yes, generally market related and operated as a business.	Yes, as market related. Conservancies often profitable for communities, particularly when hunting and photographic nature-based tourism are both operated.	Turnover often poor (rarely have business plans). Wages/operating costs may be subsidized by NGO. Success varies between countries and institutional structures.
Dividends	Not to communities (to private sector shareholding).	Variable annual dividends distributed related to turnover. Trust and community decides how distributed. Dividends include flat fees, bed night levies, rental fees, percentage of income, and meat from hunting.	Variable annual dividends distributed in relation to turnover. Trust and community decides how distribution is done (e.g. split between households; for local infrastructure, etc.).
Institutional support	Not necessary. Sometimes within a conservancy.	Elected community trust. Sometimes transparency problems with Trust. Sometimes within a conservancy.	Elected community trust. Sometimes transparency and power dynamics problems with Trust. Sometimes within a conservancy.
Employment	Yes. Mostly menial labour with low wages, and can be seasonal, (expatriates earn more).	Yes. Often employ local staff. Some seasonality.	Yes, at all levels. Skills are not always sufficient (e.g. book keeping, marketing, reservations) Little seasonality of labour (often retain staff on minimal wages).
Skills development	Some, for positions that require it. Limited promotion of local people.	Yes, for positions that require it. Often employ local staff and train them for promotion.	Often at initiation of enterprise at all levels, but with limited follow up.

Table 7.8 *continued*

Issue	Type of business structure		
	Private sector	*Joint venture (Community Trust and private sector)*	*Community based*
Associated SMME development	Not generally attempted. Use of existing suppliers.	Attempted, and can be successful with private sector mentorship.	Attempted, but not always successful. Requires sustained mentorship.
Procurement of goods and services	Limited spend in local communities, dependent on price, quality, reliability, etc. Major spending power.	Some local spend, and support for local businesses.	Local spend where entrepreneurs/small businesses exist.
Stakeholder support	Not necessarily.	May be NGOs, donors or government departments facilitating.	Often set up, facilitated and subsidized by NGO or donors, or government.
Impact on wildlife	Ad hoc, dependent on individual enterprise activities.	Often wildlife increases, particularly in conservancies.	Often wildlife increases, particularly in conservancies.

the local economy can be relatively small. In some areas (e.g. Botswana) it is noted that most local people are employed in menial positions, while management jobs are filled by expatriates. However, in Zambia the average proportion of expatriates employed in Luangwa lodges has declined over time (Pope, 2005). The salaries of people working in the wildlife tourism sector ranged widely depending on the standard of accommodation and country concerned, even within countries. For example, wages for locals in Botwsana range from US$816 per year in the Okavango Delta (Mbiwa, 2003), to $4295 per year in northern Botswana (Suich et al, 2005). Little information is available to explicitly link the impact of wildlife tourism on levels of poverty, but research reports frequently observe that enterprises could raise their employees, and sometimes also their dependants, above the international poverty line of US$1 per day.

Communal and household benefits

Benefits distributed to households from community-based tourism enterprises, trophy hunting or joint ventures included both cash and products (e.g. animal products, agricultural supplements). Communities use wildlife resources to generate income from both hunting and photographic tourism. Joint-venture operations, where there is a private-sector partner, tend to be more successful because of the business acumen (particularly the skills of marketing and promotion) brought to the project by the outside partner. The levels of revenue distributed depends on factors that include: (1) the turnover of the tourism business, (2) wildlife density, (3) the type of partnership arrangement, (4) the number of beneficiaries living in the community, and (5) the institutional structure through which the benefits pass (e.g. RDCs in Zimbabwe compared with community-based organizations in Botswana). The type of partnership arrangement could include bed night levies, rental fees, annual flat-rate fees and percentages of turnover. Annual dividends ranged from less than US$5 per year in CAMPFIRE regions of Zimbabwe in 2001 (Child et al, 2003) to $488 per person in Botswana (Arntzen et al, 2003). However, even small benefits can have a substantial impact on livelihoods: Long (2004), found that US$74 could support the basic grocery costs for a local household for three months in Namibia. In both Botswana and Namibia there are instances where the revenue generated for communities from joint-venture agreements can be higher than wage benefits, or from hunting (Arntzen et al, 2003; WWF-Life, 2005).

Consumptive or non-consumptive wildlife tourism?

Trophy hunting often generates more revenue than photographic tourism, and from a smaller number of tourists, but photographic tourism has a higher economic multiplier (in terms of more jobs and wages). Both forms of nature-based tourism may be operated by an enterprise: either at different stages of development of the enterprise (e.g. the Makuleke), during different seasons (e.g. in Botswana) or in different locations on a property or within a conservancy.

Conclusion

Research on the economic impacts of wildlife tourism is patchy across southern Africa: in terms of geographical location, number of studies and the type of information that is reported. The benefits accrued by employees and host communities vary widely, depending on the institutional structures, partnership arrangements, business viability of a particular venture, the indigenous wildlife and location. Also, the policy framework and political environment heavily influence the structure and delivery of community-based natural resource management, community-based tourism and joint-venture activities. These factors make comparisons between regions difficult, and also complicate the extraction of sound recommendations.

Wildlife that directly contributes to livelihoods is most important to the poor, and is the main determinant of people's attitude towards wildlife. The more livelihood benefits that are obtained (or the higher the user value), the more widely wildlife is appreciated. If wildlife does not generate benefits or the benefits do not reach the rural population (for example, due to a skewed distribution of the direct use value), people are unlikely to appreciate and conserve it (Arntzen, 2003). Emerton (2004) argues that the livelihood benefits from wildlife tourism are not always sufficient to make up for the costs of living with wildlife, and that both the costs and benefits are unequally distributed. Therefore, generating broad development benefits does not ensure that wildlife will produce net local economic gains, and it is not the same as providing economic incentives for conservation. Local people often suffer costs from living with wildlife and close to protected areas, due to crop-raiding, damage to infrastructure and even danger to their personal safety. Therefore, when people can generate benefits from wildlife tourism – for example, through community levies, revenue sharing or employment – this can lead to more positive attitudes (Lindberg et al, 2003).

Therefore it is clear that a business model approach should be adopted wherever possible, to ensure that tourism enterprises are commercially viable, and individuals perceive benefit. Maximizing opportunities for local employment and training, promoting local ownership or equity in enterprises, enhancing local procurement of goods and services to support tourism, conserving viable populations of wildlife, promoting good governance and decision making structures, are all factors that can improve the net benefits accrued by host communities. Also, more systematic and standardized evaluations of wildlife tourism, and dissemination of their findings, would make the positive and negative impacts of this activity more widely understood, and would allow future initiatives to learn from prior experiences.

Acknowledgements

Thanks to the IUCN Southern Africa Sustainable Use Specialist Group who supported the production of this paper. Many thanks to individuals who contributed grey literature comments, particularly Fred Nelson, Jon Barnes, Jean-Michel Pavy, Vernon Booth, Brian Child, Rowan Martin and Russell Taylor. Also thanks to Myles Mander who made valuable comments on a draft version of the paper.

Notes

1   Exchange rate was 0.16977 on 1 June 2006.
2   Exchange rate from US$ to Rands was 0.1773 on 1 June 2001.
3   Exchange rate was 0.14409 on 1 June 2000.
4   Constant 2004 US$ values.
5   Constant 2004 US$ values.
6   N$ to US$ exchange rates for 1 June each year: 1999=0.16038; 2004=0.15104.
7   Exchange rate was 0.11819 on 1 June 2003.
8   Exchange rate of 4.78.
9   Exchange rate was 0.14355 on 1 June 2000.
10   Suich considers that most tourism enterprises in Livingstone host visitors interested in nature-based activities, (Suich, pers. com. 2007), and therefore these enterprise results are included here.
11   The DNPWLM data collated in the early stages of the CAMPFIRE programme differ significantly from the WWF CAMPFIRE data for this period. Given that the DNPWLM data were based on regular field audits, and on quotas set by DNPWLM, and that WWF was not directly involved in data collection at the time, some doubt must be cast on this early data in the WWF database. While there is minor variation in income data, trophy data and standard values differ significantly in the period 1989 to 1993.
12   Ammonium nitrate, for application in the early stages of maize cultivation.

References

Alexander, J. and McGregor, J. (2000) 'Wildlife and politics: CAMPFIRE in Zimbabwe', *Development and Change*, vol. 31, 605–627. Cited in Zeppel, H. (2006) *Indigenous Ecotourism: Sustainable Development and Management*, Ecotourism series 3, CABI, Trowbridge

Arntzen, J. (2003) 'An economic view on wildlife management areas in Botswana', CBNRM Network Occasional Paper no.11. CBNRM Support Programme SNV/IUCN

Arntzen, J. W., Molokomme, D. L., Terry, E. M., Moleele, N., Tshosa, O. and Mazambani, D. (2003) *Final Report of the Review of Community-based Natural Resource Management in Botswana*, Centre for Applied Research for the National CBNRM forum, Maun, Botswana

Ashley, C. and Barnes, J. (1996) 'Wildlife use for economic gain: The potential for wildlife to contribute to development in Namibia', Directorate of Environmental Affairs Research Discussion Paper 12. Ministry of Environment and Tourism, Windhoek

Ashley, C. and Elliott, J. (2003) 'Just wildlife?' or a source of local development? ODI Natural resource perspectives, No 85, April

Ashley, C. and Garland, E. (1994) 'Promoting community-based tourism development: Why, What and How?' Research discussion paper no. 4. Ministry of Environment and Tourism, Windhoek, www.met.gov.na/pub_all.htm. Cited in Zeppel, H. (2006) *Indigenous Ecotourism: Sustainable Development and Management*, Ecotourism series 3, CABI, Trowbridge

Aylward, B. (2003) 'Actual and potential contribution of nature tourism in Zululand: Considerations for Development, Equity and Conservation', in Aylward, B. and Lutz, E. (eds), *Nature Tourism, Conservation, and Development in KwaZulu-Natal, South Africa*, World Bank, Washington, DC

Baker, J. (1997) 'Trophy hunting as a sustainable use of wildlife resources in southern and eastern Africa', *Journal of Sustainable Tourism*, vol 5, pp306–321

Barnes, J., Burgess, J. and Pearce, D. (1992) 'Wildlife tourism', in Swanson, T. M. and Barbier, E. B. (eds), *Economics for the Wilds: Wildlife, Wildlands, Diversity and Development*, Earthscan, London, pp136–151

Barnes, J. I,. MacGregor, J. and Weaver, C. (2002) 'Economic efficiency and incentives for change within Namibia's community wildlife use initiatives', *World Development*, vol. 30, no. 4, 667–681

Bond, I. (2001) 'CAMPFIRE and the incentives for institutional change', in Hulme, D. and Murphree, M. (eds) *African Wildlife and Livelihoods: The Promise and Performance of Community Conservation*, James Currey, Oxford

Buckley, R. (2003) 'CAMPFIRE, Zimbabwe', in *Case Studies in Ecotourism*, CABI Publishing, Wallingford, UK, pp29–30, Cited in Zeppel, H. (2006) *Indigenous Ecotourism: Sustainable Development and Management*, Ecotourism series 3, CABI, Trowbridge

Child, B., Jones, B., Mazambani, D., Mlalazi, A. and Moinuddin, H. (2003) *CAMPFIRE: Communal Areas Management Programme for Indigenous Resources*, Final Evaluation Report: Zimbabwe Natural Resources Management Program – USAID/Zimbabwe Strategic Objective No. 1, 29 July

Collins, S. (2003) 'Optimising community benefits from conservation: Visual tourism versus hunting in the Makuleke Contractual Park in South Africa's Kruger National Park', cited in Spenceley, A. (2005) *Tourism Investment in the Great Limpopo Transfrontier Conservation Area: Scoping report*, Report to the Transboundary Protected Areas Research Initiative, University of the Witwatersrand, Johannesburg

Conningarth Consultants (2002) *Social accounting matrix for North Eastern KwaZulu-Natal (RSA). A report to the World Bank*. Conningarth Consultants, Johannesburg. Cited in Aylward, B. (2003) 'Actual and potential contribution of nature tourism in Zululand: Considerations for Development, Equity and Conservation', in Aylward, B. and Lutz, E. (eds), *Nature Tourism, Conservation, and Development in KwaZulu-Natal, South Africa*, World Bank, Washington DC

Crawford, S. (2000) 'Communal Areas Management Program for Indigenous Resources (CAMPFIRE)', in *Designing Tourism Naturally: A Review of the World Best Practice in Wilderness Lodge and Tented Safari Camps*. WA Tourism Commission, Perth, pp54–56. Cited in Zeppel, H. (2006) *Indigenous Ecotourism: Sustainable Development and Management*, Ecotourism series 3, CABI, Trowbridge

de la Harpe, D. (2001) *The Malilangwe Trust: Development through conservation, Annual Report 2000*, cited in Spenceley, A. and Barnes, J. (2005) *Economic Analysis of Rhino*

Conservation in a Land-Use Context within the SADC region, SADC RPRC Task 6.3-1.2 (Phase II), SADC Regional Programme for Rhino conservation, Report to IUCN-ROSA

Department of Environmental Affairs and Tourism (DEAT) (1996) *The Development and Promotion of Tourism in South Africa*, White Paper, Government of South Africa, Department of Environmental Affairs and Tourism

DEAT (2004) 'About us: Biodiversity and conservation', available from www.environment.gov.za (accessed 18 January 2004)

Elliffe, S. (1999) 'Guidelines for the Release/development of Dormant state or community assets for ecotourism development in the context of community involvement, land issues and environmental requirements'. Unpublished paper presented at the Community Public Private Partnerships Conference, Johannesburg, 16–18 November, cited in Rogerson, C. M. (2001) 'Spatial development initiatives in Southern Africa: The Maputo Development Corridor, discourse and the making of marginalised people', *Journal of Economic and Social Geography*, vol 92, no 3

Emerton, L. (2004) 'Economics, incentives and institutional change, The nature of benefits and the benefits of Nature: Why wildlife conservation has not economically benefited communities in Africa', in Hulme, D. and Murphree, M. (eds), *African Wildlife and Livelihoods: The promise and performance of community conservation*, Heinemann & James Currey, Oxford and Portsmouth, NH

Gujadhur, T. and Motshubi, C. (2000) The Khoadi/Hoas Conservancy: Wildlife management and tourism development. In Sustainable Development of Tourism: A compilation of Good Practices. WTO, Madrid, pp125–126, available from www.cbnrm.bw/pages_sub_dir/CBT.htm

Hamilton, K., Tembo, G., Sinyenga, G., Bandyopadhyay, S., Pope, A., Guillon, B., Muwele, B., Simasiku, P. and Pavy, J. M. (2007) 'Economic and poverty impact of nature-based tourism, Economic and sector work', The World Bank – Zambia, Draft 22 August 2007

Jansen, D., Bond, I. and Child, B. (1992) 'Cattle, wildlife, both or neither. Economic analysis of commercial ranches in Zimbabwe', in Proceedings of the 3rd International Wildlife Ranching Symposium, Pretoria, South Africa, paper No. 8A 2

Jones, B. T. B. (1998) 'Namibia's approach to community-based natural resource management (CBNRM): Towards sustainable development in communal areas'. Scandinavian Seminar College. African perspectives of Policies and Practices Supporting Sustainable Development in Sub-Saharan Africa. www.cdr.dk/sscafrica/jones-na.htm

Jones, B. T. B. (2004) 'CBNRM, poverty reduction and sustainable livelihoods: Developing criteria for evaluating the contribution of CBNRM to poverty reduction and alleviation in southern Africa', *Commons southern Africa occasional paper series*, No. 7, CASS and PLAAS, March 2004

Jonga, C. (2003) CAMPFIRE experiences in Zimbabwe, Global Transboundary Protected Area Network. www.tbpa.net/workshops_01.htm cited in Zeppel, H. (2006) *Indigenous Ecotourism: Sustainable Development and Management*, Ecotourism series 3, CABI, Trowbridge

Lewis, D. M. and Alpert, P. (1997) 'Trophy hunting and wildlife conservation in Zambia', *Conservation Biology*, vol 11, no 1, 59–68

Lindberg, K., James, B. and Goodman, P. (2003) 'Tourism's contribution to conservation in Zululand: An ecological survey of private reserves and protected areas', in Aylward, B. and Lutz, E. (eds), *Nature Tourism, Conservation, and Development in KwaZulu-Natal, South Africa*, The World Bank, Washington DC, pp201–244

Long, S. A. (2004) 'Livelihoods in the conservancy study areas', in *Livelihoods and CBNRM in Namibia: The findings of the WILD Project. Final technical report of the Wildlife*

Integration for Livelihood Diversification Project (WILD), edited by S. A. Long. Windhoek, Ministry of Environment and Tourism. Cited in Jones, B. T. B. (2004) 'CBNRM, poverty reduction and sustainable livelihoods: Developing criteria for evaluating the contribution of CBNRM to poverty reduction and alleviation in southern Africa', *Commons southern Africa occasional paper series*, No. 7, CASS and PLAAS, March 2004

Maluleke, M. L. (2003) Presentation by Mashangu Livingston Maluleke on behalf of the Makuleke Community to the World Parks Congress 2003, cited in Spenceley, A. (2005) *Tourism Investment in the Great Limpopo Transfrontier Conservation Area: Scoping Report*, Report to the Transboundary Protected Areas Research Initiative, University of the Witwatersrand

Manwa, H. (2003) 'Wildlife-based tourism, ecology and sustainability: a tug-of-war among competing interests in Zimbabwe', *Journal of Tourism Studies*, vol 14, 45–54

Mauambeta, D. D. C. (2003) 'Private investments to support protected areas: experiences from Malawi', Vth World Parks Congress: Sustainable Finance Stream, September 2003

Maveneke, T. N. (1998) 'Local participation as an instrument for natural resources management under the Communal Areas Management Programme for Indigenous Resources (CAMPFIRE) in Zimbabwe', Proceedings of an International Workshop on Community-based Natural Resource Management (CBNRM), May, Washington, DC

Mbaiwa J. E. (1999) 'Prospects for Sustainable Wildlife Resource Utilisation and Management in Botswana: A Case Study of East Ngamiland District'. MSc Thesis. Department of Environmental Science, University of Botswana, Gaborone. Cited in Mbaiwa, J. E. (2005c) 'Wildlife resource utilisation at Moremi Game Reserve and Khwai community area in the Okavango Delta, Botswana', *Journal of Environmental Management*, vol 77, no 2, 144–156

Mbaiwa, J. E. (2000) 'The impacts of tourism in the Okavango Delta in north-west Botswana', a paper presented at a Workshop on Climate Change, Biodiversity, Multi-Species Production Systems and Sustainable Livelihoods in the Kalahari Region, Maun Lodge, Botswana, 1–13 October

Mbaiwa, J. E. (2003) 'The socio-economic and environmental impacts of tourism development on the Okavango Delta, north-western Botswana', *Journal of Arid Environments*, vol 54, 447–467

Mbaiwa, J. E. (2004) 'The socio-economic impacts and challenges of a community-based safari hunting tourism in the Okavango Delta, Botswana', *Journal of Tourism Studies*, vol 15, no 2, 37–50. Cited in Mbaiwa, J. E. (2005c) 'Wildlife resource utilisation at Moremi Game Reserve and Khwai community area in the Okavango Delta, Botswana', *Journal of Environmental Management*, vol 77, no 2, 144–156

Mbaiwa, J. E. (2005a) 'Community-based tourism and marginalized communities in Botswana: The case of the Basarwa in the Okavango Delta', in Ryan, C. and Aicken, M. (eds) *Indigenous Tourism: The commodification and management of culture*. Elsevier, Oxford, pp87–109

Mbaiwa, J. E. (2005b) 'Enclave tourism and its socio-economic impacts in the Okavango Delta, Botswana', *Tourism Management*, vol 26, 157–172

Mbaiwa, J. E. (2005c) 'Wildlife resource utilisation at Moremi Game Reserve and Khwai community area in the Okavango Delta, Botswana', *Journal of Environmental Management*, vol 77, no 2, 144–156

Ministry of Environment and Tourism (MET) (2005) 'Community funding facility (CFF). Information kit. MET'. Cited in Zeppel, H. (2006) *Indigenous Ecotourism: Sustainable development and management*, Ecotourism series 3, CABI, Trowbridge

Muchapondwa, E. (2003) 'The economics of community-based wildlife conservation in Zimbabwe', PhD thesis, Department of Economics, Goteborg University

Muir-Leresche, K., Bond, I., Chambati, W. and Kkhumalo, A., (2003) An analysis of CAMPFIRE Revenue generation and Distribution: The First Decade (1989–2000), WWF-SARPO, Harare. Cited in Child, B., Jones, B., Mazambani, D., Mlalazi, A. and Moinuddin, H. (2003) *CAMPFIRE: Communal Areas Management Programme for Indigenous Resources, Final Evaluation Report*: Zimbabwe Natural Resources Management Program – USAID/Zimbabwe Strategic Objective No. 1.29, July 2003

Murphree, M. (2003) 'Lessons from non-lease projects in the communal lands of Zimbabwe', in Sihlophe, H. (ed) *Leadership Lessons for Best Practice in Estuary Based Enterprise Development. Part II – Case Study Presentations*, Beahrs Environmental leadership program, University of California, Berkeley, available at http://nature.berkely.edu/BeahrsELP/reports/03safinal.html

Namibian Association of CBNRM Support Organisations (NACSO) (2004) *Namibia's Communal Conservancies: A Review of Progress and Challenges*, Namibian Association of CBNRM Support Organisations (NACSO), Windhoek

Ndubano, E. (2000) 'The economic impacts of tourism on the local people: The case of Maun in the Ngamiland-sub district, Botswana', MSc thesis, Department of Environmental Science, University of Botswana, Gaborone. Cited in Mbaiwa, J. E. (2003) 'The socio-economic and environmental impacts of tourism development on the Okavango Delta, north-western Botswana', *Journal of Arid Environments*, vol 54, 447–467

Novelli, M. and Humavindu, M. N. (2005) 'Wildlife tourism – wildlife use vs local gain: Trophy hunting in Namibia', in M. Novelli (ed.), *Niche tourism: Contemporary Issues, Trends and Cases*, Elsevier, Oxford, pp171–182. Cited in Zeppel, H. (2006) *Indigenous Ecotourism: Sustainable Development and Management*, Ecotourism series 3, CABI: Trowbridge

Pope, A. (2005) Tourism Study. Report to the Luangwa Safari Association, April 2005

Porter, S., Ferrer, S. and Aylward, B. (2003) 'The profitability of nature tourism in Zululand: A survey of private reserves and public protected areas', in Aylward, B. and Lutz, E. (eds), *Nature Tourism, Conservation , and Development in KwaZulu-Natal, South Africa*, The World Bank, Washington DC, pp287–234

Relly, P. (2004) 'Employment and investment in Madikwe Game Reserve, South Africa', Masters dissertation, University of the Witswatersrand, School of Human Sciences

Roe, D., Leader-Williams, N. and Dalal-Clayton, B. (1997) *Take Only Photographs, Leave Only Footprints: The Environmental Impacts of Wildlife Tourism*, International Institute for Environment and Development, Wildlife and Development Series, No. 10

Rozemeijer, N. (2000) *Community Based Tourism in Botswana: The SNV experience in 3 community tourism projects*. Community based tourism in Botswana

Scheyvens, R. (2002) *Ecotourism: The CAMPFIRE programme in Zimbabwe. In Tourism for Development: Empowering Communities*, Prentice Hall, Essex, pp73–80

Scholes, R. J. and Biggs, R. (eds) (2004) *Ecosystem Services in Southern Africa: A Regional Assessment*, CSIR, Pretoria

Sims-Castley, R., Kerley, G. I. H., Geach, B. and Langholtz, J. (2005) 'Socio-economic significance of ecotourism-based private game reserves in South Africa's Eastern Cape Province', *Parks*, vol 15, no 2, 6–17

Skyer, P. (2004) 'CBNRM, The conservancy programme and Nyae-Nyae Conservancy case study', *Game and Wildlife Science*, vol 21, no 3, 157–177

Spenceley, A. (2005) *Tourism Investment in the Great Limpopo Transfrontier Conservation Area: Scoping Report*, Report to the Transboundary Protected Areas Research Initiative, University of the Witwatersrand, Johannesburg

Spenceley, A. and Barnes, J. (2005) *Economic Analysis of Rhino Conservation in a Land-Use Context within the SADC Region*, SADC RPRC Task 6.3-1.2 (Phase II), SADC Regional Programme for Rhino conservation, Report to IUCN-ROSA

Spenceley, A. and Seif, J. (2002) *Sabi Sabi Imvelo Responsible Tourism Assessment,* Confidential Report to the Federated Hospitality Association of South Africa, cited in Spenceley, A. and Seif, J. (2003) *Strategies, Impacts and Costs of Pro-poor Tourism Approaches in South Africa,* Pro-Poor Tourism working paper No. 11, January 2003

Steenkamp, C. (1998) 'The Makuleke Land Claim signing ceremony: Harnessing social justice and conservation', *African Wildlife,* July/August 1998, vol 52, no 4, downloaded from http://wildnetafrica.co.za/wildlifearticles/africanwildlife/1998/ julaugust_makuleke.html, 8 April 2002, cited in Spenceley, A. (2005) *Tourism Investment in the Great Limpopo Transfrontier Conservation Area: Scoping Report,* Report to the Transboundary Protected Areas Research Initiative, University of the Witwatersrand, Johannesburg

Steenkamp, C. and Grossman, D. (2001) People and Parks: Cracks in the Paradigm, IUCN Policy Think Tank Series, No. 10. May 2001, cited in Spenceley, A. (2005) *Tourism Investment in the Great Limpopo Transfrontier Conservation Area: Scoping Report,* Report to the Transboundary Protected Areas Research Initiative, University of the Witwatersrand, Johannesburg

Suich, H., Busch, J. and Barbancho, N. (2005) 'Economic impacts of transfrontier conservation areas: baseline of tourism in the Kavango-Zambezi TFCA', Paper No. 4. Conservation International, Cape Town

Taylor, R. D. and Murphree, M. W. (2007) Case studies on successful southern African NRM initiatives and their impacts on poverty and governance: Zimbabwe: Masoka and Gairesi, USAID-FRAME & IUCN, Draft, February 2007

Turpie, J., Lange, G.-M., Martin, R., Davies, R., and Barnes, J. (2004) *Strengthening Namibia's system of national protected areas: Subproject 1: Economic analysis and feasibility study for financing,* Anchor Environmental Consultants cc

Virtane, P. (2003) 'Local management of global values: Community-based wildlife management in Zimbabwe and Zambia', *Society & Natural Resources,* vol 16, 179–190 Cited in Zeppel, H. (2006) *Indigenous Ecotourism: Sustainable development and management,* Ecotourism series 3, CABI, Trowbridge

Weaver, C. and Skyer, P. (2003). *Conservancies: Integrating wildlife land-use options into the livelihood, development and conservation strategies of Namibian communities.* WWF/LIFE Project and NACSO, Windhoek, Namibia

Weaver, D. B. (1998) Ecotourism in the less developed world. CABI, Wallingford, UK. Cited in Zeppel, H. (2006) *Indigenous Ecotourism: Sustainable development and management,* Ecotourism series 3, CABI, Trowbridge

Wolmer, W. (2003) 'Transboundary conservation: The politics of ecological integrity in the Great Limpopo Transfrontier Park', *Journal of Southern African Studies,* vol 29, no 1 261–278

WWF–LIFE on behalf of the CBNRM programme (2005) 'Conservancy income data', cited in Spenceley, A. and Barnes, J. (2005) *Economic Analysis of Rhino Conservation in a Land-Use Context within the SADC Region,* SADC RPRC Task 6.3-1.2 (Phase II), SADC Regional Programme for Rhino conservation, Report to IUCN-ROSA

Zeppel, H. (2006) *Indigenous Ecotourism: Sustainable Development and Management,* Ecotourism series 3, CABI, Trowbridge

8

Tourism in Transfrontier Conservation Areas: The Kavango–Zambezi TFCA

Helen Suich

Introduction

Transfrontier conservation areas (TFCAs) are areas of land and/or sea that strad-dle international (or sub-national) borders, that are jointly or cooperatively managed for conservation and/or sustainable natural resource utilization. Recognizing that borders are political rather than ecological, such initiatives aim to ensure that key ecological processes continue to function where such borders have divided ecosystems, river basins and/or wildlife migration routes. Although there are various definitions and categories of TFCAs, they can all be managed jointly or cooperatively, using legal or other effective means. In southern Africa, TFCAs are usually developed in anticipation of the achievement of multiple objectives, most commonly relating to biodiversity conservation, local economic development and the promotion of peace and cooperation across international borders (see World Bank, 1996; Griffin et al, 1999; SADC, 1999; Hanks, 2002; IUCN, 2003).

At least 22 sites have been identified in southern Africa as having the potential to become transfrontier parks or TFCAs (Hall-Martin and Modise, 2002). (Transfrontier parks typically include only state protected areas, differing from TFCAs which can include a variety of conservation and multiple use areas under different land tenures – including state protected areas, game and wildlife management areas, forest reserves, community and private conservation areas, etc.). Both types of initiatives are being given increasing levels of support from stakeholders including governments, donors and non-government organizations (NGOs), and have been endorsed by both the New Partnership for African

Development and the Southern African Development Community as instruments that can contribute to local economic development, regional integration and cooperation, and poverty alleviation through biodiversity conservation activities (SADC, 1999; NEPAD, 2001). Tourism is seen to be a driving force in achieving these objectives – indeed all of the international agreements relating to transfrontier parks and TFCAs in southern Africa refer specifically to tourism as a means to achieve economic development and poverty alleviation objectives.

The proposed Kavango–Zambezi Transfrontier Conservation Area (KAZA TFCA) involves parts of Angola, Botswana, Namibia, Zambia and Zimbabwe. The initiative stems from an idea in the early 1990s to create a southern African wildlife sanctuary, which later developed into the Okavango Upper Zambezi International Tourism Initiative, the aim of which was to take advantage of the region's network of protected areas, wildlife, cultural and natural resources to become a premier tourism hub (DHV Consultants, 1999). More recently, the idea of a conservation and tourism initiative has been revitalized by the tourism ministers of those five countries, who signed a Memorandum of Agreement in late 2006 committing them to work towards the establishment of a TFCA. The KAZA TFCA focuses on the Okavango and Upper Zambezi rivers, and will incorporate approximately 36 national parks, game reserves, community conservation areas, game management areas, as well as internationally important wetlands and World Heritage Sites. The area contains the largest contiguous population of African elephants on the continent (said to number 250,000), as well as world famous tourism attractions such as the Victoria Falls, the Okavango Delta and Chobe National Park, among others, and will reportedly be the largest on the continent (Gosling, 2006).

The specific purpose of the KAZA TFCA is to 'establish a world-class transfrontier conservation area and tourism destination in the Okavango and Zambezi river basin regions of Angola, Botswana, Namibia, Zambia and Zimbabwe within the context of sustainable development' (Anon, 2003). A number of key elements have been identified as crucial to the success of the initiative, which include (among others) improving natural resource management in the region, active support for sustainable tourism development, and the creation of a framework for public and private sector investment and community participation in tourism and other economic activities based on the natural resources of the area (Anon, 2003).

Recognizing the importance of tourism to the achievement of the TFCA objectives, a study was undertaken to determine the existing size of the industry within the KAZA TFCA region, prior to the implementation of any TFCA activities.[1] The aim of the research was to provide baseline information regarding the size, structure and direct economic impact of the tourism industry within the KAZA region, to enable changes in the industry to be monitored as the KAZA TFCA developments are implemented. This chapter reports the results from this research, and discusses strategies that could be adopted to assist the KAZA TFCA maximize the local economic benefits from the tourism industry, in order to achieve its rural development goals.

Methods

The research was designed to determine the level of tourism characteristic products; that is 'those products which in most countries would cease to exist in meaningful quantities, or those for which the level of consumption would be significantly reduced in the absence of visitors' (UN et al, 2000, 35). Within the proposed KAZA TFCA, the only tourism characteristic products were considered to be accommodation and tour operations. Other usual tourism characteristic products were not considered as few are provided by operators within the region and it was expected that much of their economic impact would leak out of the KAZA region (being felt at either the national or international level). Induced and indirect impacts were expected to be small, as is characteristic of relatively small and non-diverse economies, and so were not considered in determining the baseline.

A survey of accommodation establishments and tour operators was conducted in 2004, in northern Botswana (focusing along the Chobe River and in nearby areas, but excluding the Okavango Delta), in Livingstone and along the Upper Zambezi (Zambia), in parts of Victoria Falls (Zimbabwe), and in the Caprivi Region of Namibia. Almost 60 per cent of accommodation establishments and almost 40 per cent of tour operators open for trading in 2004 were surveyed (see Table 8.1). Logistical issues meant that only the nine largest hotels in Victoria Falls were able to be surveyed, and no tour operators in that town were surveyed, thus the results reported below are likely to underestimate the importance of the town as a tourist hub. A total of 30 tour operators were surveyed, although only 26 of these were trading in 2004; the results reported below are only for those enterprises that were operational during 2004. As a result of the omission of tour operators in Victoria Falls, the results reported for the tour operator sector (and thus the tourism industry as a whole) are likely to be underestimated.

Where results are reported below as being 'local' (e.g. 'local employment') this was considered to be an area within the country in question falling within the

Table 8.1 *Sample and population size of establishments open in 2004 surveyed, by region, 2004*

| Area | Accommodation | | Tour operators | |
	Surveyed	Total	Surveyed	Total
Botswana – Kasane, Kazungula, Leshoma, Pandamatenga, Ngoma	19	19	10	14
Zimbabwe – Victoria Falls	9	37	0	37
Zambia – Livingstone	37	71	16	18
Zambia – Upper Zambezi (to Senanga)	13	21	0	0
Namibia – Caprivi Region	24	30	0	0
Total	102	178	26	69

proposed boundaries of the KAZA TFCA. Thus, a 'non-local' Namibian employee was considered to come from outside of the Caprivi region in Namibia. It was assumed that profit earned by 'locally owned' tourism businesses remained within the KAZA region, while that earned by (non-local) corporate enterprises, foreigners and other non-locals was remitted outside of the proposed KAZA TFCA borders.

The survey covered several topics, including the type of business (e.g. capacity, origin of guests, type of ownership, owner residence and ethnicity), the finances of, and employment by the business. The final section was devoted to questions regarding the level of knowledge regarding the KAZA TFCA, and to gaining respondents' impressions of its potential impacts and opportunities.

Survey results

Accommodation

In terms of the total surveyed accommodation capacity in the region (see Table 8.2), northern Botswana offered 17 per cent, Livingstone 35 per cent, Victoria Falls 32 per cent, the Upper Zambezi only 4 per cent and Caprivi the remaining 12 per cent.[2] These proportions contrast quite sharply with the proportion of surveyed establishments in each region – northern Botswana was home to 14 per cent of establishments, Livingstone to 52 per cent and Victoria Falls hosted just 7 per cent of accommodation businesses. The Upper Zambezi was home to 10 per cent and Caprivi to 18 per cent of establishments. Of the guests to these establishments, 39 per cent were from KAZA countries, and 61 per cent were foreign.

The total number of bednights sold in the region in 2004 was 782,200. Each establishment sold on average 5751 bednights, with median sales of 1743. Across the region, bednights sold per enterprise ranged between less than 100 to almost 150,000; 39 per cent of bednights were sold in Livingstone, 25 per cent in Victoria Falls, 23 per cent in northern Botswana, 9 per cent in Caprivi and 4 per cent in the Upper Zambezi establishments.

The provision of accommodation services generated 64 per cent of total accommodation sector revenue, restaurant and bar sales generated 31 per cent, with 4 per cent generated by tour services and 1 per cent by 'other' – which included curio and shop sales, casino operations, a golf course, sales of firewood, transfers and commissions on tour sales (see Table 8.3). Of the total revenue

Table 8.2 *Capacity of accommodation establishments, KAZA region, 2004*

	Average	Median	Total
Number of rooms	24	8	3214
Number of beds	49	16	6629
Camping capacity	12	3	1683
Annual (bednight) capacity	22,308	8578	3,033,880

Table 8.3 *Revenue and operating expenditures, accommodation sector ('000s), KAZA region, 2004*

	Enterprise average ($US)	Enterprise median ($US)	Regional Total ($US)
Revenue			
Total	657	60	89,370
Accommodation	419	33	56,802
Bar and restaurant	203	4	27,635
Tours	27	0	3663
Other	9	0	1270
Operating expenditures			
Total wages and salaries	130	13	17,720
Non-wage operating costs	302	26	41,042
Taxes	60	0.8	8139

generated in the region, 34 per cent was generated by surveyed establishments in Victoria Falls, 28 per cent in Livingstone, 26 per cent in northern Botswana, and just 6 per cent each in Caprivi and the Upper Zambezi.

As can be seen in Table 8.4, just in excess of 4900 people were employed in accommodation establishments within the KAZA region in 2004. Within the accommodation sector, 95 per cent of workers were local employees, 2 per cent were non-local nationals, 1 per cent KAZA nationals and 3 per cent were expatriates. Livingstone provided 44 per cent of total tourism employment, 23 per cent was in Victoria Falls, 14 per cent in northern Botswana, 11 per cent in Caprivi and the remaining 8 per cent was in enterprises along the Upper Zambezi. The total annual salary bill for these employees was approximately US$17.7 million (see Table 8.3). The differences in wages paid across countries were stark – for instance, while Victoria Falls provided 23 per cent of the workforce, these workers earned 35 per cent of the total salary bill; in contrast, Livingstone establishments provided 44 per cent of total employment, but paid workers only 36 per cent of the total salary bill.

Of the 4913 employees in the accommodation sector, a total of 4662 local workers were employed, 688 of them in part-time employment; equating to 4318

Table 8.4 *Employment in accommodation establishments, KAZA region, 2004*

	Total	Average	Median
Total employment	4913	36	12
Local male	2843	20	5
Local female	1819	12	4
Non-local national	92	1	0
KAZA national	33	0	0
Expatriate	126	1	0

Table 8.5 *Local financial impacts of accommodation establishments ('000s), KAZA region, 2004*

	Total (US$)
Local wages	12,592
Local expenditure	19,364
Profit retained locally	4467

full time equivalents; 61 per cent of the local workforce was male, the remaining 39 per cent female. Although local employees made up 95 per cent of the tourism workforce, they earned only 71 per cent of the total wage bill (Table 8.5). Differences in wage levels between countries were significant, with average annual local wages estimated to range between just US$974 in Livingstone and US$5368 across the Zambezi River in Victoria Falls.

Across the KAZA region, approximately 47 per cent of non-wage operating expenditures (approximately US$19.3 million) were made locally, with regional averages ranging between 36 and 61 per cent – the lowest in Livingstone and the highest in northern Botswana. It is estimated that profits of almost US$4.5 million were retained within the KAZA region earned by locally-owned enterprises – 67 per cent of this amount was earned by establishments in northern Botswana, 18 per cent by those along the Upper Zambezi, 6 per cent in Victoria Falls and Livingstone (each) and the remaining 2 per cent by establishments in Caprivi.

Tour operators

As can be seen from Table 8.6, tour operating capacity exceeded 1 million tourists during 2004, with approximately one-third of capacity in northern Botswana, and two-thirds in Zambia. (As noted above, these results underestimate the total size of the tour operator sector due to the lack of results for enterprises operating in Victoria Falls.)

Approximately 314,200 individual tourists were estimated to have gone on tours in the region in 2004. Of the revenue generated in the region, enterprises in northern Botswana generated 64 per cent of the total, while Livingstone operators generated the remaining 34 per cent. Of the tour operators' guests, 11 per cent were from KAZA countries and 89 per cent were foreign (Table 8.7).

Of the 616 workers employed in the tour operator sector (see Table 8.8), only 1 was employed in a part-time position. Approximately 88 per cent of employees were locally employed, 1 per cent were non-local nationals, 1 per cent were KAZA

Table 8.6 *Capacity of operators, KAZA region, 2004*

	Total	Average	Median
Number of vehicles	226	9	8
Number of seats	2926	113	58
Annual capacity	1,067,990	41,077	21,170

nationals and 10 per cent were expatriates. One-third of total employment in this sector was found in northern Botswana, though these employees earned 64 per cent of the total wage bill (see Table 8.7). That is, approximately 200 employees earned $US1.3 million in northern Botswana, while in Livingstone 416 employees earned $US740,000.

Table 8.7 *Revenue and operating expenditures ('000s), KAZA region tour operators, 2004*

	Regional Total ($US)	Enterprise average ($US)	Enterprise median ($US)
Revenue			
Total	10,833	387	213
Tours	10,398	371	213
Food and drinks	435	16	0
Operating expenditures			
Total wages and salaries	2052	73	21
Non-wage operating costs	4791	171	53
Taxes	1242	44	9

Table 8.8 *Employment in KAZA region tour operators, 2004*

	Total	Average	Median
Total employment	616	24	13
Local male	425	17	9
Local female	117	5	3
Non-local national	4	0	0
KAZA national	9	0	0
Expatriate	61	2	0

In 2004, a total of 542 local workers were employed, just 1 of them in part-time employment. Of these workers, 78 per cent were male and only 22 per cent female; 32 per cent of local workers were employed in northern Botswana operations and 68 per cent worked for Livingstone tour operators.

Across the region, tour operators spent on average 58 per cent of non-wage operating costs locally – with these expenditures ranging between 10 and 100 per cent for different enterprises. Of the total spent locally on non-wage operating costs, 74 per cent was made by enterprises in northern Botswana; only 26 per cent of total non-wage operating expenditures were made by enterprises in and around Livingstone.

Of the profit earned by locally-owned operations, 64 per cent of total local tour operator profit was earned by northern Botswana enterprises, with Livingstone entrepreneurs making only 38 per cent of locally retained profit in the tour operator sector (Table 8.9).

Table 8.9 *Local financial impacts of tour operators ('000s), KAZA region, 2004*

	Total (US$)
Local wages	1847
Local expenditure	2769
Profit retained locally	674

Tourism activity in the Kavango–Zambezi TFCA

In 2004, surveyed accommodation establishments in the KAZA region had the capacity to house 8312 guests each night. It is estimated that just over 318,640 guests spent 1 or more nights in these accommodation enterprises, and 782,200 bednights were sold in the region during 2004, while approximately 314,200 guests were taken on a tour by operators in that year.

Table 8.10 shows details of enterprise turnover and employment according to business ownership type, illustrating the dominance in the region of a very small number of corporately owned enterprises, which earned approximately 50 per cent of total tourism enterprise revenue generated in the KAZA TFCA region.

Table 8.10 *Share of tourism market by ownership type, KAZA region, 2004*

n = 162	Total operations (%)	Turnover (%)	Employment (%)
Private	88	49	58
Communal	3	0	0
State/Government	—	—	—
Corporate	7	50	40
Community/Private Joint venture	—	—	—
Other	2	1	2

Information regarding the residence and ethnicity of business owner(s) was also collected (Table 8.11), and illustrates the large number of enterprises that generate very small financial returns for their owners – particularly black enterprise owners.

The tourism industry generated US$100.2 million in 2004; $US89.4 million in the accommodation sector, and US$10.8 million by tour operators. Notable from Table 8.12 is the fact that although the number of enterprises in Victoria Falls is small, they generate significant revenues. The Caprivi and Upper Zambezi regions contribute only a small proportion to the total revenue generated in the KAZA region, however, these enterprises are important local revenue generators, with few other economic activities (aside from subsistence farming) present in the regions.

In 2004, 5529 people were employed in the tourism industry in the KAZA region. Of these, 5204 were local employees, 689 of them in part-time jobs. Table 8.13 shows the breakdown by region by sector.

Table 8.11 *Share of tourism market by owner residence and ethnicity,*
KAZA region, 2004

n = 162	Total operations (%)	Turnover (%)	Employment (%)
Owner's residence			
Local	49	19	25
KAZA	21	19	17
Foreign	12	6	8
Other	11	6	11
Corporate	7	50	40
Owner's ethnicity			
Black	45	6	13
White	34	29	34
Black/white partnership	6	8	5
Other	8	7	9
Corporate	7	50	40

Table 8.12 *Total revenue and operating expenditures (US$'000s),*
KAZA region, 2004

Region	Kasane	Livingstone	Victoria Falls	Upper Zambezi	Caprivi	Total
Accommodation revenue	22,908	25,227	30,822	5437	4976	89,370
% of accommodation revenue	26	28	34	6	6	100
Tour operator revenue	6891	3942	–	0	0	10,833
% of tour operator revenue	64	36	–	0	0	100
Total tourism revenue)	29,799	29,169	30,822	5437	4976	100,203
% of total revenue	30	29	31	5	5	100

Table 8.13 *Total employment in KAZA region, 2004*

Region	Kasane	Livingstone	Victoria Falls	Upper Zambezi	Caprivi	Total
Accommodation employment	698	2144	1151	391	529	4913
% of accommodation emp.	14	44	23	8	11	100
Tour operator employment	204	412	–	0	0	616
% of tour operator emp.	33	67	–	0	0	100
Total employment	902	2556	1151	391	529	5529
% of total employment	16	46	21	7	10	100

Local wages paid as a proportion of the total wage and salary bill across the
KAZA region were just 73 per cent, although 94 per cent of employees were
locally employed, illustrating the disparity in earnings between local and non-local

Table 8.14 *Total local financial impacts ('000s), total KAZA region, 2004*

	Accommodation (US$)	Tour Operators (US$)	Total (US$)
Local wages	12,809	1847	14,656
Local expenditure	19,364	2769	22,133
Profit retained locally	4444	673	5117

employees. Across tour operators and accommodation establishments in the KAZA TFCA, males made up 61 per cent of the local workforce, with 39 per cent of positions filled by women. In the accommodation sector, women accounted for 38 per cent of the local workforce; in the tour operator sector, they accounted for just 22 per cent of local employees.

Just 48 per cent of non-wage operating costs were spent 'locally' across the KAZA TFCA region, although the proportion varied massively between regions and enterprises (see Table 8.16). The 52 per cent spent outside of the KAZA region represents a significant leakage, compounded by the fact that ultimately, many of the goods and services purchased locally are not produced locally – much of what appears to be local spending leaks from the local economy eventually, as local suppliers import goods and services in order to meet local demand. (The survey did not determine which goods and services were supplied locally and which were imported, although this would be a useful avenue of research in order to determine if there were additional goods or services that could be locally supplied in the future.)

Only 20 per cent of the estimated profit earned by tourism enterprises was generated by local owners, and was therefore assumed to remain in the KAZA region. Remittances of corporate and private profits represent an enormous leakage from the local economy, as such leakages reduce the potential income and investments able to be made locally. However, few of the enterprises were foreign owned, accounting for only a small proportion of turnover and profit, therefore much of the leakage from the KAZA region is assumed to remain within the five countries, and so is not lost to national economic development.

Table 8.15 *Total local employment and wages, KAZA region, 2004*

	Local employees as % of total employees	Local wages as % of total wage bill	Average local salary (US$)[a]
Kasane	91	81	3531
Livingstone	96	49	1281
Victoria Falls	100	100	5368
Upper Zambezi	82	50	1321
Caprivi	88	64	1847

Note: a Accommodation sector only.

Table 8.16 *Total non-wage operating expenditures, KAZA region, 2004*

Region	Non-wage operating expenditures made 'locally' (US$)	Local expenditure as % of non-wage operating costs
Kasane	8,918,000	62
Livingstone	4,903,000	40
Victoria Falls	5,707,000	49
Upper Zambezi	1,141,000	57
Caprivi	1,464,000	75
Total	22,133,000	

The future

Tourism in the KAZA region has grown rapidly over the last decade – with one-third of tour operators and almost half of all accommodation establishments opening for business since 2000 (and 85 per cent and 84 per cent, respectively, opening since 1990). This trend is predicted to continue into the foreseeable future, with 5–6 per cent growth per annum predicted in the region, and growth estimates as high as 10–15 per cent in some countries (Yunis, 2004; Perkins, 2005). In this context, the KAZA initiative could almost certainly increase the rate of tourism growth within the TFCA, above that of existing predictions. However, governments and tourism planners will need to decide whether they wish to accelerate this growth beyond predictions, or identify other methods of extracting value from the industry. Rapid rates of growth are likely to be desirable only if the growth can be properly planned and managed, rather than occurring in an uncontrolled and *ad hoc* manner. In terms of achieving the multiple aims of the KAZA TFCA initiative, simply increasing the size of the industry will not necessarily contribute to its sustainability or to the achievement of biodiversity, social or economic objectives. As can be seen from the results presented above, leakages of revenue, operating expenditures, profits and salaries are already a feature of the industry, and continued reliance on passive approaches to tourism planning and development will mean that local benefits from growth remain comparatively small. The adoption of sustainable tourism principles has already been identified as a primary means of shaping and managing this growth to assist in the achievement of the economic development and poverty alleviation objectives of the TFCA, while jointly achieving its biodiversity and natural resource management goals.

Maximizing returns

Several options are available to increase returns from the industry – to increase the total size of the industry, to maximize the value extracted from the industry, or some combination of the two. Tourism planners must decide whether they wish to accelerate growth beyond predictions or identify other methods of extractive value from the industry. Increasing the size of the industry will not necessarily contribute to its sustainability or the achievement of the biodiversity, social or economic objectives of the TFCA, particularly in the light of survey results that show leakages of revenue, operating expenditures, profits and salaries are already a feature of the industry. Relying on passive rather than pro-active approaches to tourism development will mean that benefits from growth remain trickle-down in nature, and will be unlikely to achieve the 'triple bottom line' sustainability desired by the KAZA TFCA. Further, it is not certain that increases in tourist numbers are desirable, or even appropriate across the whole of the KAZA region – particularly given the ecological sensitivity of some areas, combined with the fact that some areas, according to anecdotal evidence, are already close to saturation (see Perkins, 2005). In order to maximize impacts at the local level, additional strategies will be required, as discussed below.

Local employment

Employment impacts positively on local livelihoods and economies, and in the KAZA region, the employment of locals in the tourism industry is already high (approximately 94 per cent across the region). However, few seem to be employed in management or supervisory positions (except in Victoria Falls), the benefits of which are obvious when examining the differences in average wages across the region and the difference between local and non-local salaries. This deficiency could be addressed by improving the skills base of local employees through the provision of appropriate training. In terms of ensuring positive impacts of employment in the tourism industry, it is vital that living wages are paid to all employees – particularly in light of the finding that tourism has been noted as paying, on average, 20 per cent less than other economic sectors (ILO, 2001 cited in Mastny, 2001).

Local participation

One of the key strategies of the KAZA initiative should be to increase the participation and success of local entrepreneurs in the tourism industry. While half of enterprises are already locally owned, the financial returns to these entrepreneurs – and in particular to black-owned enterprises – are low in absolute terms (i.e. revenues and profits generated) as well as relatively (i.e. compared to the corporates). Increasing local participation and crucially, increasing the returns to local operators, will require significant commitments of resources for capacity building, skills development, tourism and business training. The availability of financial resources targeted specifically at improving the profitability of existing locally owned enterprises and enabling new local businesses to open will be vital to maximizing the flow of benefits from the initiative to the local economy.

Partnerships

Many of the sites of high tourism development potential within the KAZA TFCA fall on communal land. In such areas, where local entrepreneurs tend not to have the necessary expertise or financial resources to start a new business, it may be possible to form partnerships between the private sector and the communities who hold traditional rights over an area. Such agreements recognize the profit motive of tourism enterprises, while acknowledging local community resource rights and encouraging their participation in the KAZA initiative and the tourism industry. If well designed and monitored, joint venture agreements can provide benefits to all parties – private sector enterprises can operate in high tourism potential areas while rural communities can benefit from local employment and revenue generation (e.g. through lease fees, revenue sharing or other arrangements), as well as being rewarded for their sustainable resource management activities.

Local procurement

Procurement policies favouring local suppliers can provide an important means of increasing local economic impact by creating opportunities for local entrepreneurs to become involved in providing goods and services to tourism businesses. By increasing local inter-industry linkages through sourcing inputs locally, the indirect and induced impacts of the tourism industry on the local economy can also be improved. Although local procurement is already almost 50 per cent within KAZA, there are considerable regional differences that could be addressed in future.

While local procurement strategies can also be viewed as a form of partnership (as discussed above), local procurement contracts would be expected to be of much shorter duration than those governing tourism operations. There is also a need to be realistic regarding what goods and services can reasonably be expected to be produced and supplied locally.

Equitable distribution

Ensuring equitable distribution of opportunities and benefits within the KAZA TFCA will require careful planning and balance. An inequitable distribution of opportunities and benefits may stimulate conflicts over land and other resources that generate benefits for a minority. There would seem to be most potential for such conflicts in communal areas, where tenure over land and other resources is not always secure. Incoherent land allocation policies (e.g. land leases for tourism sites) may also stimulate conflict between operators and residents. Although, obviously, some sites will always have a higher tourism demand than others due to their unique and/or spectacular characteristics, land allocation policies that are fair, widely understood and adhered to are extremely important in avoiding conflicts. Spatially planning future tourism development should improve the likelihood of the equitable distribution of opportunities to enter the industry across the KAZA region.

Cost mitigation

In addition to benefits that may flow from the KAZA TFCA, the mitigation of costs associated with the initiative must also be considered. Human–wildlife conflict (HWC) is likely to be one of the most important costs to residents of the TFCA, and refers mostly to damage to crops by wild herbivores and stock losses to predators, and can have significant negative effects on agricultural livelihoods and household food security. The limited data available suggest that up to 80 per cent of agricultural households suffer some level of crop damage caused by wildlife, while almost 20 per cent of stock-owning households suffer losses to predators (Suich, 2003; Cullis and Watson, 2004). Innovative measures will need to be developed and trialled (as is happening in some areas) to determine the best possible method(s) of damage limitation. It will also be necessary to introduce successful mitigation methods in a timely manner into areas where wildlife populations expand as resource management improves (particularly in Zambia and Angola). By implementing such programmes, it will be possible to provide direct and positive impacts at a household level to a significant proportion of the rural population.

Infrastructure development and service delivery

The necessity of improving and extending infrastructure within the KAZA region has been identified as one means to increase tourist access to the KAZA TFCA, and will obviously impact on access to individual sites within it. National plans for infrastructure development and the provision of ancillary services (e.g. communications, electricity, health, finance, etc.) will guide the spatial development of the tourism industry, and should be coordinated amongst the five countries.

In regions that currently have limited or no access to infrastructure or services, its provision is likely to have more widespread positive impacts on poverty, and contribute more to local economic development, than the opportunities offered by the tourism industry. Thus, infrastructure development and service delivery must be carefully planned and implemented to ensure that proposed developments meet not only the needs of the tourism industry, but also those of residents.

Additional challenges

A number of challenges will face KAZA TFCA institutions in their attempts to support and facilitate sustainable tourism, support local economic development and poverty alleviation. As the five countries are at very different stages of economic and tourist industry development, policy makers will face significant challenges in attempting to harmonize relevant policy and legislation. The need for coherent tourism and related policies within the KAZA region will need to be balanced with the needs of the tourism industry elsewhere in each of the five countries. A balance will also need to be achieved between regulations and policies that encourage sustainable tourism, and those that are so complex or bureaucratic that they stifle the growth of the industry. In many cases, offering incentives for desired outcomes will be more successful than attempting to regulate undesired behaviour.

Governments are ideally placed to create an enabling environment that stimulates desired outcomes, particularly if the initiative increases the levels of cooperation and coordination. However, the creation of an enabling environment should not become confused with being an active participant in the tourism industry. It has been demonstrated within the region, and elsewhere in the world, that the private sector is typically more efficient than government at managing industries such as tourism.

One of the major issues that will require an innovative solution will be how to incorporate the needs and wishes of local residents in all aspects of the planning, decision making and implementation of the KAZA TFCA. The institutional structures set up to manage transfrontier parks and TFCAs elsewhere in southern Africa do not provide explicitly for active community participation in decision making and planning, and lessons should be learned from the lack of participation of local communities in other regional transfrontier initiatives. Problems could be avoided in the KAZA region if management institutions allow for direct community participation in processes at the local, national and international level. Support for, and strengthening of, existing transboundary tourism and natural resource management institutions should occur as one means of encouraging local input into planning processes. However, in order to achieve the effective participation of local communities, significant resources will be required for capacity building and associated activities in rural communities.

In terms of managing the tourism industry, a balance will need to be achieved between the benefits accruing to the tourism industry based on the extensive natural and wildlife attractions of the region, and the cost of managing these resources. While profits from the nature-based tourism industry in KAZA accrue predominantly to private and corporate tourism enterprises, the costs of managing wildlife populations and conservation areas fall largely on the national governments of the five countries. (The exceptions to this are community and private conservation areas, which are expected to generate sufficient revenues to manage the resources within their boundaries with little assistance from the state.) Methods of ensuring that the tourism industry in the region, which relies almost entirely on well managed wildlife populations (inside and out of protected areas) contributes to the cost of their management must be determined. There are many examples of innovative methods of achieving such a goal, and feasibility studies should be conducted to determine which methods are most appropriate within the KAZA TFCA. One example is the implementation of an environmental levy on tourists and/or tourism businesses in the region, with revenues returned to institutions responsible for natural resource and protected area management within the KAZA TFCA.

There is a demonstrated willingness on the part of existing operators to contribute to the development of local areas, with around half of all existing businesses already making voluntary financial and/or in-kind contributions to local communities. Raising the awareness of industry participants of ways in which they can maximize the social and economic benefits of their business practices, coupled with some combination of incentives and regulations regarding local employment, local procurement policies and partnership arrangements would be likely to stimulate significant positive changes within the industry.

Although there will always be a proportion of operators who are disinterested in contributing to, or participating in, TFCA activities, if even a minority of operators were to change their business practices, it is likely that significant additional positive local economic impact will follow.

In conclusion, it can be seen from the survey results presented above that the tourism industry as it currently operates already contributes to economic growth, revenue generation, government tax revenues and job creation within the KAZA region. However, the KAZA countries are characterized by high levels of inequality and poverty – where 25–66 per cent of the population live on less than $US1 per day, and between 55 and 90 per cent live on less than $US2 per day (World Bank/UNDP, 2005). Within the KAZA region, much of the population is rural, reliant on rainfed agriculture, often food insecure and with inadequate access to infrastructure and government services. In the region covered by this survey, the total population is in excess of 1 million people (GeoHive, 2005). In 2004, approximately 5500 people were employed in the tourism industry – just 0.5 per cent of the population. Assuming that each employee provides support to one household, the indirect impact rises to around 5 per cent of the population. It would be expected that with the anticipated continued growth in the tourism industry, combined with a widespread adoption of sustainable tourism principles as outlined above, the industry could make an important contribution to achieving the economic development and poverty alleviation objectives of the KAZA TFCA – particularly as very few alternative development programmes currently exist in the region. However, this contribution should be neither over- nor under-emphasized; sustainable tourism development should be recognized as one element of a suite of development strategies that are required to overcome poverty and stagnant economies in the region. Given that the majority of residents within the KAZA region are reliant on subsistence agriculture, consideration should also be taken of implementing programmes to improve the efficiency and sustainability of resource use within agriculture and pastoralism, while increasing production and productivity levels in those sectors.

Notes

1   This research was funded by the Swiss Agency for Development and Cooperation through the Transfrontier Conservation Unit of Conservation International, South Africa.
2   More detailed results are available in Suich et al, 2005.

References

Anon. (2003) 'Minutes of the Meeting of Ministers responsible for tourism in Angola, Botswana, Namibia, Zambia and Zimbabwe on the Okavango Upper Zambezi Tourism Initiative (OUZIT)'. Katima Mulilo, Namibia, 24 July

Cullis, A. and Watson, C. (2004) 'Winners and losers: Privatising the Commons', *Briefing Paper*. London: International Institute for Environment and Development/Resource Conflict Institute

DHV Consultants (1999) 'Preliminary project scan for the scoping assessment for the Okavango Upper Zambezi International Tourism study (OUZIT)', Unpublished paper for the Development Bank of Southern Africa

GeoHive (2005) 'GeoHive population data – Angola administrative units; Botswana administrative units; Namibia administrative units; Zambia administrative units; Zimbabwe administrative units'. available at www.212.204.253.230/cd/link.php?xml=ao&xsl=neo1

Gosling, M. (2006) 'Green light for landmark African nature park', *Cape Times*, 12 December

Griffin, J., Cumming, D., Metcalfe, S., 't Sas-Rolfes, M., Singh, J., Chonguiça, E., Rowen, M. and Oglethorpe, J. (1999) *Study on the development of Transboundary Natural Resources Management Areas in Southern Africa*. Biodiversity Support Programme, Washington, DC

Hall-Martin, A. and Modise, S. (2002) 'Existing and potential transfrontier conservation areas in the SADC region. Status report', PPF/RETOSA/DBSA, Stellenbosch

Hanks, J. (2002) 'Transfrontier conservation areas (TFCAs) in southern Africa: Their role in conserving biodiversity, socio-economic development and promoting a culture of peace', *Journal of Sustainable Forestry*, vol 17, no 1/2, 127–148

IUCN (2003) 'A typology of transboundary protected areas: Different approaches for different needs', in IUCN, *Transboundary Conservation: Promoting peaceful Cooperation and Development While Protecting Biodiversity*. ITTO/IUCN, Yokohama/Gland

Mastny, L. (2001) 'Travelling light. New paths for international tourism', *Worldwatch Paper No.159*. Worldwatch Institute, Washington, DC

New Partnership for Africa's Development (NEPAD) (2001) *New Partnership for Africa's Development (NEPAD)*. NEPAD, Abuja. http://www.uneca.org/nepad/nepad.pdf

Perkins, J. (2005) 'Status and perspectives of regional tourism in the context of the Kavango–Zambezi initiative, KAZA TFCA', Unpublished support document to local consultation and national stakeholder workshops/InWEnt

Southern African Development Community (SADC) (1999) *Protocol on Wildlife Conservation and Law Enforcement*. SADC, Gaborone

Suich, H. (2003) 'Summary of partial results from the socio-economic household survey regarding community based natural resource management and livelihoods in Caprivi and Kunene', *WILD Project Working Paper No. 12*, Ministry of Environment and Tourism/WILD, Windhoek

Suich, H., Busch, J. and Barbancho, N. (2005) 'Economic impacts of transfrontier conservation areas: Baseline of tourism in the Kavango–Zambezi TFCA', Paper No. 4 prepared for Conservation International, Cape Town

UN-EUROSTAT-OECD-WTO (2000) *Tourism Satellite Account (TSA): Methodological references*. World Tourism Organisation, Madrid

World Bank (1996) 'Mozambique. Transfrontier Conservation Areas Pilot and Institutional Strengthening Project', *Report No. 15534-MOZ*. World Bank, Washington, DC

World Bank/UNDP (2005), 'Income and poverty 2005', www.worldbank.org (accessed 10 February 2006)

Yunis, E. (2004) 'Sustainable tourism and poverty alleviation', Presentation given at the Annual World Bank Conference on Development Economics, Brussels, Belgium, 10 May

9

The Realities of Ecotourism Development in Botswana

Joseph E. Mbaiwa

Introduction

Ecotourism has, since the 1990s, become a buzzword among tourism practitioners and those in academia. The term 'ecotourism' was coined by a Mexican conservationist, Hector Ceballos-Lascarain, in 1983 (Ceballos-Lascurain, 1996). Despite its global impact, ecotourism as a concept is surrounded by confusion (Bjork, 2000). This is because different researchers and practitioners have defined it differently. Dowling (2000) states that between 1993 and 1994, over 30 definitions of ecotourism were created and marketed. Because of its many definitions, ecotourism has become a subject of controversy among those in academia. Valentine (1993) and Bjork (2000) state that ecotourism is a fuzzy concept defined and named in many different ways. However, the theme that runs across most of the definitions of ecotourism is that which describes ecotourism as nature-based tourism that includes an educational component, promotes the socioeconomic well being of local people and is managed on a sustainable basis. As such, ecotourism implies a tourism industry that is mostly nature-based, promotes environmental conservation, environmentally friendly tourists and the socioeconomic well being of the local people. Ecotourism is thus seen as an alternative to mass tourism due to its small-scale infrastructure development and its ability to minimize environmental impacts (Mbaiwa, 2005). This responsibility also applies to other stakeholders such as tour operators and the government. This approach to tourism management and environmental conservation contributes to the ecological sustainability and sustainable tourism in the tourism destination areas.

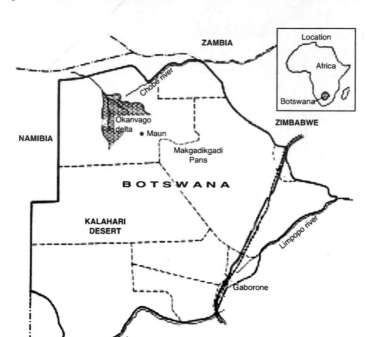

Figure 9.1 *Map of Botswana showing the Okavango Delta*

In Botswana, located in southern Africa (Figure 9.1), tourism was almost non-existent at the time of independence in 1966. However, by 2006, it had grown to be the second largest economic sector contributing 5 per cent to Botswana's gross domestic product (GDP) (Gaolatlhe, 2006). In 2000, the total visitor arrivals in Botswana were 1,424,669 of which 81,632 of them were ecotourists/holiday tourists and visited the country's national parks, game reserves and other wildlife areas (Botswana Government, 2003). Much of Botswana's holiday tourists (that is, photographic and safari hunters) visit the Okavango Delta and rich wildlife habitat located in northwestern Botswana.

While tourism development in Botswana, particularly in wildlife areas such as the Okavango Delta, is on the increase, a number of studies (e.g. Fidzani et al, 1999; NWDC, 2003; Kgathi et al, 2005) have found that most of the people in the Okavango Delta live in what the United Nations has defined as 'human poverty'. Human poverty is a composite measure of life span, health, knowledge, economic provisioning and degree of social inclusion (UNDP, 2005). Poverty has created conditions for the over-harvesting of natural resources by local people in the Okavango Delta. It is from this perspective that, in the late 1980s, an approach to involve local communities in natural resource conservation through tourism development was adopted by government. This approach has come to be known as Community-Based Natural Resource Management (CBNRM) and ecotourism in Botswana is embedded in this approach. That is, there is a thin line that can be drawn between CBNRM projects and ecotourism projects in Botswana. Ecotourism activities in Botswana largely involve game viewing, bush walks, safari hunting, camping, lodging, boat driving, mekoro (dug-in canoe) safaris, story telling, dancing and many others. Some scholars have a narrower definition of ecotourism that restricts it to tourist visits to nature-based areas and excludes small-scale enterprises which rely on nature's resources to produce artefacts such as baskets and the collection of veld products like devil's claw, which are produced for sale to tourists and the tourist market. In addition, safari hunting has been excluded by a number of scholars on the grounds that it is not an ecotourism activity. However, in Botswana, rural communities which have ecotourism projects use hunting as one of the main activities in their areas. Safari hunting on a remote community level is conducted at a small scale and involves selective and seasonal hunting; which animals are to be hunted is determined after an annual total population survey of existing game is carried out. Considering that these activities are produced on a small scale by rural communities in order to make a living from tourism development, the definition of ecotourism in this chapter is broadened to include these products and operations.

Many tourism operators in Botswana and around the world have misused the term 'ecotourism', mostly for marketing purposes. Some operators who practise mass tourism describe their businesses as ecotourism in order to attract tourists. In Botswana, there are two forms of tourism developing in parallel to each other. The first form is enclave tourism (Mbaiwa, 2005). Ceballos-Lascurain (1996) defines enclave tourism as tourism that is concentrated in remote areas where the types of facilities and their physical location fail to take into consideration the needs and wishes of surrounding communities. The goods and services available are beyond the financial means of the local communities and any foreign currency generated may have only a minimal effect upon the economy of the host location (Ceballos-Lascurain, 1996). Enclave tourism is well developed in the Okavango Delta and is dominated by foreign safari companies and practitioners. The second form is ecotourism implemented through the Community-Based Natural Resource Management (CBNRM) programme. The CBNRM began in the mid-1990s as a strategy to foster rural community and natural resource conservation in remote areas. Botswana adopted an Ecotourism Strategy in 2002 to strengthen local participation in tourism and conservation. Among some of its goals, the strategy aims to (1) contribute actively to environmental conservation; (2) involve local communities in tourism planning, development and operation and contribute to their well being; and (3) promote nature-based tourists who are environmentally friendly (Department of Tourism, 2002). The objective of this chapter, therefore, is to explore in general the realities of ecotourism development in Botswana. The chapter will focus on the success achieved and the problems associated with ecotourism development in the country. The chapter will finally make suggestions on how some of the problems of ecotourism development can be minimized in Botswana.

The contribution of ecotourism to rural livelihoods

Since ecotourism began in the mid-1990s in Botswana, it has had several success stories, including the following:

- participation of local communities in ecotourism;
- employment creation in remote areas;
- income generation for local communities;
- investment in community development projects and facilities; and
- empowerment of communities in conservation and tourism development.

These stories of successful ecotourism development in Botswana are discussed below.

Participation of local communities in ecotourism

There is no doubt that the adoption of ecotourism has increased social capital in many villages in Botswana. This is demonstrated by the ability of various communities in Botswana to have formed ecotourism institutions known as Trusts or community based organisations (CBOs) to enable them to participate and benefit from the growing tourism industry. Trusts or CBOs are specifically formed to enable local participation in ecotourism development in rural areas of Botswana. Trusts, as local institutions, fulfil a leadership role in the use of land and resources such as wildlife for tourism purposes by participating communities. The Chobe Enclave Conservation Trust in the Chobe region was the first community tourism institution to be established in 1993. The second was the Sankuyo Tshwaragano Management Trust in the Okavango Delta, established in 1995. Many more Trusts have been established and, in total, 91 Trusts with the basic aim of promoting ecotourism development are currently registered in Botswana (Schuster, 2007). These ecotourism projects cover approximately 150 villages in all of the 10 districts of Botswana. A total of 135,000 people or 10 per cent of Botswana's population is thus participating in ecotourism (Schuster, 2007). However, the level of participation and success of these ecotourism projects differs, some – like that of Sankoyo village – are more successful while others have only reached the point of registration with no measurable output. The increase in the number of Trusts, people and villages involved in ecotourism demonstrates the interest of local communities to derive socioeconomic benefits from the growing tourism industry in Botswana.

The formation of Trusts is an important achievement by local communities, since it has given them access to land and related natural resources for ecotourism purposes. Trusts act as intermediaries between the Government, NGOs and their communities. Trusts are guided by constitutions agreed upon by their respective communities. Trusts also have land use management plans for their ecotourism areas. As such, Trusts are *de facto* owners of the wildlife resources in their respective community areas. Trusts are engaged in tourism activities such as sub-leasing community tourism areas and selling their wildlife quotas to safari companies, managing cultural tourism, marketing baskets and crafts, photographic tourism and marketing reeds and grass (National CBNRM Forum, 2001). Trusts also sign legal documents such as leases and contracts with safari companies, and maintain a close contact with the trust lawyers. They also keep trust records, financial accounts and reports, and present them to the general membership at the annual general meetings (Mbaiwa, 2004a). Trusts therefore conduct and manage all the affairs of the community on behalf of its members, who are generally people aged 18 years and above in the respective participating villages.

The level of social capital between communities differs. However, it can be stated in general terms that the formation of Trusts and their ability to manage ecotourism projects on behalf of their communities demonstrate the fact that the establishment of ecotourism has increased the level of social capital in many villages involved in ecotourism in Botswana. The formation of local institutions is therefore a form of local empowerment where communities make decisions to improve their livelihoods.

Employment creation in remote areas

The creation of employment opportunities is one of the key indicators of how successful ecotourism can be in promoting rural livelihoods. Ecotourism has increased employment figures in participating villages in different parts of Botswana. According to Schuster (2007), in 2006, there were more than 8000 local people employed in a wide range of ecotourism projects and activities in Botswana (Table 9.1).

In Botswana terms, an employment estimate of 8000 people in ecotourism projects represents a substantial number of people. This is because most of the ecotourism projects are carried out in remote parts of Botswana where there are no industrial or manufacturing sectors to create employment opportunities for local people. As a result, the development of ecotourism in Botswana can be described as one of the tools used to improve rural livelihoods and rural development.

Table 9.1 *Employment in ecotourism projects and activities*

Activity	Employment
Trophy hunting	560
Photographic and cultural tourism	420
Veld production (e.g. basket selling)	At least 3100
Crafts e.g. wood carving	At least 4000
Total	At least 8800

Source: Schuster, 2007

Financial benefits of ecotourism

Ecotourism projects in Botswana generate huge sums of money and income for participating communities. For example, a total of P16.3 million[1] in revenues was generated by various ecotourism projects in 2006 (Schuster, 2007). The majority (72 per cent) of the income in 2006 came from wildlife-based ecotourism activities, particularly from trophy hunting (Table 9.2). As shown in Table 9.2, other ecotourism activities, particularly photographic and cultural tourism, the sale of veld products and craft production, contribute a significant amount of income to the ecotourism sector in Botswana.

The income generated from ecotourism is important because it is one way for communities to sustain their livelihoods. Much of the revenue from ecotourism is used for community development projects and only benefits individual households in the form of income from employment. There is, however, some income, such as that from Sankoyo, which the community receives in the form of household dividends. For this reason, Arntzen (2003) notes that income from ecotourism subsequently ends up in the households in the form of dividends. Schuster (2007) argues that even though a substantial level of income is generated from ecotourism projects in the Okavango Delta, it translates to a theoretical average annual income of only P50 for each household for those participating in ecotourism development. For example, between 1996 and 2001, each household at Sankoyo Village in the Okavango Delta was paid P200, this sum increased to P250 in 2002, P300 in 2003 and P500 in 2004. In 2005 and 2006, households at Sankoyo also got P500 each (Schuster, 2007). This income is distributed every October/November to each household by the Trust. Schuster (2007) argues that income to households is small, and it can therefore be concluded that benefits generated through natural resource use or ecotourism are at best a supplementary income. However, the distribution of income to the various households is an important element in improving rural livelihoods. It is also an aspect of income diversification in that villagers are able to diversify their existing revenue base. Income levels in villages which are not involved in ecotourism development in wildlife areas are low, since employment opportunities are very limited for rural communities. As a result, most people in non-ecotourism villages rely on agricultural production, veld production collection and remittances from relatives and family members working in bigger centres like Maun.

Table 9.2 *Revenue generated from ecotourism projects*

Activity	Amount in Pula	Percentage of Total
Trophy hunting	11,900,000	72
Photographic and cultural tourism	3,100,000	20
Veld marketing	710,801	4
Craft production	600,000	4
Total	16,310,801	

Source: Schuster, 2007

Table 9.3 *Income generated by ecotourism projects in different regions of Botswana*

Community Trusts Okavango Delta/ Chobe Regions	Type of Ecotourism Project 1997	Income in Pula,[a] 1995–2005		
			2000	2005
Sankoyo Tshwaragano Management Trust	Photographic, camping, hunting and sale of crafts	285,000	595,460	1,630,400
Chobe Enclave Community Trust	Photographic, camping and hunting	464,000	1,030,000	1,500,000
Okavango Community Trust	Photographic, camping and hunting	400,000	950,000	1,800,000
Kalepa Trust	Photographic, camping and hunting	2930 (1998)	270,000	1,500,000
Kgalagadi/Ghanzi Regions				
Nqwaa Khobe Xeya Trust	Photographic, camping, hunting and sale of crafts	–	180,000	109,150
Huiku Trust	Photographic, camping, hunting and sale of crafts	–	59,200 (2002)	66,000
Kweneng/Central Regions				
Gaing-O Community Trust	Photographic, camping, hunting and sale of firewood	11,000 (1999)	74,000 (2001)	78,586
Baikago Development Trust	Harvesting and marketing devil's claw, veld products, trees etc	–	12,580	–

Note: a Income being tourist expenditure on accommodation, land rentals, sale of wildlife quota, sale of crafts, etc.

Source: Schuster, 2007

Ecotourism projects found in northern Botswana where there is an abundance of wildlife resources generate more income than those found in the western, central and eastern parts of the country where wildlife resources are less than those in the north. This is illustrated by Table 9.3 which shows that communities in the Okavango and Chobe regions generate more income than those in the Kgalagadi, Kweneng and Ghanzi areas. Ecotourism projects in the Okavango and Chobe regions also employ more people than those in the Kgalagadi, Kweneng and Ghanzi regions.

As noted earlier, in this chapter the definition of ecotourism is not restricted to tourists visits to nature-based areas but also involves the small scale production of natural resources for the tourist market. Based on this understanding, most of the ecotourism projects in the Kweneng, Central, Ghanzi and Kgalagadi regions were found to rely on the production of craft products, thatching grass and the harvesting of natural resources such as devil's claw (*Harpogophytum procumbens*). This shows that communities in these regions have diversified ecotourism beyond the use of wild animals, birds or forests to use veld products such as the devils claw, thatching grass and other natural resources but all with the basic aim of benefiting from the ecotourists visiting their areas.

Access to land for ecotourism development

Access to land for ecotourism development is one of the major benefits which remote communities in Botswana have achieved since the mid-1990s. Before the 1990s when ecotourism was introduced in Botswana, people living in wildlife areas did not have land for tourism development. The Wildlife Conservation Policy of 1986 and Tourism Policy of 1990 laid the foundation for ecotourism development in Botswana. The two policies called for increased opportunities for local communities to benefit from wildlife and natural resources through tourism development (Mbaiwa, 2004b). Through the Wildlife Conservation Policy of 1986, land in wildlife areas was sub-divided into smaller land zones known as Controlled Hunting Areas (CHAs) while the Tourism Policy of 1990 allows local communities to participate in ecotourism projects (Mbaiwa, 2004b). Figure 9.2 shows CHAs that have been demarcated and allocated to various communities for tourism purposes in the Okavango Delta. There are 91 registered Trusts in Botswana (Schuster, 2007) and most of these Trusts have been allocated CHAs for ecotourism purposes.

CHAs are administrative blocks or land units used by the Department of Wildlife and National Parks to allocate wildlife quotas to local communities for tourism purposes. After the allocation of a CHA, a community decides on the type of land use for that particular area, that is, either for hunting or photographic purposes. CHAs are not a uniform size. Botswana is divided into 163 CHAs which are zoned for various types of wildlife utilization (both consumptive and non-consumptive uses), under commercial or community management (Darkoh and Mbaiwa, 2005). The zoning of wildlife areas for ecotourism purposes

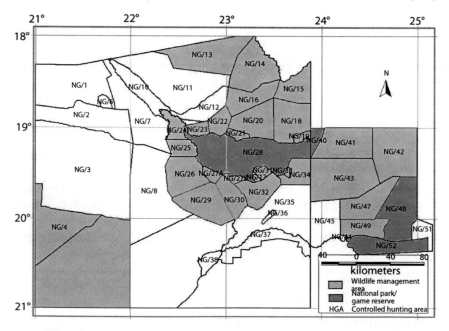

Figure 9.2 *Controlled Hunting Areas (CHAs) in the Okavango Delta*

indicates a partial return of custodianship and stewardship of natural resources to local communities. Studies (e.g. Thakadu, 1997; Mbaiwa, 2002; Bolaane, 2004) have shown that local people were disposed from resource areas such as the Moremi Game Reserve a century ago when Botswana came under British colonial rule in 1885. At independence from British rule in 1966, Botswana's post-colonial government adopted colonial policies and continued with the process of centralizing natural resources, particularly wildlife (Mbaiwa, 2002). Access to land for ecotourism by rural communities can be described as local empowerment to natural resource use. The empowerment of local people has the potential to improve rural livelihoods and encourage sustainable natural resource use.

Reinvestment of revenue generated from ecotourism

In some communities, funds generated from ecotourism have been ploughed back into other tourism enterprises and community development projects. For example, Sankoyo has established a 16-bed photographic lodge (Santawani Lodge), a cultural tourism centre (Shandrika) where tourists can view the cultural activities and way of life of the people of Sankoyo and a campsite (Kazikini) (Mbaiwa, 2004a). Some of the Trusts have ploughed back revenue generated from ecotourism into the provision of social services and community development projects (Table 9.4).

Livestock farming, dryland crop production and remittances from relatives and family members working in urban centres play a significant role in promoting rural livelihoods. At present, there is no study that has measured the monetary value of the agricultural output and remittances obtained by communities in wildlife-based tourism areas. However the social services provided as a result of ecotourism to the various communities demonstrate that ecotourism plays a significant role in rural livelihoods and economic development in Botswana.

Table 9.4 *Social services provided by trusts to their villages*

Type of Social Services	Amount Given & Comments
Assistance for funerals	P200 to P3000 per household
Support for local sport activities	P5000 to P50,000 per village
Scholarships	P7000 to P35,000 per village
Services and houses for elderly people	P150 to P300 per month per person
Assistance for orphans	P40,000 per Trust
Assistance for disabled people	P15,000 per village
Provision of communication tools such as radios	Available for use by all community members
Transport services particularly in the use of vehicles	Available for use by members
Installation of water stand pipes in households	Every household in Sankoyo and Mababe Villages have been provided with this

Source: Arntzen et al, 2003; Mbaiwa, 2004a, 2007; Schuster, 2007

Table 9.5 *Assets owned by communities involved in ecotourism*

Assets	Total no of assets owned by Trusts	No of communities that own assets
DSTV		
(Satellite television)	2	2
Internet access	7	7
Computers	23	17
Printers	24	14
Cars/vehicles	42	15

Source: Schuster, 2007

Schuster (2007) argues that ecotourism has transformed the people living in some rural communities in the Okavango Delta from being beggars who survive on handouts from the Botswana Government and donor agencies into productive communities that are moving towards achieving sustainable livelihoods. In addition to providing social services, communities involved in ecotourism have invested a certain percentage of their funds in physical development projects and into assets that are made accessible to most of the people in their villages (Table 9.5). The majority of the communities involved in ecotourism in the Okavango Delta operate grocery and bottle stores in their villages, own vehicles for transportation, have built their own offices and have access to radios and computers (Arntzen et al, 2003; Mbaiwa, 2007; Schuster, 2007). These assets are owned by communities and managed by Trusts. Some of the assets include buildings for offices, grocery and bottle stores.

Assets owned by the community are bought using communal funds generated from ecotourism enterprises. As a result, Schuster (2007) argues that even though vehicles bought by ecotourism projects are meant for business, they are also used as a form of transportation by community members for personal reasons between one village and another. Community members can also hire these vehicles in case they want to transport their goods from one point to another. These vehicles can also be used to transport the dead and mourners – yet another important aspect of community and rural development in Botswana. As noted earlier, most of these projects are located in remote areas which only a decade ago were very difficult to access. The availability of transportation has increased the accessibility of these once remote areas to big regional centres like Kasane and Maun in northern Botswana or Molepolole in Kweneng, Ghanzi in Ghazi area and Hunkuntsi or Tsabong in Kgalagadi in the south. The introduction of television sets, modern computer technology, internet and radios in the remote villages of Botswana is an important aspect of rural development, particularly because it enables the people to keep informed of the latest developments not only in Botswana but in most parts of the world. The reinvestment of funds from ecotourism into other economic activities by rural villages is an important aspect of community development. In this sense, ecotourism can be described as one of the tools promoting economic development in rural areas of Botswana.

Ecotourism and the conservation of natural resources

The introduction of ecotourism in Botswana was driven by a number of factors such as: the threat of species extinction due to the over-utilization of resources (especially wildlife through poaching); the inability of the state to protect its declining wildlife resources; land use conflicts between rural communities living in resource areas and resource managers (especially wildlife managers); and the need to link conservation and development (Mbaiwa, 2004b). While ecotourism has been in operation in Botswana since the mid-1990s, it has not yet been established how much it has contributed to biodiversity conservation. According to Arntzen et al (2003) and Mbaiwa (2004a), the economic benefits of ecotourism and access to land for ecotourism purposes have resulted in the development of positive attitudes by indigenous communities towards wildlife conservation. This has in turn led to a reduction in poaching levels in ecotourism areas in comparison to non-ecotourism areas. Table 9.6 shows that the level of poaching reported between 1998 and 2006 in ecotourism areas in the Okavango Delta was lower than levels in non-ecotourism.

The reduction in poaching is an important aspect of wildlife conservation in the Okavango Delta. Arntzen et al (2003) note that even though animal species such as buffalo, lechwe, hippo and sitatunga are still declining, numbers of some species are stabilizing or showing an increase. For example, populations of steenbok, impala and elephant have increased by 5 per cent in the last decade (Arntzen et al 2003). The low rates of wildlife poaching in ecotourism areas shows that when local communities began to derive economic benefits from ecotourism and the natural resources of their area, they start to place a value on those natural resources and to use them – particularly the wildlife – sustainably.

The case for conservation in ecotourism areas is strengthened by government requirements for each project. For example, all the Trusts in Botswana are required by the Government to incorporate natural resource management goals in their constitutions. In addition, Trusts are required to produce management plans in which they specify how environmental management will be carried out in their CHAs or ecotourism areas. Communities are also required to provide an annual report on how natural resource management was carried out in their areas before annual wildlife quotas are provided by the Department of Wildlife and National Parks. In order to meet these requirements, communities have appointed community escort guides to ensure proper environmental management in their areas.

Table 9.6 *Reported cases of illegal hunting in the Okavango Delta*

Area	1998	1999	2001	2002	2003	2004	2005	2006
CBNRM areas	4	0	0	0	1	2	2	1
Non-CBNRM areas	23	9	12	13	12	12	10	5
Total	27	9	12	13	13	15	12	6

Source: Arntzen et al, 2003, DWNP Annual Illegal Hunting Records, 1998–2006

Escort guides patrol ecotourism areas and enforce the agreed community regulations on environmental management. Schuster (2007) notes that 14 Trusts in the Okavango Delta (but also in Kgalagadi and Kweneng) had a total of 111 escort guides who control poaching and ensure compliance with hunting regulations. Escort guides have proved effective in ensuring that hunting is controlled in CHAs. They accompany hunters on hunting safaris. The effectiveness of escort guides and their desire to conserve resources in their CHAs is further demonstrated by their numerous patrols in their areas. For example, in 2004, this author travelled with and observed community escort guides of Sankoyo Village when they caught two men who had illegally killed an impala in NG 34 (Sankoyo's CHA). They subsequently handed the two men to the police for prosecution. The second incident that this author witnessed was when I was driving in NG 32 after the permitted time of 18:00 hours. Escort guides responsible for that CHA suspected me of being an illegal wildlife hunter and stopped my vehicle. After a few minutes of questioning and satisfaction that I was not an illegal hunter, they allowed me to proceed on my journey with the advice that in future, I should refrain from driving in the area outside the permitted time. All these efforts indicate the role communities are playing in natural resource conservation in their ecotourism areas.

Challenges for ecotourism in Botswana

Ecotourism development in Botswana faces a number of challenges that affect its objectives to improve rural livelihoods and natural resource conservation, including the following:

*   competition from enclave tourism;
*   a lack of marketing and entrepreneurship skills among local people;
*   a lack of re-investment of the funds generated by ecotourism;
*   mismanagement of the funds generated by ecotourism; and
*   the lack of a fair or equitable distribution of benefits from ecotourism.

Enclave tourism and ecotourism

The main challenge that faces ecotourism development in Botswana is competition from a predominently foreign-owned and well developed tourism industry described as 'enclave tourism'. Enclave tourism in Botswana also has the characteristics of mass tourism, particularly in terms of poor environmental management. Ecotourism and enclave tourism in Botswana, particularly in the rich wildlife areas of the Okavango Delta and Chobe regions, compete for the same natural resources of land, wildlife and scenic beauty. Land allocated on concession to safari operators who practise enclave tourism is right next to that allocated to rural communities for ecotourism purposes. Enclave tourism and ecotourism also compete for the same clientele –mostly from North America, Europe and Australia/New Zealand (Mbaiwa, 2005). Enclave tourism in

Botswana is characterized by tourism facilities being under foreign ownership, top management positions that attract better salaries being held by expatriates, the repatriation of funds from Botswana to developed countries; and its failure to contribute effectively to poverty alleviation in Botswana (Mbaiwa, 2005). While enclave tourism brings insignificant benefits (e.g. employment, income, ownership of facilities, etc.) to local people, ecotourism revenue benefits accrue to the communities participating in ecotourism development.

Even though enclave tourism and ecotourism development in Botswana compete for the same resources and clientele, local communities cannot match their foreign counterparts, particularly when the competition is the foreign-owned safari companies. Foreign-owned companies possess the necessary entrepreneurial skills in tourism, such as the ability to market their product in developed countries where the tourists originate. They also have management skills and technological know-how which are not readily available among local groups. Foreign-owned companies also have strong financial capital with which to establish tourism projects while local investors lack the necessary funds. In this respect, enclave tourism remains one of the main challenges to ecotourism development in Botswana.

Lack of entrepreneurial skills in tourism development

Local communities involved in ecotourism face problems because of their limited entrepreneurial skills, especially in the marketing of their ecotourism products. The level of education among indigenous populations is low and the ability to communicate in English, French, German, Spanish or any other foreign language by rural communities is meagre or almost non-existent. Similarly, limited skills in marketing will mean a lack of the necessary negotiating business skills in ecotourism development, especially with clients and other safari operators involved in joint-venture partnerships. For this reason, most Trusts have opted for joint partnerships with international safari companies who have the skills and experience in tourism development. The Government of Botswana expect joint-venture partnerships to transfer entrepreneurial and management skills from safari operators to the local people (DWNP, 1999). However, the joint-venture partnership system in Botswana is very weak and there has been no significant transfer of such skills between safari hunting operators and Trusts (Mbaiwa, 2007). There has been no quantifiable collaboration and learning between safari companies and communities as was expected by the Government. The acquisition of entrepreneurial and managerial skills therefore remains one of the major challenges for communities involved in ecotourism in Botswana.

Lack of re-investment, mismanagement and misappropriation of funds

The lack of entrepreneurial skills by communities has also led to funds obtained from ecotourism projects either being kept in the bank without being re-invested, or being misappropriated or mismanaged (Mbaiwa, 2007). For example, in 2000,

DWNP (2000, p4) noted there had been a misappropriation of funds amounting to P12,500 by some members of the Okavango Kopano Mokoro Community Trust (OKMCT) in the Okavango Delta. Another example is that of the Khwai Development Trust (KDT), where the Board of Trustees misappropriated about P400,000 between 2002 and 2003. This money was unaccounted for following an audit conducted by Meyer and Associates (Potts, 2003). Potts (2003, p4) notes that the KDT board members were not following proper financial or accounting procedures. He notes, 'the KDT does not have a business or annual work plan – no proper budgeting was done and hence no control over trust finances. Money was just spent in a willy-nilly and haphazard fashion resulting in there being no receipts, supporting documents or paper to follow'. The misuse and poor management of trust funds by the KDT board is a reflection of what happens in most of the Trusts in the Okavango Delta.

Lack of fair distribution of benefits from ecotourism

Trusts generally lack a mechanism for the equitable or fair distribution of benefits derived from ecotourism (Mbaiwa, 2007). This problem threatens the sustainability of ecotourism projects in Botswana. Poor distribution of benefits is a result of factors such as ineffective coordination between those in Trust leadership and the rest of the general membership (Mbaiwa, 2004b). For example, the Okavango Community Trust has been cited for poor communication between trusts board members and the wider community members (DWNP, 2000). The Board of Trustees has been accused by general members of running the trust with little participation by other community members leading to disparities in benefit sharing (Rozemeijer and van der Jagt, 2000). This indicates that only the emerging elite, who are at the helm of trust management teams, benefit from ecotourism while the majority of the community members derive little or no benefit. The distribution of benefits is probably the most crucial component of ecotourism development in Botswana. As such, if it is not worked out in sufficient detail, it becomes a potential stumbling block for the success of ecotourism in Botswana. This, however, does not suggest that all ecotourism projects are not performing well, some – particularly that of Sankoyo – are reported to be doing far better than other projects in achieving the goal of rural development in remote areas of Botswana (Arntzen et al, 2003). Table 9.7 shows the progress made by some of the ecotourism enterprises in the Okavango Delta.

Response to mismanagement of funds in ecotourism projects

In order to address problems of financial mismanagement in ecotourism projects, most of the projects have resorted to employing qualified people in management and financial accounting positions. For example, some of the ecotourism projects have employed Trust Managers who are charged with the responsibility to manage ecotourism projects as executive officers and report to the Board of Trustees. The Trust Manager is responsible for the day-to-day business operation

Table 9.7 *Brief review on progress made by CBNRM Projects, 2000*

Name of CBO	Village(s) Involved	Comments on progress
Sankuyo Tshwaragano Management Trust	Sankuyo	• households get annual dividends of P500.00 • built 40 Enviro Loo toilets for 40 households (not operating) • purchased a Land Cruiser, built an office and social centre • running a Santawani Lodge, Kazikini Campsite, etc. • kiosk stopped operating due to losses • leasing land for hunting and photographic tourism to other safari companies
Okavango Community Trust	Seronga, Eretsha, Gunotsoga, Beetsha, Gudigwa	• bought a plot at Seronga with shop, bottlestore, guest house and office (shop and bottlestore closed due to mismanagement of funds • built a shop at Beetsha (shop operating) • kiosks in Gunotsoga, Eretsha and Gudingwa closed down due to mismanagement of funds • purchased 2 Land Cruisers, I truck and a motor boat (motor boat not operational due to break down)
Mababe Zokotsana Community Trust	Mababe	• bought a vehicle, besides sub-leasing their land and sale of wildlife quota, they have no immediate plans for what to do in terms of investing in the tourism business • leasing land for photographic and hunting purposes
Okavango Kopano Mokoro Community Trust	Ditshiping, Boro Xaxaba, Daunara, Xharaxao, Xuxao	• bought a Land Cruiser • progress to invest in other activities not forthcoming
Khwai Development Trust	Khwai	• constructing two tourist camps (traditional villages) in their community areas • operating a lodge, hunting and photographic campsite
Cgaecgae Tlhabologo Trust	Xaixai	• office, campsite, trust hall, craft shop and guest house are operational • bought a Land Cruiser • future plans to operate a bakery and a vegetable garden

of ecotourism projects. In other words, Trust Managers operate as Chief Executive Officers of ecotourism projects. These are persons qualified in the field of business. In the past, the Boards of Trustees have been charged with this responsibility a system that has proved to be inadequate. In addition to having Trust Managers, the Government has resorted to demanding audited annual financial statements before communities can have their licences renewed and wildlife quota released.

In 2007, the Botswana Government took a further step and passed a CBNRM Policy, whereby 65 per cent of the funds from any community reported to be misusing funds is deposited in the government conservation fund. This policy also gives the Minister responsible –the Minister of Wildlife, Tourism and Environment –a waiver for communities that manage their finances well. The employment of Trust Managers is one of the steps that communities involved in ecotourism development have taken to address the problems of financial misuse. However, if implemented, the 65 per cent required by government has the potential to result in the collapse of ecotourism projects in Botswana. This is because, as pointed out by communities such as those of Sankoyo, the 35 per cent remaining in the communities is too little even to pay for the running costs of their office. While there are problems of a lack of entrepreneurial skills, marketing, financial mismanagement and many others in ecotourism projects, in the last decade ecotourism projects in the Okavango Delta have addressed these areas. They have provided training for their people to enable them to acquire the necessary skills to run ecotourism projects and, where they have limited capacity, they employ people from outside who do have such skills.

Conclusion

The reality of ecotourism development in Botswana is that it is still in its infancy. As a result, it has not made a considerable impact yet in terms of achieving rural development and conservation in most villages. However, there is no doubt that in some villages, especially in the Okavango Delta, it significantly contributes to the improvement of rural livelihoods. Of particular interest is the availability of game meat, the creation of employment opportunities, income generation, access to land and wildlife resources as well as funeral benefits and recreation services.

Even though ecotourism has improved rural livelihoods in some of the villages in Botswana, it is also characterized by problems such as a lack of indigenous skills in tourism development; the misappropriation of funds and a lack of re-investment of the funds generated by ecotourism. As such, if ecotourism is to improve rural livelihoods and sustainable natural resource use, the empowerment of local groups through training in entrepreneurial and managerial skills in tourism should be given priority. This will reduce the problems associated with re-investment, mismanagement or misappropriation of funds. Training of local communities can be achieved through both formal and informal training programmes. This goal has the potential to promote sustainable rural livelihoods and the conservation of natural resources in Botswana. This means that the major stakeholders involved in ecotourism development – the Government of Botswana and NGOs such as Conservation International, Kalahari Conservation Society, the SNV-Netherlands and local communities – should develop a manual that will guide the activities of Trusts, particularly in relation to financial management and environmental management of their ecotourism areas.

Ecotourism finds itself competing with an already established tourism industry, that is, enclave tourism. However, small-scale ecotourism projects, if properly managed, are less harmful to the environment and can thus promote sustainable development of natural resources in the Okavango Delta. Britton and Clarke (1987) note that small-scale projects, locally controlled, can have a significant impact on raising the living standards of local people. However, small-scale tourist projects are unlikely to meet the needs of large numbers of tourists as well as the interests of some rich tourists that currently visit the Delta from overseas. As a result, some large-scale tourism projects, involving big hotels and lodges, are inevitable in the Okavango region. Therefore, small-scale and high-cost tourism projects should complement each other. Government planners should coordinate investment in tourism infrastructure that takes into consideration the needs of small-scale entrepreneurs and those of the local communities instead of putting the focus on developing a high-cost tourism industry alone, as emphasized by the high-cost–low-volume tourism policy. Carter (1991) states that large-scale development is often the precursor to small-scale development. That is, as tourism development proceeds, indigenous firms, industries and locals gain knowledge and experience. It is from this perspective that the National Ecotourism Strategy is perceived as one means to empower rural communities to develop tourism enterprises and benefit from the growing international tourism industry in the country. In 2007, the Botswana Parliament passed a bill that reserved some of the tourism activities such as guest houses, mobile safaris and other small-scale enterprises for ecotourism communities. This approach is one way of shifting tourism from a purely enclave form to ecotourism in Botswana.

Notes

1   US$1 = P1.6 (Botswana Pula) as at June 2007.

References

Arntzen, J. W. (2003) *An Economic View on Wildlife Management Areas in Botswana.* CBNRM Support Programme Occasional Paper No. 10, Gaborone
Arntzen, J., Molokomme, K., Tshosa, O., Moleele, N., Mazambani, D., and Terry, B. (2003) *Review of CBNRM in Botswana.* Applied Research Unit, Gaborone
Bjork, P. (2000) 'Ecotourism from a conceptual perspective, an extended definition of a unique tourism form', *International Journal of Tourism Research*, vol 2, 189–202

Bolaane, M. (2004) 'The impact of game reserve policy on the River BaSarwa/Bushmen of Botswana', *Social Policy and Administration*, vol 38, no 4, 399–417

Britton, S. and Clarke, W. C. (eds) (1987) *Ambiguous Alternative: Tourism in Small Developing Countries*. University of South Pacific, Fiji

Carter, E. (1991) 'Sustainable tourism in the Third World: Problems and prospects', Discussion Paper No. 3, University of Reading, Reading, 32pp

Ceballos-Lascurain, H. (1996) *Tourism, Ecotourism and Protected Areas*, IUCN, Gland

Darkoh, M. B. K. and Mbaiwa, J. E. (2005) *Natural Resource Utilisation and Land Use Conflicts in the Okavango Delta, Botswana*, Department of Environmental Science and Harry Oppenheimer Okavango Research Centre, University of Botswana.

Department of Tourism (DOT) (2002) *Botswana National Eco-Tourism Strategy: Final Report*. Department of Tourism, Gaborone

Department of Wildlife and National Parks (DWNP) (1999) *Joint Venture Guidelines*, Department of Wildlife and National Parks, Gaborone

Dowling, R. K. (2000) 'Developing ecotourism into the millennium', *International Journal of Tourism Research*, vol 2, 203–8.

DWNP (2000) *CBNRM Progress Report for 2000*, Department of Wildlife and National Parks, Gaborone

Fidzani, B., Mlenga, W. S., Atlhopheng, M. and Shatera, M. M. (1999) *Socio-Economic Effects of CBPP in Ngamiland*, Division of Agricultural Planning and Statistics, Ministry of Agriculture

Gaolatlhe, B. (2006) *The Budget Speech of 2003/4*, Ministry of Finance and Development Planning, Gaborone

Government of Botswana (2003) *National Development Plan Eight 2003–8*, Gaborone Printer, Gaborone

Mbaiwa, J. E. (2002) 'The sustainable use of wildlife resources among the Basarwa of Khwai and Mababe in Ngamiland District, Botswana: The past and present perspectives', *Pula: Botswana Journal of African Studies*, vol 16, no 2, 110–22

Mbaiwa, J. E. (2004a) 'The socio-economic impacts and challenges of a community-based safari hunting tourism in the Okavango Delta, Botswana', *Journal of Tourism Studies*, vol 15, no 2, 37–50

Mbaiwa, J. E. (2004b) 'The success and sustainability of community-based natural resource management in the Okavango Delta, Botswana', *South African Geographical Journal*, vol 86, no 1, 44–53

Mbaiwa, J. E. (2005) 'Enclave tourism and its socio-economic impacts in the Okavango Delta, Botswana', *Tourism Management*, vol 26, no 2, 157–72

Mbaiwa, J. E. (2007) 'The success and sustainability of consumptive wildlife tourism in Africa', in B. Lovelock (ed.), *Tourism and the Consumption of Wildlife: Hunting, Shooting and Sport Fishing*. Routledge, London, pp141–154

National CBNRM Forum (2001) 'Proceedings of the Second National CBNRM Conference in Botswana, 14–16 November 2001', IUCN/SNV CBNRM Support Programme, Gaborone

Potts, F. (2003) *Khwai Development Trust-A Short Case Study*, Eco-tourism Support Services, Maun

Rozemeijer, N. and Van der Jagt, C. (2000) 'Community based natural resource management in Botswana: How community based is community based natural resource management in Botswana, Occasional Paper Series, IUCN/SNV CBNRM Support Programme, Gaborone

Schuster, B. (2007) Proceedings of the 4th National CBNRM Conference in Botswana and the CBNRM Status Report. 20–23 November 2006. IUCN Botswana, Gaborone

Thakadu, O. T. (1997) 'Indigenous wildlife management knowledge systems and their role in facilitating community based wildlife management projects in Botswana', MSc Thesis, University of Natal

Twyman, C. (2000) 'Participatory conservation? Community-based natural resource management in Botswana', *The Geographical Journal*, vol 166, no 4, 323–335

UNDP (2005) *Human Development Report 2005*. United Nations Development Program, New York

Valentine, P. (1993) 'Ecotourism and nature conservation. A definition with some recent developments in Micronesia', *Tourism Management*, vol 14, no 2, 107–115

10

Citizen Participation in the Lodge Sector of the Okavango Delta

Peter John Massyn

Introduction

Increasingly, policy makers have come to view wildlife – and the 'African safari lodge' industry based on it – as a resource uniquely suited to the needs of rural development. The safari lodge sector, in the form in which it has evolved in southern Africa, is often seen as an important source of employment and revenue generation for rural people who would otherwise exist on the margins of the societies in which they live (Ashley et al, 2000; Massyn and Koch, 2004, Poultney and Spenceley, 2001). However, there is also widespread concern that the pro-poor benefits of the sector are muted by factors such as remoteness, skills shortages, insecure land rights and generally weak levels of human and social capital. These elements typically combine to create situations in which the local poor provide only menial labour while external interests capture the lion's share of the benefits generated by the tourism market (Massyn, 2007). This results in a skewed distribution of returns that has led some commentators to question whether the African safari lodge sector is 'socioeconomically sustainable' (Mbaiwa, 2003, 2005; Perkins, 2005).

Since the 1980s, the Okavango Delta in northern Botswana's Ngamiland District has emerged as an iconic 'high value, low volume' African destination. Today, it hosts one of the continent's largest and most successful safari lodge clusters (Massyn and Koch, 2004). As such, it has attracted widespread attention from policy makers and academics interested in the poverty-reducing impacts of wildlife tourism. A leading voice in this regard is that of Mbaiwa, a scholar attached to the University of Botswana's Harry Oppenheimer Okavango

Research Centre (see Chapter 9 by Mbaiwa) , who has used the delta to exemplify what he calls the 'enclavic nature' of the safari lodge sector (Mbaiwa, 2005, p464):

> *The foreign domination and ownership of tourism facilities has led to the repatriation of tourism revenue, domination of management positions by expatriates, lower salaries for citizen workers, and a general failure by tourism to significantly contribute to rural poverty alleviation in the Okavango region. Tourism as a result has a minimal economic impact on rural development mainly because it has weak linkages with the domestic economy, particularly agriculture.*

> (Mbaiwa, 2003, p1)

To counter this situation, Mbaiwa argues for a 'sustainable' form of tourism based on local control of the industry, which will, in his opinion, ensure 'benefits to local people and the sustainable use of resources' (Mbaiwa, 2005, p463). This view falls squarely within a broader tendency in the tourism studies literature that regards mainstream tourism as necessarily exploitative of local economies and resources. These critiques – rooted in earlier dependency perspectives – argue in favour of 'sustainable' or 'alternative' tourism that is 'small-scale, indigenously owned, environmentally sensitive and ... authentic' (Mitchell and Ashley, 2006; Mbaiwa, 2003, 2005).

Recently, however, some commentators associated with the Overseas Development Institute's Tourism Programme, have rejected this approach. Mitchell and Ashley, for example, argue that it constitutes a 'strategic mistake' because it deflects the pro-poor focus away from mainstream tourism – which alone has the 'muscle' to reduce African poverty – towards 'the comfortable ghetto of small, niche operations' (Mitchell and Ashley, 2006, p1). They argue that the depiction of high value, international tourism as a 'neo-colonial' activity characterized by huge 'leakage' of benefits is not generally supported by rigorous empirical analysis. Moreover, it involves a turning away from the broad thrust in contemporary thinking, which regards outward-orientated global processes, rooted in the market and private enterprise, as the main drivers of global poverty reduction (Mitchell and Ashley, 2006, p2).

Against the background of these debates, this chapter draws on new data (sourced from recent government statistics, an industry survey and focus group discussions) to re-examine the Okavango's high value lodge sector. It shows that tourism in the delta already brings significant benefit to local citizens, primarily through employment in safari lodges. But it also supports the view that the sector is not well integrated, especially at the local level, and that a relatively low percentage of tourist spend is earned by local and national interests. Unlike Mbaiwa it does not regard this as a neo-colonial affront that requires radical 'indigenization'. Instead, the chapter argues that a degree of 'leakage' is a necessary consequence of the socio-cultural roots and global structure of wildlife tourism and may be better regarded as a form of 'gearing' that is necessary to attract tourist spend at the local level. The policy challenge is therefore not so much the radical restructuring of the sector to break 'foreign domination' and ensure local control; the question is rather what practical measures may be taken to increase the participation of local people – especially the local poor – in a robust but globally integrated sector.

Ownership

The northern Botswana tourism cluster has its roots in the late 1950s when hunting safari companies from East Africa began visiting with their clients. Trophy hunting dominated until the 1970s when the photographic tourism sector started to emerge led largely by expatriates from east and southern Africa who obtained tribal or state leases in the prime areas of the delta. International media exposure, proclaiming the Okavango as the 'jewel of the Kalahari', rapid growth in the disposable income of northern source markets as well as improvements in land and air communications, provided a stimulus for long haul tourists to visit northern Botswana and resulted in rapid growth of the sector during the following two decades. As these new markets developed, the number of establishments burgeoned and the quality of tourism accommodation and services improved, but the ownership patterns set in the early years remained largely intact (Massyn and Koch, 2004).

By the early 1990s, the first generation of tourism leases in the delta terminated. Second-round 'concessions' were subsequently awarded within a framework set by a raft of new regulatory instruments (including the 1991 Land Use Plan, the 1990 Tourism Policy and the 1992 Tourism Act). Under the new dispensation, 15-year leases were offered via competitive tender, ostensibly to Botswana citizens (or legal entities registered in Botswana). Despite these restrictions, incumbents – particularly a South-African-based group known as Wilderness Safaris – were exceptionally successful in recapturing the prime concession areas mainly through the use of subleasing arrangements. Although industry players are reluctant to disclose such arrangements, it is known that citizen leasees often collect substantial premiums in what appears to be classic rent-seeking manoeuvres. This practice forms part of a complex – but rarely discussed – system of rent apportionment that characterizes the Botswana system. It allows Botswana nationals to interpose themselves between the state and (mostly expatriate) third parties to appropriate a portion of the rents generated by commerce in Ngamiland (Massyn and Koch, 2004).

Interestingly, the leases awarded during the 1990s do not contain explicit provisions regarding citizen participation. It appears the land leases do not impose contractually enforceable obligations on lodge operators to ensure greater equity in their labour and procurement practices. Operators are required to submit a 'localization and training plan' to the Commissioner of Labour and to submit annual reports providing information on their practices in this regard. But it appears there is no consistent monitoring or enforcement of these plans by the Botswana authorities and that Government has therefore not used its position as landowner and regulator to advance citizen participation at the operational level of the Okavango's lodge sector.

This short historical sketch highlights an important facet of tourism in the delta: the development of the sector was largely driven by expatriates (or Botswana nationals of European descent) with links to east and southern Africa who – sometimes in rent-sharing partnerships with members of the Botswana nationals elite – have continued to dominate ownership patterns. This trajectory is strengthened by the global structure of high value tourism, which finds its source markets in the (mainly white) north-Atlantic world and relies on complex sets of personal, cultural and commercial linkages between in-country operators and northern suppliers (and markets). This racialized pattern is further reinforced by the branding strategies associated with African safari lodges. The sector typically taps into a semiotics of wild Africa rooted in a romanticized vision of the continent as a place of spectacular but savage beauty sparsely populated by exotic tribesmen and heroic Western explorers. This notion is deeply embedded in the Western imagination and provides a rich repository of images, continually reinforced in the popular media:

> *Europeans invented a mythical Africa, which soon claimed a place of privilege in the Western imagination. We cling to our faith in Africa as a glorious Eden for wildlife. The sights and sounds we instinctively associate with wild Africa – lions, zebra, giraffe, rhinos, and especially elephants – fit into the dream of a refuge from the technological age. We are unwilling to let that dream slip away... The march of civilization has tamed or destroyed the wilderness of North America and Europe, but the emotional need for wild places, for vast open spaces like the plains of Africa, persists*
> (Adams and McShane, 1996, pxii).

This dream – which is rooted in the colonial era and generally denies or ignores the history of dispossession and struggle that shaped the continent's rural landscapes – has formed popular perceptions of Africa in the West and provided fertile soil for the branding of the Okavango Delta in its main source markets. Typically, the experience on offer in the Okavango is marketed as a journey into the authentic and pristine mediated by skilled, mostly expatriate (white) guides assisted by unskilled local (black) labourers (Massyn and Koch, 2004; Turner, 2004; Wells, 1996). These expectations tend to entrench racialized employment patterns by focusing on the safari guide as a latter day version of the early Western explorer. Disrupting such expectations may reduce the appeal of the Okavango in its principal (northern) markets (Turner, 2004; Wells, 1996).

However, the rise of demand from tourists for a more ethical approach coupled with people-friendly reforms in the conservation sector has seen the beginnings of a shift in the expectations and practices associated with the lodge sector. Some enterprises – often located on communal land or based on some other form of partnership with local people – have self-consciously promoted beneficial linkages with the rural poor. But generally the new pro-poor practices

Table 10.1 *Ownership of tourism businesses in Ngamiland (by number)*

Ownership	2000	2005	% change
Citizen-owned	16	62	46
Joint venture	36	59	23
Foreign-owned	51	80	29
Totals	103	201	98

Source: Botswana Department of Tourism, 2005

sit uncomfortably in a sector steeped in the imagery of colonialism on land formerly occupied by the rural poor. One of the deep, but often unrecognized, challenges of the African lodge sector is therefore to renovate not only its business practices by building stronger linkages with the rural poor but also to discover a new brand based on imagery appropriate to changed circumstances.

Against this background, the latest ownership statistics for Ngamiland compiled by the Botswana authorities makes for interesting reading.

The figures indicate that the tourism industry in Ngamiland continued to expand rapidly between 2000 and 2005 with the overall number of enterprises nearly doubling. During this period, the number of citizen-owned businesses increased by almost 300 per cent, but 139 (or nearly 70 per cent) of the 201 businesses operational in 2005 were still either wholly or partly owned by non-citizens.

Table 10.2 indicates that most Category A businesses in Ngamiland (hotels, bed and breakfasts, and motels) are citizen-owned. Ownership of Category B facilities (safari lodges), which include most of the high value lodges in the Okavango Delta, is still dominated by foreigners either through direct holdings or via joint ventures with citizens. Of the 107 enterprises in this category, nearly 77 per cent (82 of 107) have some form of foreign ownership. Likewise, 66 per cent (47 of 71) of the Category C businesses (mobile operators) and 72 per cent (8 of 11) of the Category D businesses (travel agencies) involve foreign ownership (Figure 10.1).

The ownership figures provided by the Department of Tourism segment the industry by number and category of enterprise. They do not provide an indication of the scale or value of the individual enterprises nor do they disaggregate the

Table 10.2 *Ownership of tourism businesses in Ngamiland (by category)*

Category	Totals	Ownership		
		Citizen	Joint-venture	Foreign
A	12	10	2	0
B	107	25	41	41
C	71	24	13	34
D	11	3	3	5
Totals	201	62	59	80

Source: Botswana Department of Tourism, 2005

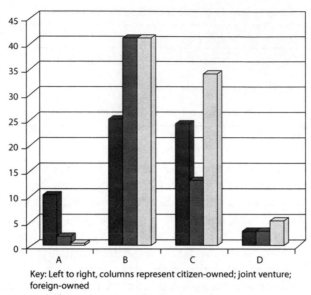

Key: Left to right, columns represent citizen-owned; joint venture; foreign-owned

Figure 10.1 *Ownership by business category*

'citizen' category by race or locality. But it is clear that so-called Category B enterprises include the flagship products of Ngamiland's tourism sector (the high value lodges of the Okavango) and that this category is dominated by foreign ownership either through direct holdings or via joint ventures with Botswana nationals. Although the figures are not available, it is evident that, if segmented by value, foreign ownership of tourism assets in Ngamiland would be even more prominent than in the numbers presented above (Category B enterprises include a large proportion of the sector's high value enterprises). The relatively high number of joint ventures are probably also an indication of the rent-seeking participation by Botswana nationals referred to above.

The high levels of foreign ownership evident in the lodge component of the Ngamiland tourism cluster – especially at the higher value end of the industry – is not surprising given the introductory discussion of this chapter. It is almost certainly a consequence of the expatriate-driven history of the cluster as well as the global character of high value tourism in general (which relies on worldwide linkages to penetrate its mainly international markets). Industry stakeholders in individual interviews and focus group discussions cited further reasons for the relatively low level of domestic ownership in the Ngamiland tourism sector. Some claimed that citizen participation was inhibited by a domestic culture that is risk-averse and non-entrepreneurial. Others referred to the absence of appropriate financial products designed to accommodate the specific cash flow needs of ecotourism enterprises while at the same time promoting citizen participation in the sector. It was claimed that the financial products offered by Botswana's Citizen Entrepreneurial Development Agency were not appropriate to the needs of the high value ecotourism sector, which is capital-intensive but typically suffers from long product development cycles and early liquidity problems. Cash-strapped citizens therefore struggled to raise the capital needed to finance equity in the sector.

Citizen participation survey

The Botswana authorities do not collate industry-wide figures summarizing tourism employment, procurement spend, lease incomes, etc. Tourism enterprises do submit annual reports to the land and labour authorities. As part of a rapid survey of citizen participation in the Ngamiland tourism sector, access was obtained to the 2005 returns of a number of high value lodge operations in the Okavango Delta (on condition that the individual enterprises remained anonymous). The survey was designed to assess the extent to which Botswana nationals participate in the core industry of the Okavango, especially as employees. It targeted 20 tourism operations involving 17 individual companies, employing 646 full-time employees and disbursing a total annual wage bill of P13,246 million.[1] Information was gleaned from the annual returns of the companies as well as follow up interviews and a brief focus group discussion with operators and representatives of local communities.

Structural arrangements

Three distinct landholding arrangements underpin the lodges surveyed in the Ngamiland cluster. Two of the operations fall within the Moremi Game Reserve and are held on medium-term leases from the Department of Wildlife and National Parks via the Tawana Land Board. Another two of the operations are situated on community-held leases and have been subleased to photographic tourism operators. The rest of the operations sampled are held on direct lease from the Tawana Land Board.

Employment

The 20 operations surveyed employed a total of 646 persons of which 585 were Botswana nationals and 61 were expatriates (Figure 10.2).

The total annual wage bill at the surveyed operations amounted to P13,246 million of which citizens captured P7718 million and non-citizens P5528 million. Citizens thus made up 90.6 per cent of the total workforce at the operations surveyed but captured only 58.3 per cent of the total payroll. Conversely, non-citizens, representing 9.4 per cent of total employees, earned 41.7 per cent of the total payroll.

There was very little variation between the surveyed operations, with all the lodges showing broadly similar trends. There was, for example, no evidence that citizens captured a greater percentage of the payroll at the operations on community-held leases.

Despite the significant disparity between the remuneration levels of citizens and expatriates, it is important to note that the operations surveyed employed an

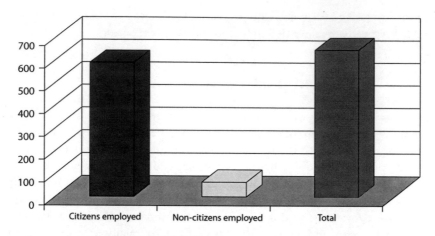

Figure 10.2 *Employment survey (n = 646)*

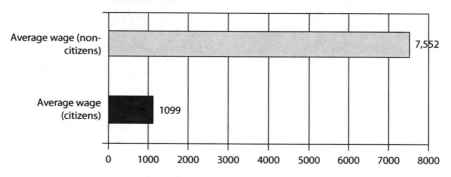

Figure 10.3 *Comparative wage levels*

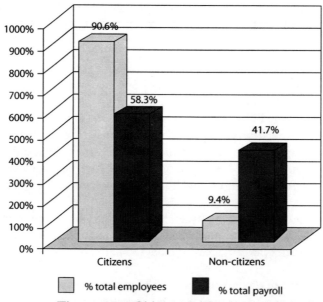

Figure 10.4 *Citizen participation (employment)*

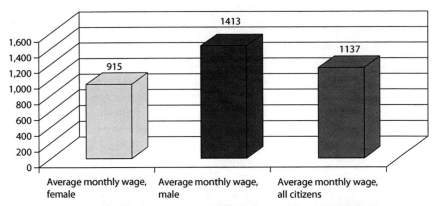

Figure 10.5 *Citizen employment: wages by gender*

average of 29.25 citizens and paid annual wages of P385,900 per lodge to citizens in 2005. Extrapolated across the 107 enterprises in Category B (see Table 10.2) this means the Ngamiland lodge sector probably disbursed a citizen payroll of more than P41 million and provided jobs to over 3000 citizens in 2005. This represents a very considerable pro-poor impact, particularly if one considers the deep rural status of Ngamiland.

Ten of the surveyed operations employing a total of 236 citizens provided information on the gender composition of their citizen workforces. These operations employed 116 citizen males (49.2 per cent of citizen employees) and 120 citizen females (50.8 per cent). Although women made up 50.8 per cent of the sample, they captured only 42.2 per cent of the total citizen payroll. The average monthly wage for women was P915 compared to P1137 for all citizen employees and P1413 for male citizens. Women earned only 64.8 per cent of the average wage paid to their male counterparts (Figure 10.5).

The survey confirms similar findings by Massyn and Koch (2004): Botswana women employed in high value lodges appear to be at a 'double disadvantage' compared to their male counterparts. The local workforce already receives much lower average pay than their expatriate colleagues but local women's average wage is lower still. The challenge in the Okavango lodge sector is therefore not only to increase the proportion of citizens – especially local residents – employed in higher paying positions but also to improve the position of Botswana women relative to their male compatriots.

Business linkages

Four of the operations surveyed provided estimates of the value of goods and services purchased from local rural residents. Local procurement at the four operations averaged just under P59,000 for the year. This amounts to approximately 8.9 per cent of the total local payroll benefits generated by the operations over the same period. This represents a small proportion compared to, for example, typical patterns in countries such as South Africa. It also confirms that the most important pro-poor impact of lodge tourism in the Okavango – like elsewhere in southern Africa – results principally from local employment rather than secondary business linkages (Mitchell, 2006; Massyn and Koch, 2004).

There is a small but high quality basket weaving sector in the Okavango Delta, which accounts for most local sales to the lodges. But overall, the very low level of secondary enterprise associated with the surveyed lodges probably reflects the fact that local settlements are generally geographically distant from the operations. In addition, low levels of local economic capacity in the hinterland of the lodges and the sophisticated needs of operations aimed at the upper end of the international tourism market combine to discourage the purchase of goods and services from so-called remote area dwellers. There is an inherent asymmetry between the consumption needs of high value tourism lodges and the supply capacity of the local rural economy, which hampers greater local integration and small business stimulation. This means that virtually all supplies and services are purchased outside the local economy, mainly from the district capital (Maun), which, in turn, is supplied mainly from Gaborone and South Africa.

Lease fees

Two lodges in the sample are located in areas held by community trusts under an arrangement whereby the state leases land at nominal rents to local communities who then sublease the land to private partners on conditions set by the state. This arrangement is a variation of the widespread practice of 'rent-collecting' partnerships in the Okavango: it gives certain communities – like their elite compatriots – the opportunity to obtain valuable land leases at relatively low prices which they then sublease at market rates earning them substantial incomes.

The resource rental paid to the community trusts for the rights to operate the photographic lodges on their land amounted to more than P555,000 per year for each of the two subleases. At these operations, lease income represented about one-third of the total local financial benefit generated by the lodges, employment about two-thirds and secondary enterprise an almost insignificant proportion (Figure 10.6).

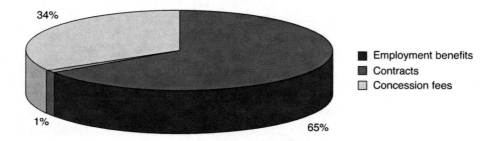

Figure 10.6 *Local benefits by category*

Conclusion and recommendations

This chapter has argued that safari lodge tourism in the Okavango already generates significant pro-poor benefit. There was a significant increase in the number of tourism businesses owned by citizens in the five years to 2005 and local nationals already capture a large proportion of the annual payroll associated with the sector. But the chapter also confirms the widespread view that, while tourism is the mainstay of the Ngamiland economy, increasing the participation of Botswana nationals – especially the local poor – remains an important challenge. The high value end of the sector is still dominated by foreign ownership (sometimes in partnership with rent-collecting nationals). This is probably a consequence of the fact that tourism in the Okavango was historically largely developed by expatriates and continues to rely on global linkages to secure market share. But it may also reflect the absence of a strong domestic entrepreneurial culture as well as appropriate financial products to help citizens capitalize equity, especially in the high value sector of the industry.

Citizens make up the vast majority of the workforce at each of the operations surveyed but large disparities exist between the remuneration levels of expatriates and citizens. Individual interviews and focus group discussions suggested a number of reasons for this disparity. They include skills shortages amongst Botswana nationals as well as reluctance amongst skilled citizens to work in the remote areas where many of the Ngamiland's tourism enterprises are located.

More than 50 per cent of the citizen workforce at the surveyed lodges was female but these women captured less than half the total citizen wage bill. This 'double disadvantage' gap is similar to patterns observed elsewhere in southern Africa. It strongly reinforces the notion that women are at a disadvantage both as citizens (compared to expatriates) but also as women (compared to their male compatriots) and that gender (as well as race) plays a role in structuring patterns of employment and remuneration in the Okavango.

From the above it is clear that employment equity in the Okavango's tourism sector has lagged, especially at senior employment levels where the use of expatriate labour is widespread. Given the fact that employment is by far the largest pro-poor impact of the lodge sector (Mafisa , 2002), this is an area of high strategic importance. Remedying this situation may be partially achieved through more efficient implementation of current government regulation coupled with targeted skills development initiatives. Weaknesses in the public sector's ability to administer existing regulations must be remedied and strategic interventions promoted that build the civil service's capacity in this regard.

Current tourism leases in the Okavango do not contain systematic provisions promoting citizen participation. Using land allocation procedures and instruments to promote greater domestic participation in a land-based sector such as tourism is a widely used method in other jurisdictions. Within the Southern African Development Community, countries such as Mauritius, Namibia and South Africa have successfully used a combination of regulation, licensing and conditional award of commercial rights to promote broad-based indigenous empowerment across a suite of categories (including ownership, employment, procurement, etc.). Many of the leases to the Okavango's prime areas are due to expire shortly; their imminent reallocation represents a strategic opportunity to advance citizen participation by integrating conditions promoting broad-based citizen participation into the new agreements.

This recommendation needs to be carefully qualified. While it is a critical function of government to create an enabling environment for greater citizen participation, it is nevertheless important that it does not adopt policies and practices that inhibit the market or create new opportunities for passive rent collecting by politically connected local elites. The policy test faced by the Botswana authorities is therefore to find an approach that encourages broad-based – especially local – citizen participation but avoids being so onerous and bureaucratic that it stifles the industry or forces it into a set of narrow alliances with a few powerful local individuals. Tourism – especially the high value lodge sector – depends on continual innovation and external linkages. The difficult but vital challenge is to use government's land leasing system to leverage greater citizen inclusion while continuing to foster the extraordinary success of the Okavango in international tourism markets. Importantly, this does not involve a turning away from outward-oriented, private sector-led tourism in the Okavango Delta. In this sense, it seeks to avoid the 'strategic mistake' referred to by Mitchell and Ashley (2006). Instead of advocating a withdrawal into 'alternative' forms of small-scale tourism, it promotes practical measures to use public 'planning gain' in the interest of greater local integration into the sector. In effect, it challenges government to use its position as public custodian to promote greater citizen participation while continuing to foster a sector that already generates significant economic activity in one of the remotest corners of Botswana.

Note

1   US$1 = 5.5371 Pula on 1 June 2005.

References

Adams, J. S. and McShane, T. O. (1996) *The Myth of Wild Africa – Conservation Without Illusion*, University of California Press, Los Angeles

Ashley, C., Boyd, C. and Goodwin, H. (2000) 'Pro-poor tourism: Putting poverty at the heart of the tourism agenda', *Natural Resource Perspectives*, no 61, Overseas Development Institute, London

Mafisa (2002) 'African game lodges and rural benefit: Key findings of six southern African case studies,' www.mafisa.co.za, accessed 20 July 2005

Massyn, P. J. and Koch, E. (2004) 'African game lodges and rural benefit in two southern African countries', in C. Rogerson and G. Visser (eds), *Tourism and Development Issues in Contemporary South Africa*, Africa Institute of South Africa, Pretoria, pp102–138

Massyn, P. J. (2007) 'Communal land reform and tourism investment in Namibia's communal areas: A question of unfinished business?' *Development Southern Africa*, vol 24, no 3, 381–392

Mbaiwa, J. E. (2003) 'The socio-economic and environmental impacts of tourism development in the Okavango Delta', *Journal of Arid Environments*, vol 54, 447–467

Mbaiwa, J. E. (2005) 'Enclave tourism and its socio-economic impacts in the Okavango Delta, Botswana', *Tourism Management*, vol 26, no 2, 157–172

Mitchell, J. and Ashley, C. (2006) 'Can tourism help reduce poverty in Africa?' *ODI Briefing Paper*, Overseas Development Institute, London

Perkins, J. S. (2005) 'Status and perspectives of regional tourism in the context of the KAZA-TFCA initiative', Unpublished paper, Biotrack Botswana (Pty) Ltd, Gaborone

Poultney, C. and Spenceley, A. (2001) 'Practical strategies for pro-poor tourism, Wilderness Safaris South Africa: Rocktail Bay and Ndumu Lodge,' www.propoor-tourism.org.uk, accessed 30 August 2005

Turner, R. (2004) 'Communities, conservation, and tourism-based development: Can community-based nature tourism live up to its promise?' http://repositories.cdlib.org/cas/breslauer/turner, accessed 31 August 2006

Wells, M. P. (1996) 'The economic and social role of protected areas in the new South Africa', unpublished policy paper 26, Land and Agriculture Policy Centre, Johannesburg

11

The Impacts of Tourism Initiatives on Rural Livelihoods and Poverty Reduction in South Africa: Mathenjwa and Mqobela

Murray C. Simpson

This chapter gives the summary results of two case studies conducted to analyse the impacts of tourism on rural livelihoods and poverty reduction in Maputaland, South Africa. The chapter reflects critically on the analyses, considers the potential roles of the private sector and elements that are important for communities to receive appropriate and effective livelihood benefits from tourism initiatives. The data were gathered through a structured and integrated assessment approach designed to evaluate more accurately the impacts of tourism initiatives on rural livelihoods and poverty reduction.

Background

Tourism neologisms such as ecotourism, pro-poor tourism, community tourism, sustainable tourism, responsible tourism and community benefit tourism (Goodwin, 1996; Mowforth and Munt, 1998; Swarbrooke, 1999; Ashley et al, 2001; WWF, 2001; Goodwin and Francis, 2003; Simpson, 2008a) are based on the premise that tourism in a generic sense should develop in an environmentally, economically and socially sustainable manner. However, despite the undoubted importance of these goals it has been difficult to assess the success of tourism initiatives that aim to benefit the environment and local communities whilst also being financially viable (Ashley, 2002; WTO, 2004). One of the most problematic areas of assessment has been to quantify the impacts of tourism on communities, poverty reduction and local livelihoods.

The relationships and interactions between tourism, poverty reduction and rural livelihoods are complex, requiring considerable debate and research, which to date has been somewhat lacking (Cheong and Miller, 2000; Jafari, 2001; Sofield, 2003; Rogerson, 2006; Hall, 2007; Scheyvens, 2007; Simpson, 2008b). Proponents of poverty alleviation and rural development through tourism have ambitious goals (Sharpley, 2002; Briedenhann and Wickens, 2004; Saarinen, 2007). Critics of such high objectives question core concepts such as: the level and type of benefits being delivered to the rural poor; the roles of tourists, tour operators and other stakeholders in the poverty–tourism equation; the value and effect of trade-offs between the negative impacts on the environment and communities' culture and traditions in comparison to the supposed livelihood enhancements; and the lack of research into the intricate relationships between the development goals of marginalized communities and the objectives of tourism initiatives (Mowforth and Munt, 1998, 2003; Cheong and Miller, 2000; Davis, 2001; Gossling et al, 2004; Hall, 2007; Scheyvens, 2007; Simpson, 2008a).

In addition to the paucity and fragmented nature of research on the topic and despite on-going conceptual discussions concerning the relationships between development and tourism (De Kadt, 1979; Lea, 1988; Eadington and Smith, 1994; Mowforth and Munt 1998, 2003; Deloitte & Touche et al, 1999; Scheyvens, 2007; Harrison, 2007), there also appears to be a lack of consensus about appropriate and effective methodologies with which to assess whether in fact tourism is reducing poverty and enhancing livelihoods in given situations. The majority of work conducted is highly subjective and difficult to compare (Visser and Rogerson, 2004; Zhao and Ritchie, 2007; Spenceley and Goodwin, 2007; Harrison, 2007). Tourism's relationship with rural development, poverty and livelihoods is convoluted and fraught with conflicts and challenges, and the surge of tourism to rural and peripheral areas has wide-ranging implications for development and the livelihoods of rural communities (Sharpley and Roberts, 2004; Hall, 2007; Scheyvens, 2007; Simpson, 2008a). The limited amount of critical debate combined with a lack of primary research and the use of methodologies that are inadequate and extremely difficult to replicate has led to calls for an elemental reassessment of the interrelationships between tourism, development and rural livelihoods and poverty reduction (Visser and Rogerson, 2004; Gossling et al, 2004; Scheyvens, 2007; Chok et al, 2007). There is clearly a pressing requirement not only for a replicable and robust analytical framework to evaluate the relationships, processes and impacts associated with the issues surrounding tourism and development but also a need to evaluate more critically tourism's interactions with poverty and rural livelihoods.

The protocol and the results

To provide a comprehensive and valid assessment of the impacts of tourism on livelihoods, data were gathered through a structured and integrated assessment protocol that included participatory methods, secondary/archival data collection, semi-structured interviews and structured questionnaires used in a household survey (see Simpson, 2008b for a detailed discussion of the integrated methodology). Data collection and research was carried out in the field at the study sites, in the administrative centres of South Africa and KwaZulu-Natal and through the analysis of secondary data in 2004 and 2005. An initial livelihood analysis of the existing socioeconomic conditions was carried out through the collection of baseline data.

Whilst there are no specific methods or tools prescribed for carrying out livelihood analysis (Ashley and Carney, 1999; Simpson, 2008b), participation is one of the underlying principles of sustainable livelihoods (SL) approaches and this stage of the methodology broadly followed similar lines to those described by Ashley (2002). However, these studies conducted in Maputaland were considerably strengthened by more detailed and clearly sequenced techniques such as participatory mapping, 'H' diagrams and ranking exercises (SEI, 1998; Ashley and Hussein, 2000; Guy and Inglis, 1999; Mayoux, 2001; Simpson, 2008b). The methodology used in these studies also extended and enhanced SL approaches and earlier tourism impact assessments through the use of a household level survey (analysed using SPSS v14.0) and the semi-structured interviewing of a purposeful sub-set sample (De Vaus, 2001) which, when integrated with the livelihoods analysis, provided a robust assessment and monitoring tool. As part of this integrated approach, participatory techniques were used in the initial stages and continued throughout the life of the fieldwork. Throughout the assessment process participatory techniques also provided a mechanism for ensuring the representation of less vocal groups or individuals within the community. To provide structure and the ability to replicate the approach in different spatial and temporal scales the integrated assessment protocol was divided into a seven stage process (Simpson, 2008b) (Figure 11.1).

The protocol was implemented in two case studies in South Africa. Rocktail Bay Lodge and Ndumo Wilderness Camp are located in Maputaland, northeastern KwaZulu-Natal (see Figure 11.2). These study sites were chosen due to their geographic position on the continent of Africa, the poorest in the world. These two initiatives, with their ground-breaking ownership structure and complex stakeholder relationships also provided interesting and unique case studies in different locations with which to better examine the processes, impacts and interactions occurring at the tourism–poverty livelihoods nexus.

Both enterprises are nature-based tourism lodge initiatives operated by Wilderness Safaris (WS), a safari specialist that operates camps and safaris mainly in Southern Africa. WS is over 24 years old and has an ethos focused on environmental protection and community development. In Maputaland, WS are engaged in community–private–public partnerships (CPPP). Local residents and

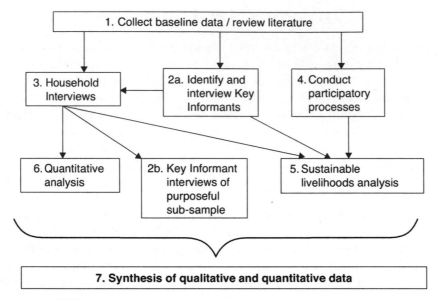

Source: Simpson, 2008b

Figure 11.1 *Integrated assessment protocol for measuring and monitoring the impacts of tourism on community development and sustainable livelihoods*

the park authority became shareholders in the lodges at their inception; this was the first time in South Africa that the conservation authorities, the surrounding local communities and the private sector had jointly built lodges within a proclaimed park where each party owned equity in the operation. The communities involved in each of the tourism initiatives; the Mathenjwa in the case of Ndumo Wilderness Camp and the Mqobela in the Rocktail Bay Lodge initiative, are rural based, with approximately 1000 and 200 households respectively in the community areas adjacent to the reserve where the tourism initiative is located.

In the case of Ndumo Lodge, WS own 50 per cent of the lodge operating company (LOC). Isivuno is a Section 21 (not for profit) company formed as the trading arm of what is now KwaZulu-Natal Nature Conservation Services (KZNNCS) and owns 37.5 per cent of the LOC, while the Mathenjwa Community Trust hold the remaining 12.5 per cent. The LOC's tenure is based on a 20-year lease arranged with the Lodge Owning Company (LOC#2) which commenced in 1995. The LOC#2 ownership structure is as follows; Ithala Bank 42 per cent, Isivuno 43.5 per cent and the Mathenjwa Community Trust 14.5 per cent. This ownership structure mirrors that of the arrangement entered into by WS with the Mqobela Community in Rocktail Bay Lodge, a tourism initiative on the coast of Maputaland commenced in 1992 (Poultney and Spenceley, 2001; Massyn and Koch, 2004; Simpson, 2008b). Due to the involvement of the Mathenjwa community at both owning and operating company levels, the Mathenjwa Community Trust receive a fixed amount every quarter, being 14.5 per cent of the lease and in addition they also expect to receive a variable amount

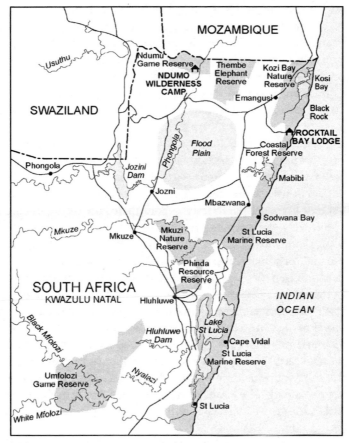

Figure 11.2 *Map of Maputaland, Northern KwaZulu Natal*

every quarter this being 12.5 per cent of the turnover of the LOC. The Mathenjwa Community Trust, its directors and trustees are appointed to operate the trust and spend the funds received on behalf of and in consultation with the Mathenjwa community who live adjacent to the area of the coastal reserve where Ndumo Wilderness Camp is located (Simpson, 2007).

In the case of Rocktail Bay Lodge there are in fact two communities virtually equidistant from the lodge. In addition to the Mqobela community there is the Mpukane community, of approximately 150 households, who are also located adjacent to the area of the coastal reserve where the lodge is based. There are different opinions as to where the borders of each community meet, suffice to say that, whilst the lodge is within the coastal reserve, each community and its various community leaders believe that the lodge's buildings lie either exactly on the historical boundary line of the communities or just one side or the other. It is believed that during the period that the arrangement was reached with the Mqobela community regarding their ownership percentage of LOC and LOC#2, there was some confusion in the Mpukane community with regard to leadership and direction. The community's Nduna (headman) had recently passed away and there does not seem to have been a strong executive at the time and neither an immediate replacement at Nduna level nor a willingness to become quickly involved in the negotiations taking place. At the same time certain members of the Mqobela community were strongly in favour of reaching an agreement as quickly as possible and were involved in pressing for a resolution and hence for one reason and another ownership arrangements were made solely with the Mqobela community.

In recent times the Mpukane and Mqobela communities have found themselves in growing conflict and disagreement. The Mpukane community have gradually been feeling more isolated from what they see as the benefits, predominantly economic, flowing from the lodge to Mqobela for a range of reasons: from an individual employment perspective, from their lack of involvement from an ownership point of view and also from seeing lodge guests visiting Mqobela community on Community Tours approximately twice a week, bringing with them the potential for philanthropic donations. These key issues and the perceived potential livelihood benefits have created tensions both between the two communities and between the individual communities and the lodge management and staff. Given the proximity of the Mpukane community to the tourism initiative and knowing that despite the disagreements and tensions between the two communities some members of the Mpukane community were employed at the lodge, a further study was conducted incorporating the analysis of both the Mpukane and the Mqobela communities, the results of this study are examined in Simpson (forthcoming). The focus of this chapter is on the Mathenjwa community adjacent to Ndumo Wilderness Camp and the Mqobela community adjacent to Rocktail Bay Lodge.

In following the first stage of the protocol; the collection of baseline data and the literature review, considerable relevant data were gathered concerning both study sites by making contact with stakeholders such as the KwaZulu-Natal (KZN) Tourist Board, the local police, health and education officials and obtaining archive materials, in both electronic and paper format. In order to collect as much data as possible in this phase, informal interviews were held with representatives of the tourism operator; Wilderness Safaris, and also with the KZNNCS officials, the Inkosis and Ndunas (community leaders) and the elders in each relevant community.

This initial profile was significantly augmented by stages two, three and four of the protocol. These three stages of the approach were conducted simultaneously in the field. In stage two, following the further identification of key informants, semi-structured interviews were held with all of those identified at each study site. The interviewees included those working in local government, tourism and conservation authorities, health, education, police, local business, religious leaders, community members and tourism enterprises.

In stage three a structured household questionnaire was developed. The questionnaire was split into several thematic sections: house and household; health; education; food security; savings, borrowings, household budget and income; and lastly, facilities, infrastructure, environment and general information. Questions were designed to give adequate opportunity for the respondents to provide data on changes in level of assets, house construction, size and dates of acquisition of a range of possessions including furniture and any consumer items. The questionnaire was translated into IsiZulu, the local language, to assist potential respondents in their understanding of the questions and to better facilitate the implementation of the survey and collection of relevant information; the questionnaire was then piloted and further refined. A survey response sheet was also designed so the information gathered could be recorded in an organized manner.

Since no official documentation existed for the number and location of households in each community in the study sites, the sampling areas (the communities) were surveyed and the location and number of households were recorded and coded. Huts, houses and compounds were numbered and a random sample of approximately 17 per cent of the households in Mathenjwa and around 35 per cent in Mqobela were selected for the implementation of the questionnaire. Assistance in the implementation was secured from a small team of seven local people in each study site. The team were trained and accompanied in the collection of data and the fulfilment of the household surveys in order to ensure that data gathering was as accurate as possible and to minimize any potential bias. During the implementation of the questionnaire survey, regular meetings were held between the researchers to ensure consistency and data quality. The quantitative data collected were then subjected to analysis in stage six of the protocol using SPSS version 14.0 computer software.

Twelve respondents ($N - 171$) in the Mathenjwa community stated that a member of their household was earning an income as a direct result of the presence of the tourism initiative; seven households in the Mqobela community ($N = 77$) stated the same. Average earnings from tourism by these household members in both communities were stated as being between ZAR50 and ZAR200 per month. Approximately 50 per cent of respondents in each sample stated that their total household income from all sources varied throughout the year and generally there was an optimistic perception that overall the household will earn more in the future. However the perception of households in both communities when asked if they anticipated more or less people in the household earning an income from tourism deriving from the lodge was mixed, with the majority believing that the number of people earning an income as a result of the tourism initiative would stay the same; the results are shown in Table 11.1. Table 11.1 also shows the responses of the households to questions concerning how the infrastructure and environment in and around the community may have changed since the inception of the tourism initiative and indicates their perception of the effect that the tourism initiative may have had on these aspects of their livelihoods.

In the Mqobela community 32.9 per cent of respondents ($N = 73$) stated that members of their households had attended training courses or acquired new skills since the start of Rocktail Bay Lodge, 9.5 per cent of the households sampled in the Mathenjwa community responded that they also had members who had attended training courses or acquired new skills since the start of Ndumo

Table 11.1 *Perception of future income and changes to infrastructure and the environment as a result of the tourism initiatives*

Selection from Household Survey	Mathenjwa Community (Ndumo Wilderness Camp) (N = 171)	Mqobela Community (Rocktail Bay Lodge) (N = 77)
More or less people in the household earning an income from tourism deriving from the lodge or camp in the future.	More people – 27.5% Less people – 20.5% Same number – 52% (N = 171)	22.2% 8.3% 69.4% (N = 72)
Quality of the roads to and around the community and the household since the start of the tourism initiative.	Improved – 4.8% Worsened – 40.5% Stayed the same – 54.8% (N = 168)	0% 22.1% 77.9% (N = 77)
Quality of the drainage systems in and around the community and the household since the start of the tourism initiative.	Improved – 0.7% Worsened – 37.5% Stayed the same – 61.8% (N = 144)	0% 22.1% 77.9% (N = 77)
Quality of the water system in and around the community and the household since the start of the tourism initiative.	Improved – 20.6% Worsened – 25.3% Stayed the same – 54.1% (N = 170)	7.8% 19.5% 72.7% (N = 77)
Quality of the wildlife and fauna in and around the community and the household since the start of the tourism initiative.	Improved – 83.6% Worsened – 7% Stayed the same – 9.4% (N = 171)	25.3% 0% 74.7% (N = 75)
Quality of the trees, plants, flowers, flora in and around the community and the household since the start of the tourism initiative.	Improved – 50.3% Worsened – 33.7% Stayed the same – 16% (N = 171)	2.6% 19.5% 77.9% (N = 75)

Source: Simpson, 2008b.

Wilderness Camp. The courses and skills concerned in both cases were broadly an even mixture of hospitality/waiting skills, computer skills, higher education degrees and a smaller number were management and financial skills. 61 per cent of households surveyed in Mqobela (*N* = 59) were members of social or community organizations (such as the safety committee or the church) as opposed to just 4.2 per cent (*N* = 168) in the Mathenjwa community sample.

In stage two 'b' semi-structured interviews were conducted with a purposeful sub-sample of individuals from the household survey for more in-depth qualitative analysis. The individuals were chosen so as to be representative of the range of livelihoods present in the original sample of the community in the study site. In stage four, two participatory events were held in each community to provide forums so that as large a number and as wide a spectrum of the community as

Source: Simpson, 2008b

Figure 11.3 *Participatory events in Maputaland, KwaZulu-Natal*

possible were able to take part in the assessment process, articulate their feelings, beliefs and knowledge. They communicated information concerning their livelihoods in the village, the impact of the tourism initiative and on other topics they believed relevant such as the protected areas adjacent to their communities.

Source: Simpson, 2008b

Figure 11.4 *Participatory events in Maputaland, KwaZulu-Natal*

The participatory events took place in the open, under trees, and in a community hall and they were attended by between 70 and 100 people on each occasion (see Figures 11.3 and 11.4). The techniques used included asset mapping and community mapping (Mayoux, 2001; Guy et al, 2002; Kerka, 2003); the participants drew maps of their community illustrating the position of those structures and locations within the village that the members of the community perceived as assets such as households, roads or tracks, water supply, schools, health clinics, shops, community buildings, the tourism initiative, any boundaries and natural assets, for example, the sea, a lake, rivers or a forest. The maps enabled the collection of a range of qualitative data such as people's localities, resources, social institutions, wealth and status.

At the events members of the community also participated in other PRA techniques such as the creation of an 'H-Diagram'; a variation of the 'H-Form' introduced by Guy and Inglis (1999), to indicate their likes, dislikes and desired changes (see Table 11.2).

At every stage of the protocol the qualitative data that were gathered were collated into a series of livelihood matrices in order to complete stage 5, the Sustainable Livelihoods Analysis (SLA). Drawing on livelihood issues identified during the course of the studies, earlier livelihoods analyses and discussion of livelihoods including work by Chambers and Conway (1992), DFID (1997), Scoones (1998), Carney (1999), Ashley (2000, 2002) and Poultney and Spenceley (2001) the analysis was conducted by integrating the summary data into a series of matrices focusing on categories of impacts on the communities' livelihoods, assets and activities that are characteristic of tourism initiatives.

Livelihoods analysis matrices included: positive and negative impacts of the tourism initiative on community and individual livelihood assets, key impacts on livelihood issues such as policy, empowerment and migration, barriers to participation in tourism and the financial earnings of the community. For the purposes of this chapter, summary data from the SLA giving the impacts of the tourism initiative are provided in Tables 11.3 a, b, c, d, e and f, using simplified matrices based on the five livelihood assets (financial, physical, human, natural and social) identified in early work on sustainable livelihoods.

Table 11.2 Communities' likes, dislikes and desired changes summarized and organized into themes

Themes:	Ndumo wilderness camp	MATHENJWA COMMUNITY Village/community	Game reserve	Rocktail Bay Lodge	MQOBELA COMMUNITY Village/community	Coastal reserve
LIKES	Provides employment for some Sponsors of the Zulu dance, the football tournament, and 'Children in the Wilderness'	Nothing / no good things about the village Water access has been improved a little	Opportunity to buy meat Cheap meat Some contract jobs exist	Provides employment for some Helps with transport in the area and helps the country develop Brings tourists who help the school	Natural vegetation and the sea School has improved a little Rocktail Bay Lodge	Position of cattle pasture Some of the flora has improved
DISLIKES	Not enough job opportunities Not enough local people working in the lodge Not enough training opportunities	Roads are very poor Not enough jobs Not enough schools, no community hall, no training colleges, not enough sports fields No electricity	No job opportunities There is nothing good about the game reserve No communication between the game reserve managers, staff and the community Bad roads	Employs very few people and shortage of vacancies Low wages No roads have been constructed	No roads No electricity, no drainage, no toilets, no water to the houses Poverty and no employment opportunities Lack of good health clinic close to the village, school could be better	KZNNCS shouldn't be here No work opportunities KZNNCS doesn't help or support the community Taken ancestors graves

Table 11.2 *continued*

		MATHENJWA COMMUNITY			MQOBELA COMMUNITY	
Themes:	Ndumo wilderness camp	Village/community	Game reserve	Rocktail Bay Lodge	Village/community	Coastal reserve
		Too far to get water, too far to the clinic	Broken promises such as providing work and enough meat	Discriminates between people and communities	There is nothing good about the village	Stops the community collecting wood, and finding fish and sea food
DESIRED CHANGES	Employ different people in the community	Better roads, shops, job opportunities and more facilities such as banks, telephones	If there are job opportunities they should contact the community	Money from lodge that is given to the trust should go to the community	Better roads and improve the school and its buildings	Access to the trees to be able to collect wood
	Provide education and training on tourism and the environment	More water, more schools, more clinics, electricity, and dams for livestock water	Everything must change	Improve the roads and buildings in the community should be improved	Require electricity	Employment
	Provide more employment	Build a community hall	Provide fruit and reeds for the community	More jobs	Better access to water and toilets	
	More benefits to the community and sponsor more events	Change everything		Management of the lodge should communicate more and train the community	More jobs	

Source: Simpson, 2008b

Table 11.3a *Positive and negative impacts of the tourism initiative on community and individual assets and livelihoods – financial*

Financial Assets	Negatives		Positives	
	Matheniwa	Mqobela	Matheniwa	Mqobela
Access to investment funds, loans	• No significant change since opening of the lodge • Loans not accessible for all community members • No record of any loans made to community members living adjacent to the lodge • Loans being distributed by the community trust to members of Matheniwa Inkosi's (chief's) family (no record of these loans being repaid)	• Loans not accessible to all community members • No record of any loans made to community members being paid back to the Community Trust, general acceptance that they will never be repaid • Loans given to staff by the tour operator now ceased	• Bank accounts for some full-time staff provide potential for loans • Loans given by the tour operator to staff in the past (now ceased) • Access to Matheniwa Community Trust money for community members related to Inkosi and directors of the trust • Equity for the community trust in the tourism initiative • Loans given by the tour operator to staff in the past • Bank accounts for some full-time staff provide potential for loans	• Access to Mqobela Community Trust money for some community members in the form of loans • Equity for the community trust in the tourism initiative • Loans given by the tour operator to staff in the past • Bank accounts for some full-time staff provide potential for loans
Earnings	• No significant change for community as a whole • Very few full-time employees • Allegations of misuse and misappropriation of funds by the Community Trust • No accountability	• No significant change for the community since 2000 • Very few full-time employees • Allegations of misappropriation of funds by the Community Trust	• Earnings for a small minority as full-time employees (21 people earning an average of ZAR 857 pcm affecting approximately 21 households (approx 2% of households) average of 7.06 people per household) • Approximately ZAR 1500pcm given by the lodge to Matheniwa Community Trust as part of lease • Some additional money derived from initiative into community trust account in the past (ceased prior to study)	• Earnings for a minority as full-time employees (23 people earning an average of ZAR1 340 pcm affecting approximately 23 households (approx 11% of households) average of 5.09 people per household) • Some seasonal casual work (approximately 50 people working 19 days per year on an average wage of ZAR30 per day) • Approximately ZAR2500 pcm given by the lodge to Mqobela Community Trust as part of lease • Some additional money derived from initiative into community trust account in the past (e.g. ZAR17,784 in 1998)

Table 11.3a *continued*

Financial Assets	Negatives		Positives	
	Mathenjwa	*Mqobela*	*Mathenjwa*	*Mqobela*
Other funds or donations to the community	• No access to donations • Dependent on lodge staff bringing visitors to the community sites (visits to households in the past – ceased prior to study)	• Dependent on lodge staff bringing visitors to the community sites	• Donations to community via visitors making visits to members of the community (ceased prior to study)	• Donations to the school and the community via visitors taking tours of the community • Lodge give ZAR 700 pcm for Police Forum • Food (e.g. bread and muffins) from the lodge is given sometimes on every second day sometimes weekly (dropped off at the school for members of the community
Informal sector and secondary business; opportunities and effects	• Opportunities for additional and follow on business not fulfilled • Vegetable garden created to provide food for lodge guests not producing sufficient quality or quantity	• Little or no 'trickle down effect' • Opportunities for additional and follow on business not fulfilled • Vegetable garden created to provide food for lodge guests not producing sufficient quality or quantity	• Some income derived for taxi drivers and transport • Small amount of handicrafts sold • Opportunities available e.g. for more curios, food supply, lodge furnishings and niche tours if occupancy levels were higher	• Some income derived for taxi drivers and transport • Small amount of curios and handicrafts sold • Opportunities available e.g. for more curios, food supply, lodge furnishings and niche tours

Note: 1 ZAR = 0.17714 US$ on 1 January 2005.

Table 11.3b *Positive and negative impacts of the tourism initiative on community and individual assets and livelihoods – physical*

Physical Assets	Negatives		Positives	
	Mathenjwa	Mqobela	Mathenjwa	Mqobela
Infrastructure: • Water, waste • Roads, transport • Telephone, communication	• No evidence of any significant change in quality of roads, drainage or access to water or electricity as a result of the lodge	• Quality of roads worsened • Drainage worse • Access to water improved only marginally	• Some improvement in access to water; cell phone communications and electricity as a result of existing government policies and the presence of game reserve (no evidence this was as a result of the tourism initiative)	• Access to water improved marginally • Bicycles (4 each) given to the communities jointly for use by the Police Forum
Special projects	• Lack of special projects affecting the community at large	• Not clear to people how the work carried on in the community on buildings is funded (not transparent)	• Mobile water containers; 'Hippo Rollers' provided by the lodge to selected community members • Curio shop built at the entrance to the game reserve and lodge drive (used by women in the community to make and sell curios)	• Building of airstrip in 2003 (cost of ZAR 1 million) • Improved community building
Health and education		• Permanent clinic is still approx 6km away	• Improvement work on 3 classrooms in local school conducted by KZNNCS (though no concrete evidence this was as a result of the lodge)	• Improved school building with new classrooms • Equipment donated to the school by foreign visitors • KZN Wildlife to renovate 4 more classrooms at the local school and secured commitment from Wilderness Safaris to do the rest

Note : 1 ZAR = 0.17714 US$ on 1 January 2005.

Table 11.3c *Positive and negative impacts of the tourism initiative on community and individual assets and livelihoods – human*

Human resources	Negatives		Positives	
	Mathenjwa	Mqobela	Mathenjwa	Mqobela
Skills	• Only training and skills development for minority with full-time employment • Not enough people with accounting and bookkeeping skills to track finances of Community Trust	• Only training and skills development for minority with full-time employment • Not enough people with accounting and bookkeeping skills to track finances of Community Trust	• Training and skills development for minority with full-time employment • Small number of the community have more skills e.g. computer skills, hospitality	• Training and skills development for minority with full-time employment • More people in the community have more skills e.g. bookkeeping, computer skills, hospitality
Education (access and level)	• No change since lodge opened • Bursaries provided by Mathenjwa Community Trust only to family of Inkosi	• Bursaries stopped as loans from the Community Trust funds stopped • No incentive for recipients of bursaries to return to the community	• Small number of people studying higher level courses • Small number of bursaries exist	• More people studying higher level courses • Bursaries from the Community Trust for community members to study courses in the past
Access to health care	• No evidence of any change as a result of the tourism initiative	• Not improved	—	—

Table 11.3d *Positive and negative impacts of the tourism initiative on community and individual assets and livelihoods – natural*

| Natural resources | Negatives | | | Positives | |
	Mathenjwa	Mqobela	Mathenjwa	Mqobela	
Natural resources (access to, use/productivity)	• No access to game reserve	• Limited access to coastal reserve • Quota system for fishing not functioning/not effective • Conflict with conservation authorites	• Quality of flora and fauna improved significantly • Cheap meat available	• Quota system for fishing set up by KZNNCS • Some firewood provided by KZNNCS available for collection • Sea turtle protection project attracts more visitors • Improved cattle pasture • Quality of flora and fauna improved

Table 11.3e *Positive and negative impacts of the tourism initiative on community and individual assets and livelihoods – social*

Social capital	Negatives		Positives	
	Mathenjwa	Mqobela	Mathenjwa	Mqobela
Community organization, cohesion, pride	• Unrealistic expectations • Mistrust and resentment of perceived misuse of funds by (physically distant) community trust and elite members of tribal authority • Community Trust not respected or trusted and not in communication with community adjacent to the lodge • Expectations not met • Sponsored events are one-off occasions with no regularity leading to discontent and disillusionment within the community	• Internal mistrust and conflict over possible embezzlement of funds by Community Trust and elite members of community • Conflict with neighbouring community • Community Trust not respected or trusted • Expectations not met	• Community Trust established • Community support for lodge and pride of association with the enterprise • Employment provides possible reasons to stay in the area • High aspirations • Football tournament organized by the lodge (extremely well supported by the community) • 'Children in the Wilderness' project organized by the lodge for children of the community to go and visit and stay at the lodge, learning about the environment • Traditional dance event sponsored by the lodge generated great support and attendance form the community	• Community Trust established • Community Trust Directors replaced by community when they lost faith in existing people • Strengthened social coherence • Community support and pride in infrastructure enhancements and educational advancements • Employment provides possible reasons to stay in the area • High aspirations
Physical safety	• Some carjacking of tourists taking place (average 2 incidents per year)	• Still some carjacking of tourists taking place (average 2 incidents per year)	–	• Strengthened community and tourist security due to Police Forum
Local culture	• Sangoma performances may lead to commodification of local culture (not taking place over period of study)	• Sangoma performances may lead to commodification of local culture	• Sangoma performances create value for local culture and assist in keeping alive traditional practices and customs (not taking place over period of study)	• Sangoma performances create value for local culture and assist in keeping alive traditional practices and customs

Table 11.3f *Positive and negative impacts of the tourism initiative on community and individual assets and livelihoods – other livelihood issues*

Other livelihood issues	Negatives		Positives	
	Mathenjwa	Mqobela	Mathenjwa	Mqobela
Migration	• Very little mobility due to low skills base • Some jobs going to 'incomers' from other communities (including from Mozambique)	• More people leaving the community • Some jobs going to 'incomers' from other communities	• People staying within the community	• Some community members moving on to other areas to 'better' themselves educationally and for higher paid employment
Markets, market opportunities; tourism and other industries and livelihood activities such as farming	• Interest in other tourism initiatives may be misguided • Expectations of potential from follow on and secondary industries such as curio sales may be too high • No significant change in other livelihood activities	• Expectations of potential from follow on and secondary industries such as curio sales may be too high • No significant change in other livelihood activities	• Perceived benefits have encouraged interest in other possible initiatives • Experience and knowledge of the tourism industry have created some degree of a culture of ideas and opportunities • Women's group making and selling curios in purpose built shop at the entrance to the reserve	• Experience and knowledge of the tourism industry has created a culture of ideas and opportunities
Policy environment	• No significant change • Expectations that the partnership policy would deliver significant benefits too high	• Expectations that the partnership policy would deliver significant benefits too high	• Community, Public, Private, Partnership (CPPP) model being considered for future initiatives with other communities	• Community, Public, Private, Partnership (CPPP) model being considered for future initiatives with Mqobela and other communities

Table 11.3f *continued*

Other livelihood issues	Negatives		Positives	
	Mathenjwa	*Mqobela*	*Mathenjwa*	*Mqobela*
Empowerment and influence over policy makers	• No significant change • Uneasy and difficult relationship with KNNCS due to lack of communication and differing agendas on game reserve • Little influence over local government	• Uneasy and difficult relationship with KNNCS due to lack of communication and differing agendas on coastal reserve • Little influence over local government	• Gender empowerment in a small number of households (61% of community members employed are women) • For a small minority an increased level of control over own destiny within the community and ability to exercise some degree of influence externally	• High level of gender empowerment (73% of community members employed are women) • Increased level of control over own destiny within the community and ability to exercise some degree of influence externally
Access to information	• No significant change • Lack of communication between lodge and community and Community Trust	• No significant change • Lack of communication between lodge and community and Community Trust	—	—
Overall vulnerability of households	• No significant change • Potential for small minority of households to be over reliant on the initiative	• Potential for over reliance on the initiative	• Vulnerability marginally lowered in a number of areas for a minority of households	• Vulnerability marginally lowered in a number of areas for a minority of households

Conclusions

During the course of the study it became clear from the data collected through the semi-structured interviews, the purposeful sub-sample of the household survey and observation by the researchers that occupancy levels at Ndumo Wilderness Camp were extremely low and had been this way for years. From interviews with WS staff and secondary data it appeared that WS had been running the lodge at a loss for some time. In the second half of 2004, some time after the fieldwork for this study was completed, Ndumo Wilderness Camp finally closed down. According to one WS official, quoted in Honey (2007), the company lost 5 million South African Rand (approximately US$860,000) between 1995 and 2004 and would have closed the lodge earlier if it had not been for their 'social commitment' to the area.

Perhaps unsurprisingly, the case studies demonstrated that the tourism initiatives had influenced community development and the communities' livelihoods and assets in both positive and negative ways and as a result had enhanced livelihoods only marginally. Whilst the positive impacts generally seem to outweigh the negative, the financial benefits are limited to a select few households who have members directly employed. Other livelihood assets such as physical assets, for example, school infrastructure, have improved only marginally as a result of the tourism initiatives and these improvements have not met the expectations of the community or the tourism industry stakeholder. Improvements in human resource assets were also limited to those few who have been trained for work in the lodges, although some gender empowerment took place in the Mathenjwa community as a result of the curio shop being built and a group of women taking on the manufacture of products to sell there. This outlet will now have negligible, if any, benefit to the community as the lodge is currently closed down. In the case of Rocktail Bay Lodge and the Mqobela and Mpukane communities this was the first time in South Africa that the conservation authorities, an adjacent local community and the private sector had jointly built a lodge within a proclaimed park where each party owned equity in the operation. Expectations were high, challenges and conflicts appeared almost inevitable. The Mqobela community were found to have received livelihood benefits in a number of areas, however, these benefits are less than they would have wished and affect relatively few households. Perhaps predictably, mainly due to the absence of a formal involvement with the tourism initiative, the benefits delivered as a result of tourism to the Mpukane are considerably less. In both case studies benefits in social capital and natural resource assets seem to have been offset by negative impacts such as conflicts (internal and external), mistrust, allegations of misuse of funds and restrictions in access and use of the game and coastal reserves.

The research revealed that not only can conflicts be created and challenges raised by the presence of tourism initiatives in a local area but that unrealistic expectations on the part of the community are generated. Expectations of economic and livelihood benefits from tourism initiatives to communities run high, and poverty alleviation and other development goals are often anticipated when a tourism initiative is commenced in a rural area. These expectations seem to arise as a result of the emphasis by government, development agencies, tour operators and international organizations on tourism as a possible source of economic development. These expectations seem particularly acute if the community have some form of tenure or ownership in the business (Jenkins et al, 1998; Briedenhann and Wickens, 2004; Saarinen, 2007; Simpson, 2008a). However, the ability of tourism initiatives to meet communities' expectations appears to be questionable and their expectations seem in the main to be unrealistic and unfulfilled as the economic and livelihood benefits communities receive from tourism are not only lower than expected but also limited to a small minority of the community (Sharpley, 2002; Saarinen, 2007; Spenceley and Goodwin, 2007; Simpson, 2008a, 2008b).

Whilst the protocol provided a coherent and effective framework within which to capture relevant information, implementation posed several challenges. In addition to significant demands on time, finance and human resources, the study identified a wide range of challenges relating to the assessment of impacts, relationships and processes, and difficulties associated with capturing diverse and complex information were experienced. The availability of baseline data with which to gauge the type and rate of changes in the communities since the commencement of the tourism initiatives was limited, including specific figures on health and education, income levels, population size and the numbers of people in households. This was to be expected due to the location of the study sites and rural nature of the environment, but despite these constraints an acceptable baseline profile was established of the tourism initiatives and their communities. Causality was also difficult to establish: in some instances it was problematic to define categorically whether the presence or actions of the initiative had affected change in any way, and secondary effects were also hard to attribute to the tourism initiative. In order to overcome these problems comprehensive long-term studies would be required; the protocol could be implemented again after a suitable period of time had passed, perhaps two to five years, allowing impacts to become clearer and hence the analysis more accurate.

The collection and interpretation of the data were further complicated by the presence of hierarchies and elites. Within the communities these long-established tribal systems were accentuated by the ownership arrangements in the tourism initiatives at the case study sites. In each case the community involved in the tenure of the tourism initiative was represented by a community trust which ostensibly was independent from the tribal system, however, the established hierarchies appeared to be so strong that they resulted in the existing elite system subsuming the appointed directors of the trust. This situation appeared to have fostered a culture of secrecy with regard to the finances of the community trusts and made it extremely difficult to gather precise data on amounts that had been paid to the respective community trusts and what the money had been spent on. Information collected through the series of semi-structured interviews and the participatory approaches suggested that in both case studies there had been incidences of misappropriation and corruption and very little, if any, of the money had found its way to benefiting the community as a whole.

Through the analyses of the case studies, characteristics and roles for the private sector/tourism industry were identified that could contribute to minimizing the conflicts and meeting the challenges that occur in the interrelationships between tourism initiatives and rural livelihoods. The roles and characteristics identified could also address some of the constraints and barriers to the communities receiving appropriate and effective livelihood benefits, and raise awareness within the community concerning the realistic potential of tourism to deliver effective and appropriate benefits. Communication, or rather the lack of it, seemed to play a significant role in engendering and sustaining the conflicts that were present in both case study areas and the absence of regular meetings between stakeholders and the lack of other formal and informal interactive structures such as participatory events, community meetings and feedback sessions was also a notable contributor to an absence of understanding and interaction. Communication appears to be a vital element at all stages of the development and operation of any tourism initiative but especially in one designed to deliver benefits to a community. It seems to be essential to provide a forum for greater understanding of the realistic potential of a tourism initiative and to overcome some of the barriers to the involvement of community members in the tourism industry and associated secondary industries. Community knowledge and awareness of the markets, their pitfalls and possibilities are clearly important. If we assume that this knowledge is typically held by the private partner (Hall, 2007; Simpson, 2008a), then it could be argued that the private sector is best positioned to impart this knowledge and understanding to the community. During the establishment and negotiation phase, open communication is necessary to create trust and to ensure that agreements match the expectations of all parties. The research indicated that this communication and a facility for the community and its individual members to express their views, needs and desires should be maintained throughout the life of the initiative by using structured channels of communication and encouraging regular participatory events.

The private sector appears broadly to recognize the issues of sustainability, and to recognize the importance of the community as a stakeholder in the paradigm of successful tourism, with the more aware operators and investors understanding something about the needs and requirements of the community (Swarbrooke, 1999; Scheyvens, 2002; WTO, 2005). However, when investors and private operators consider an initiative in a rural area, there appear to be a number of other serious considerations and potential constraints to the commencement and long-term success of the project, including: a limited manpower and skills pool; regulatory and policy restrictions regarding fundamental issues such as construction and operation; cultural and language barriers; political constraints, i.e. support or objections by local, regional and national government or conflicts with current political agendas; an additional economic cost of conducting business in a remote location; decisions about whether or not to involve the community in the ownership structure or give the community some other level of tenure in the business; and if one of the defined objectives of the initiative is to benefit the community then weighing up the potential environmental, economic

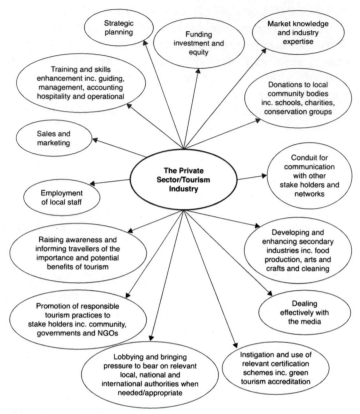

Source: Adapted from Simpson, 2008a

Figure 11.5 *Potential roles of the private sector and the tourism industry in maximizing the delivery of benefits to communities*

and socio-cultural costs to the community against the potential benefits (Rattanasuwongchai, 1998; Simpson, 2008a).

The private sector is more sensitive to the market than any other stakeholder; this is of course not surprising as private sector stakeholders are interested in financial stability, remuneration and economic sustainability. However, the support and cooperation of the local community is frequently integral to those objectives and the path by which to achieve commercial and economic goals may often involve the preservation of essential natural assets, fundamental to the tourism product, and the maintenance of good relations with communities adjacent to or affected by the tourism initiative (Roe et al, 2002; Wearing and MacDonald, 2002; WTO, 2005; Beeton, 2006; Hawkins and Mann, 2007). During the course of conducting the case studies, potential roles available to the private sector and the tourism industry in maximizing the delivery of livelihood benefits to communities were identified and these are given in Figure 11.5.

Negative impacts and adverse change as a result of the tourism and community nexus can take many forms and manifest themselves through social, economic, environmental and/or political factors (MacLeod, 2004). Attitudes and actions of controlling stakeholders such as the private sector can be interpreted as neo-colonialism, other negative impacts can include environmental degradation, destruction of traditional social structures, alteration of local identity, beliefs, values and politics, adverse shifts in power, the growth of unwanted secondary industries and other sectors, the instigation of negative attitudes to the environment, the world, foreigners and women, and the commencement of unknown and potentially detrimental business and employment structures (Young, 1973; Butler and Hinch, 1996; Krippendorf, 1987; Swarbrooke, 1999; Fagence, 2003; MacLeod, 2004). However, change generated by tourism is multifaceted: whilst enterprises can present problems within a community, threaten its stability and harmony, and trigger a range of other challenges, where the private sector understands the issues and fully embraces their variety of roles, tourism initiatives do possess the potential to bring appropriate and effective livelihood benefits to communities (Murphy, 1985; Mowforth and Munt, 1998; Ashley et al, 2001; Simpson, 2008a).

The private sector appears to be best placed to identify opportunities, realize the potential of a destination, drive forward the development of product and has the potential to adopt a range of highly effective strategies for the benefit of communities and their livelihoods.

The studies examined in this chapter suggest that the relationship between tourism and rural livelihoods is fragile and complex and that one of the key factors for a tourism initiative's success as an instrument for enhancing rural livelihoods is the adoption of effective and practical roles by the private sector, including the development of systems of good governance, administration and logistics, and above all economically sustainable business practices. The implementation of a series of case studies assessing the impacts and benefits of tourism on communities and investigating various aspects of different initiatives and the roles of their stakeholders will provide opportunities to examine other areas for the further development of tourism initiatives that can provide livelihood benefits. A consistent and coherent analytical framework such as the one implemented in these studies will be essential and should be applicable in a range of spatio-temporal situations in order to learn from the experiences of others and advance knowledge in the field of tourism and development through cumulative critical understanding. The importance of on-going monitoring cannot be understated in order to refine strategies, mitigate costs, maximize benefits to communities and ensure the long-term sustainability of individual tourism initiatives. These monitoring and assessment projects should take place over a range of diverse tourism initiatives in various geographic locations. Elements of 'worst practice', i.e. problems and failures in tourism initiatives aimed at benefiting communities, will need to be subjected to rigorous scrutiny along with ostensibly successful community benefit tourism initiatives (CBTIs, see Simpson, 2008a), in order that thoroughly effective strategies can be developed. It appears to be the responsibility of researchers, practitioners, policy makers and stakeholders to strive continually to raise the level of awareness of tourism's potential for communities and thereby to contribute to raising the standards of tourism practice which will assist in the enhancement of rural livelihoods and the alleviation of poverty.

References

Ashley, C. (2000) *The Impacts of Tourism on Rural Livelihoods: Namibia's Experience*, Working Paper 128, Overseas Development Institute (ODI), London

Ashley, C. (2002) *Methodology for Pro-Poor Tourism Case Studies*, PPT Working Paper 10, Overseas Development Institute (ODI), London

Ashley, C. and Carney, D. (1999) *Sustainable Livelihoods: Lessons from Early Experience*, Department for International Development (DFID), London

Ashley, C. and Hussein, K. (2000) *Developing Methodologies for Livelihood Impact Assessment: Experience of the African Wildlife Foundation in East Africa*, Sustainable Livelihoods Working Paper 129, Overseas Development Institute (ODI), London

Ashley C., Roe, D. and Goodwin, H. (2001) *Pro-Poor Tourism Strategies: Making Tourism Work for the Poor: A Review of Experience*, Pro-Poor Tourism Report No. 1, ODI, International Institute for the Environment and Development (IIED) and Centre for Responsible Tourism (CRT), London

Beeton, S. (2006) *Community Development Through Tourism*, Landlinks Press, Victoria, Australia

Briedenhann, J. and Wickens, E. (2004) 'Rural tourism – Meeting the challenges of the New South Africa', *International Journal of Tourism Research*, vol 6, 189–203

Butler, R. W. and Hinch, T. (1996) *Tourism and Indigenous Peoples*, International Thomson Business Press, London

Carney, D. (1999) *Approaches to Sustainable Livelihoods for the Rural Poor*, ODI Poverty Briefing 2, Overseas Development Institute (ODI), London

Chambers, R. and Conway, G. R. (1992) *Sustainable Rural Livelihoods: Practical Concepts for the 21st Century*, Institute of Development Studies (IDS), University of Sussex, Brighton

Cheong, S. and Miller, M. (2000) 'Power and tourism: A Foucauldian observation', *Annals of Tourism Research*, vol 27, no 2, 371–390

Chok, S., Macbeth, J. and Warren, C. (2007) 'Tourism as a toll for poverty alleviation: A critical analysis of "Pro-Poor Tourism" and implications for sustainability', *Current Issues in Tourism*, vol 10, nos 2&3, 144–165

Davis, J. B. (2001) 'Commentary: Tourism research and social theory – expanding the focus', *Tourism Geographies*, vol 3, no 2, 125–134

De Kadt, E. (ed.) (1979) *Tourism: Passport to Development?* Oxford University Press, New York

Deloitte & Touche, IIED & ODI (1999) *Sustainable Tourism and Poverty Elimination: A Report for the Department of International Development*, IIED and ODI, London

Department for International Development (DFID) (1997) *Tourism: Key Sheets for Sustainable Livelihoods*, DFID, London

De Vaus, D. A. (2001) *Research Design in Social Research*, Sage, London

Eadington, W. and Smith, L. (1994) 'Introduction: The emergence of alternative forms of tourism', in L. Smith, and W. Eadington, (eds), *Tourism Alternatives: Potential and Problems in the Development of Tourism*. Wiley, Chichester

Fagence, M. (2003) 'Tourism and local society and culture in tourism communities', in S. Singh, D. J. Timothy and R. K. Dowling (eds), *Tourism in Destination Communities* (pp 55–78), CAB International, Oxford

Goodwin, H. (1996) 'In pursuit of ecotourism', *Biodiversity and Conservation*, vol 5, no 3, 277–291

Goodwin, H. and Francis, J. (2003) 'Ethical and responsible tourism: Consumer trends in the UK', *Journal of Vacation Marketing*, vol 9, no 3, 271–284

Gossling, S., Schumacher, K., Morelle, M., Berger, R. and Heck, N. (2004) 'Tourism and street children in Antananarivo, Madagascar', *Tourism and Hospitality Research*, vol 5, no 2, 131–149

Guy, S. and Inglis, A. (1999) 'Tips for trainers: Introducing the "H-Form": A method for monitoring and evaluation', PLA Notes Issue 34, pp84–87, International Institute for Environment and Development (IIED), London

Guy, T., Fuller, D. and Pletsch, C. (2002) *Asset Mapping: A Handbook*, Canadian Rural Partnership, Ottawa, Ontario, www.rural.gc.ca/conference/documents/mapping_e.phtml

Hall, C. M. (2007) 'Editorial, Pro-poor tourism: Do "Tourism exchanges benefit primarily the countries of the South"?' *Current Issues in Tourism*, vol 10, nos 2 & 3, 111–118

Harrison, D. (2007) 'Towards developing a framework for analysing tourism phenomena: A discussion', *Current Issues in Tourism*, vol 10, no 1, 61–86

Hawkins, D. E. and Mann, S. (2007) 'The World Bank's Role in Tourism Development', *Annals of Tourism Research*, vol 34, no 2, 348–363

Honey, M. (2007) *Ecotourism and Sustainable Development: Who Owns Paradise?* 2nd ed, Island Press, Washington DC

Jafari, J. (2001) 'The scientification of tourism', in Smith, V. L. and Brent, M. (eds), *Hosts and Guests Revisited: Tourism Issues of the 21st Century*, Cognizant Communication, New York

Jenkins, J., Hall, C. M. and Troughton, M. (1998) 'The restructuring of rural economies: Rural tourism and recreation as a government response', in R. Butler, C. M. Hall and J. Jenkins (eds), *Tourism and Recreation in Rural Areas*, Wiley, Chichester

Kerka, S. (2003) *Community Asset Mapping*, Educational Resources Information Centre (ERIC), Clearinghouse on Adult, Career and Vocational Education, Trends and Issues Alert 47. www.cete.org/acve/docs/tia00115.pdf

Krippendorf, J. (1987) *The Holiday Makers: Understanding the Impact of Leisure and Travel.* Butterworth Heinemann, Oxford

Lea, J. (1988) *Tourism and Development in the Third World*, Routledge, London

MacLeod, D V I. (2004) *Tourism, Globalisation, and Cultural Change: An Island Community Perspective*, Channel View Publications, London

Massyn, P. J. and Koch, E. (2004) 'African game lodges and rural benefit in two African countries', in Rogerson, C. M. and Visser, G. (eds) *Tourism and Development Issues in Contemporary South Africa*, Africa Institute of South Africa, Pretoria

Mayoux, L. (2001) Participatory Methods. *EDIAIS Application Guidance Note.* available from www.enterprise-impact.org.uk/word-files/ParticMethods.doc

Mowforth, M. and Munt, I. (1998) *Tourism and Sustainability: New Tourism in the Third World*, Routledge, London

Mowforth, M. and Munt, I. (2003) *Tourism and Sustainability: Development and New Tourism in the Third World*, 2nd ed, Routledge, London

Murphy, P. E. (1985) *Tourism: A Community Approach*, Methuen, London

Poultney, C. and Spenceley, A. (2001) *Practical Strategies for Pro-Poor Tourism, Wilderness Safaris South Africa: Rocktail Bay and Ndumu Lodge*, Pro-Poor Tourism (PPT), Working Paper 1. PPT Partnership, London

Rattanasuwongchai, N. (1998) *Rural Tourism: The Impacts on Rural Communities II*, Department of Career Services, Kasetsart University Press, Thailand, www.agnet.org/library/eb/458b

Roe, D., Goodwin, H. and Ashley, C. (2002) 'The tourism industry and poverty reduction: A business primer. *Pro-Poor Tourism Briefing 2*, available from www.propoortourism.org.uk/final%20business%20brief.pdf

Rogerson, C. M. (2006) 'Pro-poor local economic development in South Africa: The role of pro-poor tourism', *Local Environment*, vol 11, no 1, 37–60

Saarinen, J. (2007) 'Commentary – Contradictions of rural tourism initiatives in rural development contexts: Finnish rural tourism strategy case study, *Current Issues in Tourism*, vol 10, no 1, 96–104

Scheyvens, R. (2002) *Tourism for Development: Empowering Communities*, Pearson Education, Harlow

Scheyvens, R. (2007) 'Exploring the tourism–poverty nexus', *Current Issues in Tourism*, vol 10, nos 2 & 3, 231–254

Scoones, I. (1998) *Sustainable Rural Livelihoods: A Framework for Analysis*, Institute of Development Studies (IDS), Working Paper 72. IDS, Brighton

Sharpley, R. (2002) 'Rural tourism and the challenge of tourism diversification: The case of Cyprus', *Tourism Management*, vol 23, 233–244

Sharpley, R. and Roberts, L. (2004) 'Rural tourism – 10 years on', *International Journal of Tourism Research*, vol 6, 119–124

Simpson, M. C. (2007) 'The impacts of community benefit tourism on rural livelihoods and poverty reduction', DPhil Thesis, School of Geography, Oxford University Centre for the Environment

Simpson, M. C. (2008a) 'Community benefit tourism initiatives – a conceptual oxymoron?, *Tourism Management*, vol 29, no 1, 1–18

Simpson, M. C. (2008b, in press) 'An integrated approach to assessing the impacts of tourism on communities and sustainable livelihoods', *Community Development Journal*, vol 43

Simpson, M. C. (forthcoming) 'Conflicts and challenges in South African communities: Tourism's impact on the livelihoods of Mqobela and Mpukane'

Sofield, T. (2003) *Empowerment for Sustainable Tourism Development*. Pergamon, Oxford

Spenceley, A. and Goodwin, H. (2007) 'Nature-based tourism and poverty alleviation: Impacts of private sector and parastatal enterprises in and around Kruger National Park South Africa', *Current Issues in Tourism*, vol 10, nos 2&3, 255–277

Stockholm Environment Institute (SEI), (UNDP) (1998) *Participatory Assessment and Planning for Sustainable Livelihoods*. SEPED/BDP Draft No.1, United Nations for Development Program (UNDP), www.vulnerabilitynet.org/OPMS/ getfile.php?bn=seiproject_hotel&key=1140130220&att_id=950

Swarbrooke, J. (1999) *Sustainable Tourism Management*. CABI Publishing, Oxford

Visser, G. and Rogerson, C. M. (2004) 'Researching the South African tourism and development nexus', *GeoJournal*, vol 60, 201–215

Wearing, S. and MacDonald, M. (2002) 'The development of community based tourism: The relationship between tour operators and development agent as intermediaries in rural and isolated communities', *Journal of Sustainable Tourism*, vol 10, 191–206

World Tourism Organization (WTO) (2004) *Indicators of Sustainable Development for Tourism Destinations: A Guidebook*. WTO, Madrid

World Tourism Organization (WTO) (2005) *Making Tourism More Sustainable: A Guide for Policy Makers*, WTO, Madrid

World Wildlife Fund (WWF) (2001) *Guidelines for Community-Based Ecotourism Development*, WWF International, London

Young, G. (1973) *Tourism: Blessing or Blight?* Penguin Books, London

Zhao, W. and Ritchie, J. R. B. (2007) 'Tourism and poverty alleviation: An integrative research framework', *Current Issues in Tourism*, vol 10, nos 2&3, 119–143

12

Madikwe Game Reserve, South Africa – Investment and Employment

Piers Relly

Introduction

This chapter will briefly explore the debate around tourism research in relation to poverty relief for local residents – and look at the ongoing economic impacts of investment and employment in a large wildlife reserve.

Madikwe Game Reserve (MGR) is a 60,000ha provincially managed reserve located in the north-west Province of South Africa on the Botswana/South Africa border (see Figure 12.1). The reserve was established from scratch in the early 1990s and stocked with around 10,000 head of wildlife. It ranks as a 'big five' destination (offers viewing of buffalo, elephant, leopard, lion and rhinoceros) but has also established a reputation for its wild dog sightings. Madikwe serves the international and domestic tourism markets targeted mainly at the mid- to high-spending tourist. Included in the offerings within the park is a mixture of commercial and corporate lodges. The corporate lodges are owned and used privately by syndicate members, enjoying the same game viewing privileges as the commercial tourists. Commercial lodges are operated for profit and take paying customers.

The reserve was established by the provincial tourism authority, North West Parks and Tourism Board (NWPTB) primarily for socioeconomic reasons with conservation being a desirable but secondary objective (Davies, 1997). This makes it somewhat of an anomaly in the larger game reserve genre, where the *primary* purpose for establishment historically in South Africa (prior to the 1990s) was usually preservation or biodiversity related.

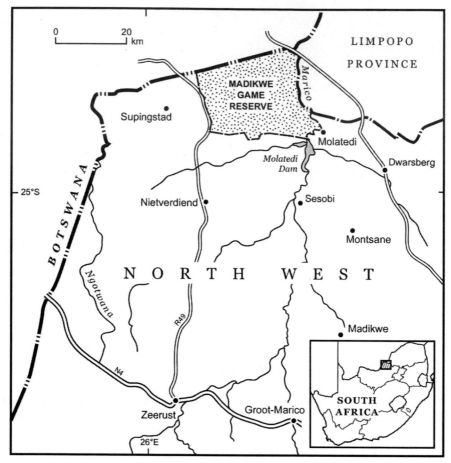

Figure 12.1 *Location map of Madikwe Game Reserve*

Relly (2004a) submitted and later condensed (2004b) a quantitative research study detailing some of the interim economic outcomes of the reserve, specifically the levels of investment, subsequent employment creation and cash remuneration to various categories of employee (female, local (i.e. prior to employment they resided within 50km of the park boundaries) and previously disadvantaged (i.e. individuals not entitled to vote prior to 1994 under the Apartheid government)). This chapter revisits the study where the baseline data have been augmented by further developments in the park, dating from 2003 to mid-2007.

Theoretical background and purpose of study

The intention of this research study was to provide useful benchmarks for a small number of economic and socioeconomic indicators, particularly investment, employment and remuneration in an impoverished and drought-prone area of

South Africa, formerly offering little opportunity for employment and wealth creation. African wildlife as a product is presented in so many locations, with so many thematic and aesthetic variants, that it can be particularly difficult to hold a vision of what a new or developing product should offer by way of differentiating itself.

Here some questions are posed: Does the government measure and understand the relationships between its investment and the socioeconomic 'dividends'? How do the investment 'dividends' compare with other projects/sectors competing for scarce funds? Is a Madikwe-sized project being used to effectively inform tourism policy/strategy? Also, whether this product (being a destination, in this study) could or should be developed at all. Does this destination or product fit comfortably into a portfolio of available provincial, national and regional offerings?

South Africa has shown that it regards tourism as a lead economic sector in the overall Growth Employment and Redevelopment strategy (Republic of South Africa, 1996, 1998). Large game reserves and wildlife products are a central part of the leisure tourism economy in South Africa, so it seems sensible to plan carefully where large, government-led projects are tabled for development.

Wildlife tourism has been researched from a variety of angles. Much of the recent research has been driven by the following:

1   The need to demonstrate how the benefits of this form of tourism actually manifest in the hands of local indigenous populations, who are frequently poor, and often marginalized. The results of these studies can be fed back into the policy environment informing issues such as land tenure and access to capital. Tourism is seen as a sector in which Africa has a natural competitive advantage and most developing countries have included it as a lead sector for their economies. But the sector has to converge with national employment and poverty alleviation targets.

2   The important research driver of nature conservation. It is well understood that many protected areas in southern Africa have seen government funding diminish and surrounding local populations grow. The result has often been a rising gap between the economies of those enterprises (mainly tourism) within reserves and those without (often subsistence economies). This competition for economic and physical space has prompted a variety of research projects aimed at understanding and bringing economic benefit from various forms of tourism closer to local populations, whilst achieving the objectives of conservation.

Wildlife and nature tourism is so important to Namibia for instance, that it has seen focused, community-level research studies such as those summarized by Ashley (2000) and many others, evolve through to macroeconomic studies such as Tourism Satellite Accounts (TSAs) recently produced by the World Travel and Tourism Council (WTTC, 2006). The WTTC study indicates that 16 per cent of jobs in Namibia are created directly or indirectly by tourism.

In his study of Fiji, Britton (1982, 1983) has shown how one type of tourism growth can lead to 'crumbs from the table' for host countries. In Fiji (and other destinations cited by Britton), it was found that the foreign entities owned airlines, resorts and other tourism service providers in the value chain. These entities also employed mostly expatriate staff in senior employment positions. The outcomes resulted in a high outflow of profits and benefits from the host country back to foreign entities while the local economies received a low percentage of tourists' total trip expenditure. These benefits were mainly in the form of low paying employment positions.

Other studies (Wunder, 2000) have demonstrated how relatively low levels of tourism investment and expenditure (from domestic capital sources) can have significant, positive direct and indirect effects on participating communities who own a greater percentage of the tourism enterprises. We can use the emerging global experience and research information to see where and how policy has led to more responsible and equitable forms of development that help host nations or destinations to capture a higher percentage of the tourism expenditure (i.e. through the value chain) and retain it within the host economies. A well-directed policy environment should minimize leakage from the national and, in the instance of Madikwe and similar tourism initiatives, from the local economy too. Failure to produce more than 'crumbs from the table' in a modern tourism environment could indicate either a lack of tourism policy or, as is more often the case, an existing but poorly implemented set of tourism and economic policies.

There are a variety of studies being conducted under rubrics like Community Based Tourism, Pro-Poor Tourism, Fair Trade in Tourism and Responsible Tourism. Research methods and tools include Value Chains, Social Accounting Matrices and statistical sampling to qualitative interviews, to name a few. All work from different measurement perspectives but share the common goal of how to use the results to re-slice, remix or re-bake the tourism pie so that employment and poverty are addressed and participant communities get a greater chance of improved living standards or better still – wealth creation. As Mitchell and Ashley (2007, p1) have noted '*review [by the World Bank and the ODI in 2006] revealed that there is more evidence available than is generally marshalled into pro-poor tourism arguments. But at the same time, evidence is piece-meal, use of definitions sloppy, and methodological divisions fragment the body of knowledge and researchers*'. Further, they noted that not 1 of 300 + studies in the review has examined a 3-tiered approach to tourism and poverty being; (1) direct (labour income, small enterprise income, non-labour income and livelihood effects); (2) indirect (i.e. supply chain effects and associated income/employment multipliers); and (3) dynamic impact effects (i.e. a basket of economic effects which include changes to infrastructure, communications, human resource capabilities, cross-sector effects, etc.). (For full details see Mitchell and Ashley (2007, pp3–4).

Madikwe revisited

If the exchange between researchers and policy makers in tourism needs to be underpinned by a comprehensive and collaborative research framework such as the one outlined by Mitchell and Ashley (2007), Madikwe is certainly providing visible benefits to a poor area of South Africa, even if the economy of the reserve is not comprehensively researched. This research study looks at labour income effects covered by category (1) enumerated by Mitchell and Ashley above.

In 1992, the newly established protected area had provided only a few marginal employment opportunities in agriculture. Planning ahead, Davies et al (1997) provided some economic scenarios which included an employment estimate of around 1200 tourism jobs at full development. The employment figure in Madikwe is an important one from the poor household perspective. Much of the local (direct) benefit goes to people who reside outside the reserve and occupy formal employment positions within. Little is known about the multiplier effects of their spending within the local economy but the anecdotal evidence suggests that there may be a high level of leakage to more distant urban centres and metro-politan service providers.

In Madikwe, cash benefits from formal employment constitute a dominant proportion of total economic benefits associated with this destination economy. Relly (2004a, 2004b) conducted a review of investment and employment in 2003 and some of these data have been augmented by recent developments to June 2007.

There are five chosen categories of employer in the Madikwe area: commercial lodges, corporate lodges, peripheral tourism enterprises contiguous with the reserve, small and micro enterprises (SMMEs) providing goods and services to the aforementioned and finally NWPTB being the provincial wildlife authority and protected area manager. Collectively they are referred to as the Madikwe 'Cluster' being a geographically and thematically linked group of inter-connected enterprises in and around MGR.

Two categories of employer were reviewed and updated: 'Commercial Lodges' and 'Corporate Lodges' The 2003 study has been used as a baseline for earnings increases and employee profiling. Profiling refers to the categories mentioned above: female, local and previously disadvantaged. Where indicated in this study, 2003 *employee earnings* figures are brought forward unchanged from that study and show nominal earnings in 2003 US$.

Investment figures (at cost) from 2003 have been inflated at 5 per cent per annum in the base currency (SA rands) to obtain nominal parity figures for all investment amounts in June 2007, and then converted to US$, the reporting currency. Table 12.1 shows the total investments made to June 2007 in US$ and provides a backdrop for other data within the reserve (US$ figures converted at the exchange rates on 30 June 2007 at 7 SA Rand to 1 US$).

The total investment in the reserve amounts to around $93 million. Government investment has attracted private sector capital in a multiple of 2.34, that is, private sector investment at $65.14 million is 2.34 times the $27.85 million

Table 12.1 *Madikwe – investment and employment summary*

Madikwe – investment and employment	2003	2007	Notes
Investment NWPTB	$27.14m	$27.86m	1
Investment private sector	$41.57m	$65.14m	1
Ratio private sector:			
NWPTB investment	1.53	2.34	
Beds (within reserve)	386	552	2
Employees (total cluster)	539	773	3
Wages and salaries –			
whole Madikwe Cluster	$2,609,143	$5,254,838	4
Wages and salaries —			
local employees	$1,111,857	$2,544,098	4
Number employed – local	353	575	4
Percentage local employees			
by numbers	65.5%	74.4%	
Above local employees			
percentage share of total			
cash earnings	42.6%	48.4%	

Notes:

1 Includes all investment made *within* the reserve.

2 Includes all guest beds pertaining to above investments.

3 Includes employment numbers for five enterprise categories (the cluster).

4 Includes only formal cash income earned for employees of all enterprise categories and excludes non-cash remuneration such as fringe benefits. It also excludes cash remuneration from casual labour and gratuities.

Source: 2003 – Relly, 2004b; 2007 – author research

invested by the government to date. This multiple is likely to rise further depending on what NWPTB decides is the final bed capacity (originally 500–700 beds according to Davies et al, 1997).

There are land claims for instance which have recently been settled and these will add bed capacity in the south of MGR. The number of beds in the reserve was targeted within a range set by NWPTB who manage both the reserve (as a protected area) and the tourism development within the reserve. The main constraints on total bed capacity in the reserve are the number of operational game-drive vehicles and the number of operational roads and tracks. Put simply, too many vehicles and too few roads results in higher traffic volume which compromises the guest experience. It appears that NWPTB has a flexible approach to total capacity and it interacts with existing lodge operators. Much of the southern area of the reserve remains undeveloped due to land claims and this area offers some scope for new road development once the land claims issues are finalized.

If the investment figure for privately owned properties (contiguous with the reserve) is added to the $65.14 million figure above, private sector investment could at present be in the range of $78–88 million for the whole cluster. The 'cluster', as previously mentioned, includes the five categories of enterprise either within the reserve or outside but proximal to the reserve fences.

There are insufficient comparative data elsewhere in the tourism sector to make comparisons between Madikwe and other large wildlife reserves. Nonetheless there are plans to extend the reserve and the research data may provide a basis for socioeconomic scenario plans. The creation of the Heritage Park (approaching 300,000ha in extent), linking MGR with Pilanesberg some 80km distant, will continue to provide a strong stimulus to the expansion of these reserves (Boonzaier and Lourens, 2002). This Heritage Park appears to offer the best long-term prospects for land use, employment and poverty alleviation in the local economy. It will have a variety of areas with low to high tourism densities and a mixture of leisure activities. A core corridor will provide the means for larger game species to migrate between the two reserves.

Total formal employment (within the geographic locale) has risen to 773 persons from 539 in 2003. This is likely to be an underestimate given that, other than the additions for new lodges, only six new jobs (in the SMME category) were added to the 2003 employment figures. Within the whole Madikwe cluster, local employees held 74.5 per cent of the total jobs in the cluster and earned 48.4 per cent of the total cluster remuneration by value (Table 12.1).

Business linkages between lodges and local service providers remain weak, unlike those experienced in countries such as The Gambia where Ashley (2006) recently reported that poor members of the population derived more benefit from the supply chain to tourism than direct sales or employment. Handicraft sales were also cited by Ashley as an important component of poor peoples' economies. From current and previous research (Relly, 2004b) in Madikwe there is little evidence of handicraft production/sale playing any role in the local economy. However, most lodges have curio shops or kiosks and the benefits from handicraft sales arise in communities in Zimbabwe, Namibia, east Africa and elsewhere in South Africa. Some transport providers ferry employees to and from local villages and there are a few suppliers of firewood collected under concessions. Laundry services are also offered by a few enterprises outside the reserve. The most significant service provider is a company engaged to manage the various access gates at the reserve. It employed 25 per cent of total employees in the SMME category and probably a similar percentage in 2007. The earnings of all SMME employees in the cluster amounted to 5 per cent of the total annual earnings for the cluster in 2003 (Relly, 2004b, p384) and this figure is not likely to have changed substantially. Madikwe still remains (other than direct employment at lodges) a fairly limited market to employment for the surrounding small enterprise economy. This is to say that the employment multipliers in the local supply chains are low considering the size of the inner-reserve economy. Whilst this is a common phenomenon at many destinations in South Africa in particular, with similar findings elsewhere in the country, the supply chains would have to be thoroughly understood to assess where and how much of the benefit accrues to poorer people. It is probable that where it does, it is likely mostly to occur outside of the geographic area of MGR.

The research sample does not incorporate the other direct employment created in various metropolitan businesses which provide various services to these lodges (as employees thereof). One such enterprise (a bookings and marketing agency) employs around 20 people. Another enterprise, an air charter business, now conveys around 1000 passengers per month to the reserve. NWPTB also employs a number of people outside of MGR in its administrative offices and procures various services such as game capture, etc. The total number of jobs and economic effects are, likewise, not evaluated or incorporated in the total direct economic effect from an employment perspective but the effect is substantial, even if not within the geographic area of the MGR cluster.

At June 2007, there were 20 commercial and 14 corporate lodges (in 2003: 12 and 12). Inflation and increased lodge numbers have boosted the employee cash earnings in the reserve (here we are examining corporate and commercial lodges as well as SMMEs, NWPTB and private sector lodges outside of but contiguous with the reserve fences) to nearly $5.3 million/annum of which nearly $2.6 million accrues to residents defined as 'local' (prior to employment they resided within +/– 50km of the reserve).

Some adjustments to the $2.6 million figure

In 2003 (Relly 2004a, 2004b) determined from a sample of 192 non-management, non-guide staff, that annual gratuities constituted an important cash boost to staff earnings at lodges within the reserve. It was calculated that around $857/annum was earned per staff member in the sample. This figure has been kept at the 2003 level and multiplied by qualifying staff in 2007; total gratuities amount to $420,000/annum with an estimated $343,000 going to local employees. Interviews (with new lodge owners) and 2003 data suggest that *gratuities continue to be a significant category of cash earnings!* In 2003, gratuities to a sample of 192 qualifying staff (excluding guides) provided a boost of 22 per cent to cash earnings for these staff members at commercial lodges (Relly, 2004b, p390).

Guides earn the lion's share of gratuities, sometimes up to and above $1430/month in high season. In the last study a conservative average of $429/month per guide was used to estimate their gratuities. For guides, a frustrating array of qualifications is in place at Madikwe and to date these have been a barrier to larger scale participation in this employment category by local residents. The qualifications require tertiary studies in guiding, public driving permits, medical aid certification, rifle shooting competency and 'jungle lane' training (the latter two have to be renewed by testing every year). The shooting competency places far too much emphasis on actual shooting and virtually none on safe guiding in the bush. In the event that an animal has to be shot by a guide, reports from around Africa indicate that this has usually been the consequence of the guide not following correct safety procedures. Besides the high failure rate in the shooting competency (amongst all guides), local residents face a much longer learning curve in order to catch up with the pool of trained guides being drawn in from elsewhere in South Africa. Using a current estimate of gratuity income of $571,429 per annum for all guides, less than $71,429 (12.5 per cent) ends up in the hands of local residents.

Recent legislation, effective from July 2007 stipulates a minimum cash wage of R1650/month ($236 at the exchange rate of R7 to 1US$) for employees in the hospitality industry. In Madikwe this will increase total annual earnings (only lodge employees) by R275,000 (an average increase of around 18.7 per cent for those qualifying), mostly to local employees. Assuming a household size of six persons dependent on one earner's minimum wage (using a dependency ratio suggested by Massyn and Swan, undated), the average earnings per household dependant amount to around $40/month or $1.33/day. This is a low figure but this should be seen in the context of a region which in the early 1990s employed fewer than 100 poorly paid individuals on cattle ranches.

Casual labour (commissioned for ad hoc projects and not covered by formal employment contracts) has not been investigated for the current study but ongoing repairs and maintenance and works projects in the reserve add anywhere between $285,000 and $715,000 per annum to local pockets.

In total, from the enterprises evaluated in both the 2003 and 2007 studies, with some adjustments referred to in preceding paragraphs, *cash* income earned at the Madikwe cluster is estimated at somewhere between $6.43 and $7.43 million/annum. The minimum and maximum are dependent on the extent of casual wages and gratuities for which accurate 2007 figures are not available. Using the known employment profiles, at least $3.29 million per annum is likely to end up in local households. By comparison – under a livestock ranching, dry-land farming regime – cash income to local employees would amount to possibly $100,000/annum, 3 per cent of the above figure.

In 1999 Rutec (cited in Koch and Massyn, 2003) estimated that the villages and settlements around Madikwe numbered 1775 households. Allowing for some growth to 1850 households in 2007, this translates to an average of $1778 cash earnings/household/annum or $148/month/household. This figure should be added to the pre-existing average 1999 estimate of $225/household/annum (SA rands, inflated for seven years and converted to US$). The approximate total household earnings are therefore now in the region of $373/month. Based on these figures, tourism has boosted average local household income by 65.7 per cent, a considerable average increase over eight years.

Concluding from Table 12.1 and the analysis above, the figures for local residents show a rising proportionate share of numbers of people employed in 2007 (74.4 per cent) compared with 2003 (65.5 per cent) showing far greater recruitment of local residents as defined, but the distribution ratio (ratio of local employee numbers to earnings) shows little change. This indicates that the rapid growth of numbers in the Madikwe cluster has not been accompanied by an even more rapid conversion of local earners from unskilled to skilled labour. The local skills deficiency identified in the area by Relly (2004b) persists in 2007. If destination developers aim to maximize *local* socioeconomic benefit, they must include training in their capital/revenue expenditure budgets. Madikwe was fortunate to benefit from a DfID programme which helped to address this policy failure to some extent.

Table 12.2 *Madikwe – commercial lodge statistics*

Madikwe – Commercial Lodges	Total Dec 2003	Additions	Total June 2007
Investment private sector	$29,325,122	$19,512,000	$48,837,122
Total beds	266	146	412
Total employees	356	215	571
Investment/employee (averages)	$82,374		$85,529
Investment per bed (averages)	$110,245		$118,537
Bed:employee ratio	1.34		1.39
Total cash salaries and wages (annualized)	$2,020,948		$3,901,784
Average, annual, cash salary/person	$5677		$6833
Female employees			
No. female employees	171		285
Total earnings female employees	$827,105		$1,631,193
Percentage of total employed	48.0%		49.9%
Percentage of total cash remuneration	40.9%		41.8%
Average, annual, cash salary	$4837		$5723
Local employees			
No. local employees	249		424
Total earnings local employees	$829,892		$1,802,241
Percentage of total numbers	69.9%		74.3%
Percentage of total cash remuneration	41.1%		46.2%
Average, annual, cash salary	$3333		$4251
Previously disadvantaged employees			
No. PDI employees	264		443
Total earnings PDI employees	$911,972		$1,932,802
Percentage of total numbers	74.2%		77.6%
Percentage of total cash remuneration	45.1%		49.5%
Average, annual, cash salary	$3454		$4363

Source: 2003 Relly (2004b), 2007 – Author Survey

Apart from SMMEs engaged directly in the reserve, the study does not account for the various financial and non-financial benefits arising in the villages outside of the game reserve, nor does it assess non-cash benefits included in the remuneration of employed staff members (more relevant to higher paid staff members who, depending on seniority, receive more than a basic unemployment benefit contribution, i.e. private medical aid, private pension contributions, free meals, motor vehicle allowances and accommodation for family are the principal benefits). If it were possible to research and quantify guidelines (for a broader variety of benefits and multipliers) suggested in the SNV/ODI Toolkit (Ashley, 2006), it is likely that a monetized figure for value added to local community could be in excess of $4.3million per annum.

Table 12.2 examines figures only from *commercial lodges within* MGR. Included in these are two local community-owned, commercial lodges which were not operational in 2003 and some of the data pertaining to these lodges are discussed shortly under a separate heading. Table 12.2 provides a breakdown of employee profiles for female, local and previously disadvantaged persons. The commercial lodges form the backbone of the local economy, providing three-quarters of direct employment and employee earnings in the cluster. In the latest study, most of the focus on new data was aimed at these enterprises. Where applicable, assumptions relevant to Table 12.1 apply also to Table 12.2.

Investors from the private sector have continued to opt for the high end of the tourism market (the intention of the planners from the outset) and the investment/bed has increased in the past few years. The job:bed ratio supports this observation.

Female employees make up half of the workforce and earn nearly 42 per cent of total remuneration. Local employees now constitute nearly three-quarters of total employed and earn 46.2 per cent of the total cash remuneration paid by commercial lodges.

Community-owned lodges

A significant development in the reserve has contributed to the shift in the 2003:2007 figures when compared. Two community-owned commercial lodges have become operational since 2003. Local village communities have collectively obtained the right to develop and own commercial lodges. This falls within part of the NWPTB objectives to give some preference to local communities in the securing, development and ownership of lodge sites.

With the exception of one staff member, 57 of the 58 employees in these lodges are from local villages, indicating the significant bargaining power gained from direct ownership. With 40 beds in community lodges, the job:bed ratio is 1.45, slightly above the average of 1.39 for all of the commercial lodges combined.

Significantly, although the Madikwe study does not address *total* local community benefit (i.e. does not include all non-cash benefits and other unassessed multiplier effects, development in social capital, etc.), the community-owned lodges have turnover clauses with their appointed operator (including a minor base rental) and the combined revenue at present from this source is around $157,000 per annum. This revenue accrues to two village communities who fall within the Madikwe cluster. As these lodges become more established, this figure can be expected to rise.

Massyn and Swan (undated, p1) estimated that one of the community lodges (Lekgophung village, 16 bed lodge) would generate average returns in the order of $450 per household/annum in the estimated 600 household community. This figure has now reached the $371/annum mark (cash returns only) bearing in mind that the lodge has not yet reached its optimal, annual bed-occupancy. As the lodge moves towards this level, one could expect the annual household benefit to be close to the original estimate (excluding the non-cash items, multipliers, etc. mentioned in the paragraph above). Data were not available for the other community-owned lodge (Molatedi village) but turnover and occupancy levels at their 24 bed lodge are significantly higher in absolute and percentage terms than the Lekgophung village lodge.

The communities have been able to secure all but one of the employment positions through their greater bargaining power. In addition they earn turnover royalties/levies discussed above. In due course they will also become owners of the lodges, debt-free with significant capital value estimated at $4.7 million. The revenue flows from these assets (profits and/or royalties) can be directed at a number of community projects in the future.

Some comparative data from lodge clusters in southern Africa

For comparative purposes, in Figure 12.2, studies by Koch et al (2001a, 2001b, 2001c, 2001d) show samples of top-end lodges in four southern African clusters compared to Madikwe in 2003. The sample sizes are small, but some regional differences are apparent. Zimbabwe for instance has a low percentage of female employees (23 per cent). The cleaning and room service positions – usually taken by women in the industry are, in the instance of the region reviewed in Zimbabwe, often taken by men. Notably, South Africa has the lowest percentage of local employees and this partly reflects the skills shortage in the area, which is not densely populated, and also the relative newness of the community to the tourism industry. The remoteness of many of the lodges, in the non-SA lodges sampled, may also pose a substantial barrier to the employment or development of non-local employees. However, given that Madikwe is a socioeconomic model developed for local benefit it is hoped that the reserve managers and policy makers will pay more attention to local skills development and promotion

In the commercial lodges, aside from the effect the community lodges have on the averages, it appears that after 10+ years, the villages around the reserve continue to capture a greater proportional share of the available jobs. However, the gap between percentage of locals employed (74.3 per cent) and percentage earned (46.2 per cent) compared to 2003 indicates that the skills gap persists and skills have to be recruited from more distant areas. For semi-skilled or skilled positions (defined very broadly in this study as annual cash wages of $4286 upwards and consisting of 241 of the 571 formal jobs at commercial lodges) 102 or 42.3 per cent were occupied by local residents. From the data available, it appears that 19.4 per cent or 19 out of 98 jobs, in the 20 commercial lodges paying above $10,000 per annum for those positions, were occupied by local residents.

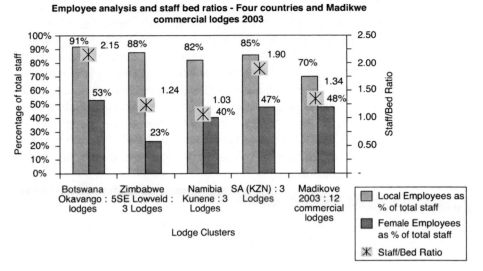

Source: Botswana, Zimbabwe, Namibia & SA (KZN) from Relly 2004a, adapted from Koch et al, 2001a, 2001b, 2001c, 2001d

Figure 12.2 *Madikwe Cluster 2003 compared with clusters in four countries – employee numbers only*

Summary and conclusions

The ongoing evaluation of Madikwe has been conducted in a relative vacuum of comparable published data. However, the evaluation of new lodges within the reserve has produced some noteworthy data.

The state's investment of nearly $28 million (mainly infrastructure, fencing and wildlife) has attracted a further $65.14 million worth of private sector, fixed investment *within* the reserve in the form of lodge superstructure and fittings – and is well in excess of this if one considers the capital that has been invested in land and tourism plant on farms not officially incorporated in the reserve to date. Within the reserve, investment at the 20 commercial lodges averages around $118,570 per bed or $85,570 per permanent job.

The reserve has created 773 full-time employment positions within the cluster of five enterprise categories. Nearly 75 per cent of these jobs are occupied by local employees, a significant percentage increase on the 2003 figure of 65.5 per cent. The 2007 figure suggests that the 12+ years of MGR's operational existence has started to manifest in increased local recruitment. This is supported by the increased local capture of cash remuneration to 48.4 per cent (2003, 42.6 per cent). The total formal cash earnings going to local employees are now close to the $2.57 million/annum mark and this figure can be reckoned to be in the region of $3.29 million/annum with various estimated adjustments for cash income sources not reflected on the payrolls.

Although the primary purpose of the study has been to evaluate the economic effects for local residents, it shows that in the commercial lodges, there have also been slight improvements in employment and earnings for female and previously disadvantaged groups. The distortions between employment and earnings percentages however indicate that these groups still reflect the gender and skills gaps that existed in 2003. Using adjusted 1999 figures for households, approximately 1850 households in the area will, on average, have experienced an income rise from a base of $225/household/month to $373/household/month in cash income. Using an estimate of seven persons/household, the effect translates from $1.06/person/day prior to the reserve's existence to $1.75/person/day in 2007, a 65 per cent increase in nominal terms.

The two community lodges which are now operational must provide satisfaction to planners and policy makers in regard to returns to community, considering how recently they were established. It appears that there could be room for more of these operations as the relationships between private sector partners and communities are operating in harmony and also indicate economic viability. In the two lodges, local employees occupied 57 of the 58 formal employment positions. They (the larger communities) also participated in turnover levies which, provided they remain on track, will allow them to repay all debt which has been structured at a manageable level. In due course the communities will have full ownership of their lodges, debt free. If we use the bed investment figures established in this study, the present day (net asset) value of those lodges should be in the region of $4.7 million.

In Madikwe, the research undertaken at this reserve would benefit from further studies, deepening the research to household level, investigating multiplier effects and analysing (non-labour) lodge expenditure and profitability to name but three potential areas. The exercise would require inputs from individuals with professional experience in statistics, economics, resource economics and research methodology in human sciences. These inputs are costly and information may be sketchy, particularly where confidentiality is concerned. In the end, would we finally have a replicable model showing impacts for the poor? The model may only be area specific and the next step would be to assess whether such a model could be adapted to serve policy makers for other types of tourism, urban scenarios, provincial or national scenarios and so on.

Nonetheless, without these augmentations, the data as presented indicate that Madikwe continues to bring opportunities and substantial income to a once marginal economic area.

References

Ashley, C. (2000) *The Impacts of Tourism on Rural Livelihoods: Namibia's experience*, Working Paper 128, Overseas Development Institute, London

Ashley, C. (2006) *Participation by the Poor in Luang Prabang Tourism Economy: Current Earnings and Opportunities for Expansion*, ODI Working Paper 273, ODI and SNV, London and The Hague

Ashley, C., SNV and ODI (2006) *How Can Governments Boost the Local Economic Impacts of Tourism? Options and Tools*, Netherlands Development Organization (SNV) and Overseas Development Institute (ODI), The Hague and London

Boonzaier, W. B. and Lourens, M. (2002) *Heritage Park Concept Plan*, 2nd ed, Pilanesberg National Park Management Series for the North West Parks and Tourism Board by Contour Project Managers and Grant Thornton Kessel Feinstein, Rustenburg

Britton, S. G. (1982) 'International tourism and multinational corporations in the Pacific', in M. Taylor and N. Thrift (eds), *The Geography of Multinationals*, Croom Helm, London, 252–274

Britton, S. G. (1983) *Tourism and Underdevelopment in Fiji*, Development Studies Centre Monograph 31, Australian National University, Canberra

Davies, R. (1997) 'A description and history of Madikwe Game Reserve', *Madikwe Development Series Number 1*, North West parks and Tourism Board

Davies, R., Trieloff, C. and Wells, M. (1997) 'Financial and economic objectives and management of the Madikwe Game Reserve', *Madikwe Development Series Number 5*, North West Parks and Tourism Board

Koch, E. and Massyn, P. J. (2003) 'The Madikwe Initiative: A programme designed to optimize local benefit by integrating the conservation of wildlife with local economic development' in M. Brett (ed.), *Madikwe Game Reserve – A decade of progress*, North West Parks and Tourism Board, Mafikeng, pp21–33

Koch, E. and Massyn, P. J. with Relly, P. and Hartley, R. (2001a) 'African game lodges and rural benefit in Botswana – a survey of five lodges in the Okavango Delta', Report by Mafisa – commissioned by the Ford Foundation, available from www.mafisa.co.za

Koch, E. and Massyn, P. J. with Relly, P., Johnson, S. and Metcalfe, S. (2001b) 'African game lodges and rural benefit in Zimbabwe', Report by Mafisa – commissioned by the Ford Foundation, available from www.mafisa.co.za

Koch, E. and Massyn, P. J. with Relly, P. and Jones, B. (2001c) 'African game lodges and rural benefit in Namibia', Report by Mafisa – commissioned by the Ford Foundation, available from www.mafisa.co.za

Koch, E. and Massyn, P. J., with Relly, P. (2001d) 'African game lodges and rural benefit in South Africa', Report by Mafisa – commissioned by the Ford Foundation, available from www.mafisa.co.za

Massyn, P. J. and Swan N. (undated) 'Case study of Lekgophung Tourism Lodge – South Africa', available from www. Livelihoods.org/post/docs/legophung.doc

Mitchell, J. and Ashley, C. (2007) 'Can tourism offer pro-poor pathways to prosperity – Examining evidence on the impact of tourism on poverty', Briefing Paper 22, Overseas Development Institute, London

Relly, P. (2004a) 'Employment and investment in Madikwe Game Reserve – South Africa', Unpublished research report submitted to The Graduate School of Human Sciences – University of the Witwatersrand in partial fulfilment of requirements for the degree of Master of Arts in Tourism Studies, Supervised by Prof. C. Rogerson

Relly, P. (2004b) 'Madikwe Game Reserve – The local impacts of wildlife tourism', in C. Rogerson and G. Visser (eds), *Tourism and Development Issues in Contemporary South Africa*, Africa Institute of South Africa, Pretoria, 372–398

Republic of South Africa (1996) *White Paper on the Development and Promotion of Tourism in South Africa*, Department of Environmental Affairs and Tourism, Pretoria

Republic of South Africa (1998) *Tourism in Gear: Tourism Development Strategy 1998-2000*, Department of Environmental Affairs and Tourism, Pretoria

World Travel and Tourism Council (WTTC) (2006) *Namibia – The impact of travel and tourism on jobs and the economy*, WTTC, London

Wunder, S. (2000) *Big Island, Green Forests and Backpackers: Land Use and Development Options on Ilha Grande, Rio de Janaeiro State, Brazil,* Working Paper 4, Centre for Development Research, Copenhagen, available from www.propoortourism.org.uk

Part 3

Community-based Tourism

13

Local Impacts of Community-based Tourism in Southern Africa

Anna Spenceley

Purpose and scope of the chapter

A review of southern African community-based tourism enterprises (CBTEs) was undertaken as an initiative from the United Nations World Tourism Organization (UNWTO), the Regional Tourism Organization for Southern Africa (RETOSA), and the Dutch development Agency SNV. The objective was to use the information collected to develop an online CBTE directory that would help the enterprises reach tourists and tour operators internationally, and thereby improve their market access.

This chapter presents an analysis of how 218 CBTEs in 12 southern African countries (Botswana, Lesotho, Madagascar, Malawi, Mauritius, Mozambique, Namibia, South Africa, Swaziland, Tanzania, Zambia and Zimbabwe) impact on the local environment and people. The review includes information on the type of tourism operated, their commercial viability (i.e. visitation, revenue, human resources) and their socioeconomic impacts on local communities (i.e. employment, revenue generation, visitation, local procurement of goods and services). The chapter also presents the constraints faced by CBTEs, and a review of interventions that the enterprises deem necessary to improve their commercial viability.

Background to community-based tourism in southern Africa

International agencies increasingly promote tourism, and particularly community-based tourism as a means to reduce poverty in developing countries. Community-based initiatives have proliferated across Africa, Asia and the Neotropics (Walpole, 1997) and there have been many theoretical and practical studies examining them (Kiss, 1990; Zube and Busch, 1990; Wells and Brandon, 1992; von Loebenstein et al, 1993; Wells and Brandon, 1993; IIED, 1994). In Zimbabwe (as reviewed in Chapter 7), landowners and rural district councils are granted the appropriate authority to utilize wildlife on their land (Murphree, 1996). The devolution of control has allowed community-based resource use schemes such as the Communal Areas Management Programme for Indigenous Resources (CAMPFIRE) to develop. CAMPFIRE is a system of harvesting wildlife where associated benefits are accrued by local communities. Local Authorities are able to manage wildlife resources on communal land, and harvest wildlife in accordance with National Parks quotas. Hunting is a favoured tourism activity in CAMPFIRE regions as it requires little infrastructural and institutional support (Grossman and Koch, 1995). Money reaching the communities is distributed by them, in accordance with their wishes; either split between all the inhabitants equally, or invested in infrastructure such as schools, roads and clinics (Baker, 1997).

Community involvement in tourism has been widely supported in the literature as essential (Murphy, 1985; Wilkinson, 1989; de Kadt, 1990; Drake, 1991). It is emphasized from a moral point of view, an equity perspective, a developmental perspective and from a business management view (de Kadt, 1990; Cater, 1996; Wilkinson, 1989; Brohman, 1996). Community ownership provides livelihood security, minimal leakage, efficient conflict resolution, increases in the local populations social carrying capacity, and improved conservation (Steele, 1995). From a conservation perspective, using local populations to protect resources rather than external people is more effective (Chambers, 1988). Local knowledge of wildlife and forest products can also greatly enhance tourism services, and may have implications for practical infrastructural development through the use of vegetation products (Hawkins et al, 1995), reduces leakage, lowers costs and enhances local multiplier effects (Cater, 1996).

Costs associated with community tourism projects include the fact that they are expensive, they generate high expectations which may not be achievable, new conflicts may arise as marginal groups become more empowered while elites gain greater benefits through networks (Zazueta, 1995). They may fail because authority has not been devolved to the appropriate lowest level and so benefits from activities are not returned to the community (Attwell and Cotterill, 2000). Donor support may be fickle, and may be removed by the donor at any time, as there are no contracts to state that a donor must remain until a project is sustainable. In addition, despite attempts to empower communities to exploit tourism markets, they are frequently unable to provide the standard of service the foreign tourists require, leaving large tourism operations without competition or any incentives to distribute wealth (Yu et al, 1997).

Kiss (2004) notes that the level and distribution of economic benefits from CBTs depend on many factors including the attractiveness of the tourism asset, the type of tourism operation, the nature and degree of community involvement, and whether earnings become private income or are channelled into community projects or other benefit-spreading mechanisms (Wunder, 2000). She notes that projects that simply generate local employment opportunities are sometimes a good start. Joint ventures between community groups and private tourism operators, which are increasingly popular, might have the greatest potential for generating significant revenues for communities, and might also be more likely to succeed than wholly community-run enterprises, particularly in the early stages. However, communities will often need outside assistance to organize themselves, obtain and assert their legal rights and understand their obligations in such partnerships (Wunder, 2000; Wells, 1997; Ashley and Garland, 1994).

There have been many case study examples of livelihood impacts of specific tourism enterprises on local people (e.g. Spenceley and Goodwin, 2007; Simpson, Chapter 11; Mbiwa, Chapter 9; Spenceley, 2001; Ottosson, 2004; Ntshona and Lahiff, 2003), but few systematic evaluations of many enterprises (e.g. Dixey, Chapter 15; Kibicho, 2004; Williams et al, 2001; Roe et al, 2001), and no systematic evaluations where hundreds of enterprises have been compared.

The aim of the review was to establish how 218 CBTEs in southern Africa impact on the local environment and people. The analysis includes information on the type of tourism operated, their commercial viability and their socioeconomic impacts on local communities. The chapter also presents a review of the constraints faced by CBTEs, and a review of interventions that the enterprises deem necessary to improve their commercial viability.

Method

Scope

The geographical scope of the study was the 14 Southern African Development Community (SADC) countries, which are members of the Regional Tourism Organization for Southern Africa (RETOSA). The SADC countries are Angola, Botswana, Democratic Republic of Congo, Lesotho, Madagascar, Malawi, Mauritius, Mozambique, Namibia, South Africa, Swaziland, Tanzania, Zambia and Zimbabwe.

Defining community-based tourism enterprises

A working definition of CBTEs that would be used to guide the directory development was developed. In the absence of an internationally recognized and standard definition of CBTE in the academic or institutional literature, a definition used by RETOSA during the compilation of an existing CBTE directory was taken as a starting point. Following review and comment by the project team, the working definition for the project was established as having three criteria:

1   located within a community (e.g. on communal land, or with community benefits such as lease fees); or
2   owned by one or more community members (i.e. for the benefit of one or more community members); or
3   managed by community members (i.e. community members could influence the decision-making process of the enterprise).

It was acknowledged that in general, communities involved in CBT are:

- relatively remote from national centres of learning, economy and industry;
- constrained by poor infrastructure, in terms of roads, electricity and water;
- economically poor, with little or no capital for investment in the tourism industry;
- inexperienced and under-skilled at developing and managing tourism enterprises, working with tourists,
- rich in distinctive cultures and histories firmly rooted in the local area; and
- largely dependent on local natural resources (such as trees, medicinal plants and wildlife).

Information on community-based accommodation and their associated activities (e.g. guided tours, traditional performances) was prioritized for collection. The working definition ensured a broad scope for CBTEs that could be proposed for evaluation: CBTEs could have government assistance, they could be partnerships with the private sector or non-profit organizations, they could be township B&Bs run by individual indigenous entrepreneurs, or they could be operations run by collective community groups and managed through elected Trusts.

Identifying enterprises

The literature sources and institutional sources that were used included guide books, existing directories (from RETOSA and the Open Africa Initiative) and consultancy reports. Many individuals and institutions facilitated the initiative by providing additional information on CBTEs operating in the region.

CBTE evaluation process

The evaluation process of the CBTEs was as follows:

1   Agreements were made with in-country institutions to recruit and coordinate, and pay volunteers to undertake CBTE evaluations, in return for an administration fee for the institution.
2   Volunteers recruited by the institutions collected information on the CBTEs in their country using questionnaires and guidelines provided (see below).

Evaluations consisted of a site visit, completion of a questionnaire, and entry of that information onto an online database. In return, volunteers were paid an honorarium for each assessment and their transportation and associated expenses.

3   A proportion – 12 per cent – of the CBTEs were re-assessed by another volunteer to ensure the reliability of data, and the validity of the evaluation process.

Development of assessment materials

Since a central training programme for all volunteers was not feasible given the logistics and budget for the research, assessment materials were developed to assist the volunteers in the assessment process. These consisted of the following:

Introductory text, explaining what the data collection was for; how communities would benefit; what community-based tourism is; how institutions could get involved; how volunteers could get involved; how volunteers could use the website; downloads (i.e. the assessment and guidance materials); and links to various websites and sources of information.

Guidelines to plan assessments, including useful information that volunteers could use to plan safe and interesting assessments. Suggestions were included regarding how they should contact the enterprise (i.e. to see if they were interested in participating, to ensure that they were still operating, and to arrange a site visit), how to plan their travel, how to conduct the site visit, and how to enter the information on an online database when they returned from the site visit.

The questionnaire to be completed by the volunteers at each enterprise, to collect information on:

• the type of accommodation, facilities, tours and prices;
• levels of quality and security;
• how the enterprise benefited members of the local community;
• skills and training needs;
• how they advertised and marketed their product; and
• how their customers made bookings.

The questionnaire went through several iterations and reviews by the project team. Two pilot tests at CBTEs were conducted by volunteers in South Africa, before a final version was produced. The content and evaluation criteria addressed incorporated aspects of other tourism questionnaires previously developed by WorldHotelLink (WHL, 2005), a USAID study of CBTEs undertaken in Zambia (Dixey, 2005), the Tourism Grading Council of South Africa (TGCSA, undated a, undated b), and the WTO's Sustainable Tourism-Eliminating Poverty (ST-EP) guidelines (WTO, 2004). The criteria included indicators that would elicit information regarding enterprise viability – including details of their visitation, their booking systems, limitations to their business, and training both received and required.

Training was provided to volunteers during workshops in Tanzania and South Africa, at the request of the two coordinating institutions based in these countries.

On site evaluations

The site visits entailed a volunteer visiting the enterprise, and through discussions with the manager and observation, completing a detailed questionnaire. During each on-site evaluation, the volunteer would leave a briefing document with the enterprise. This provided them with information about the data collection process, the online directory that was to be developed and how they could benefit from the new market access channel.

In all there were 251 assessments undertaken, of which 28 were audits (repeat assessments to check evaluation quality), 3 enterprises were no longer operating, 1 was incomplete, and 1 was found not to be a CBTE under the criteria used. Therefore in total 218 CBTEs were assessed.

All of the CBTE entries compiled by volunteers on the online database were checked by the project team, and comments and corrections were relayed to the coordinating institutions for amendment. Assessment audits of 12 per cent of the enterprises were undertaken for quality assurance purposes. A comparison of the 25 enterprises that were audited revealed that on the quality issues, of 375 data entries, only 9 (0.8 per cent) revealed completely different responses (e.g. one volunteer rating quality 'very good', and the auditor rating it as 'poor'). This indicates that the system of using volunteers who are provided with guidance information was highly reliable.

Results

The data from the CBTEs that were of sufficient quality to accept tourists were placed on a searchable website www.community-tourism-africa.com that could be used by tourists and tour operators to identify and select enterprises to visit, and also to contact them to make bookings. More information on all of the enterprises analysed here can be found at this site.

Location

The majority of enterprises evaluated were located in South Africa (50.3 per cent), followed by Namibia (10.8 per cent), Zimbabwe (8.7 per cent), Zambia (6.7 per cent), Botswana (5.6 per cent), Madagascar and Malawi (4.1 per cent each), Lesotho, Mozambique and Swaziland (3.1 per cent each) and Mauritius (0.5 per cent). No CBTEs were identified in Angola or the DRC.

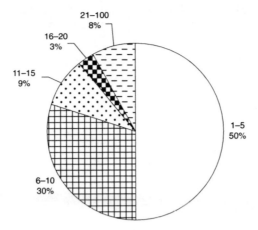

Figure 13.1 *Room capacity of CBTEs (number of rooms, and % of enterprises)*

Facilities and services

Nearly half the enterprises were Bed and Breakfasts (47.7 per cent) or campsites where people bring their own tents (44.5 per cent). Traditional chalets (24.8 per cent) were also frequently identified, in addition to game lodges, guest houses and homestays (17.4 per cent each), self catering flats (11.5 per cent), backpackers (10.6 per cent), campsites with electricity (6.0 per cent) or with fixed tents (5.5 per cent). Only a small proportion of the enterprises were hotels (4.1 per cent) or campsites without electricity (2.3 per cent). Some of the CBTEs had more than one type of accommodation (e.g. backpackers and camping). Most of the enterprises were small, with 1 to 5 rooms or units (49.5 per cent) (see Figure 13.1).

The enterprises cumulatively offered 4146 beds or spaces (i.e. for camping), with capacity for 6531 people to stay (see Table 13.1). The World Travel and Tourism Council's Tourism Satellite Accounts estimate that there were 27.4 million overnight international visitors in southern Africa in 2007 (see www.wttc.travel/eng/Research/Tourism_Satellite_Accounting_Tool/index.php). Therefore only a tiny fraction of these visitors could possibly be accommodated by CBTEs in the region.

The themes of most of the enterprises was cultural (67.4 per cent) and rural (55.0 per cent), followed by natural area/park (47.3 per cent), safari/game

Table 13.1 *Room and bed capacity*

Type of accommodation	Total number of beds/spaces	Total number of people who can stay
Rooms	3388	3792
Dormitory	234	214
Campsite	524	2525
Totals	4146	6531

Table 13.2 *Third-party support for CBTE*

Type of organization	No.	% of enterprises
Non-governmental organization	39	17.89
Destination management organization	20	9.17
Community-based organization	11	5.05
Conservation parastatal	9	4.13
Private sector – accommodation	8	3.67
Private sector – tour operator	8	3.67
Local authority	5	2.29
Private sector – tourism association	5	2.29
Private sector – other	5	2.29
Donor	4	1.83
Government	4	1.83
National government	4	1.83

viewing/wildlife (29.8 per cent), mountain (26.2 per cent), urban (18.4 per cent), adventure/sport (15.6 per cent), conference/business (12.4 per cent), highway/roadside (8.3 per cent), or beach/coastal (7.8 per cent). A small number of enterprises were desert based (2.3 per cent), offering casinos or gaming (1.4 per cent), with a health spa or golf (0.9 per cent each).

Support by third-parties

CBTEs were asked whether there was a contact partner or champion agency involved. This might be an organization or company that helps the enterprise with funding or heavily supports it in some way. Institutions might include non-governmental organizations (NGOs), donors, tourism enterprises or tour operators. Over half the enterprises reported receiving support from a third party (55 per cent), and most of these were aided by an NGO (17.89 per cent of enterprises) or a destination management organization (DMO) (9.17 per cent enterprises) (see Table 13.2). For example, all of the CBTEs assessed in Tanzania received support from the Tanzanian Tourism Board. Interestingly, only 5 per cent of CBTEs were supported by a community-based organization, such as a community trust.

Business administration

Most described themselves as budget accommodation (71.9 per cent) or mid-range (28.1 per cent). There were no luxury or high-end CBTEs in the sample. A review of the prices charged for accommodation at the CBTEs indicates that most enterprises charge per person, per night, rather than per unit or space. The average per person high season prices ranged from $31.24 for a room, $12.83 for a dormitory and $11.69 for camping (see Table 13.3). There is little variation between low and high season prices for rooms, dormitories and campsites: the

Table 13.3 *Accommodation prices*

Prices (US$)	Per person		Per room/space	
	Low season average	High season average	Low season average	High season average
Rooms	29.23 (n = 226)	31.24 (n = 226)	37.54 (n = 139)	39.08 (n = 139)
Dormitory	12.83 (n = 18)	12.83 (n = 18)	19.81 (n = 2)	19.81 (n = 2)
Campsite	8.54 (n = 59)	11.69 (n = 59)	10.23 (n = 12)	10.48 (n = 12)

Note: Where figures were cited in local currency the exchange rate on 1 November 2006 was used for conversion. Some of the enterprises had more than one type of room, with more than one price scale, which is the reason why the number of rooms indicated is greater than 218.

greatest variation being a 36 per cent increase for camping rates per person between seasons.

The occupancy levels at the CBTEs were relatively low, with the majority of enterprises ranging between 11 and 500 visitors over the previous year (60.9 per cent). On average, the enterprises had 884.8 visitors, ranging from none to 32,000. One fact of concern, was that 14 enterprises could not say how many people had stayed during that period, and 33 could not report the number of day visitors, indicating poor levels of record keeping (Figure 13.2). Most of the enterprises reported that visitors stayed for 2 nights (40.4 per cent of CBTEs), with an average of 3.9 nights reported.

The CBTEs were asked to indicate the most important limitations they faced in developing their tourism businesses. The most frequently cited limitation was

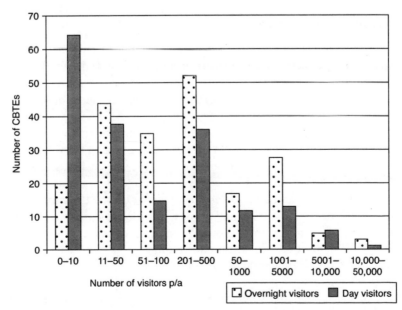

Figure 13.2 *Number of overnight and day visitors during the past year at CBTEs*

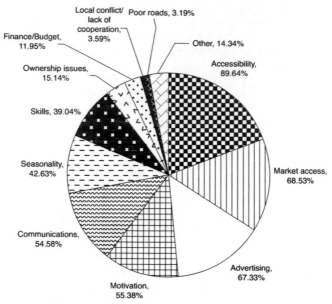

Figure 13.3 *Limitations to tourism enterprise*

accessibility (90.8 per cent) followed by market access (71.6 per cent) (Figure 13.3). This has implications for the planning of new CBTEs in the future (i.e. to ensure that their location in relation to source markets and transport infrastructure is commercially viable) and also regarding training and capacity building to improve linkages between existing enterprises and the market.

Sustainable development

Most of the enterprise managers indicated that they knew what sustainable tourism was (74.3 per cent), and a similar proportion believed they were practising sustainable tourism (74.8 per cent). A third of CBTEs' statements or policies on sustainable tourism mentioned conservation or sustainable resource use (33.0 per cent), and a fifth mentioned community benefits and employment (20.6 per cent). Many others indicated the importance of community development and cultural conservation and celebration (11.5 per cent). Some of the CBTE's definitions provided were related to guest satisfaction (17.9 per cent), service quality and commercial viability, rather than 'triple bottom line' sustainable tourism (6.0 per cent). The type of sustainable tourism activities reflected their understanding of sustainable tourism, and concerned conservation or sustainable resource use (34.9 per cent) and community benefits or employment (27.0 per cent). Enterprises also mentioned education and training (18.8 per cent), community development (14.2 per cent) and cultural conservation and celebration (11.5 per cent) (Table 13.4).

Some notable sustainability statements by the enterprises include the following:

Table 13.4 *Sustainable tourism commitment and activities*

Factors mentioned in sustainability commitment	No	% of enterprises	Types of activities implemented	No	% of enterprises
Conservation/sustainable resource use	72	33.03	Conservation/sustainable resource use	76	34.86
Community benefits/ employment	45	20.64	Community benefits/ employment	59	27.06
Guest satisfaction	39	17.89	Education/training	41	18.81
Community development	25	11.47	Community development	31	14.22
Cultural conservation/ celebration	25	11.47	Craft/product development	27	12.39
Service quality/ commercial viability	13	5.96	Cultural conservation/ celebration	25	11.47
Future generations	10	4.59	Local ownership	13	5.96
Local participation	10	4.59	Local participation	13	5.96
Local ownership	8	3.67	Hospitality	11	5.05
Education	7	3.21	Empowering women	8	3.67
Gender	4	1.83	Access to finance	8	3.67
Health	2	0.92	Recycling	5	2.29
Indigenous knowledge	1	0.46	Economic feasibility	5	2.29
			Clean up operations	3	1.38
			Environmentally friendly products	1	0.46

[The enterprise is] An intimate part of the community that believes wholeheartedly in engaging with the local people and sharing the benefits of tourism with the entire community.

Efforts are made to minimize impact on the environment; water use is restricted to river water, while waste water uses natural filtration processes before re-entering the river. They use solar panels for their power. Local people are employed at the camp, thereby supporting several local families with each employee.

Our vision is to balance community development with conservation through the creation of a sustainable wilderness reserve.

A fifth of CBTEs had received some form of award for quality, conservation, or providing local benefits (20.1 per cent), and a quarter had received some form of certification (25.2 per cent). The certification schemes mostly related to quality of the enterprise (40.3 per cent), such as a 'star' rating, followed by social (37.1 per cent) or environmental criteria (14.5 per cent).

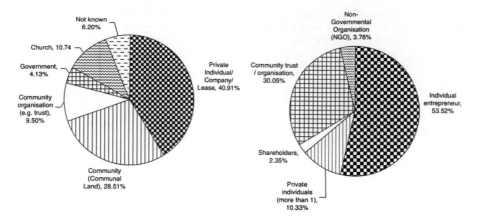

Figure 13.4 *Land ownership (left) and business ownership (right)*

Community involvement

The land that most of the enterprises were based on was owned by private individuals, a company or was leased (45.4 per cent). The host community or a community-based organization owned the land of many enterprises (42.2 per cent). The owners of most businesses were individual entrepreneurs (52.3 per cent) followed by community trusts or community organizations (29.4 per cent) (Figure 13.4). Increasing the extent of equity that people have in destinations can be a powerful way to enhance local benefits and participation in the tourism industry.

Half of the CBTEs reported that members of the community made decisions about how the tourism enterprise was run (50.0 per cent). The mechanism for doing so included meetings (27.5 per cent), through an elected community trust or committee (19.3 per cent), joint decision making (10.6 per cent), using a village representative or council (7.3 per cent). Some indicated that the community was involved in planning (5.1 per cent), and decided how to use funds (3.2 per cent), or that there were informal visits or discussions (1.8 per cent).

Socioeconomic impact

The 218 enterprises employed a total of 2644 people between them, including 1587 men (60.0 per cent), 1048 women (39.6 per cent) and 9 youths under the age of 17 (0.3 per cent). Of these, 2504 employees were from the local community (94.7 per cent). The average number of employees per enterprise was 12.1 people, ranging between 0 and 300 staff. These figures have very good implications for local wages and also for the role of women in tourism.

Enterprises reported a wide range of benefits that the local community gained from the enterprise. Most frequently they reported access to finance (45.0 per cent), employment (38.5 per cent) and community infrastructure development (30.3 per cent), followed by training (28.9 per cent) and product purchasing

Table 13.5 *Local benefits from the CBTE*

Type of benefit	No.	% of enterprises
Access to finance (loans, profit, donations)	98	44.95
Employment	84	38.53
Community infrastructure development	66	30.28
Education/training (and support of education institutions)	63	28.90
Craft/product development and purchasing	61	27.98
Service provision	48	22.02
Access to resources	40	18.35
Health facilities	26	11.93
Conservation/sustainable resource use	25	11.47
No benefit	17	7.80
Cultural conservation/celebration	16	7.34
Community benefits	15	6.88
Local ownership	12	5.50
Decision making	11	5.05
Cultural exchange	10	4.59
Enterprise development	8	3.67
Helping orphans	7	3.21
Empowerment women/youth	6	2.75
Voluntary work (by tourists or staff)	6	2.75
Local participation	5	2.29
Sports development	5	2.29
Local enterprise management	5	2.29
Institutional development	2	0.92

(28.0 per cent). However, some indicated that the community received new benefits (7.8 per cent) (Table 13.5).

Cumulatively, the amount of money that was given to local projects by the CBTE over the previous year was the equivalent of US$4,461,331. On average, 186 of the enterprises (85.3 per cent) had provided $35,129 to local projects, with a median of $450. A total of 30 of the enterprises (14.8 per cent) could not determine what amount of money was provided, while 2 provided in-kind benefits.

Local procurement of products and services was practised by many of the enterprises. When asked what they purchased, many reported buying craft (39.5 per cent), fruit and vegetables (28.9 per cent) and using services such as cultural dancing, singing and entertainment (42.7 per cent), guiding (28.9 per cent) and catering (13.8 per cent) (Table 13.6). On average, 196 of the enterprises (89.9 per cent of the sample) spent the equivalent of US$6616 per year on products and services from the local community. Cumulatively, they spent $965,954 locally, with a median of $667, although 22 of the enterprises could not report how much money they spent locally (10.1 per cent of the sample). Examining the procurement chains within the local economy in detail for a sample of these enter-

Table 13.6 *Local products and services procured by CBTEs*

Local products	No.	% of enterprises	Local services	No.	% of enterprises
Craft	86	39.45	Cultural dance/singing/ entertainment	93	42.66
Fruit and vegetables	63	28.90	Guiding	63	28.90
Décor (including pots)	34	15.60	Catering	30	13.76
Food	29	13.30	Making/selling craft	24	11.01
Meat & meat products	29	13.30	Employees	24	11.01
Fabric/clothes	27	12.39	Construction	18	8.26
Wood	26	11.93	Transport	18	8.26
Building materials	22	10.09	None	18	8.26
Groceries	21	9.63	Maintenance	16	7.34
None	18	8.26	Horse/donkey rides	12	5.50
Pulses (e.g. rice)	16	7.34	Security	10	4.59
Thatch/grass	14	6.42	Housekeeping	9	4.13
Cleaning/maintenance materials	12	5.50	Walks	8	3.67
Drinks	10	4.59	Local services	6	2.75
Furniture	10	4.59	Fishing	5	2.29
Products	9	4.13	Boat trips	5	2.29
Accommodation (including homestays)	8	3.67	Traditional healer	4	1.83
Traditional foods (e.g. mopane worms)	8	3.67	Making furnishings	4	1.83
Tools	7	3.21	Porters	3	1.38
Fish	5	2.29	Babysitters	3	1.38
Dairy products	5	2.29	Story telling	2	0.92
Honey	3	1.38	Access to natural resources (e.g. wood, water)	2	0.92
Plants	2	0.92	Hair and beauty	2	0.92
Restaurant	2	0.92	Laundry	2	0.92
Bread	1	0.46	Environmental clean up	2	0.92
Internet	1	0.46	Gardening	2	0.92
			Washing cars	2	0.92
			Scuba diving	1	0.46
			Information	1	0.46

prises, would help to establish which additional small businesses might benefit from exploiting the CBTEs' needs. Those enterprises could subsequently be provided with support (i.e. access to finance and training) to establish those businesses, and so grow the local economy.

Lessons learnt and critical issues

This review has found that the vast majority of CBTEs in southern Africa are small enterprises with between one and ten rooms. The total capacity identified was for 6531 people in either rooms, dormitories or camping areas, across 12 countries. Prices were generally budget, ranging between an average of US$10.23 to $39.08 per room. Occupancies were relatively low, and on average the enterprises had 885 visitors per year, and the average length of stay was 3.9 nights.

Many of the businesses were owned by individual entrepreneurs (52.3 per cent) or by community trusts (29.4 per cent), which showed an encouraging level of local equity. Landowners were often private individuals, companies, or properties were leased (45.4 per cent) or were on communal (31.7 per cent) or community organization land (10.6 per cent). Half of the CBTEs reported that the host community made decisions about how the enterprise was run, through meetings, elected community trusts/committees, or using a village representative or council. Playing an active role in decision making is very important in CBTEs that are collectively owned, but not as relevant to individual entrepreneurs or SMMEs from the community, which could be a reason behind this figure.

Several of the enterprises were able to provide very limited information about their business. For example, 14 enterprises could not report how many visitors they received during the past year. Key business limitations reported included accessibility (90.8 per cent), market access (71.6 per cent), advertising (70.2 per cent) and communications (57.3 per cent). Similarly, 22 of the enterprises could not state how much money they spent locally each year. This has critical implications for the commercial viability of CBTEs operating in southern Africa. It is clear that substantial efforts need to be made to provide training and small business support to many struggling small businesses. Since more than half the CBTEs have some form of external support from a third party, and yet these problems were still widespread, and therefore it may be beneficial for a regional capacity building programme to be considered. Only a small proportion of the enterprises had the support of the private sector – either directly from a particular accommodation enterprise, tour operator or tourism association – and this lack of a 'mentoring' support base may be part of the problem. A key focus of NGO and donor agency interventions should be building the business and tourism management capacity of CBTE managers and employees. Where they have not previously been implemented, business plans built on solid market research should be used to establish the commercial viability of CBTEs. Also important, and potentially controversial, should be the ability of CBTEs to accept that they are unviable, if market research and business plans deem ventures to be commercially unsound, and concentrate efforts on alternative livelihood activities instead. Anecdotal evidence suggests that stakeholder institutions establish and then support the operation of well-intentioned, but commercially unsound community-based tourism ventures, in the name of 'capacity building'. Such a condescending attitude fails to respect the people living in 'beneficiary' communities, and certainly undermines any opportunity for sustainable development.

Tourism is a business, in addition to being a conservation and development tool. If the business plan is flawed, and the enterprise unprofitable, the continuation of the enterprise will likely frustrate those whose expectations were raised unrealistically. If tourism is not viable, other, more sustainable livelihood opportunities should be sought. Fundamental problems with the way that donor agencies and NGOs have approached CBT have been highlighted by Häusler (2008). She found that in proposals for funding in South America and Asia, agencies frequently considered participation, gender, empowerment and capacity building. However, their proposals were not required to address business plans, administration, marketing strategies, product development, target groups, cooperation with private sector or communication channels. Therefore it is perhaps not surprising that so many CBTEs struggle with the basic principles of business management: they were established without a business focus.

It was interesting to find that most of the CBTEs believed they practised sustainable tourism, and many had sustainability commitments and activities that incorporated conservation, sustainable resource use, community benefits, employment, cultural conservation, local ownership, empowerment of women and participation. The enterprises cumulatively had provided the equivalent of US$4.46 million to local projects over the previous year. In impoverished, and particularly in rural areas, the extent of this support could make substantial impacts on the quality of life of people affected by them, and also potentially on the conservation of biodiversity. Further work, and site visits by ecologists, would be required to establish the actual extent of the conservation benefit of CBTEs. They would need to compare baseline data (i.e. before the CBTE) with current survey data to establish the difference, and would also need to consider other factors affecting biodiversity unrelated to tourism.

The CBTEs appeared to have a substantial impact on the local economy. The 218 enterprises employed a total of 1587 men and 1048 women, of which 94.7 per cent were local. Other local benefits cited included access to finance (e.g. loans, profits, donations) (45.0 per cent), community infrastructure development (30.3 per cent), education and training support (28.9 per cent), craft purchasing and product development (28.0 per cent), service provision (22.0 per cent) and access to resources (18.4 per cent). Local products and services were extensively procured by the enterprises. Products purchased included craft (39.5 per cent), fruit and vegetables (28.9 per cent) while services used included cultural entertainment (42.7 per cent), guiding (28.9 per cent) and catering (13.8 per cent). On average, 196 of the CBTEs spent the equivalent of US$6616 per year on local products and services, or almost US$1 million cumulatively. As shown in Chapter 6 by Ashley and Haysom, promoting local procurement through the value chain can have substantial implications for poverty alleviation, and therefore this element of the CBTEs' business practice (and potentially related to one of the main limitations: accessibility) is one of its pro-poor strengths.

In conclusion, this review reveals that the CBTEs in the region contribute positively and substantially to local economic development, and presumably poverty alleviation through their operation. The level of local employment, purchasing and support of local projects is substantial when viewed collectively. Clearly there are also limitations and constraints to the enterprises, in particular in terms of access. Therefore, business planning and market research should be undertaken prior to the development of any tourism business, not least a CBTE. Where enterprises are already established, interventions from NGOs, government and donor agencies can help improve the viability of CBTEs by addressing their specific concerns, needs and constraints. The promise of CBTEs can raise expectations within communities to unrealistic levels, particularly within poorer areas. Therefore undertaking studies to evaluate the viability of enterprises, establishing whether the location is appropriate, and forging links to the rest of the tourism industry increases the chances for the success, and for the sustainability, of CBTEs.

Acknowledgements

This research was coordinated by the author supported by the UNWTO ST-EP, RETOSA and SNV, in partnership with Zachary Rozga. Institutions that coordinated volunteers across the region included the Centre for Applied Social Sciences at the University of Zimbabwe, GeoSavvy Development, NACOBTA, Ulendo, University of Botswana, University of KwaZulu-Natal, Sky Trails Ltd, Swaziland Tourism Authority, Tanzania Tourism Board, TechnoServe, WWF Quirimbas.

References

Ashley, C. and Garland, E. (1994) 'Promoting community-based tourism development: What, why and how?' Research Discussion Paper 4. Department of Environmental Affairs, Ministry of Environment and Tourism, Namibia

Attwell, C. A. M.and Cotterill, F. P. D. (2000) 'Postmodernism and African conservation science', *Biodiversity and Conservation*, vol 9, no 5, 559–577

Baker, J. E. (1997) 'Trophy hunting as a sustainable use of wildlife resources in Southern and Eastern Africa', *Journal of Sustainable Tourism*, vol 5, no 4, 306–321

Brohman, J. (1996) 'New directions in tourism for Third World development', *Annals of Tourism Research*, vol 23, no 1, 48–70

Cater, E. (1996) 'Community involvement in third world ecotourism', Discussion Paper 64, Geographical Papers: Series B, Department of Geography, University of Reading, Reading, UK

Chambers, R. (1988) 'Sustainable rural livelihoods: A key strategy for people, environment and development', in C. Conroy and M. Litvinoff (eds), *The Greening of Aid: Sustainable Livelihoods in Practice*, Earthscan, London

de Kadt, E. (1990) *Making the Alternative Sustainable, Lessons from Development for Tourism*, Oxford University Press, Oxford

Dixey, L. (2005) 'Inventory and analysis of community based tourism in Zambia', Unpublished report to Production, Finance and Technology (PROFIT), a USAID Private Sector Development Programme, Lusaka, Zambia, November

Drake, S. P. (1991) 'Local participation in ecotourism projects', in T. Whelan (ed.), *Nature Tourism*, Island Press, Washington DC, 132–156

Grossman, D. and Koch, E. (1995) 'Nature tourism in South Africa: Links with the reconstruction and development programme', Report for SATOUR, Pretoria

Häusler, N. (2008) 'Community-based Tourism (CBT) – What works and what does not work? Drawing on experiences in South America and Asia', Presentation at the 2nd International Conference on Responsible Tourism in Destinations, 21–24 March, Kerala, India

Hawkins, D. E., Epler Wood, M. and Bittman, S. (1995) *The Ecolodge Sourcebook*, Ecotourism Society, North Bennington

International Institute for Environment and Development (IIED) (1994) *Whose Eden?* International Institute for Environment and Development/Overseas Development Administration, London

Kibicho, W. (2004) 'Community tourism: A lesson from Kenya's coastal region', *Journal of Vacation Marketing*, vol 10, no 1, 33–42

Kiss, A. (ed.) (1990) 'Living with wildlife: Wildlife resource management with local participation in Africa', World Bank Technical Paper 130 (Africa Technical Department Series). World Bank, Washington, DC

Kiss, A. (2004) 'Is community based ecotourism a good use of biodiversity conservation', *Trends in Ecology and Evolution*, vol 19, no 5, 232–237

Murphree, M. (1996) 'The cost/benefit approach to wildlife management and the "producer community" in the CAMPFIRE program', CAMPFIRE Association Publication series, 1, 16–18

Murphy, P. E. (1985) *Tourism: A Community Approach*. Methuen, New York

Ntshona, Z. and Lahiff, E. (2003) 'Community-based eco-tourism on the Wild Coast, South Africa: the case of the Amadiba Trail', *Sustainable Livelihoods in Southern Africa Research Paper 7*, Institute of Development Studies, Brighton, available at www.ids.ac.uk/UserFiles/File/knots_team/wRP07.pdf

Ottosson, C. (2004) 'The rise of community based tourism approaches – Case studies from Kabarole and Kisoro district, Uganda 2002', School of Economics and Commercial Law, Gotheburg University, Gotheburg

Roe, D., Greg-Gran, M. and Schalken, W. (2001) *Getting the Lion's Share from Tourism: Private Sector-community Partnerships in Namibia, Volume 1: Background Report and Review of Experience*, Poverty, Inequality and Environment series no 1, IIED in association with NACOBTA

Scheyvens, R. (1997) 'A framework for analysing the impacts of ecotourism on local communities', Paper presented at the First National Tourism Students' Conference, Dunedin, New Zealand, September 26–27

Spenceley, A. (2001) 'A comparison of local community benefit systems from two nature-based tourism operations in South Africa', *Industry and Environment: Ecotourism and Sustainability, United Nations Environment Programme*, vol 24, no 3–4, 50–53

Spenceley, A. and Goodwin, H. (2007) 'Nature-based tourism and poverty in South Africa', *Current Issues in Tourism*, vol 10, nos 2&3, 255–277

Steele, P. (1995) 'Ecotourism: An economic analysis', *Journal of Sustainable Tourism*, vol 3, no 1, 29–44

Tourism Grading Council of South Africa (TGCSA) (Undated a) Backpacker and Hostelling minimum requirements, © Tourism Grading Council of South Africa, available at www.tourismgrading.co.za/tgcsa/view/tgcsa/en/page45, last accessed 20 October 2006

Tourism Grading Council of South Africa (TGCSA) (Undated b) Grading criteria for Backpacking and Hostelling, © Tourism Grading Council of South Africa, available at www.tourismgrading.co.za/tgcsa/view/tgcsa/en/page45, last accessed 20 October 2006

von Loebenstein, K., Trix, A. and Welte, T. (1993) *Compensation and Reconciliation of Interest in the Field of Buffer Zone Development*, Deutsche Gesellschaft fur Technische Zusammenarbeit (GTZ), Bonn

Walpole, M. (1997) 'Dragon Tourism in Komodo National Park, Indonesia: Its contribution to conservation and local development', PhD thesis, Durrell Institute of Conservation and Ecology, UK

Wells, M. (1997) 'Economic Perspectives on Nature Tourism, Conservation and Development', Environment Department Paper 55 (Environmental Economics Series), The World Bank, Washington, DC

Wells, M. P. and Brandon, K. E. (1992) *People and Parks: Linking Protected Area Management with Local Communities*, World Bank/WWF/USAID, Washington DC

Wilkinson, P. F. (1989) 'Strategies for tourism in island microstates', *Annals of Tourism Research*, vol 16, 153–177

Williams, E., White, A. and Spenceley, A. (2001) 'UCOTA – The Uganda Community Tourism Association: A comparison with NACOBTA', Pro-Poor tourism working paper 5, ODI/CRT/IIED, May

WorldHotelLink (WHL) (2005) 'Hotel Information Form, HIF – Version 2' October 2005

World Tourism Organisation (WTO). (2004) *Tourism and Poverty Alleviation Recommendations for Action*, World Tourism Organisation, Madrid

Wunder, S. (2000) 'Ecotourism and economic incentives: an empirical approach', *Ecological Economics* vol 32, 465–479

Yu, D. W., Hendrickson, T. and Castillo, A. (1997) 'Ecotourism and conservation in Amazonian Peru: Short-term and long-term challenges', *Environmental Conservation*, vol 24, no 2, 130–138

Zazueta, F. (1995) *Policy Hits the Ground Running: Participation and Equity in Environmental Decision Making*, World Resources Institute, Washington DC

Zube, E. H. and Busch, M. L. (1990) 'Park–people relationships: An international review', *Landscape and Urban Planning*, vol 19, 117–131

14

Livelihoods, Conservation and Community-based Tourism in Tanzania: Potential and Performance

Fred Nelson

Introduction

For the past two decades, Tanzania has had one of Africa's most rapidly growing tourism industries. Following the liberalization of the country's economic policies beginning in 1986, the tourism industry has expanded from annual revenues of US$65 million in 1990 to over US$800 million today, accounting for around 10–15 per cent of the country's gross domestic product (GDP). The country's tourism industry is based on a suite of natural and biological assets that few other African nations can match: the unparalleled abundance of wildlife in the Serengeti ecosystem; Africa's largest wildlife protected area in the Selous Game Reserve; Mount Kilimanjaro; and 1000km of pristine reef-fringed Indian Ocean coastline. Just as tourism has come to play a major role in the country's sustained macroeconomic growth of the past decade, tourism revenues underpin national investments in biodiversity conservation through a protected area network that covers over 25 per cent of the country's land area. For example, the Serengeti National Park generates about US$8.5 million annually in revenue from visitor entry fees and other levies. This revenue not only funds management of the Serengeti but other, newer parks elsewhere in the country (TANAPA, 2005).

At the national level, the growth of Tanzania's tourism industry has thus had important and often positive economic and environmental impacts. However, one of the foremost characteristics of the Tanzanian economy since the abandonment of socialism 20 years ago is that macroeconomic growth and stability have not

necessarily translated into broad reductions in poverty or improvements in livelihoods at the local level (URT, 2005). The failure to translate increasing growth
and investment into widespread livelihood improvements, in a country where
three-quarters of the population still lives in rural areas, reflects political economic
factors causing a concentration of wealth in the hands of the governing and affili-
ated elites, and widening inequality. Tourism in Tanzania is embedded in these
broader economic and institutional dynamics, which fundamentally shape
tourism's developmental impacts.

Tourism is a source of significant potential livelihood diversification and
economic opportunities for local communities, and of conservation incentives at
both national and local levels. At the same time, however, tourism's rapid growth,
in the context of Tanzania's institutional environment, is a source of growing
tensions and conflicts over the natural resources – lands, wildlife, forests and
marine resources – that this industry relies on. These conflicts occur at national,
district and local levels, and reflect challenges relating to the governance of
common pool resources at different scales. While Tanzania's tourism industry will
most likely continue to play a major role in supporting macroeconomic growth, at
least over the course of the next decade, the broader impact of tourism on conservation and development objectives will depend on political economic and
governance factors. The outcomes of institutional struggles over the new sources
of wealth that tourism creates in a poor and largely rural country such as Tanzania
will be pivotal in efforts to translate the industry's growing potential into broader
beneficial socioeconomic impacts.

This chapter provides a brief history of the Tanzanian tourism industry's
development over the past two decades, including the emergence of innovative
models for community-based tourism partnerships that channel benefits directly
to rural landholders. It reviews several local case studies of community-based
tourism in northern Tanzania in order to examine outcomes and impacts and the
factors underlying them in greater detail. The chapter concludes with a discussion
of the institutional forces and trends that shape tourism's impacts in Tanzania, and
what this implies for the future of tourism as a development and conservation
strategy.

The rise of community-based tourism in Tanzania

The origins of Tanzania's tourism industry trace back to the safari hunting era of
the early colonial period. After independence, Tanzania had high expectations of
developing wildlife-based tourism as a significant source of foreign exchange, but
the country's socialist economic policies and regional conflicts with Kenya and
Uganda in the late 1970s largely undermined that aim (Honey, 1999). In 1986,
following the severe economic crises of the early 1980s, a prolonged debate with
foreign donors over economic policy, and the departure from power of independence leader and President Julius Nyerere in 1985, Tanzania adopted a Structural
Adjustment Agreement with the International Monetary Fund (Campbell and

Stein, 1991). This marked the beginning of broad market-oriented economic reforms – on-going for over 20 years now – and also facilitated the shift, in 1992, from a single-party state to pluralist politics. These changes were central to unleashing growth in Tanzania's moribund tourism industry, which by 1989 was earning only US$60 million annually from 138,000 visitors (Honey, 1999).

Aided by policies that liberalized financial regulations and sought to encourage foreign and private investment, the tourism industry grew at over 10 per cent per annum throughout the 1990s, and by 1999 was estimated to be generating over $700 million annually (World Bank/MIGA, 2002). This rapid growth was centred in three emerging 'circuits': the northern game and mountain parks including the Serengeti, Ngorongoro Crater and Kilimanjaro; the less-developed southern parks of Ruaha, Selous and Mikumi; and the coastal islands of Zanzibar (Unguja and Pemba) (MNRT, 2002). The northern wildlife and mountain circuit is by far the most important of these; half of all tourists to Tanzania visit Ngorongoro Crater and Kilimanjaro National Park, despite its small size, accounts for about 45 per cent of the total annual income of the Tanzania National Parks (TANAPA) authority (TANAPA, 2005).[1]

As tourism boomed in the 1990s, it brought increasing national revenues but also growing congestion in the core destinations, particularly the famous parks in the northern part of the country. Ngorongoro Crater gradually became a scene of dozens of safari vehicles carving up its verdant caldera floor, racing from end to end in pursuit of lions and rhinos. In Tarangire National Park, for example, the number of tourists in its 2600km^2 increased from 7290 in 1987/88 to 58,061 in 1996/97 (Sachedina, 2006).

As tourism's importance grew, other socioeconomic forces posed growing threats to the wildlife that the expanding industry depended on. Tanzania, like Kenya to the north, underwent an epidemic of commercial poaching in the 1970s and 1980s that led to a loss of about half of its elephants and nearly all its black rhinos (WSRTF, 1995). Other wildlife species had also become widely depleted by bushmeat poaching, a result of a declining law enforcement capacity on the part of the state authorities, rural poverty and a lack of any local ownership rights in wildlife that might encourage local conservation measures (WSRTF, 1995). These trends, coupled with the growing influence of foreign donors, forced Tanzania to re-examine its conventional centralized wildlife management approach. In 1998, a new wildlife policy was approved which called for devolving management rights and control over benefits from wildlife outside protected areas, such as revenue from tourist hunting concessions, to rural communities (MNRT, 1998).

Actors within the tourism industry also responded to existing conservation challenges in ways that both contributed to and fed off of the policy reform movement of the 1990s. In the country's ecologically rich northern savannahs, wildlife was under pressure from land use changes, as investment in agriculture and land sales picked up following liberalization (Igoe and Brockington, 1999).

Wildlife in savannah parks such as the Serengeti and Tarangire moves across much larger landscapes, often migrating over 50km between wet and dry season ranges. During the past several centuries these same landscapes have been inhabited by pastoralist groups such as the Maasai whose livestock management strategies also reflect the ecological importance of seasonal mobility and spatial flexibility (Homewood and Rodgers, 1991). These livestock production systems are highly compatible with mobile wildlife populations and have been an important force shaping the region's savannahs and grasslands. However, extensive pastoralist land use systems have come under increasing pressure through state land appropriation and investment schemes, starting in the 1960s and 1970s, and increasing after the economic reforms of the mid-1980s (Shivji, 1998). In key wildlife dispersal areas such as the lands to the east of Tarangire National Park, rangelands have been fragmented as land has been sold and allocated to agriculture, resulting in both the loss of wildlife habitat and less viable livestock production systems (Borner, 1985; Mwalyosi, 1992; Igoe and Brockington, 1999).

A few pioneering tour operators recognized these growing socioeconomic pressures on wildlife and pastoralist land use systems, and the need for wildlife to provide direct economic returns as a way of encouraging local communities to maintain large unfragmented and uncultivated land holdings.[2] The result was a set of pilot initiatives by two relatively small, high-end tour operators to formulate tourism agreements with pastoralist communities located adjacent to Serengeti and Tarangire National Parks (Dorobo Tours and Safaris and Oliver's Camps Ltd, 1996). These agreements were based on the legal framework for local governance and land tenure in Tanzania, which makes village councils the elected representatives of the community and gives them corporate powers to enter into contracts and own property.[3] Village councils also are the chief statutory decision-making authority over local community lands held under customary rights of occupancy.[4] The essence of the agreements was that the tour operators would be granted a concession area for camping and walking safaris where traditional livestock grazing (mainly dry season use) could continue but agricultural cultivation and settlement were excluded.[5] In return, the communities received a fixed annual rent and bed-night payments based on the number of clients entering the area. The agreements ran for 5 years on a renewable basis; some of them have now been operating for 17 years, making them the longest-running community-based tourism ventures in the country.

These initial community-based tourism agreements were motivated principally, at the outset, by broader conservation interests on the part of the individuals and companies involved, and the desire to build a socially and ecologically sustainable approach to community management of rangelands using tourism as the economic lever to promote conservation. The companies noted early on that the agreements could not be justified from a purely commercial perspective, as a result of the time-intensive nature of community negotiations and the logistical challenges to providing a high-end tourism product in remote communal lands (Dorobo Tours and Safaris and Oliver's Camps Ltd, 1996). At first, the initiatives' conservation objectives received strong backing from government authorities, including the Wildlife Division in the Ministry of Natural Resources and

Tourism.[6] One initial challenge facing such community-based tourism ventures at this time, which made Wildlife Division support vitally important, was that most wildlife-rich community lands were allocated as centrally controlled tourist hunting concessions, posing a significant conflict with the development of tourism activities in these areas. The ventures initiated in the early 1990s were predicated on an assumption that these areas would not be allocated for hunting, or at least that control over all commercial activities would be transferred to communities as the new wildlife policy, then in draft, called for (Dorobo Tours and Safaris and Oliver's Camps Ltd, 1996). But rather than abate, the conflict with hunting and between central and local authority was destined to grow substantially over time.

Although their initial social, environmental and business objectives would continue to face challenges from without and within, these pilot efforts were key in establishing a conceptual and procedural model for private sector tourism partnerships with local villages in Tanzania. This effectively established wildlife-based tourism as a potential component of local common property management systems in a way that created both collective (through village revenues) and individual (through employment and the sale of goods) economic opportunities. A critical aspect of this Tanzanian model, which differentiates it from many community-based tourism concessions in other countries such as Kenya, is the way that it integrates wildlife-based tourism with existing pastoralist production systems and land use patterns. This greatly reduces the opportunity costs local communities incur in granting tourism concessions over large portions of their land; helps to maximize tourism's value as a complement to rather than replacement for transhumant livestock production; and enhances the resilience of local livelihoods through economic diversification.

By the late 1990s, as the northern circuit's visitor numbers grew and national parks became more congested, more mainstream tour operators began to look at community lands as an untapped business opportunity. Community lands have a number of key attributes that have attracted growing interest from operators over the past decade (see Nelson, 2004):

- opportunities for fairly large and exclusive 'wilderness' concession areas; such exclusivity is greatly valued by high-end operators and in decreasing supply in many parks as visitor numbers rise and lodges proliferate;
- opportunities for alternative activities such as walking or night drives which are prohibited or heavily curtailed in the parks; and
- opportunities for cultural interactions that are also unavailable in national parks.

Driven by these market incentives and government policy reforms supportive of community-based tourism ventures, the late 1990s were a period of rapid proliferation of village–operator agreements.[7] In the Loliondo area to the east of Serengeti National Park, for example, six villages bordering the park increased their revenues from new agreements to over $100,000 annually by 2003, up from perhaps a few thousand dollars only 5 years earlier. The following section examines some of the outcomes of these local ventures in greater detail.

Community-based tourism ventures in Northern Tanzania: Outcomes and impacts

Community-based tourism in Tanzania has demonstrated the potential to generate significant returns on its conservation, socioeconomic and business objectives as ventures have spread and evolved during the past 15 years. But major challenges have also crystallized, mainly relating to the governance of these enterprises at both local and national levels. This section examines local experiences with community-based tourism in the Serengeti and Tarangire ecosystems of northern Tanzania.

Community-based tourism in the Serengeti

Serengeti National Park is the world's premier terrestrial wildlife area and forms the core of the greater Serengeti ecosystem, which spans the Kenya–Tanzania border and includes six formal state protected areas, including Kenya's Maasai Mara National Reserve. The ecosystem's boundaries are defined by the annual seasonal migration of wildebeest and zebra – approximately 1.5 million animals – between the dry season refuge of the Mara to the north, and the wet season calving grounds on the Serengeti plains to the south (Sinclair, 1995). Although the Serengeti ecosystem contains about 30,000km² of state protected lands, this is not enough to contain the entire annual range of the migratory ungulates. In November, when the short rains usually arrive and the animals begin to head south from the Mara, they pass through community lands in Loliondo Division, which borders the northeastern side of Serengeti National Park. In May and June, when the long rains end and the wildebeest head back north, they move in a clockwise pattern through the Serengeti's western corridor along the Grumeti River, and then swing to the north-east on their way back to the Mara. Along this route they pass through large expanses of community lands in Serengeti and Tarime Districts. Both of these areas, to the west and east of Serengeti National Park, have become foci of community-based tourism over the past decade, although this review will only examine experiences in Loliondo.

The Loliondo area contains the eastern fringes of the greater Serengeti system. The area is inhabited by Maasai agro-pastoralists, some of whom formerly lived in what is now Serengeti National Park prior to the area's gazettement in 1959. Maasai communities in Tanzania co-exist extremely well with large wild animals, as a result of both their mobile livestock-based land use systems and traditions of not eating most species of wildlife (Homewood and Rodgers, 1991). In the Loliondo area, game surveys have found no discernible difference in wildlife densities on either side of the park boundary in Loliondo, at least as of the early 1990s (Campbell and Borner, 1995). Other research has found densities of some large predators in Loliondo equivalent to those inside the park (Maddox, 2002).

With some of the best wildlife and scenery of any locale in the country, Loliondo is a highly desirable tourism destination and was one of the areas included in the original community-based tourism ventures established starting in 1991. However, shortly thereafter the entire Loliondo area was allocated as a hunting concession to a member of the royal family of the United Arab Emirates, in an arrangement that prompted considerable national and international controversy and local resistance (Honey, 1999).[8] The tension between village level contracts with tour operators, and centrally allocated hunting concessions, presented a physical and jurisdictional conflict which has dominated community-based tourism in northern Tanzania for the past decade (Masara, 2000; Nshala, 2002; Nelson, 2004).

In Loliondo, the hunting concession has provided a constant source of conflict among parties, but this has not been enough to stem a substantial rise in community-based tourism investments in the area. Most of these new initiatives followed the model of high end operators contracting with village councils for access to areas used for camping and walking, without any permanent structures. But one much more substantial investment agreement, financially and in terms of infrastructure, was forged between Ololosokwan village and Conservation Corporation Africa (CCA).[9]

Ololosokwan is located in the north-western corner of Loliondo, adjacent to the Kenyan border and the Maasai Mara, as well as Klein's Gate, an entry-point to Serengeti National Park. In 1996 CCA purchased a 10,000ha piece of land which the village had sold to another investor a few years before. The circumstances surrounding the initial land sale were highly disputed, however, and the source of on-going legal wrangling between the village and the investor, a case which CCA subsequently inherited following their acquisition of the property. To end these disputes, in 1999 the village and CCA agreed to a contract which paid the community an annual land rent – starting at $1 per acre and increasing at 5 per cent annually – in addition to bed-night levies of around $3 per client per night (Nelson and Ole Makko, 2005). By 2003, the village was the top-earning community in the country, in terms of tourism revenues, capturing about $55,000 in annual income in addition to various employment and side benefits. This transformed the village council's ability to improve service provision to its constituency of about 3000–4000 people without relying on external government or donor funds, as the annual village budget leaped from about $2500 in 1995–1997 to over $50,000 in 2001–2003 (Nelson and Ole Makko, 2005). The community invested in educational facilities, individual bursaries for secondary and university students from the village, health facilities and individual medical expenses, a nursery school and a re-constructed village office.

Ololosokwan has not only become Tanzania's most successful example of community-based tourism in terms of generating revenue through a private joint venture, but also highlights the importance of strong local governance and accountability. The village's tourism income arose in the first place largely because the village was able to contest – legally and politically – its claims over the land sold to CCA after that land was allegedly acquired through dubious and improper means. This strong capacity for advocating its land and resource rights has been essential to the development and maintenance of the village's tourism revenues during the past decade (Nelson and Ole Makko, 2005). Just as importantly, the village has demonstrated a relatively open and transparent decision-making process in relation to tourism planning and the use of revenues. Particularly notable has been the strong role of the village assembly in demanding accountability from the village council and effectively performing its oversight functions to ensure decisions are made in the broader community's interests.[10] For example, the village assembly has in the past demanded special audits be performed on the village council's financial records. As more investors seek land in Loliondo adjacent to Serengeti National Park for tourism campsites, a range of new developments have been proposed in Ololosokwan, including another contested land allocation dating from a title granted by the village more than 20 years ago. Recently, stemming from debate over contractual negotiations with the owner of this disputed property and concerns about the transparency of village council deliberations, the village assembly in Ololosokwan successfully demanded the removal of the entire village council and a new council election (S. Ole Makko, pers comm.). While this may reveal some level of internal conflict over tourism development in the village, it also illustrates the high level of engagement, awareness and assertiveness of the overall community and its ability to hold village leadership accountable for decisions.

The socioeconomic benefits generated by tourism in Ololsokwan and other villages in Loliondo have motivated significant investments in conservation on the part of the communities. In addition to the CCA concession in Ololosokwan, much of the traditional dry season livestock grazing areas which run along the villages' border with Serengeti National Park are now formally set aside for tourism and wildlife, mixed with seasonal livestock grazing, and these land uses are enforced through village by-laws. The area remains high quality wildlife habitat. For example, recently wild dogs, which went extinct in the Serengeti ecosystem in 1994 following a rabies outbreak, have re-colonized at least two villages in Loliondo. Tourism revenues are an important incentive for the pastoralist communities to accept and value the presence of these predators (Masenga and Mentzel, 2006), which seem to prefer Loliondo's community lands to Serengeti National Park itself, possibly because of the abundance of lions in the latter.[11] The link between conservation and community tourism revenues in Loliondo is thus fairly well established, and is particularly important given the overlap of the local tourism concessions with the Serengeti wildebeest herds' migration routes.

Two key points emerge from Loliondo's experiences with community-based tourism during the past 15 years. First, the villages there have come perhaps the closest of anywhere in Tanzania to translating the potential of tourism as a development and conservation tool into reality. Tourism in Loliondo has created tangible economic benefits for villages, and these benefits have increased markedly in the past ten years. Community-based tourism has also created substantial benefits for conservation of the Serengeti ecosystem. However, tourism has been beset with constant conflicts characterized by a lack of central or district support for community ventures. The externally-imposed hunting concession has been a constant source of conflict for villages and tour operators, and prevents use by tourists of much of the Loliondo area for several months each year. Another conflict emerged from the government effort, supported heavily by international conservation organizations, to have the area declared a Wildlife Management Area (WMA), which would have removed much of the control over tourism ventures from village governments (Nelson and Ole Makko, 2005; Nelson, 2007). Despite the empirical success of the Loliondo ventures from a developmental and environmental perspective, there has been very limited support for community-based tourism in the area from policy makers or district administrators since the late 1990s.

Community-based Tourism in Tarangire-Simanjiro

To the south-east of the Serengeti system, below the Gregory Rift Valley escarpment, the Tarangire-Simanjiro ecosystem comprises another vast savannah and grassland mosaic where migratory wildlife moves across a landscape of about 35,000km². Two core areas used by migratory wildebeest, zebra and antelopes are the dry season habitat along the Tarangire River in Tarangire National Park, and the wet season calving grounds on the Simanjiro plains. Unlike the Serengeti, though, the vast majority of land in this ecosystem (over 80 per cent), including the Simanjiro plains, lies outside formal protected areas on community and private lands (Borner, 1985).

As in Loliondo, community lands in the Tarangire-Simanjiro system were among the first areas where community-based tourism ventures were initiated in the early 1990s. Unlike Loliondo, though, this area has much better infrastructure and relatively easy accessibility; Arusha, the urban centre of the safari industry, is only a couple of hours away, and a tarmac road runs between Tarangire and Lake Manyara National Parks. A range of tourist camps and lodges now encircle the northern end of Tarangire National Park, closest to this road.

As in Loliondo, tourism ventures on community lands have created significant local revenue flows and led to land being set aside for wildlife. In an ecosystem where wildlife is so heavily dependent on village lands, the latter outcome is particularly important. Lolkisale village, for example, is situated along the north-eastern border of Tarangire National Park. The village has set aside about 20,000ha of land for several small tourism lodges, in an area heavily used by elephants and buffalo during the wet season. As tourism enterprises have expanded in this area, substantial areas have reverted from commercial farming back to wildlife habitat.

However, several factors have undermined the generation of local economic benefits from tourism around Tarangire. First, not all tourism ventures have been developed through the model of contractual agreements between village councils and operators; a number of developments have arisen on lands that were simply allocated or sold by villages, often under unclear terms and conditions. This 'individualization' of tourism developments prevents benefits from reaching the entire community,[12] and may also reflect the relative weakness of local collective institutions in this locale compared to other pastoralist areas such as Loliondo.[13]

Even where contracts have been formed transparently between the village council and tour operators, problems with local revenue management are apparent. In Emboreet village,[14] tourism revenues generated $126,889 in payments to the village from 2001–2005, or an average of $25,338 annually (Sachedina, 2006). Despite these high earnings, Sachedina (2006) finds that 93 per cent of Emboreet villagers claim that they do not receive any household benefits from wildlife. He explains this discrepancy by noting that audits of village financial records have showed mismanagement and significant levels of fraud in the use of tourism revenues at the village level (Sachedina, 2006). Village governance organs are thus effectively failing to translate substantial annual tourism revenues into collective benefits and services, with the downward accountability of local elites to the community that is so important in Ololosokwan apparently weak in Emboreet.

The outcome of this local governance failure is that substantial wildlife-based tourism revenues have not resulted in strong local conservation incentives, and collective incentives do not emerge to control land fragmentation and conversion to agriculture. Consequently, the quality of the wildlife-based tourism resource has declined, with negative implications for both conservation and local economic options.

Opportunity or threat? The political economy of tourism in Tanzania

Community-based tourism in Tanzania demonstrates the potential for generating substantial revenues at the local level, providing new tourism products for private operators to market, and has led to significant actions by local communities in support of wildlife conservation in savannah landscapes. Despite these positive outcomes, the first decade of widespread community-based tourism ventures in Tanzania has been beset by major challenges.

Locally, the transparent and collectively accountable management of tourism revenues has been the exception rather than the rule. In many instances tourism revenues are captured by elites within village governments and few economic benefits reach community members except for those benefiting directly through employment at tourist camps. Beyond this, there are numerous examples of decision-making processes that violate collective consensual norms, whereby a few leaders allocate tourism concessions without involving the broader community. Such failures of local collective decision-making undermine the objectives of community-based tourism and serve to degrade both the tourism product and long-term community resource interests.

While community-level governance represents a significant challenge, these problems are greatly exceeded, and often exacerbated, by institutional factors at higher levels of government. Government policy has consistently provided rhetorical support for community-based tourism, but legal and administrative actions belie such rhetoric. Starting in 2000, community-based tourism ventures faced something of a crisis when regulations issued by the Wildlife Division declared all tourism activities occurring within hunting blocks on village lands subject to the authority of the Director of Wildlife (Masara, 2000; MNRT, 2000). This measure was motivated by the incentives on the part of wildlife authorities to maintain exclusive access to village lands in the hands of the hunting companies. The regulations effectively tried to replace village authority for developing commercial agreements with tour operators, as had emerged during the 1990s, with a much more centralized regulatory framework. Since the Wildlife Division's main interest has always been maintaining stability in tourist hunting management on community lands, this measure could have served to shut down many community level tourism ventures. This outcome did not occur, mainly because most tour operators and village governments never recognized the authority of the Wildlife Division to regulate these ventures, and simply carried on business as before. The government, perhaps recognizing its weak legislative basis for controlling commercial tourism ventures on village lands, only forced the matter intermittently, and most areas continued in a state of moderate conflict over jurisdictional authority, occasionally boiling over into localized crises. The regulations have, however, greatly increased the costs of doing business in community areas for most operators, and served to discourage entry into new community-based ventures for many mainstream firms. The government's approach has greatly impeded the spread of community–private tourism partnerships, which have existed for the past 8 years in an institutional environment that is effectively hostile to their existence. Another outcome of this situation is the weakening of facilitation for community–operator ventures; many NGOs have been discouraged from working to promote community-based tourism, since such ventures are now nominally illegal in most high-potential areas. It is thus something of a testament to the extremely high market potential of community-based tourism in the region, and the resilience of both private operators and local communities, that most initiatives have continued to operate, and even expand, within this institutional context.

Understanding the discrepancy between policy and institutional practice requires placing community-based tourism within the broader configuration of political economic trends and dynamics in modern Tanzania. The past 20 years of economic reforms have led to the growth of commercial markets and investment activity, but this has occurred within the context of a heavily centralized state based around patron–client relations and interests. As investment in Tanzania has increased, so have the private interests of public functionaries (Kelsall, 2002). Although the narrative of 'economic liberalization' in Tanzania presents an image of government withdrawal from direct control of markets and economic production, this is partially illusory. Most key productive resources remain under the control of central institutions, which manage their use and allocation in pursuit of patron–client interests that bridge private and public spheres of activity.[15] There are strong disincentives for those central interests and institutions to devolve control over valuable resources to local communities. For example, Tanzania's land tenure reform process in the late 1990s began with a strong push for more secure local tenure but was eventually shaped by key Ministerial officials in a way that maintained key discretionary powers over land in the hands of state agents (Sundet, 1997; Shivji, 1998). Over 15 years of donor-led efforts to devolve greater powers over wildlife to local communities has had little impact on this heavily centralized sector (Nelson, 2007).

This political economy of centralized resource control set against a backdrop of reformist narratives is a fundamental characteristic of many African economies during the past 20 years (Van de Walle, 2001). African states seek to maintain control over key patronage resources, and thus ensure their own stability, meanwhile seeking international legitimacy for their policies through the adoption of 'liberalization' discourses. In the case of natural resource management, the outcome is the widespread endorsement of decentralization and devolution of authority as a narrative discourse, but the practical reality of 'aborted devolution' or recentralization (Murphree, 2000; Ribot, 2004; Ribot et al, 2006). The management of Tanzania's tourism industry fits within this much broader political economic pattern of natural resource governance, not only in Africa but in parts of Asia and Latin America as well.

Within this political economic environment, growing levels of tourism investment in rural Tanzania often serve to exacerbate tensions among actors operating at different institutional scales. For example, in northern Tanzanian savannahs, traditional pastoralist rangelands are subject to growing external pressures as their value for tourism investment rises. Such pressures can be manifested in various ways, including as pressure from state agencies to allocate land to commercial investors, or direct pressure from investors to purchase lands, which is often pursued through illegitimate means at the village level.[16]

The other side of the coin, though, is that if communities are able to secure commercial tourism agreements that recognize their jurisdiction over village lands and create economic opportunities at the local level, it can support local interests in maintaining their resources in the face of external appropriative pressures. In other words, community-based tourism can create financial capital that is transformable into political capital at the local and national level.[17] In a political economic environment that strongly promotes capital markets as the key to improvements in Tanzania's living standards, often at the expense of the security of local resource tenure, the ability of communities to enter formal markets as competent actors is critical to their long-term security and resilience.

Conclusion

Some contemporary critiques of ecotourism (e.g. Kiss, 2004; Walpole and Thouless, 2006) argue that the prospects for tourism to contribute to biodiversity conservation goals are in fact limited by market demand and weaknesses in the community-level incentives that these ventures establish. Others argue that tourism's contributions to rural livelihoods are often marginal or insignificant. This review of Tanzania's experiences with community-based tourism suggests that, by contrast, there is substantial evidence of large-scale conservation benefits and local economic benefits in northern Tanzanian landscapes. Certainly, community-based tourism has been the main force behind rural communities voluntarily setting aside land for wildlife conservation in different parts of northern Tanzania, and it has also had a significant economic impact in certain settings. That said, it should be highlighted that Tanzania, and particularly northern Tanzania, has a potential for community-based tourism, with respect to both environmental and rural economic objectives, that exceeds most areas in sub-Saharan Africa. Tanzania's wildlife populations are unparalleled, and its savannahs and grasslands create comfortable viewing and travelling conditions for tourists. The migratory nature of wildlife in these landscapes, coupled with the traditional co-existence and conservation ethic of local pastoralists, creates tremendous opportunities for integrating tourism with local land uses and economic activities that few other areas can offer.

But despite this potential and the development of relatively practicable and transparent institutional models for private–community partnerships, community-based tourism has been fighting against the tide for most of the past decade. These countervailing forces are institutional and political economic in nature, and reflect the efforts of political elites to monopolize control over valuable resources and commercial activities. Tanzania's modern economy is highly contested terrain, with rural communities struggling to access the opportunities that growing markets like tourism create, in the face of competition from more powerful public institutions and some private sector actors.

Tourism is thus both an opportunity and a threat for rural communities negotiating this institutional environment. Tourism increases the incentives for other, usually more powerful, actors to encroach on and appropriate local lands and resources, but it also creates the opportunities that rural people need to diversify their livelihoods and generate economic and political capital to support them in long-term contests over resources.

Ultimately community-based tourism has a major role to play in Tanzania in the attainment of both conservation and local developmental objectives, but capitalizing on its potential is a generational institutional process. It should be noted, though, that the same institutional struggles over control of tourism investments apply to the entire political economy of Tanzania; private elite capture of public resources is increasingly the dominant theme in the country's social and political discourse. Tourism is but a single, albeit important, part of this broader developmental process, the outcomes of which are largely unpredictable and unknown.

Acknowledgements

I am grateful to Anna Spenceley and Dan Brockington for comments made on earlier drafts of this chapter. Support for the work in northern Tanzania that provides the basis for this analysis was provided at various times by the WISDOM Foundation, the Sand County Foundation and the Bradley Fund for the Environment. My understanding of community-based tourism in Tanzania has benefited immeasurably from the insights and experiences of many individuals, but in particular from Sinandei Ole Makko, Dismas Meitaya and Maanda Ngoitiko; David, Mike and Thad Peterson; Hassan Sachedina, Peter Lindstrom, Damien Bell, Andrew Williams and Christopher Kissyoki Ole Memantoki. Nevertheless the author bears sole responsibility for the analysis contained in this chapter and any factual errors are mine alone.

Notes

1   Kilimanjaro and Serengeti National Parks (out of 14 parks in total) accounted for about 24 million Tshs out of 33 million Tshs (72 per cent) in total revenues for TANAPA during the 2004/05 financial year.

2   The lead operator was and remains Dorobo Tours, whose directors, three American brothers, grew up in Tanzania, developing a deep grassroots understanding of conservation and development issues. The eldest brother carried out a study of wildlife and livestock ecologies in the Maasai Steppe in the mid-1970s which provided a key baseline understanding in Dorobo's later community-based tourism ventures in the region.

3   Village councils are elected every 5 years and comprise between 15 and 25 members. The village council reports to the village assembly, which consists of all adult members of the community. Key legislation is the Local Government (District Authorities) Act of 1982.

4   In the 1980s and early 1990s village councils had in many instances been given title deeds, under provisions in the Land Ordinance of 1923, over the village's lands which gave them freehold ownership. This gave the communities secure title but also resulted in many village councils, often through corrupt transactions, selling land to outsiders and the broader community having no legal recourse in such instances. In 1999 Tanzania reformed its land tenure framework so that village councils would be more clearly answerable to the village assembly and would not hold title deeds but only be a management authority over village lands (see Wily, 2003).

5   The operators were not to build any permanent structures in the concession areas.

6   The Wildlife Division is responsible for all wildlife outside national parks and Ngorongoro Conservation Area. The Wildlife Division wrote the following to the companies: 'The venture you are about to engage in is in keeping with departmental policy objectives, i.e. enhancing the value of wildlife to the immediate local community through fees paid to the village councils. In due course the beneficiaries will appreciate the value of wildlife to them and therefore be responsive to and responsible for its conservation ... please be informed that your intended operation has the support of the Department of Wildlife.' (Letter from C. Mlay, Director of Wildlife, for the Principal Secretary, Ministry of Lands, Natural Resources & Tourism, Reference No. PA/GWC/177).

7   The new wildlife policy, for example, advocated 'Locating future major tourist developments outside PAs [protected areas] in order to reduce negative impacts and enhance benefit sharing with local communities' (MNRT, 1998).

8   Although the area was previously used as a hunting concession managed by the Wildlife Division of the Ministry of Natural Resources and Tourism, and, as noted before, most wildlife-rich community lands are included in centrally-allocated hunting concessions, the apparent influence of foreign political and financial clout on this allocation caused an unusual amount of controversy to surround the decision.

9   CCA is a large South African ecotourism company, and one of Tanzania's largest tourism sector investors. Klein's Camps is its only contractual partnership with a local village.

10   See footnotes 3 and 4 in reference to basic functions of village councils and village assemblies.

11   Lions are a major predator upon wild dogs and account for the majority of natural mortalities in some wild dog populations (Creel and Creel, 1996).

12   This situation is reminiscent of that documented by Thompson and Homewood (2002) with regards to tourism on community lands outside the Maasai Mara National Reserve in Narok District, Kenya. There, the bulk of tourism revenues are captured by individuals, and collective institutions do not effectively function to distribute benefits equitably among the resident population. Most of the best lands, closest to the reserve, have been allocated to individuals or groups of elites, who reap the lion's share of tourism revenues.

13   Relatively weaker collective institutions may in turn reflect greater local heterogeneity in the human population; the area around Tarangire, situated along the main road and close to the urban centre of Arusha, has seen substantial immigration from other areas. This includes 'Waswahili' (a Maasai term for Kiswahili-speaking Bantu peoples) and Waarusha (a more agricultural and sedentary Maa-speaking subgroup), who have both come to this area in large numbers searching for land as a result of overpopulation in adjacent highlands.

14   Emboreet was one of the villages included in the original Dorobo Tours and Oliver's Camps projects initiated in 1991.

15   For example, Cooksey (2003) describes how the liberalization narrative ignores the actual trend towards increasing bureaucratic control over key export crops in recent years. Milledge et al. (2007) describe how timber production in Tanzania comprises US$58 million worth of informal (i.e. illegal) exports, most of which is closely linked to senior government officials. Newspapers in Tanzania provide new evidence on a daily basis with respect to the large-scale private appropriation of Tanzania's public resources, both natural and financial.

16   For example, payments to individual village leaders to allocate lands outside the formal community decision-making process.

17   This was once made most clear to me by a local elected leader from Loliondo, who explained the importance of tourism to local land rights struggles in this way: 'We need financial capital to help us fight those who want to take our land away.' Another example would be Ololosokwan's ability to hire professional attorneys at various stages when facing land tenure conflicts.

References

Borner, M. (1985) 'The increasing isolation of Tarangire National Park', *Oryx*, vol 19, no 2, 91–96

Campbell, H. and Stein, H. (1991) *The IMF and Tanzania*, SAPES Trust, Harare, Zimbabwe

Campbell, K. and Borner, M. (1995) 'Population trends and distribution of Serengeti herbivores: Implications for management', in A. R. E. Sinclair and P. Arcese (eds), *Serengeti II: Dynamics, Management, and Conservation of an Ecosystem*, University of Chicago Press, Chicago, IL

Cooksey, B. (2003) 'Marketing reform? The rise and fall of agricultural liberalisation in Tanzania', *Development Policy Review*, vol 21, no 1, 67–91

Creel, S. and Creel, N. M. (1996) 'Limitation of African wild dogs by competition with larger carnivores', *Conservation Biology*, vol 10, no 2, 526–538

Dorobo Tours and Safaris and Oliver's Camp Ltd (1996) 'Potential models for community-based conservation among pastoral communities adjacent to protected areas in northern Tanzania', in N. Leader-Williams, J. Kayera and G. Overton (eds), *Community-based Conservation in Tanzania*, IUCN, Gland, Switzerland and Cambridge, UK

Homewood, K. M. and Rodgers, W. A. (1991) *Maasailand Ecology: Pastoralist Development and Wildlife Conservation in Ngorongoro, Tanzania*, Cambridge University Press, Cambridge

Honey, M. (1999) *Ecotourism and Sustainable Development: Who Owns Paradise?* Island Press, Washington, DC

Igoe, J. and Brockington, D. (1999) *Pastoral Land Tenure and Community Conservation: A Case Study from North-east Tanzania*, International Institute for Environment and Development, London

Kelsall, T. (2002) 'Shop windows and smoke-filled rooms: Governance and the re-politicisation of Tanzania', *Journal of Modern African Studies*, vol 40, no 4, 597–619

Kiss, A. (2004) 'Is community-based ecotourism a good use of biodiversity conservation funds?', *Trends in Ecology & Evolution*, vol 19, 232–237

Maddox, T. (2002) 'The ecology of cheetahs and other large carnivores in a pastoralist-dominated buffer zone', PhD thesis, University of London

Masara, Y. B. (2000) 'The conflict of legislations and collision of jurisdictions: An impediment to the realization of community based conservation in Tanzania?', Unpublished consultancy prepared for the African Wildlife Foundation, Arusha, Tanzania

Masenga, H. E. and Mentzel, C. (2006) 'Bouncing back', *Swara*, vol 29, no 4, 16–19

Milledge, S. A. H., Gelvas, I. K. and Ahrends, A. (2007) *Forestry, Governance and National Development: Lessons Learned from a Logging Boom in Southern Tanzania*, TRAFFIC East/Southern Africa/Tanzania Development Partners Group/Ministry of Natural Resources and Tourism, Dar es Salaam, Tanzania

Ministry of Natural Resources and Tourism (MNRT). (1998) *The Wildlife Policy of Tanzania*, Government Printer, Dar es Salaam, Tanzania

Ministry of Natural Resources and Tourism (MNRT) (2000) *Wildlife Conservation (Tourist Hunting) Regulations*, Government Printer, Dar es Salaam, Tanzania

Ministry of Natural Resources and Tourism (MNRT) (2002) *Tourism Master Plan: Strategy and Actions*, CHL Consulting Group/United Republic of Tanzania, Dar es Salaam, Tanzania

Murphree, M. W. (2000) 'Boundaries and borders; the question of scale in the theory and practice of common property management', Paper presented to The Eighth Biennial Conference of the International Association of Common Property (IASCP), Bloomington, IN

Mwalyosi, R. B. B. (1992) 'Land-use changes and resource degradation in south-west Masailand, Tanzania', *Environmental Conservation*, vol 19, no 2, 146–152

Nelson, F. (2004) *The Evolution and Impacts of Community-based Ecotourism in Northern Tanzania*, Drylands Issue Paper no 131, International Institute for Environment and Development, London

Nelson, F. (2007) *Emergent or Illusory? Community Wildlife Management in Tanzania*, Drylands Issue Paper no 146, International Institute for Environment and Development, London

Nelson, F. and Ole Makko, S. (2005) 'Communities, conservation, and conflict in the Tanzanian Serengeti', in B. Child, and M. W. Lyman (eds), *Natural Resources as Community Assets: Lessons from Two Continents*, Sand County Foundation and The Aspen Institute, Madison, WI, and Washington, DC

Nshala, R. (2002) 'Village rights relating to land management, tourism, and tourist hunting', Unpublished report by Lawyers' Environmental Action Team, Dar es Salaam, Tanzania

Ribot, J. C. (2004) *Waiting for Democracy: The Politics of Choice in Natural Resource Decentralization*, World Resources Institute, Washington, DC

Ribot, J. C., Agrawal, A. and Larson, A. M. (2006) 'Recentralizing while decentralizing: How national governments reappropriate forest resources', *World Development*, vol 34, no 11, 1864–1886

Sachedina, H. (2006) 'Conservation, land rights and livelihoods in the Tarangire ecosystem of Tanzania: Increasing incentives for non-conservation compatible land use change through conservation policy', Paper presented to Pastoralism and Poverty Reduction in East Africa: A Policy Research Conference International Livestock Research Institute Safari Park Hotel, Nairobi, Kenya

Shivji, I. G. (1998) *Not Yet Democracy: Reforming Land Tenure in Tanzania*, International Institute for Environment and Development/HAKIARDHI/Faculty of Law, University of Dar es Salaam, Dar es Salaam, Tanzania and London, UK

Sinclair, A. R. E. (1995) 'Serengeti past and present', in A. R. E. Sinclair and P. Arcese (eds), *Serengeti II: Dynamics, Management, and Conservation of an Ecosystem*, University of Chicago Press, Chicago, IL

Sundet, G. (1997) 'The politics of land in Tanzania', PhD thesis, University of Oxford

Tanzania National Parks (TANAPA) (2005) *Annual Report 2004/2005*, TANAPA, Arusha, Tanzania

Thompson, M. and Homewood, K. (2002) 'Entrepreneurs, elites and exclusion in Maasailand: Trends in wildlife conservation and pastoralist development', *Human Ecology*, vol 30, no 1, 107–138

United Republic of Tanzania (URT) (2005) *National Strategy for Growth and Reduction of Poverty*, Vice President's Office, Dar es Salaam, Tanzania

van de Walle, N. (2001) *African Economies and the Politics of Permanent Crisis, 1979–1999*, Cambridge University Press, Cambridge

Walpole, M. J. and Thouless, C. R. (2006) 'Increasing the value of wildlife through non-consumptive use? Deconstructing the myths of ecotourism and community-based tourism in the tropics', in R. Woodroffe, S. Thirgood and A. Rabinowitz (eds), *People and Wildlife: Conflict or Coexistence?*, Cambridge University Press, Cambridge

Wildlife Sector Review Task Force (WSRTF). (1995) *A Review of the Wildlife Sector in Tanzania. Volume 1: Assessment of the Current Situation*, Ministry of Tourism, Natural Resources and Environment, Dar es Salaam, Tanzania

Wily, L. A. (2003) *Community-based Land Tenure Management: Questions and Answers about Tanzania's New Village Land Act, 1999*, Drylands Issue Paper no 120, International Institute for Environment and Development, London

World Bank Group/Multilateral Investment Guarantee Agency (MIGA) (2002) *Tourism in Tanzania: Investment for Growth and Diversification*, MIGA and United Republic of Tanzania, Washington DC

15

The Unsustainability of Community Tourism Donor Projects: Lessons from Zambia

Louise M. Dixey

Introduction

Community tourism has grown significantly in popularity, often as part of community conservation strategies aiming to reduce poverty and increase biodiversity conservation. Indeed, the approach has been elevated to such an extent that it has become a 'privileged solution', in that debate about the merits and demerits of community tourism is limited in official discourses. There is a rising number of practitioners and academics, however, warning of a high failure rate and stressing the need for more rigorous analysis and accountability. This chapter introduces international developments, reviews critical appraisals and reflects on empirical findings in Zambia that are relevant elsewhere in the world where donors are funding community tourism projects. The author asserts that experiences in Zambia and other destinations have demonstrated that community tourism is challenging, complex and precarious to develop and that it will only be a useful development tool if lessons learnt are assimilated – particularly the need for a market orientation. It is also important to acknowledge that community tourism is likely to remain on the margins of the industry and therefore it has limited potential in terms of pro-poor tourism development. The challenge is to mainstream approaches to harness tourism for poverty reduction so practitioners must respond to emerging opportunities in policy with more dynamic approaches and demonstrated results.

The promotion of community tourism

Conservationists and development practitioners have promoted community tourism in developing countries since the 1970s. It is often incorporated into community conservation strategies that include integrated conservation and development projects and community-based natural resources management. The purported logic is that community tourism can augment the development options of resource-dependent rural communities – it has the potential to diversify livelihood activities and generate income, thereby alleviating poverty and enhancing biodiversity conservation. The profile of the approach has risen as major donors have assisted in community tourism product, organizational and programme development. For example, 32 World Bank projects supporting protected areas in Africa between 1988 and 2003 included a community tourism component (Kiss, 2004) and the large Transfrontier Conservation Area Tourism Development Project in southern Africa has an enterprise fund to support community tourism development.

Community tourism manuals have been developed to guide field practitioners and there has been a recent flurry of publications extolling 'good practice' and positive contributions to development and conservation. General guidelines for practitioners have been produced by international conservation organizations (The Mountain Institute, 2000; WWF International, 2001) and bilateral development agencies (InWent, 2002). Specific guidelines for Rwanda have been developed with support from the United Nations World Tourism Organization (WTO) ST-EP Programme (Townsend, 2006) and a market access training manual has been developed by WTO, the Regional Tourism Organization for Southern Africa and The Netherlands Development Organization, SNV (Rozga and Spenceley, 2006). Good practice compilations featuring community tourism projects have been compiled by WTO (WTO, 2006), the United Nations Development Programme (UNDP, 2006a) and the Caribbean Tourism Organization (CTO, 2007). In addition, an inventory of good practices in community tourism in protected areas in the Asia-Pacific has been developed (APEIS-RISPO, 2006).

Critical appraisals of community tourism

It has been contentiously suggested, however, that mounting empirical evidence indicates that most community tourism projects have not contributed to local poverty reduction or delivered sufficient incentives for conservation (Goodwin 2006a). Writings emanating from early reflections on integrated conservation and development projects in the 1990s cautioned that income generated from tourism had been disappointing (Goodwin and Roe, 2001). More recent publications have raised major concerns about the ineffectiveness, potential unsustainability or failure of community tourism enterprises and a lack of accountability with regards to responsibility and performance.

A quantitative assessment of 37 community projects (including but not limited to ecotourism) selected specifically for their commercial potential and funded by the Biodiversity Conservation Network in Asia and the Pacific, found that '*in many cases, it may be hard for the enterprise ever to cover all its costs*' (Salafsky et al, 2001, p1593). Four enterprises had no revenue, 3 had minimal revenues, 13 only covered variable costs, 10 covered variable and fixed costs and just 7 made a profit. Key factors that influenced enterprise performance included the level of competence in management and book-keeping, market conditions especially competition, the adequacy of market research and whether business development was based on skills and technologies pre-existing in the community.

A Mid-Term Review of the €12.8 million European Union (EU) funded Wild Coast Spatial Development Initiative Pilot Programme in 2003 demonstrated '*very low deliverables from a massive community tourism programme*' (Ashley, 2006, p23). The review found that the main programme outcome was the establishment of a community-based horse and hiking trail along the coast but that this had come at a high cost and the sustainability of the enterprises and jobs created had yet to be ascertained. The programme faced many challenges but a key failure had been inadequate involvement of private sector tourism companies (Mid-Term Review, 2003). The final evaluation of another EU-funded programme in Swaziland in 2006 concluded that eight new community tourism enterprises that had been developed were likely to fail unless further financial subsidy was provided (Final Evaluation, 2006). The evaluation noted that of major concern was a lack of linkages between the community enterprises and commercial tour operators as this would undermine the new products and was contrary to government policy that tourism development should be private sector led. A review of 54 members of the Namibia Community Based Tourism Association estimated that after many years of intensive support, only between 5 to 10 enterprises would survive without further assistance (Hitchens and Highstead, 2005). A study in Kenya found that six community tourism enterprises remained heavily reliant on donor funds after several years in operation and faced daily problems running their enterprises (Manyara et al, 2006).

The growing evidence that projects are failing to deliver viable tourism enterprises has been accompanied by strong suggestions that interventions do not necessarily protect species or their habitats (Brechin et al, 2002). The review of 37 community conservation projects in Asia and the Pacific concluded that '*a community-based enterprise strategy can lead to conservation, but only under limited conditions and never on its own*' (Salafsky et al, 2001, p1585). Initiatives to develop community tourism and conservation projects in Honduras '*exacerbated local conflicts*' and '*the great disparity between the rhetoric and the reality of such efforts has caused many people to begin to give up on such efforts entirely*' (Stonich, 2005, p77). The failure of community conservation carries the danger of amplifying calls for stricter enforcement of protected area boundaries and '*this resurgent focus on authoritarian protectionist practices ... could lead to morally and pragmatically questionable prescriptions that most likely will not safeguard biodiversity over the long term*' (Brechin et al, 2002, pp41–42).

The reasons for poor performance

The reasons given to explain the poor performance of community tourism are similar and resound throughout the literature. Hitchens and Highstead (2005) identify the major causes in Namibia as the isolation of community tourism from the mainstream private sector, the remoteness from tourism routes, as well as dependency on external support. Goodwin (2006a) also suggests that failure is driven by a lack of commercial orientation, engagement with the private sector and proximity to tourism centres. Additional reasons appear to be that community projects had developed inappropriate tourism facilities and enterprises were in competition with national parks for business. Analysis in South Africa also highlighted the fact that community enterprises may not be well positioned to compete against state-supported protected areas and private ventures making tourism a risky strategy (Turner, 2006).

An examination of community tourism case studies from Namibia, Uganda, St Lucia, Ecuador and Nepal also identified critical factors of access of the poor to markets and commercial viability (Ashley et al, 2001). This review of experience also highlighted the importance of institutional and policy frameworks and implementation challenges in the local context. The main obstacles to a community-based heritage trail in Uganda that was strongly supported by donors, government and traditional cultural institutions included a low level of development and lack of skills in communities in poor rural areas and limited international tourism arrivals (Holland et al, 2003). A study of the Amadiba horse and hiking trail in South Africa also stressed that a lack of skills in communities imposed real limitations on collective and participatory forms of management as professional skills and specialist knowledge of the tourism market were needed for successful enterprise development (Ntshona and Lahiff, 2003). These findings are reinforced by a review of 54 community tourism enterprises in Namibia which concluded that '*the starting point of many communities in terms of their understanding, social and institutional organization and capacity to manage community tourism effectively appears extremely low*' (Hitchens and Highstead, 2005, p2). A review of five community tourism initiatives in the Windward Islands of the Caribbean identified similar key constraints including a lack of management capacity and market research, poor marketing and weak institutional arrangements (CANARI, 2004).

A few studies argue that the challenges in community tourism development must be seen from a broader political economy perspective. Turner (2006) explores the historical legacies of exclusion and dispossession and shift to liberalization and democratization in his study of community tourism in the Makuleke region of South Africa. Duffy (2002) highlighted that the constraints working against the success of community tourism in Belize were inextricably linked to wider processes that continue to marginalize the Mayan communities involved. Manyara et al (2006, p30) assert that community tourism is used as an additional conservation strategy in Kenya and therefore '*reinforces the anachronistic colonial model of tourism development.*'

A lack of accountability and rigorous assessment

Accountability is a thorny issue as it is challenging to guarantee the responsibility and performance of multilateral donors, international NGOs, commercial businesses, states and community leaders. Mowforth and Munt (1998) suggested that despite donor and government rhetoric of support for community tourism in Belize, the Toledo Ecotourism Association was undermined by multilateral donors as well as national and local politics. Wright (2005) reflected on the EU-funded Wild Coast Spatial Development Initiative Pilot Programme and contentiously argued that South Africa needs to develop a legislative framework to ensure that multilateral donor agencies are held contractually accountable for programme outcomes. Responsibility for poor performance can also lie within the community. The study of the Amadiba Trail on the Wild Coast highlighted that collective funds generated by community tourism are liable to be misused in ways that do not enhance livelihoods if there is a lack of accountability, transparency and democracy within local organizations (Ntshona and Lahiff, 2003).

Insightful critical appraisals of and lessons learnt about community tourism development have emerged, yet few community conservation projects in sub-Saharan Africa have been studied critically and in-depth (Adams and Hulme, 1998), and the evaluation of the impact of tourism projects on poverty continues to be constrained by a lack of good quality research, monitoring and evaluation, reporting and data (Pro-Poor Tourism Partnership, 2005; Goodwin, 2006b). Many proponents of community tourism have endured – or conveniently ignored? – increasing scrutiny of the approach and assertions that 'there are too many failed community-based tourism projects around the world' (Ashley, 2006, p23). However, given the amount of funding new projects continue to absorb, even donors are now calling for much more rigorous assessment as '*resources for conservation and for development are too scarce to waste on wishful thinking*' (Kiss, 2004, p236).

The research on community tourism in Zambia

The need for good quality information and more robust assessment of community tourism was a major reason why research in the Republic of Zambia was undertaken (Dixey, 2005). The practitioner study was commissioned by a private-sector development programme, Production, Finance and Technology (PROFIT) funded by the US Agency for International Development (USAID). The research was undertaken in 2005 when community tourism was rising on the national political agenda. PROFIT had a grants programme and wanted to ensure that resources were targeted effectively. It required an assessment as there was no inventory or adequate understanding of the range of community tourism initiatives and their impact in Zambia. The assignment focused on providing an overview of tourism and its relationship to poverty reduction in Zambia; outlining relevant policy, planning and institutional frameworks; developing an inventory of community tourism enterprises; assessing income-generation and making recommendations. Assessment centred on the business performance of enterprises and did not assess the impact of community tourism on livelihood strategies, socio-cultural or environmental aspects. Qualitative research methods used were a desk review of published and 'grey' literature, questionnaire surveys, field visits, participant observation and semi-structured interviews. Three different questionnaire surveys comprising of open questions were completed by 25 NGOs and donors, 29 commercial tourism companies (a 40 per cent response rate) and 22 community tourism enterprises. Interviews with relevant government agencies were also held.

Tourism and poverty in Zambia

Zambia (formerly Northern Rhodesia) is a large landlocked country in southern Africa that borders the Democratic Republic of the Congo, Tanzania, Malawi, Mozambique, Zimbabwe, Botswana, Namibia and Angola. The country is one of the poorest in Africa, ranking 38th out of 50 African countries according to the Human Development Index (UNDP, 2006b). Zambia has a population of 11 million and the UK Department for International Development categorizes 68 per cent as living in poverty (DFID, 2007). A long-lasting dominance of urban-based copper mining has led to a strong bias against the agricultural sector and consequently poverty has remained concentrated in marginalized rural areas (Lofgren et al, 2004). Although a tourism master plan was developed in 1979, this sector was also neglected until instability in the copper market focused attention on tourism in the drive for economic diversification (Rogerson, 2003).

Tourism is a small but steadily growing economic sector. The destination is marketed by the National Tourist Board as 'The Real Africa' and Victoria Falls is the country's leading tourism attraction. The nearby town of Livingstone is marketed as the 'Adventure Capital of Africa' and tourism has emerged as the 'key sectoral driver' for local economic development (Rogerson, 2005). Other major tourism attractions include the Mosi-oa-Tunya, South Luangwa, Lower Zambezi, Kafue and Kasanka National Parks. Zambia has 19 national parks and 34 game management areas (GMAs) covering a third of the country but few of these assets have been developed for tourism (GRZ, 2002).

According to WTO, international tourism arrivals more than trebled between 1990 and 2004 from 141,000 to 515,000. The most reliable data indicate that approximately one-third of arrivals are holiday makers (Dixey, 2005). Research suggests that almost 90 per cent of holiday makers are nature tourists visiting the falls, viewing wildlife or taking an adventure trip, and that the majority visit only one site with an average duration of stay of 6.3 days – low compared to Botswana (8.6 days) or Namibia (12.4 days) (Sinyenga et al, 2007). Regional tourism is crucial, particularly in South Africa, which is a source of tourists as well as investment and marketing (Rogerson, 2003). Information on the economics of tourism is limited and the value of the sector and its economic multiplier is a matter of debate. The World Tourism and Travel Council forecasts for 2007, based on the Tourism Satellite Accounting method, estimate that tourism will account for 4 per cent, directly and indirectly, of GDP; 55,000 jobs, 3.3 per cent of total employment; and grow in real terms by 4.7 per cent per annum between 2008 and 2017 (WTTC, 2007). In-depth research on the economic impact of tourism in specific locations in Zambia is limited to a study commissioned by the Luangwa Safari Association that suggested that tourism in the valley was worth US$6 million annually (Pope, 2005).

Tourism development has been slower than in some other countries in the region and shaped by internal and external factors. Economic priority in post-independent Zambia was given to copper mining and tourism development was significantly fettered by the country's involvement in protracted liberation struggles in Zimbabwe (1965–1980) and later South Africa, which reduced tourism arrivals and effectively put a brake on economic development (Teye, 1986). Tourism development has also been constrained by geographical factors such as the very short tourism season (June–October) due to the rainfall pattern, the remoteness of tourism assets, long travel distances and the dependence on air transport, and the heavy capital investment needed for infrastructure development (Teye, 1988). Challenges identified by the government include inadequate marketing of the destination and product development, poor programme implementation, lack of development finance, low level of skills, lack of private sector incentives and bureaucratic delays and high costs (GRZ, 2002). The PROFIT study established additional constraints such as shortages of material inputs (e.g. fuel), a poor relationship between the private sector and the government, poor cohesion and organization in the private sector, restrictive immigration of expatriate tourism professionals, and poor governance and transparency in government and communities (Dixey, 2005). Finally, HIV/AIDS has impacted adversely on the tourism sector reducing labour productivity, increasing labour costs and worsening skill shortages (Rosen et al, 2006).

The Tourism Policy stresses that the sector is pivotal to bringing development and poverty alleviation to rural areas (GRZ, 1999). This is reflected in the Poverty Reduction Strategy Paper 2002–2004 that states the government's vision is '*to ensure that Zambia becomes a major tourist destination of choice with unique features, which contributes to sustainable economic growth and poverty reduction*' (GRZ, 2002, p67). However, despite the recognition of the potential pro-poor benefits of tourism in the strategy paper, it has been noted that '*this support is often not reflected in sectoral policies and plans*' (ODI, 2006, p1). The Fifth National Development Plan, 2006–2010, continues to promote the potential of the tourism sector in reducing poverty (GRZ, 2006). In view of the fact that tourism has become increasingly important in poverty reduction strategies and plans, it is surprising that as noted by Rogerson (2003), tourism development in Zambia remains under-researched.

Defining community tourism in Zambia

Before presenting the key findings on community tourism in Zambia there is a need for conceptual clarity of the vocabulary. The concept of 'community' has reached the forefront of discussions on tourism and sustainability but what is meant by 'community' requires critical evaluation (Swarbrooke, 1999; Richards and Hall, 2000). This is particularly important in community tourism as the 'amorphous term' can hide the power of local elites (Mowforth and Munt, 1998, p252). For the purposes of the PROFIT study, 'community' was interpreted as locational, i.e. the people living in a geographical location. The nebulousness of the concept was acknowledged and the importance of understanding the local context with all its given ambivalences, uncertainties and divisions of power were recognized. This is particularly important in Zambia as traditional leaders are powerful. At the smallest geographic level there is one village with a village headman. Each village usually belongs to a group of villages that form a larger community organized under a chief or chieftainess. At the next level there maybe a paramount chief for an ethnic group. Customary authority presents critical challenges to community conservation and development projects in Zambia, as they are incompatible with citizenship rights, particularly equality, and the misuse of resources and accountability is problematic (Virtanen, 2003). These challenges were reflected in the PROFIT study. A plethora of definitions of community tourism exist internationally (CTO, 2007). For the purposes of the PROFIT study, it was defined as 'tourism which is owned and/or managed by communities' with the aim of generating wider community benefit. As the introduction of the term in Zambia was relatively new, it was frequently misunderstood.

Institutional frameworks and planning for community tourism in Zambia

Government departments with significant roles in tourism development fall under the Ministry of Tourism, Environment and Natural Resources (MTENR). The Department of Tourism is responsible for the implementation of policy, regulatory and legislative frameworks for tourism. Representatives interviewed envisioned a government-led approach to community tourism through regional tourism development offices to facilitate product development and tourist bookings. Officials asserted that few companies were supportive and most excluded village visits as they had an antagonistic relationship with local communities. It was also stated that outsourcing the management of community tourism assets such as lodges was against policy directives and that the licensing of community tourism was unnecessary. The PROFIT report questioned the appropriateness of the Department engaging in community tourism product development.

Two key initiatives had been undertaken by the Department of Tourism to promote community tourism. The Tourism Development Credit Facility introduced in 2004 had a revolving fund of ZMK5 billion (approximately US$1.2 million); 78 loans had been disbursed by late 2005. Only one was awarded to a community tourism project for three 'Bushcamps' in the Luangwa valley supported by the Wildlife Conservation Society. However, the enterprises had been unable to service or repay the loan during the stipulated period. The PROFIT study suggested that the Tourism Policy directive for the credit facility to act as '*a source of soft loans to local investors and local communities*' was not being met. Moreover, an advisory note of the International Monetary Fund and International Development Association concluded that the credit facility '*is not sustainable and its operations are ineffective*' (IMF and IDA, 2005, p2). The Department of Tourism received a community tourism mission from the WTO ST-EP Programme in 2004. The consultant visited two enterprises and concluded that community tourism had great potential (WTO, 2004). A proposal for the MTENR to engage hundreds of communities through a Village Action for Sustainable Tourism (VAST) Project was developed for the ST-EP Foundation. The PROFIT study strongly suggested that such an approach to community tourism was unrealistic and inappropriate.

The Zambia National Tourist Board is responsible for marketing but its promotion of community tourism was extremely limited. The Board had an internal list of four community enterprises. The PROFIT research showed that there were 21 other initiatives. The organization did profile cultural festivals, such as the Kuomboka in Barotseland, although attendance by international tourists was low. The PROFIT report suggested that the low level of attendance was due to the remoteness of event locations, no set event dates, a lack of staged authenticity and interpretation, as well as risk factors. Furthermore, it concluded that increased training, infrastructure development and promotion for festivals were unlikely to result in viable community enterprises.

The Zambia Wildlife Authority is a semi-autonomous statutory agency mandated to manage the conservation and utilization (both consumptive and non-consumptive) of wildlife and National Parks. The Authority has responsibility for regulating the formation and operation of Community Resource Boards (CRBs) in Game Management Areas (GMAs) that border National Parks and was involved with community tourism in GMAs but was not aware of all existing and planned enterprises. Community tourism appeared to fall between 'the stools' of the organization as it was relevant to the GMA Directorate as well as the Commercial Services and Tourism Development Sections. The Authority recognized many challenges including the need to develop new community institutions such as trusts as it is legally problematic for CRBs to own assets; the lack of capacity in CRBs to manage business; the danger that only the local elite benefit; conflicts between community tourism enterprises and hunting companies; and poor product quality. The Commercial Services Section was supportive of business partnerships between communities and tourism companies.

The National Heritage Conservation Commission is responsible for the conservation and management of heritage sites and many are thought to have community tourism potential. The PROFIT study advocated caution, however, as research assessing the viability of a community enterprise at the Livingstone memorial concluded that it was unlikely to generate much income (Hawkins,

2005). Overall the PROFIT study concluded that the influence of government departments on community tourism development had been minimal.

A wide range of international and local NGOs and bilateral and multilateral donors have assisted the development of community enterprises in tourism and crafts with mixed results. These include African Parks Conservation, African Wildlife Foundation, Choma Museum and Crafts Centre Trust Ltd., Conservation Lower Zambezi, Kasanka Trust Ltd., North Luangwa Conservation Project, Source Connection Foundation, West Lunga Trust, Wildlife Conservation Society, WWF Zambia, Danish International Development Agency, USAID and the World Bank.

The Fifth National Development Plan 2006–2010 reviewed past performance and acknowledged that '*although tourism has been identified as a form of rural development, the interests of the local communities have not been fully incorporated*' (GRZ, 2006, p89). The plan presents 13 programmes for tourism and 1 is community tourism development. The objective is '*to promote local community participation and ownership in tourism*' through encouraging community participation in joint ventures by using land as equity, promoting public–private and community partnerships and facilitating access to development funds by communities (GRZ, 2006, p91). It remains to be seen how this objective will be implemented.

Inventory and the impact of community tourism in Zambia

Twenty-five community tourism enterprises were identified in six out of nine Provinces with over ten more enterprises under consideration. The highest concentration of existing enterprises was located close to Livingstone followed by clusters along the borders of South and North Luangwa National Parks and the route between Kasanka National Park and Bangweulu wetlands. Several were identified in Lusaka, Lower Zambezi, Liuwa Plains National Park and Kafue National Park. No community enterprises were identified in North-Western, Copperbelt and Luapula Provinces which are marginal holiday destinations. Most community enterprises were located in GMAs bordering national parks (11 enterprises), followed by rural villages outside GMAs (8), a national park (5) and an urban area (1). It was surprising that one-fifth were located within national parks as legally the community institutions cannot own the physical assets such as the campsite facilities the tourism is based on. Overall, 52 per cent of the enterprises offered cultural products such as a village walk and 48 per cent were based on non-consumptive forms of wildlife tourism. The enterprises provided camping (16 enterprises), chalet accommodation (12), village tour (7), wildlife walk (7), entertainment (7), curio market (3) and a guesthouse (1).

The enterprises featured a range of organizational structures. The most prevalent was the CRB (8) but many were simply comprised of an informal committee (7). Most were, however, registered with the local council as a community-based organization. A few were membership associations or registered as a

Table 15.1 *Income generation of community tourism enterprises in 2004*

Enterprise	Estimated donor investment in infrastructure to date (US$)	Estimated total visitor numbers 2004	Estimated gross revenue 2004 (US$)	Estimated net income 2004 (US$)
Mukuni Development Trust	0	Unknown	15,120	Unknown
Nsongwe Village Visit Fund	0	351	1053	828
Simonga Village Visit Fund	0	769	175	175
Kawaza Village Tourism Project	250	453	8927	2250
Chiawa Community Campsite	2950	781	4200	Unknown
Natwange Community Campsite	5000	68	340	118
Muwele Cultural Village	18,200	13	260	0
Lochinvar Community Campsite	20,000	133	540	0
Dudumwenzwe Campsite	28,400	0	0	0

Source: Dixey, 2005

society. Interestingly only two were trusts that could legally hold land title deeds and thereby own property. Just one enterprise had a certificate of incorporation and none had a tax clearance certificate or liability insurance. Only two enterprises held tourism licences as these were prohibitively expensive (minimum cost US$450 per annum). Many enterprises were not aware of the legal requirements for tourism operations or ownership of assets but expressed a strong desire to become legalized to form business partnerships and prevent interference from local elites.

The available data were insufficient to compare the income-generation of all the enterprises in 2004, mainly because almost a third had not commenced operations in that year. However, the data provided for nine enterprises by community representatives, donors and tourism companies were insightful (Table 15.1).

The Mukuni Development Trust received most gross revenue from village tours, curio markets and payments from a revenue-sharing agreement with a tourism company, Ecolift Ltd. The net income accruing to the Trust is likely to be high as overheads are low. The Kawaza Village Tourism Project that was developed with technical advice from Robin Pope Safaris Ltd. was the most successful in known net income-generation. Nsongwe and Simonga Villages also received tourists through tour operators. It was notable that Nsongwe received less than half the number of tourists as Simonga, although its net income was almost five times higher, attributable to the difference in tour fees. Furthermore, although six enterprises were based on accommodation, most income was generated through revenue sharing in the case of the trust or from day visits. Moreover, the data strongly suggested that relatively high external donor funding in infrastructure development did not necessarily result in net income generation.

Only three enterprises were generating sufficient net income for wider collective benefits in the community – Mukuni, Kawaza and Nsongwe – all of which were supported by private sector tourism companies. Three new community campsites in Liuwa Plain National Park supported by African Parks Conservation also demonstrated relatively high income-generating potential and a fourth was planned. African Parks is the first private sector park management institution in Africa managing eight national parks in six countries (AP, 2006). It was notable, however, that the highest estimated gross revenue of the community tourism enterprises (US$15,000) was significantly less than the funds paid to local people by individual tourism companies surveyed in terms of annual salaries, philanthropic donations and/or purchases of goods and services. For example, Jungle Junction on Bovu Island which is a small budget camp for independent travellers pay approximately US$20,000 in wages and US$5000 for building material to the local community per annum. Robin Pope Safaris Ltd. spent US$65,000 rehabilitating Kawaza Village School in 2004 and additionally sponsors teachers and students. Sun International in Livingstone had the largest corporate social responsibility budget for local development projects that was approximately US$250,000 per year.

Furthermore, several challenges in collective income distribution from community tourism enterprises were identified. It was widely perceived that community benefits from a few enterprises were not being realized due to poor management and governance. A problem relating to CRBs was that income went into the general 'pot' rather than a separate fund allocated to a specific project, and therefore any benefits of tourism were not obvious to the community. Moreover, if several CRBs were responsible for an enterprise then any net gain for each community became negligible due to the large population. For example, the gross revenue of Lochinvar Community Campsite in 2004 was estimated as US$540 and there was no net income shared between five CRBs covering a large area.

Various business constraints were identified by the community enterprises. The main constraint was poor marketing due to a lack of resources and skills emphasizing the importance of linkages to tourism companies that can market their products. Communication for bookings was also a key constraint as many enterprises were remotely located, could not manage unexpected arrivals or deal with tourist health and safety issues adequately. A lack of skills was also highly problematic, particularly in tourism awareness, visitor handling, guiding and business development as many employees had no formal training. Finance was also perceived as a constraint, especially for upgrading accommodation. High seasonality significantly limited income as the majority of enterprises only had a six-month season as many areas are not accessible in the rainy season. Enterprises also faced other accessibility challenges as several were far from main tourism routes and/or located in areas with poor road infrastructure.

Ownership and governance issues also fettered development. Donor investment had on several occasions created assets such as lodges and campsites for CRBs that were not legally owned by the community institutions and were operating illegally. Other important issues included unaccountability for income collected and interference from the elite such as closing the enterprise or demanding tribute, for example, a form of tax for the chief to endorse the enterprise.

A couple of community tourism camps in GMAs had serious land use conflicts with nearby safari hunting outfitters as hunting in the same area discouraged non-consumptive wildlife viewing and posed threats to tourist health and safety. This was primarily due to a lack of consultation, communication and land use planning. The Mukuni Development Trust also had disputes with rafting companies in Livingstone who were reluctant to pay fees to use access routes on the chief's land. Future business projections varied from very pessimistic from those whose support from NGOs and donors had withdrawn to highly optimistic from those who continued to be supported and/or had developed good linkages with the private sector. Community members at several donor-funded accommodation facilities expressed exasperation at being effectively abandoned by NGOs and unable to manage the failing business. A few enterprises were hopeful for the future and most expressed a desire to partner with tourism companies.

Critical issues and lessons learnt in Zambia

Overall, the number of bed-nights and income captured by community tourism enterprises was extremely small. A few of the earliest projects had failed and were no longer operational such as Dudumwenze Campsite, Muwele Cultural Village and Lochinvar Community Campsite. The three 'Bushcamps' in the Luangwa valley supported by the Wildlife Conservation Society and facilitated by the Tourism Development Credit Facility remained in debt. Furthermore, many new enterprises will struggle to be profitable mainly because development had been inappropriately donor-driven and not market-led. Survey respondents from 29 private sector tourism companies suggested that on average 44 per cent of their tourists were interested in community and cultural activities suggesting a ready market for new community products. However, most companies identified constraints such as the industry not being consulted during market research and product development, attractions in the wrong place, a lack of skills and capacity, and illegal operations that resulted in highly variable and often low product quality, a lack of understanding of tourism at the community level, and barriers to cooperation. The level of donor funding and infrastructure development appeared to have a negative correlation with enterprise performance. This does not necessarily imply, however, that external assistance cannot be effective. Other factors that contributed to poor business performance were multiple and conflicting objectives, internal community disputes and poor local governance, a lack of information dissemination, coordination and planning, and sharing of common lessons learnt.

Key determinants of enterprise performance included linkages to tourism companies, proximity to main tourism routes, competitive advantage, financial management, visitor handling and community motivation. Several private sector tour operators 'championed' the most successful community enterprises, providing technical advice and marketing support. However, community tourism looked likely to remain for the most part an optional activity in existing tours as Zambia is a relatively expensive destination, time schedules are tight and it is extremely difficult to develop community tourism in remote tourism areas away from the 'tourism capital' of Livingstone. Furthermore, community tourism was in danger of being undermined by its weak legal status as there was no enabling legal framework to cater for their needs and this inhibited business partnerships with companies. The research therefore concluded that in order to increase net benefits to the poor from tourism a wider range of actions were needed that go beyond promoting community tourism, although work at the grassroots level to develop enterprises and local capacity is one key component.

Discussion

Community tourism is 'in vogue' in Zambia but the research echoed other critical appraisals in that, if the scale and the success rate of community tourism enterprises are too small, the challenge is a case of 'trickle up' not 'trickle down' (Ashley, 1995, p39). The major reason for poor performance and failure was that projects were not market-oriented. A review of community tourism in Namibia also argued that 'if tourism businesses are to succeed, they need to be understood within the context of successful business practices and the realities of markets and consumer demand' (Hitchens and Highstead, 2005, p2). Indeed, the persistent neglect of the market is of major concern as it is a key reason why pro-poor tourism approaches continue to go wrong (Ashley and Goodwin, 2007).

It has been controversially contended that conservationists are not suited to work in enterprise development, that *'far too little is known about what is really happening in the field'* and that the 'packaging' of non-governmental and donor project reports exaggerates success or downplays questionable results (Chapin, 2004, p30). Field research in Zambia supported these assertions. Several community tourism projects were alarmingly ill-conceived and/or poorly implemented giving inappropriate and unattainable roles to local people who had no business or tourism experience. Spectacular failures were not known about. Moreover, contrary to positive publicity for fundraising purposes, several interventions by NGOs had in fact resulted in wasted technical, financial and community resources, disappointed expectations and disillusioned local people.

Failures and accountability aside, the author argues that interventions in southern Africa can be more successful and cost effective if and when due diligence is paid to lessons learnt. The fact that tourism is a highly competitive service industry must be assimilated by NGOs, donor and government agencies. There are 'hidden treasures' exhibiting high potential (Dixey, 2004) but expectations of what, where and how community tourism can deliver must be realistic. Moreover, community tourism is likely to remain *'only one tiny, and difficult, aspect of participation by the poor in tourism value chains'* (Ashley, 2006, p3).

It is encouraging that Zambia, like some other African countries, has made policy commitments to harness tourism for poverty reduction. However, the author strongly cautions that community tourism, like 'community conservation', has become a privileged solution – *'so self evidently the "right" approach, on a range of grounds, that debate about its merits or demerits, about its costs and benefits, about the conditions under which it may prove effective and ineffective'* will continue to be limited in official discourses (Adams and Hulme 1998, p20). Community tourism entered the practitioners' vocabulary over three decades ago and it is time for less rhetoric, more reflexive thinking and dynamic actions. Otherwise, there is a grave danger that development interventions in Zambia and other African countries will head up a community tourism cul-de-sac.

There is an urgent need for practitioners to respond to the new opportunities provided by emerging policies with *'robust approaches and proven results'* (Ashley and Goodwin, 2007, p1). The challenge is to mainstream approaches to tourism and poverty reduction and this, uncomfortably for some, requires attention to the market and engagement with commercial tourism businesses to deliver pro-poor impacts on a significant scale.

Recommendations

The PROFIT study recommended the adoption of a market-oriented pro-poor tourism approach in Zambia. This requires small, medium and micro-enterprise development grounded in market opportunity, broader industry understanding as well as more effective management of expectations based on private sector realities. It demands a greater focus on appropriate roles for local people in tourism and the development of business partnerships between communities and companies, such as the supply of agricultural produce and joint ventures. More effective utilization of donor funding, monitoring and evaluation, and reporting is also essential.

An emphasis was placed on the need for an improved enabling environment. This requires more appropriate roles for government as a facilitator rather than as an actor in the tourism industry, improved platforms for public and private sector dialogue on industry development, investment incentives for business partnerships between communities and tourism companies, and the development of an appropriate framework to legalize and license community tourism enterprises, including minimum standards that ensure tourist safety. Better communication and planning for community tourism is necessary, especially in GMAs, to prevent land use conflicts between non-consumptive and consumptive tourism and negative environmental impacts.

A range of actions were identified to upgrade community tourism including market research, the strengthening of community institutions to ensure accountability and wider community benefit, the provision of accessible credit facilities and cost-effective skills development, as well as more concerted marketing and improved information dissemination, coordination and planning. Cautious consideration should be given to the formation of a community tourism trade association but this would have to incorporate business and legal expertise and a plan for long-term financial sustainability.

Several of the PROFIT recommendations are reflected in the Fifth National Development Plan 2006–2010 that promotes joint ventures, public–private and community partnerships, and access to development funds for communities (GRZ, 2006). However, effective implementation will depend heavily on political will and require significant improvements in communication and cooperation between the actors involved.

References

Adams, W. M. and Hulme, D. (1998) 'Conservation and communities: Changing narratives, policies and practices in African conservation', Community Conservation Research in Africa Principles and Comparative Practice Working Paper 4, Manchester

African Parks (AP) (2006) *African Parks Foundation Annual Report*, African Parks Foundation, Doorn

Ashley, C. (1995) *Tourism, Communities, and the Potential Impacts on Local Incomes and Conservation*, Directorate of Environmental Affairs Ministry of Environment and Tourism, Windhoek, Namibia

Ashley, C. (2006) *How Can Governments Boost the Local Economic Impacts of Tourism? Opinions and Tools*, Netherlands Development Organization (SNV) and Overseas Development Institute (ODI), The Hague and London

Ashley, C. and Goodwin, H. (2007) 'Pro poor tourism: What's gone right and what's gone wrong?', ODI Opinion Paper 80, Overseas Development Institute, London

Ashley, C., Roe, D. and Goodwin, H. (2001) *Pro-Poor Tourism Strategies: Making Tourism Work for the Poor – A Review of Experience*, Overseas Development Institute, London

Asia Pacific Environmental Innovative Strategies – Research on Innovative and Strategic Policy Options (APEIS-RISPO) (2006) *Good Practices Inventory on Community-Based Tourism in Protected Areas*, Asia Pacific Environmental Innovative Strategies (APEIS) Research on Innovative and Strategic Policy Options (RISPO), Japan

Brechin, S. R., Wilshusen, P. R., Fortwangler, C. L. and West, P. C. (2002) 'Beyond the square wheel: Toward a more comprehensive understanding of biodiversity conservation as social and political process', *Society and Natural Resources*, vol 15, 41–64

Caribbean Natural Resources Institute (CANARI) (2004) *Community-based Tourism Initiatives in the Windward Islands: A Review of Their Impacts*, Caribbean Natural Resources Institute, Laventille, Trinidad

Caribbean Tourism Organization (CTO) (2007) *Competing with the Best: Good Practices in Community-Based Tourism in the Caribbean*, Caribbean Tourism Organization, Bridgetown, Barbados

Chapin, M. (2004) 'A challenge to conservationists', *WORLD WATCH Magazine*, vol 7, 17–31

Department for International Development (DFID) (2007) *Zambia Fact Sheet*, UK Department for International Development, London

Dixey, L. M. (2004) *Hidden Treasures Uganda: Tourism Consultancy Services for Development of a New Tourism Guidebook and Tour Packages*, Business Services Market Development, Kampala

Dixey, L. M. (2005) *Inventory and Analysis of Community-based Tourism in Zambia*, Production, Finance and Technology (PROFIT) USAID Private Sector Development Programme, Lusaka

Duffy, R. (2002) *A Trip Too Far: Ecotourism, Politics, and Exploitation*, Earthscan, London

Final Evaluation (2006) *Final Evaluation of the Private Sector Support Programme*, The European Commission and Kingdom of Swaziland, Mbabane

Goodwin, H. (2006a) 'Community-based tourism: Failing to deliver?', *id21 insights*, no 62, University of Sussex

Goodwin, H. (2006b) 'Measuring and reporting the impact of tourism on poverty', *Cutting Edge Research in Tourism – New Directions, Challenges and Application*, School of Management, University of Surrey, UK

Goodwin, H. and Roe, D. (2001) 'Tourism, livelihoods and protected areas: Opportunities for fair-trade tourism in and around National Parks', *International Journal of Tourism Research*, vol 3, 377–391

Government of the Republic of Zambia (GRZ) (1999) *National Tourism Policy*, Ministry of Tourism, Environment and Natural Resources, Government of the Republic of Zambia, Lusaka

GRZ (2002) *Zambia Poverty Reduction Strategy Paper 2002–2004*, Ministry of Finance and National Planning, Government of the Republic of Zambia, Lusaka

GRZ (2006) *Fifth National Development Plan 2006–2010*, Ministry of Finance and National Planning, Government of the Republic of Zambia, Lusaka

Hawkins, D. (2005) 'Feasibility study of community tourism development in Chipundu, northern Zambia', Masters thesis, Kings College, London

Hitchens, R. and Highstead, J. (2005) *Community-Based Tourism in Namibia – A Discussion Paper*, The ConMark Trust, University of Sussex, Brighton

Holland, J., Burian, M. and Dixey, L. (2003) *Tourism in Poor Rural Areas: Diversifying the Product and Expanding the Benefits in Rural Uganda and the Czech Republic*, PPT Working Paper, London

International Monetary Fund (IMF) and International Development Association (IDA) (2005) *Joint IDA-IMF Staff Advisory Note on the Second Annual Progress Report*, International Monetary Fund and International Development Association

InWEnt (2002) *Training Manual for Community-Based Tourism*, Capacity Building International, Germany

Kiss, A. (2004) 'Is community-based ecotourism a good use of biodiversity conservation funds?', *TRENDS in Ecology and Evolution*, vol 19, 232–237

Lofgren, H., Thurlow, J. and Robinson, S. (2004) *Prospects for Growth and Poverty Reduction in Zambia, 2001–2015*, Development Strategy and Governance Division International Food Policy Research Institute, Washington DC

Manyara, G., Jones, E. and Botterill, D. (2006) 'Tourism and poverty alleviation: The case for indigenous enterprise development in Kenya', *Tourism, Culture and Communication*, vol 7, 19–37

Mid-Term Review (2003) *Mid-Term Review Report of Support to the Wild Coast Spatial Development Initiative Pilot Programme*, European Union and Republic of South Africa

Mountain Institute (2000) *Community-Based Tourism for Conservation and Development: A Resource Kit*, The Mountain Institute, Washington, DC

Mowforth, M. and Munt, I. (1998) *Tourism and Sustainability: New Tourism in the Third World*, Routledge, London

Ntshona, Z. and Lahiff, E. (2003) 'Community-based eco-tourism on the Wild Coast, South Africa: The case of the Amadiba Trail', Sustainable Livelihoods in Southern Africa Research Paper 7, Institute of Development Studies, Brighton, UK

Overseas Development Institute (ODI) (2006) *Briefing Paper: Can Tourism Help Reduce Poverty in Africa?*, Overseas Development Institute, London

Pope, A. (2005) *Luangwa Safari Association Tourism Study*, WHYDAH Consulting Ltd, Lusaka

Pro-Poor Tourism Partnership (2005) *Annual Register*, Pro-Poor Tourism Partnership, London

Pro-Poor Tourism Partnership (2006) *Annual Register*, Pro-Poor Tourism Partnership, London

Richards, G. and Hall, D. (2000) 'The community: A sustainable concept in tourism development?', in G. Richards, and D. Hall (eds), *Tourism and Sustainable Community Development*, Routledge, Oxford

Rogerson, C. M. (2003) 'Developing Zambia's tourism economy: Planning for the real Africa', *Africa Insight*, vol 33, 48–54

Rogerson, C. M. (2005) 'The emergence of tourism-led local development: The example of Livingstone, Zambia', *Africa Insight*, vol 35, 112–120

Rosen, S., Hamazakaza, P. and Long, L. (2006) *The Impact of HIV/AIDS on the Tourism Sector in Zambia*, Centre for International Health and Development, Boston University, Boston, MA

Rozga, Z. and Spenceley, A. (2006) *Community-Based Tourism Enterprise Market Access Training Manual*, United Nations World Tourism Organization, Regional Tourism Organization for Southern Africa and SNV

Salafsky, N., Cauley, H., Balachander, G., Cordes, B., Parks, J., Margoluis, C., Bhatt, S., Encarnacion, C., Russell, D. and Margoluis, R. (2001) 'A systematic test of an enterprise strategy for community-based biodiversity conservation', *Conservation Biology*, vol 15, 1585–1595

Sinyenga, G., Muwele, B. and Hamilton, K. (2007) *The Contribution of Nature Tourism to the Zambian Economy*, Government of the Republic of Zambia-UNDP-DANIDA-World Bank study, Lusaka

Stonich, S. C. (2005) 'Enhancing community-based tourism development and conservation in the Western Caribbean', *NAPA Bulletin*, no 23, 77–86

Swarbrooke, J. (1999) 'The host community', in J. Swarbooke (ed.), *Sustainable Tourism Management*, CABI Publishing, New York

Teye, V. B. (1986) 'Liberation wars and tourism development in Africa – The case of Zambia', *Annals of Tourism Research*, vol 13, 589–608

Teye, V. B. (1988) 'Geographic factors affecting Tourism in Zambia', *Annals of Tourism Research*, vol 15, 487–503

Townsend, C. (2006) *Guidelines for Community-based Tourism in Rwanda*, Office Rwandais du Tourisme et des Parcs Nationaux, Kigali, Rwanda

Turner, R. (2006) *Communities, Conservation, and Tourism-Based Development: Can Community-Based Nature Tourism Live Up to Its Promise?*, The Berkeley Electronic Press, Berkeley, CA

United Nations Development Programme (UNDP) (2006a) *Community Action to Conserve Biodiversity – Linking Biodiversity Conservation with Poverty Reduction. Case Studies from Latin America and the Caribbean*, United Nations Development Programme Energy and Environment Group, New York

UNDP (2006b) *Human Development Report 2006 Beyond Scarcity: Power, Poverty and the Global Water Crisis*, United Nations Development Programme, New York

Virtanen, P. (2003) 'Local management of global values: Community-based wildlife management in Zimbabwe and Zambia', *Society and Natural Resources*, vol 16, 179–190

Wright, B. B. (2005) 'A review of lessons learned to inform capacity-building for sustainable nature-based tourism development in the European Union funded support to the Wild Coast Spatial Development Initiative Pilot Programme', Masters thesis, Rhodes University, Grahamstown, South Africa

WTO (2004) *World Tourism Organization Community Based Tourism Mission to Zambia December 1-11, 2004*, United Nations World Tourism Organization, Madrid, Spain

WTO (2006) *Poverty Alleviation Through Tourism – A Compilation of Good Practices*, United Nations World Tourism Organization, Madrid, Spain

WTTC (2007) *Zambia: The 2007 Travel and Tourism Economic Research*, World Travel and Tourism Council, London

WWF International (2001) *Guidelines for Community-Based Ecotourism Development*, WWF International, Gland, Switzerland

16

Community-based Tourism and Natural Resource Management in Namibia: Local and National Economic Impacts

Jonathan I. Barnes

Introduction

In this chapter the economic characteristics of Namibian community initiatives in tourism and natural resource management are described. Community-based natural resource management (CBNRM) in Namibia has been developing since before 1990. Legislative change in 1994 made it possible for communities in Namibia's communal lands to acquire limited common property rights to manage and use their wildlife resources. These changes extended similar rights already available to private landholders in Namibia to communal lands, where residents practising traditional agro-pastoral and livestock-based land uses, had had no rights to use wildlife. Thus communities were enabled to register conservancies, through which they could take on rights, and manage and use wildlife resources with the assistance of NGOs and government. The primary motivation for CBNRM, as described elsewhere in this book, has been to give landholders incentives to invest in their natural resources. With support from donors and government, communities have established some 50 conservancies on large portions of the communal lands. Details on Namibia's CBNRM programme are given by the Namibian Association of CBNRM Support Organizations (NACSO, 2004, 2006), and Libanda and Blignaut (2007).

Namibia is a large country, embracing some 830,000km², with a mostly rural human population of some 1.7 million. It is very dry, with habitats ranging from semi-arid savanna woodland in the north-east, through to extremely arid desert in the west and south. Most land in the country is only suitable for extensive grazing by livestock or wildlife. Forty-three per cent of the country, mostly in central and southern drier parts, contains private, medium scale, commercial ranches, and 45 per cent, mostly in the more remote north, is communal land. Communal land is state-owned, but occupied by rural tribal communities – most of the country's population. Traditionally communities have practised pastoralism in the south and west, and agropastoralism in the north and north-east, but their access to markets and infrastructure has been poor. In the north-east, among San communities, some sedentary hunting and gathering is practised.

Wildlife resources of high value for tourism occur in less densely settled north-western and north-eastern communal lands. Elephant (*Loxodonta africana*), buffalo (*Syncerus caffer*), hippopotamus (*Hippopotamus amphibius*), sable (*Hippotragus niger*), roan (*Hippotragus equinus*), lechwe (*Kobus leche*), sitatunga (*Tragelaphus spekei*), lion (*Panthera leo*), leopard (*Panthera pardus*) and wild dog (*Lycaeon pictus*) are of conservation importance in the north-east. In the north-west, desert-adapted wildlife species such as elephant, black rhinoceros (*Diceros bicornis*), mountain zebra (*Equus zebra*), springbok (*Antidorcas marsupialis*), kudu (*Tragelphus strepsiseros*) and oryx (*Oryx gazella*) occur. Attractive scenery, enhancing tourism value, exists in both places.

By far the most important natural resource uses in CBNRM are non-consumptive wildlife viewing tourism and consumptive trophy-hunting tourism. Conservancies develop their own campsites from which they derive profits, and they also enter into joint ventures with private operators, where wildlife viewing and trophy hunting activities are pursued. Thus, communities offer concessions to operators where lodges and camps are developed, the communities generally contributing the site and possibly capital and the private operator contributing capital, skills, market access and other specialized inputs. Some subsistence and commercial use of natural plant and wildlife resources takes place in conservancies, for example, to produce fuelwood, poles, plant foods, meat and raw materials for crafts, but this is relatively minor. Tourism has received priority as it has been able to give communities large injections of new income.

A key policy question associated with CBNRM is whether it can generate viable and sustainable returns. Can the private benefits to communities and households resulting from CBNRM be significant and outweigh the associated costs? Can the massive donor investment that has gone into CBNRM in southern Africa be shown to be justified in terms of sustainable economic growth and rural development? The existence in Namibia of 16 years of quality data on the costs and benefits associated with CBNRM and a programme of ongoing economic analysis provides an unparalleled opportunity to answer these questions.

The economics unit of the Ministry of Environment and Tourism has analysed the financial and economic development of selected individual conservancies and the national CBNRM programme as a whole. These analyses have been aimed at determining the financial viability of conservancies and the contribution that these make to the national income (Barnes et al, 2002). They have been carried further at the national level to measure the economic impact that the

CBNRM programme as a whole makes to the national income (NACSO, 2004, 2006). This chapter reports on the findings of these analyses.

The work described here needs to be seen in the context of the 'total economic value' of wildlife and natural resources, as described by Pearce and Turner (1990) and Emerton (2001). Total economic value embraces direct use, indirect use and non-use (option, bequest and existence) values associated with natural resources. Direct use values are derived from actual utilization of the resource. They contribute tangible value in the form of income, and make up the main component of formal economic growth, which is the focus of national development efforts. This chapter deals only with direct use values. Conservation of wildlife and the tourism asset base through CBNRM could enhance the other values.

Methods for measurement of financial and economic values

Conservancy-level analysis

The economics unit of the Ministry of Environment and Tourism has developed a system of empirically-based enterprise models for natural resource use. These are developed, and periodically updated, for typical examples of different land uses. They are detailed budget and cost–benefit spreadsheets, which measure the financial returns to investors in natural resource use and also the contribution that these activities make to the national income. Barnes et al (2002) developed such models for five individual representative conservancies, which had been operating for several years. Empirical data to hand, and conservancy management plans, were used to project costs and benefits for each of the five conservancies over a ten-year life span. The conservancy 'project boundary' was defined as the investment made by donors, government and community in the development and operation of a conservancy. It embraced the investments, capital and recurrent costs, that make the conservancy function, and the benefits in the form of income to the conservancy and its employees, as a result of this investment.

Capital included expenditures by donors, government and communities, on items such as fences boreholes, buildings, vehicles and equipment, initial training workshops, etc. and wildlife stocks, if they were introduced. Excluded from capital were the costs of existing natural stock already on the land and the broader government investments in its conservation (sector conservation budgets, etc.). Recurrent costs were those for conservancy operations, including such items as payment of staff salaries and wages, maintenance and repairs to capital items, ongoing training costs, insurance, feeding and veterinary costs, etc. Included in costs were mitigation requirements for the damage that wildlife in conservancies cause to other community land uses.

Benefits included rentals and royalties paid to the conservancy by joint-venture lodges and joint-venture hunting operations, and any profits from community-operated enterprises such as campsites, cultural tourism services, guiding, sales of live game and consumption of game for meat, etc. Net benefits accruing to joint-venture tourism enterprises in the conservancies were excluded from the conservancy analysis. The conservancy budget and cost–benefit models estimated both financial and economic values. Financial analysis looked at the returns to stakeholders in the project, while economic analysis looked at the degree to which the conservancy investment affected the national economy.

In financial analysis the models provided annual net profits at stability, as well as five- and ten-year financial internal rates of return and financial net present values for the project investment. These were done for the project as a whole, to determine the returns to the donor, government and community investment combined, as well as specifically for the community, to determine the returns that the community was getting on its own investment. Wealth accumulation, in terms of residuals for capital assets, was included. Appreciation of wildlife stocks attributable to the conservancy investment was included for the project analysis but not for the community one (since they could not realize this value through sale). In the community analysis, the donor and government contributions were treated as subsidies. This meant that these contributions, treated as costs in the project financial analysis, were treated as benefits in the community analysis.

In the economic analysis, the models measured the incremental change made by each conservancy to the national income. Annual net benefits, internal rates of return, and net present values were measured in terms of net national income. National income was defined here (Gittinger, 1982) as the total net earnings of national labour, and property owned by nationals, employed in the economy over a period. Gross national income is closely similar to the GDP, which is the total of the value added in all activities in the economy. Net national income is gross national income net of asset depreciation. The financial values in the models were converted where necessary to reflect the real costs (opportunity costs) to the nation as a whole. The changes involved use of preliminary shadow pricing criteria developed by Barnes (1994), which have been more rigorously confirmed by Humavindu (2007). In an open economy such as that in Namibia, the only adjustments considered necessary were to labour prices (to reflect unemployment) and to tradable item prices (to reflect excess demand for foreign exchange). Further, some financial costs and benefits, such as taxes and subsidies, which were simply transfers and did not change the national income, were removed from the economic analysis.

The residual values, associated with capital items and wildlife stocks in the conservancy, were included as benefits in the project financial analysis. The economic analysis included the opportunity cost of the capital used, but excluded those for land, because it was partially aimed at measuring returns to land. All models were tested through sensitivity analysis, by varying key assumptions to determine how robust they were, and the strength of conclusions that can be drawn from the results. Details of the methods used are presented in Barnes et al (2002).

Programme-level analysis

In addition to the analysis of five specific conservancies, a wider economic analysis was done of the overall national CBNRM Programme of which the five are a part. The aggregate impact of the CBNRM programme on the economy is wider than the returns accruing to the communities, as it also includes all the economic activities linked to, and resulting from, the presence of the conservancies. Thus CBNRM programme expenditures generate net national income directly in community areas and this direct income generation indirectly induces generation of further net national income in the wider economy. In as much as the CBNRM Programme results in capital accumulation, such as in wildlife stocks, these form part of the aggregate impact. NACSO (2004, 2006) presented the results of the analysis to measure the aggregate impact that 16 years of CBNRM Programme investment made in the national economy.

The starting point for the aggregation of the direct economic impact was the aggregate financial income derived by communities from natural resource uses, converted to national income as described for conservancies, above. Further, tourism joint-ventures between communities and the private sector in community areas, themselves generate national income and this was included. Joint-venture income was measured from enterprise financial and economic models for tourism lodges and trophy hunting activities (Unpublished data, 2004, Ministry of Environment and Tourism). Besides their expenditures on accommodation in joint-ventures and community campsites in community areas, tourists also make other expenditures in the economy, which can be linked directly to their experience in community areas, such as those for in-country travel, urban accommodation, crafts and retail purchases. These commonly amount to some 60 per cent of their in-country expenditures (SIAPAC, 2003). The national income contribution associated with these expenditures was included in direct benefits.

All the activities that generate direct income, also create demand for inputs in the wider economy. Thus, for example, tourists' expenditures at joint-venture lodges, or with transport providers, stimulate demand for inputs such as food and fuel from food and fuel firms which, in turn, also contribute to national income. These in turn also create demand in a similar way and so on. The initial direct expenditures associated with community areas are thus responsible for indirect contributions to national income through backward linkages. This is termed the multiplier effect, which can be measured using the national social accounting matrix (SAM), an input–output model of the whole Namibian economy, which includes both firms and households. Lange et al. (2004) develop and describe this model. The indirect impact of CBNRM in the Namibian economy was measured using an income or value added multiplier derived from the SAM.

Another economic benefit measured in the programme-level analysis was the increase in wildlife stocks resulting from implementation of the CBNRM programme. The accumulated capital value of increasing wildlife stocks in conservancies is seen by many as a direct consequence of CBNRM activities. These incremental values were valued at their monetary value 'on the hoof', that is, the value they would fetch if they were to be sold or harvested commercially. The total of all the directly and indirectly generated net national income, plus the accumulated asset value of stock, generated as a result of the CBNRM activities, was measured as the economic impact of the CBNRM programme. This economic impact was compared with the investments made in CBNRM by donors and government, within a cost–benefit framework, over the life to date, of the programme (1990–2005).

Findings on local and national economic impacts

Inputs and returns in five conservancies

Table 16.1 shows some features of the five conservancies analysed by Barnes et al (2002). They ranged from near desert conditions in the north-west (Torra, ≠Khoadi //Hôas), via the northern Kalahari (Nyae Nyae), to semi-arid woodlands/floodplain habitats in the north-east (Mayuni, Salambala). They varied greatly in extent from almost a million hectares in Nyae Nyae, where non-wildlife land uses are relatively unimportant to 28,000 hectares in Mayuni where half the land was used for fairly intensive agro-pastoralism. Some conservancies possessed naturally intact wildlife resources combined with attractive scenery, on at least part of their land (Torra, Mayuni), while in others wildlife resources were depleted and required restocking or investment (Salambala, Nyae Nyae).

The potential for income generating activities varies between the five conservancies. Table 16.1 shows subjective ratings of their potential for different activities. Ratings indicate roughly the amount of income that could be generated, with 'low' signifying up to 10 per cent of income and 'high' indicating up to 80 per cent of income.

All conservancies have conditions more or less suitable for the development of lodges for non-consumptive tourism, as well as for the development of community owned and run campsites. In Nyae Nyae and Salambala the non-consumptive tourism potential is weaker than for the others. The development of trophy hunting tourism is possible in all concessions, but in Mayuni, which makes use of part of a protected area, this would require special permission. All conservancies have potential, albeit limited, for consumptive use of wildlife, including live game sale and hunting for meat. In Mayuni hunting for meat is unlikely. In ≠Khoadi //Hôas, preference might be given to live game sale, as it is situated south of the 'red line' veterinary cordon fence. All conservancies have potential for the use of forest and non-timber forest products, as well as grazing for livestock. However, the potential for these activities is higher in the higher rainfall conservancies of the north-east.

In the north-west (Torra, ≠Khoadi //Hôas, occupied by Damara communities) the traditional land use was pastoralism, that in the northern Kalahari (Nyae Nyae, occupied by San communities) was hunting and gathering with low intensity pastoralism, and that in north-east (Mayuni, Salambala, occupied by Mafwe

Table 16.1 *Comparative physical characteristics of five
Namibian conservancies in 2000*

Characteristic	Torra	≠Khoadi //Hôas	Nyae Nyae	Mayuni	Salambala
			Conservancy		
Land area (ha)	352,200	386,000	900,095	28,400	93,000
Core[a] wildlife area (ha)	108,586	177,650	900,095	13,300	11,000
Households (no.)	120	700	700	450	1200
Mean annual rainfall (mm)	90	150	450	600	650
Rangeland carrying capacity (ha per LSU equivalent)	30	25	15	12	12
Starting wildlife density[b] (ha per LSU equivalent)	427	160	464	43	3875
Expected wildlife density[b] in year 10 (ha per LSU equivalent)	257	119	251	29	85
Non-consumptive tourism potential	High	Mod High	Mod low	High	Mod low
Safari hunting tourism potential	Mod high	Mod	Mod high	Low	Mod
Consumptive wildlife use potential	Low	Low	Low	Low	Low
Other natural resource use potential	Low	Low	Mod low	Mod	Mod
Livestock keeping potential	Very low	Very low	Mod	Mod	Mod

Notes: a Core areas, allocated primarily to wildlife (rest of land shared between wildlife and livestock).

b Density calculated for the total land area, measured in terms of land occupied per unit of stock.

Source: Barnes et al, 2002

and Masubia communities) was agro-pastoralism. Mayuni was unusual among the five in that it embraces part of a protected area. ≠Khoadi //Hôas was unusual in being permitted, by the veterinary authorities, to capture and sell live game animals without quarantine. The numbers of households associated with conservancies varied from 120 in Torra to 1200 in Salambala.

The results of the conservancy-level valuation are summarized in Table 16.2. These values provided a wealth of indicative comparative information regarding the project investment, project income, community income and the economic value for conservancies in the various settings. The project financial values reflected the returns to the project investor, that is, the donors, government and community, viewed as one entity. They provided an indication of the broader financial viability of the initiative. Here, all donor contributions were treated as costs, and so were dividend payments earmarked for conservancy members, but increase in the value of wildlife stocks was treated as a benefit. Project investors do not, themselves, require large positive returns but seek only to ensure that they do not incur losses, which would require subsidization. As seen in Table 16.2, the

Table 16.2 *Base case financial and economic values for the five Namibian conservancies in 2000 (US$[a])*

Value	Torra	≠Khoadi //Hôas	Nyae Nyae	Mayuni	Salambala
			Conservancy		
Project financial values					
Initial project capital investment	166,660	121,602	493,153	107,909	198,605
Capital investment per ha	0.48	0.32	0.55	3.78	2.10
Capital investment per household	1389	174	704	240	165
Annual project net profit	13,342	9716	−37,394	46,634	18,732
Project internal rate of return	16%	19%	15%	8%	8%
Project net present value[b]	120,512	199,990	332,836	0	0
Community financial values					
Annual community net income[c]	56,916	58,598	28,654	102,579	59,648
Community net income/household	474	84	41	228	50
Community net income/ha	0.17	0.15	0.03	3.64	0.64
Community internal rate of return	133%	205%	23%	220%	40%
Community net present value[b]	298,648	469,000	191,016	517,482	188,706
Annual community dividends[d]	31,920	29,106	16,016	31,500	23,618
Dividends per household	266	42	23	70	20
Economic values					
Annual gross value added[e]	78,064	70,532	70,224	120,428	73,612
Annual net value added[f]	68,266	64,337	39,007	114,914	63,752
Net value added per ha	0.20	0.17	0.04	4.06	0.69
Economic internal rate of return	131%	66%	22%	126%	31%
Economic net present value[b]	512,722	561,414	576,086	568,260	362,292
Number of jobs created[g]	8	12	26	22	12
Economic capital cost per job	19,375	9416	24,914	4484	17,820

Notes: a In 2000 US$1.00 was equal to N$7.14 (Namibia Dollars); inflation factor to 2007 is 1.65.

b Measured over 10 years at 8% discount.

c Includes salaries and wages for conservancy employment, project profits and dividends.

d Annual surplus extracted for distribution to households.

e Gross value added to national income at opportunity cost (economic prices).

f Gross value added minus asset depreciation.

g Permanent formal employment opportunities from conservancy operations, excluding jobs created within revenue sharing and joint venture tourism operations.

Source: Barnes et al, 2002

project returns were moderate but generally positive and acceptable. The initial capital investment ranged between some US$100,000 in Mayuni to some US$500,000 in Nyae Nyae. Annual project profits at stability were mostly positive up to US$47,000, but negative for Nyae Nyae. Real project internal rates of return over 10 years of conservancy development were moderate at between 8 per cent (the discount rate) and 19 per cent.

The community financial values tell us to what extent the communities have an incentive to invest in conservancies. Here the net income accruing to the communities in the form of project profits, salaries and wages, and any dividends paid out to households is presented, ranging from some US$29,000 in Nyae Nyae to some US$103,000 in Mayuni. Community incomes, measured per household, ranged from US$41 in Nyae Nyae to US$474 in Torra. Communities invested that part of the project capital investment that was not donor or government funded and received a flow of net income described above. Community financial rates of return on investment over 10 years were generally very high, and for Mayuni, Torra and ≠Khoadi //Hôas were over 100 per cent. Rates of return were attractive but lower for Nyae Nyae and Salambala, the two conservancies with relatively weak non-consumptive tourism potential (Table 16.1).

Generally, in all cases analysed in Table 16.2, the communities could derive very favourable returns on their investments. The Torra and Mayuni conservancies were able to earn the most cash income and dividends per household, while the Mayuni, ≠Khoadi //Hôas and Torra conservancies, all showed very high financial rates of return. The Nyae Nyae and Salambala conservancies provided the least attractive returns for communities. The dominant feature of the community analysis was the fact that donors, and not the communities, bore many of the initial capital and recurrent input costs. All conservancies benefited from donor assistance in this way. Another feature of the community analysis is that it does not incorporate the accumulation of wealth in conservancy wildlife stocks, which communities cannot themselves realize through sale.

The economic values, in Table 16.2, are very useful in that they tell us whether the conservancy contributed positively to national development or not. Here the investment consists of project capital measured at its real cost to the nation, (its opportunity cost), and the benefits include the net national income generated directly within the conservancy, as well as any capital gains in stock value within the conservancy. In all cases the conservancies did, with positive annual contributions to gross and net national income, positive net present values, and generally very favourable internal rates of return. The 8 per cent real discount rate used in the cost–benefit analysis is essentially the opportunity cost for the capital used in the conservancies. It serves as a cut-off rate, in that if projects generate rates of return lower than this, their capital should be diverted and used for something else. All conservancy returns were significantly higher than the 8 per cent cut-off rate, making these investments highly desirable economically.

Conservancies with most favourable returns were found in different settings, including both the semi-desert (Torra) and the more humid north east (Mayuni). The main determinants of high investment value for conservancies appeared to be the potential of their natural resources for non-consumptive tourism (Table 16.1). The low returns for Nyae Nyae were specifically related to an artificially high costs structure, as well as low initial wildlife densities and relatively low non-consumptive tourism potential. The low returns for Salambala were also related to the low initial wildlife densities and the consequent effect this had on tourism potential.

The financial and economic values in Table 16.2 were from base-case models, and it was important to determine the degree to which these values were robust in the face of changes in model parameters. Sensitivity analysis was needed to provide an indication of the validity of the conclusions drawn from the results, as well as to provide further information on the financial and economic characteristics of the investments. Barnes et al (2002) carried out extensive sensitivity analysis on the models, assessing the effects of variation in capital expenditure, tourism development, wildlife stock densities, stock off-take rates and the inclusion, or not, of live game sales and stock purchase/acquisition. Generally the sensitivity analyses confirmed the robustness of the analytical results. Barnes et al (2002) provide a more detailed interpretation of these findings.

Community tourism development through CBNRM has involved significant donor support in southern Africa (Infield, 2001; Barnes et al, 2002). The question arises as to whether, without this support, these initiatives might be viable financially for communities. Table 16.3 shows the effects that the removal of donor grants would have on the community financial rates of return in the conservancies analysed. Thus the first row of the table shows the community financial rates of return from Table 16.2 while the next two rows show how these change if communities would have to bear all the project capital costs themselves. These effects are shown with and without the inclusion of the residual value of wildlife stocks which, because they cannot actually realize this value through sale, is only an intangible benefit for communities. Only in one conservancy (Nyae Nyae) did the community rate of return drop below the cut-off real discount rate of 8 per cent. The findings suggest that receipt, by conservancies, of donor grants very significantly enhances community returns. They also provide at least an indication that, in some conservancies, communities might have incentives to invest even without

Table 16.3 *The effect of donor grants (non-use values) on the financial rate of return to communities in the five Namibian conservancies in 2000*

Community financial rate of return (%)	Torra	≠Khoadi //Hôas	Nyae Nyae	Mayuni	Salambala
		Conservancy			
With donor grants without stock[a]	133	205	23	220	40
Without donor grants with stock[b]	44	39	18	24	17
Without donor grants without stock[c]	39	28	1	20	11

Notes: a Includes income to the conservancy from donor grants, but excludes residual value of wildlife stock appreciation (an intangible value for communities) in benefits.

b Excludes income to the conservancy from donor grants, but includes residual value of wildlife stock appreciation (an intangible value for communities) in benefits.

c Excludes income to the conservancy from donor grants, and excludes residual value of wildlife stock appreciation (an intangible value for communities) in benefits.

Source: Barnes et al, 2002

donor and government grants. In at least three of the five conservancies studied, direct use values alone might remain sufficient to attract community investment in CBNRM.

Inputs and returns in the national CBNRM Programme

Table 16.4 and Figure 16.1, derived from own calculations, NACSO (2004, 2006) and unpublished data (Unpublished data, 2007, Ministry of Environment and Tourism) show the total CBNRM programme spending in the 16 years between 1990 and 2005. This was made up predominantly of donor contributions in the provision of technical assistance for facilitation, capital developments in conservancies, and some conservancy operating costs such as payments for community game guards. Approximately 25 per cent of the total spending was made up of government matched contributions in support of the sector, and CBNRM in particular.

Similarly, Table 16.4 and Figure 16.1 show the total economic benefits attributable to the CBNRM Programme as a whole in Namibia. These benefits include the broader impacts of CBNRM on the economy as a whole, described above, including the direct on-site income generation as well as the indirect income resulting from the multiplier effect and the appreciation in the capital value of wildlife stocks. The cost–benefit analysis weighed the CBNRM programme expenditures made between 1990 and 2005, against the economic benefits arising from CBNRM activities during the same period. It can be seen from Table 16.4 and Figure 16.1, that considerable programme investments made through the period have begun to bear fruit in recent years. In 1995 there were no registered conservancies, while in 2005 there were 44, and economic impacts have been growing exponentially.

The programme analysis allows us to see whether the donor and government investments in CBNRM are contributing positively to the development of Namibia or not. The internal rate of return for the programme investment over the 16 year period was close to 15 per cent and the net present value of the investment over the period after discounting at 8 per cent was some US$7.8 million. The 8 per cent discount rate is considered to be the opportunity cost for public and donor funding, which means that if invested elsewhere these funds could be expected to provide an 8 per cent rate of return. The fact that investment in the CBNRM programme generated a higher return (15 per cent) and a positive net present value, means that it was economically efficient and contributed positively to development. After a long period, during which the economic returns to investment in the CBNRM programme were negative, the benefits generated began to rise steeply. The early significant investments appear to have borne fruit in later years.

As pointed out by Emerton (2001), Adams and Infield (2001) and Hulme and Infield (2001), costs associated with wildlife include investments in protection, costs of damage caused by wildlife and land use opportunity costs. Wildlife damage costs were considered in the conservancy models above, since they

Table 16.4 *Economic cost–benefit analysis of Namibia's CBNRM programme (US$[a], constant 2005 values, rounded)*

Year	Total programme spending[b]	Total economic benefits[c]	Benefit/cost stream
1990	478,740	0	(478,740)
1991	605,550	935,810	330,260
1992	920,390	1,099,670	179,280
1993	1,838,730	1,261,710	(577,020)
1994	5,674,010	1,451,600	(4,222,410)
1995	4,370,790	1,926,150	(2,444,640)
1996	5,298,980	2,750,870	(2,548,130)
1997	9,025,190	3,840,260	(5,184,920)
1998	9,047,180	5,309,790	(3,737,390)
1999	8,941,890	6,245,750	(2,696,150)
2000	9,451,850	6,977,820	(2,474,030)
2001	11,318,600	13,000,100	1,681,500
2002	14,449,470	21,443,570	6,994,100
2003	9,291,450	25,064,190	15,772,740
2004	6,520,820	24,851,340	18,330,510
2005	4,920,750	27,981,050	23,060,300
Total	102,154,350	144,139,640	0

Cost–benefit analysis:

Economic internal rate of return over 16 years	14.91%
Economic net present value over 16 years @ 8% discount rate	7,795,340

Notes: a In 2005 US$1.00 was equal to N$6.67 (Namibia Dollars); inflation factor to 2007 is 1.11.

b Donor and government spending specifically on CBNRM programme.

c Total direct and indirect contribution to net national income, attributable to CBNRM activities, including impact through the value added multiplier, plus appreciation of game stocks in CBNRM areas

Sources: Unpublished Data, 2007, Ministry of Environment and Tourism; NACSO, 2006

included investments in wildlife damage mitigation. More recent work on the costs of wildlife damage in the CBNRM context in Namibia's north-east (Jones and Barnes, 2007) indicates that the benefits of CBNRM tourism at community level can outweigh the costs of damage borne by households. The economic analyses, above, do not include the opportunity costs of land, but as pointed out by Barnes et al (2002) the opportunity costs of land in the arid and semi-arid lands of Namibia are low. Barnes et al (2001) analysed alternative land uses in semi-arid northern Botswana and confirmed this.

Conclusion

The findings described above help us to answer the key policy questions about CBNRM posed in the introduction.

Can the private benefits to communities and households resulting from CBNRM be significant and outweigh the associated costs?

The cost–benefit analysis of five conservancies, which represent conditions in the communal lands of the dry north-west and the more humid north-east of Namibia, indicates that the communities in these conservancies derive positive net returns to their investments in tourism-driven CBNRM. They confirm other findings, made by Barnes (1995) and Barnes et al (2001), for similar community wildlife use initiatives in Botswana. They contradict arguments made by Barrett and Arcese (1995) and Infield (2001), among others, which suggest that CBNRM initiatives in Africa are financially unsound for communities. In arid and semi-arid Namibia and Botswana, the opportunity costs for land are low, and the non-consumptive tourism potential is high. These characteristics may help to explain CBNRM's viability there.

The positive returns at community level, however, do not necessarily translate into positive returns at household level within these communities, and this analysis cannot show whether this happens. The distribution of income within conservancies is a subject requiring further research.

Donor and government grants have significantly enhanced the returns communities derive from tourism-driven CBNRM. These have no doubt been important in providing strong incentives for communities to invest in land use change and adopt CBNRM. But there are indications that CBNRM investments could be fundamentally viable for some communities even without grants.

Can the massive donor investment that has gone into CBNRM in southern Africa be shown to be justified in terms of sustainable economic growth and rural development?

At local level the cost–benefit analysis of five conservancies in Namibia indicates that community conservancy investments, in which tourism is the dominant land use, are economically efficient and contribute positively to national economic well-being.

At national level, considerable investments have been made by donors and government in the development of tourism within a CBNRM context in Namibia. The economic cost–benefit analysis of the Namibian national CBNRM Programme, described above, indicates that these donor and government investments are economically efficient and have contributed positively to national economic development. This appears to be the first evidence for the economic viability of CBNRM.

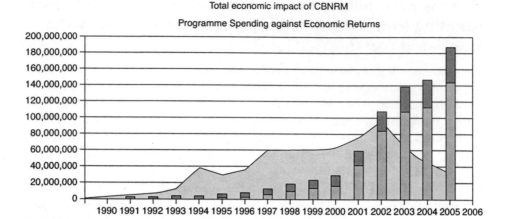

Source: NACSO, 2006

Figure 16.1 *Total CBNRM programme spending compared with total economic benefits between 1990 and 2005 (N$, 2005)*

Acknowledgements

The work reported on in this chapter has been supported through funding from the US Agency for International Development (USAID), through the World Wildlife Fund (US) LIFE Program, under terms of Agreement no. 623-02510A-00-3135-00, the Overseas Development Institute, the British Department of International Development (DFID), the Swedish Government (Sida) and the Namibian Government. Opinions expressed herein do not necessarily reflect those of any of these organizations. I thank all the many individuals who contributed to the work, through data collection, analysis and comments. Of particular help were Anna Davis, Marie Karaisl, Glenn-Marie Lange, Helen Suich and Michael Humavindu. Caroline Ashley kindly provided exhaustive comments and guidance. The responsibility for all errors is mine.

References

Adams, W. and Infield, M. (2001) 'Park outreach and gorilla conservation: Mgahinga Gorilla National Park, Uganda', in D. Hulme and M. Murphree (eds), *African Wildlife and Livelihoods: The Promise and Performance of Community Conservation*, James Curry Ltd, Oxford, 131–147

Barnes, J. I. (1994) 'Suggested criteria for shadow pricing in cost–benefit analysis of projects in Namibia', Unpublished paper, Directorate of Environmental Affairs, Ministry of Environment and Tourism, Windhoek, Namibia

Barnes, J. I. (1995) 'Economic analysis of community-based wildlife utilisation initiatives in Botswana', *Development Southern Africa*, vol 12, 783–803

Barnes, J., Cannon, J. and Morrison, K. (2001) 'Economic returns to selected land uses in Ngamiland, Botswana', Unpublished Report, Conservation International, Washington, DC

Barnes, J. I., MacGregor, J. and Weaver, L. C. (2002) 'Economic efficiency and incentives for change within Namibia's community wildlife use initiatives', *World Development*, vol 30, 667–681

Barrett, C. B. and Arcese, P. (1995) 'Are integrated conservation-development projects (ICDPs) sustainable? On the conservation of large mammals in Sub-Saharan Africa', *World Development*, vol 23, 1073–1084

Emerton, L. (2001) 'The nature of benefits and benefits of nature: Why wildlife conservation has not economically benefited communities in Africa', in D. Hulme and M. Murphree (eds), *African Wildlife and Livelihoods: The Promise and Performance of Community Conservation*, James Curry Ltd, Oxford, 208–226

Gittinger, J. P. (1982) *Economic Analysis of Agricultural Projects*, 2nd ed. Johns Hopkins University Press, Baltimore, MD

Hulme, D., and Infield, M. (2001) 'Community conservation, reciprocity and park–people relationships: Lake Mburo National Park, Uganda', in D. Hulme and M. Murphree (eds), *African Wildlife and Livelihoods: The Promise and Performance of Community Conservation*, James Curry Ltd, Oxford, 106–130

Humavindu, M. N. (2007) 'Estimating shadow pricing in the Namibian economy'. Unpublished Paper, Development Bank of Namibia, Windhoek, Namibia

Infield, M. (2001) 'Cultural values: A forgotten strategy for building community support for protected areas in Africa', *Conservation Biology*, vol 15, 800–802

Jones, B. and Barnes, J. (2007) 'WWF human wildlife conflict study: Namibian case study', Unpublished Report, Macroeconomics Programme and Global Species Programme, WWF, Gland, Switzerland

Lange, G., Schade, K., Ashipala, J. and Haimbodi, N. (2004) 'A social accounting matrix for Namibia 2002: A tool for analyzing economic growth, income distribution and poverty', NEPRU Working Paper 97, Namibia Economic Policy Research Unit, Windhoek, Namibia

Libanda, B. and Blignaut, J. (2007) 'Tourism's local benefits for Namibia's community based natural resource management areas', *International Journal for Ecological Economics and Statistics* (in press)

NACSO (2004) *Namibia's Communal Conservancies: A Review of Progress and Challenges*, Namibian Association of CBNRM Support Organisations, Windhoek, Namibia

NACSO (2006) *Namibia's Communal Conservancies: A Review of Progress and Challenges in 2005*, Namibian Association of CBNRM Support Organisations, Windhoek, Namibia. 104pp

Pearce, D. W. and Turner, R. K. (1990) *Economics of Natural Resources and the Environment*, Harvester Wheatsleaf, London

SIAPAC (2003) Visitor exit survey, prepared by SIAPAC for MET, Directorate of Tourism, Ministry of Environment and Tourism, Windhoek, Namibia

Part 4

Conclusions

17

Implications of Responsible Tourism for Conservation and Development in Southern Africa

Anna Spenceley

Can responsible tourism be used for conservation and development?

This book set out to address whether responsible tourism could be used as a development tool – for both biodiversity conservation and poverty alleviation. The practitioners who have contributed chapters to this book have supplemented the body of knowledge on this issue, by exploring these issues across southern Africa. Cumulatively, the authors provide systematic and tangible evidence of the successes and failures of tourism to fight poverty, and to enhance conservation.

Part 1: Policies, institutional interventions and market forces

In the first part of this book, practitioners working in Mozambique, Madagascar and South Africa present evidence of programmes by governments, development agencies, non-governmental agencies and the private sector that have attempted to promote conservation and poverty alleviation through tourism.

The difficulty of implementing tourism and poverty reduction policies became apparent in Andrew Rylance's analysis of the situation in Mozambique. He found that although poverty reduction was a central objective of the government, and despite the presence of relevant policies that provide a solid policy framework for responsible tourism (e.g. an Action Plan for Absolute Poverty Reduction and a

Strategic Plan for the Development of Tourism), in reality there were serious constraints on their implementation. These included corruption, land rights, poor infrastructure, laborious regulatory processes, the high costs of air travel and limited human resources. Despite these problems, there are encouraging signs that some private sector enterprises and NGOs in Nampula province were making progress in implementing responsible tourism. For example, the operator Diversecooperation was working with people living around the location of their lodge development to promote better conservation of natural resources, public infrastructure improvements and local employment. Similarly, the NGO ASARUNA was working with local craftsmen to gain access to markets and improve their business skills. These activities coupled with wider interventions in Mozambique by agencies such as the World Bank (e.g. the Transfrontier Conservation Area Program), the International Finance Corporation (IFC) (e.g. Anchor Tourism Investments), and NGOs like SNV (pro-poor tourism interventions in Inhambane) indicate that with the support of intermediaries and external agencies, the government can embark on programmes that address both conservation and poverty alleviation. However, the actual impact of these on biodiversity and rural incomes needs to be measured and reported in order to establish whether they are having a meaningful impact. Rylance's work demonstrates that it is not sufficient for countries to have good policies that provide a responsible tourism framework: governments also require stakeholders to take the initiative and implement them.

Michaela Pawliczek and Hitesh Mehta's review of ecotourism in Madagascar provides further evidence of the importance of implementing tourism policies and plans for responsible tourism. The authors found that although the Malagasy tourism masterplan had been officially adopted, it was never implemented. This appears to have been in part due to insufficient linkages between institutions and a lack of understanding of the requirements for tourism development in government. However, since some of the tourism legislation and regulations are currently under review, there is an opportunity to integrate more responsible tourism principles into the policy framework. With facilitation by the IFC, a number of up-market ecotourism lodges are in the planning phases in and around the national parks. However, training is required for local people to participate meaningfully in the ecotourism industry, and the country is hampered by few tourism training institutions. The authors stress that high quality education in tourism is required, to ensure that more local people rather than expatriates can be employed in the tourism sector, supporting tourism training research undertaken by Spenceley and Rozga (2007). Pawliczek and Mehta explore the problem of 'greenwashing' and misuse of the terms 'ecotourism' and 'ecolodge', and suggest that only a few operators are truly implementing responsible nature-based tourism. The authors urge the government to take the lead in coordinating and streamlining efforts and stakeholders into ecotourism development in the country and to improve the investment climate. This includes to channel technical assistance from donors and to assist the private sector in developing responsible tourism enterprises. With its unique biodiversity, and high levels of endemism, but widespread poverty among its inhabitants, Madagascar provides a critical testing ground for responsible tourism practices.

Planning gain is a powerful tool that protected area agencies can use to allocate tourism concessions to develop enterprises that promote both biodiversity conservation and local economic development. Giju Varghese describes the process of developing public–private partnerships in South Africa, and what has been learned through the process. Taking a business approach to tourism development, this chapter provides behind-the-scenes insights into how a conservation parastatal, South African National Parks, has integrated commercial and empowerment objectives into its policies and practices. By welcoming the private sector into national parks, the organization has not only benefited from enhanced income, but also from a higher quality of tourism product, better conservation practices, higher levels of local involvement and benefits from nature-based tourism. However, it is clear that the process has led to a number of lessons that can be used by conservation agencies in other developing countries: including how to manage contracts and how to ensure a fair and equitable system that is market-related. The chapter also shows that the participation of marginalized sectors of society (e.g. including the poor) in the commercialization process has been constrained, and that efforts need to be made to improve their level of involvement and provide more employment in remote areas. Varghese adds to the growing body of knowledge on the value of public–private partnerships in southern Africa in creating equity for local community members, tangible economic benefits, and real rather than token engagement in the private sector (e.g. Ashley and Jones, 2001 in Namibia; Gujadhur, 2001 in Botswana; Poultney and Spenceley, 2001 in South Africa; de la Harpe et al, 2004 in southern Africa).

Illustrating the role of development agencies in facilitating responsible tourism development, Steve Collins and Herman Snel describe the work of GtZ in supporting the government's Department of Environmental Affairs and Tourism in South Africa. In the Richtersveld, they engaged with a Community Property Association and local Municipality by providing financial and technical support, to draft an Integrated Development Plan that addressed tourism, conservation and local economic development. However, problems arose later in matching the expectations of the community to transform their livelihoods through tourism, and the actual market demand for community-based tourism products in that area, which was relatively low. Through the process GtZ learned of the difficulties in establishing a tourism economy, particularly in remote areas on communal land, where communities take time to agree on decisions, and when insufficient resources were invested in promotion and where there is no private sector partner. However, in the Makuleke region of Kruger National Park, activities by GtZ and other committed stakeholders had more positive impacts. Empowered to partner with the private sector on their restituted land, concession contracts and job creation was estimated at US$4.8 million in the first years of operation. The residential areas where community members live have also been enhanced with improved infrastructure and services (including electrification), and a small business support company has been developed. Here also there are constraints to responsible tourism, which include community-level politics and decision-making processes regarding how communal incomes are distributed. With regard to the role of a donor agency, the two cases illustrate implications for future interventions: that a donor agency can have a positive impact, particularly in providing facilitators to guide development processes when the target communities have been receptive, and good working relationships have been established. However, where community issues collide with requirements for good business management, tourism is more difficult to implement in a commercially viable form. The authors also stress the importance of the government in providing adequate coordination and infrastructure to support communities' endeavours in tourism development. Many research reports have considered the cases of the Richtersveld and Makuleke (e.g. Boonzaier 1996a, b; Mahony and van Zyl, 2001; Reid, 2001; Robins and van der Wall, 2008), but this is the first time people working within an implementing agency have provided perspective of the implementation process.

Within the context of a solid policy framework that exists on responsible tourism in South Africa, Nicole Frey and Richard George consider the market supply and demand in the country, and ask what interventions are necessary to encourage more responsible practices. They show that consumer trends for responsible holidays are not as strong in South Africa as they appear to be in the UK and the US, and the tourism industry is not translating the responsible tourism policy into management changes (despite an appreciation of the benefits from a marketing perspective). However, surveys of tourism enterprises in the Western Cape province revealed that few believe that government supports efforts by the private sector to become more responsible. Also, a lack of responsible tourism management is attributed to lethargy within the private sector, coupled with a lack of information about what businesses could do to implement responsible tourism. This work highlights that transforming a 'business as usual' tourism industry into a responsible one not only requires market demand, but also tools and mechanisms to assist the private sector in modifying their practices. Improvements might be more forthcoming by using policy and regulatory 'sticks' and market demand 'carrots', coupled with widely available information and assistance for the private sector to enact corporate social responsibility. Frey and George move the debate of the market demand for responsible tourism, which has generally focused on developed countries (e.g. MINTEL, 2001; Tearfund, 2000 and 2001; Müller and Landes, 2000; Goodwin and Francis, 2003) towards searching for drivers of change in tourism business. This is a critical issue for practitioners, in how to identify triggers to motivate change in the tourism enterprises towards more responsible practices.

Concluding this part of the book, Caroline Ashley and Gareth Haysom present an encouraging analysis of tourism supply chains and their implications for local economic development in South Africa. Spier's strategic shift to align its business towards a more proactive and sustainable approach, provides a positive example of what one enterprise can do when they have management support for strategic responsible business practices. Spier calculated that if it channelled only a tenth of its procurement spend towards local, small entrepreneurs, its financial impact would outweigh its philanthropy and boost the local economy substantially. Although the analysis of the enterprise supply chain was clearly a lengthy and time consuming process for the private sector operator, the results are illuminating and provide tangible evidence of 'win–wins' for both business and local economic development. For example, Spier found that even when it invested in the establishment of a local enterprise that it would procure services from (e.g. a laundry), it would save money overall, with the added benefit of creating new jobs. Two critical lessons learned were that having a champion in senior management, and a facilitator with time to work on the process are vital. This may be a defining difference between the findings at Spier, and Frey and George's disappointing evidence from other areas of the Western Cape: the private sector requires motivation and capacity to establish new responsible management practices. The process takes time and effort. Ashley and Haysom's work is indicative of an increasing trend towards the use of supply chain analysis by agencies working on tourism issues in Africa including the ODI (Mitchell and Faal, 2007), SNV, the International Finance Corporation (Ashley and Mitchell, 2008) and the International Trade Centre of UNCTAD (ITC UNCTAD, 2005). It seems likely that practitioners will continue to use these tools to explore mechanisms of expanding opportunities for the poor, particularly in the informal sector, to provide products and services to the established tourism enterprises.

The chapters in this section of the book contribute towards the body of knowledge regarding policies, institutional interventions and market forces. The interlinking themes from Madagascar, Mozambique and South Africa illustrate the complexity and importance of many interlinking factors: the policy framework and implementation of regulations; good governance and relationships, and transparency of decision making; the importance of intermediaries to guide those who wish to practise responsible tourism, such as donors and NGOs; and, of course, market demand for responsible tourism.

Part 2: Responsible nature-based tourism

Responsible nature-based tourism activities, including ecotourism and wildlife tourism, can generate income for conservation management and for rural livelihoods that are based on natural resources. However, the review of the impacts of wildlife tourism on rural livelihoods by Anna Spenceley, demonstrates substantial variations in impacts when five southern Africa countries are compared. Considering both trophy hunting and photographic tourism activities, and fragmented case studies that evaluate local economic impacts of wildlife tourism, the review establishes that the countries of Botswana, Namibia, South Africa, Zambia and Zimbabwe have a wide range of policies supporting the sector. These include policies to develop community-managed wildlife areas in Botswana, Namibia, Zambia and Zimbabwe, and the use of planning gain to establish joint ventures between conservation agencies and the private sector in South Africa (as detailed earlier by Varghese). Joint ventures of luxury lodges appear to generate the greatest returns in conservancies, when compared with community-based enterprises and trophy hunting, but photographic tourism has greater economic multipliers. Also, tourism can often be a more commercially viable option than agriculture in marginal areas, while providing higher wages and employment. Interestingly, it appears that the private sector is not always motivated by profit: sometimes the lifestyle of working in a wildlife area, and conserving biodiversity, is sufficient to engage in this sector. Also of value was identification of a robust community-based wildlife tourism enterprise in Zimbabwe that had thrived without the support of intermediaries, and despite the context of an unstable political framework. The review provides a comparison of different benefits emanating to local people from wildlife tourism through employment and household benefits. The paper also highlights the difficulty of making comparisons of the effectiveness of different tourism intervention strategies in generating benefits for the poor and biodiversity conservation. The different systems of monitoring, evaluation and reporting demonstrated in the literature are also underpinned by different policy, ecosystem and program contexts, demonstrating the complexity of synthesizing lessons to transfer elsewhere. Sometimes it can be more valuable to maintain the rich detail of case study reports, but the application of consistent monitoring and reporting frameworks will make future analyses of the impacts of wildlife tourism more effective. This may guide agencies in establishing what form of tourism is most appropriate in an area, and whether to plan joint ventures, private sector or community-based enterprises.

Transfrontier conservation areas (TFCAs) straddle the borders of two or more countries, and Helen Suich's analysis of the Kavango-Zambezi (KAZA) TFCA illustrates how they can deliver livelihood benefits to people living and working in the wildlife tourism industry. KAZA incorporates parts of Angola, Botswana, Namibia, Zambia and Zimbabwe, and in her survey of 128 accommodation enterprises and tour operators, Suich establishes a solid understanding of local socioeconomic benefits of responsible nature-based tourism. She finds that although the level of local employment in tourism was already approximately 94 per cent in the region, few local people were reaching management positions, and that greater skills development is required. Half of the enterprises are locally owned, but financial returns to investors were low, and efforts to improve the profitability were required – options may include joint ventures with experienced private sector partners. Suich identifies a need for more effective and coherent tourism policies, with less bureaucratic processes. The chapter does not comment on whether the TFCA has a cumulative or synergistic impact on responsible tourism development, and on whether local people's livelihoods, and conservation areas would have been different without KAZA. The level to which the TFCA is promoted and branded, to encourage more business in this ecologically sensitive area, will be fundamental to its outcomes. TFCAs are the subject of substantial interest among NGOs and conservation agencies and academics for their biodiversity conservation and local economic development potential (e.g. Sandwith et al, 2001; Spenceley, 2006; Ali, 2007; Bushell and Eagles, 2007, Ramutsindela, 2007). For example the World Wide Fund for Nature suggests that TFCAs have the capacity to strategically develop sustainable tourism that may support the costs of conservation management, while also providing employment and entrepreneurial opportunities for poor people in developing countries (BSP, 1999). In southern Africa, agencies including the Peace Parks Foundation, Conservation International, the African Wildlife Foundation and the World Bank have programs to support the sustainable development of TFCAs (Spenceley, 2008a). Using frameworks like Suich's, transparent evaluation of the impacts of these areas will be invaluable in establishing their effectiveness, a replication of her model has already begun in the Great Limpopo TFCA (Spenceley et al, 2008). It will be important to replicate Suich's evaluation once the KAZA TFCA has become more established to determine what impact the area has had, and also to undertake similar studies in other TFCAs in the region.

In his review of the impacts of wildlife tourism on conservation and development in Botswana, Joseph Mbaiwa provides an evaluation of a country that has been at the forefront of low-volume, high-value wildlife tourism in areas of extreme poverty. The reasons he cites for the success experienced in Botswana are the participation of local communities in ecotourism through community-based organizations (CBOs); employment; income generation; investment in community development and the empowerment of people in conservation and tourism. Through the CBOs, communities in Botswana have seemingly become truly capacitated to manage natural resources and tourism businesses. However, he states the revenue which is distributed annually to individual households from tourism based on communal land in the Okavango Delta is so small that it can only be considered as supplementary income to most people. Some of the communities have re-invested ecotourism revenues into new tourism enterprises and community development projects like water provision; scholarships; sport activities; office equipment, and assistance for orphans, the elderly and disabled people. However, there are also problems of unfair or inequitable distribution of benefits in some areas. Despite this, positive attitudes resulting from ecotourism benefits are related to lower levels of poaching, when compared with non-ecotourism areas. These conservation benefits are led by the community members, who employ community escort guides to enforce agreed environmental management regulations. However, Mbaiwa recognizes that local community members rarely have access to the same resources and understanding of the tourism industry as foreign private-sector businesses, and therefore local investors find it difficult to compete with them. This is particularly relevant to an understanding of entrepreneurship, access to finance, and skills in marketing and promotion. Although joint-venture partnerships do occur, the system is weak and partnerships rarely include a significant transfer of business skills to the community. Mbaiwa's chapter shows that although in some villages ecotourism provides substantial benefits to poor people, and considerable conservation benefits, there are still areas for improvement. Business skills and administrative controls are required, and new policies to reserve certain tourism activities (e.g. guest houses, mobile safaris, etc) for communities will promote more local engagement with ecotourism.

Also considering Botswana, Peter John Massyn argues that some degree of leakage is inevitable given the foreign domination of the market of safari lodges in the country, and that radical policy changes are needed to restructure the industry. Between 2000 and 2005 the number of tourism enterprises in Ngamiland doubled, and the number owned by Botswanan citizens increased by almost 300 per cent. However, he notes that the high level of foreign ownership at the higher-value end of the industry is a consequence of the expatriate-driven history of the sector, and there is a need for enterprises to link to the international market for clients. Massyn supports Mbaiwa's conclusion that local participation is constrained by a culture that is non-entrepreneurial, but also states that the people tend to be averse to risk. Extrapolating data from a survey of 20 tourism operations, Massyn estimates that the lodge sector in Ngamiland probably disbursed more than P41 million (~US$7.5 million[1]) and employed over 3000 Botswanans in 2005. Although Botswanans comprised 90.6 per cent of the workforce, they only captured 58.3 per cent of the total payroll. Gender inequality was apparent, and, on average, Botswanan women received lower wages than Botswanan men. Estimates of products and services purchased from local people were P59,000 per annum (~US$10,840), or 8.9 per cent of payroll: effectively a small proportion of total expenditure in 2005. In addition, lease fees paid by two lodges to community trusts amounted to P555,000 per annum (~US$10,200), or about a third of the total local financial benefit generated by the enterprises. Massyn reports that current lease arrangements do not stipulate the need for indigenous empowerment, and the imminent renegotiation of expiring leases provides an opportunity for including conditions for greater involvement of Botswanans. Recent case studies developed by the African Safari Lodges programme by Spenceley (2008b, c) and Massyn (2008) support the findings of Mbaiwa and Massyn in this volume, and demonstrate further that the development of joint-ventures frequently involve a 'donation' of equity to a host community, but that this part-ownership is rarely linked to commercial risks or responsibilities. However, he urges authorities to find an approach that does not stifle the industry by being too onerous or bureaucratic.

Murray Simpson's analysis of the impacts of two nature-based tourism lodges on the livelihoods of people in neighbouring communities had disappointing levels of benefits from a joint-venture between the private sector, a conservation parastatal and the local community. Since their inception Rocktail Bay and Ndumo Lodges in South Africa have been promoted as responsible tourism enterprises that have substantial local equity and benefit. However, through a structured and integrated assessment protocol comprising participatory methods, archival data collection, semi-structured interviews and structured questionnaires in a household survey in 2004 and 2005, Simpson reveals that the impacts were more conservative than had been previously thought. Simpson found that only a few household members from the two neighbouring communities were employed and trained at the lodges, and that there have only been small improvements in local infrastructure financed by their lodge dividends. In both communities, the benefits of social capital and natural resources have been offset by conflicts, mistrust, allegations of the misuse of funds and restrictions in access and use of coastal reserves. Unrealistic expectations of the potential positive impacts of tourism held by members of the Mqobela and Mpukane communities have led to disappointment among those who have not experienced tangible benefits. Simpson stresses the importance of open communication between communities and the private sector to ensure good relationships and to ensure a realistic appreciation of the tourism development process and its potential impacts. He also emphasizes the importance of the private sector's role in driving responsible tourism development, and engaging in mutually beneficial partnerships with host communities. The chapter provides a valuable contribution to the literature, and a basis for further exploration of the role of local equity in tourism enterprises (as in Chapter 3 by Varghese) and local supply chain linkages (as in Chapter 6 by Ashley and Haysom). The chapter also presents a research approach that could be systematically applied by other practitioners and researchers to collect comparable data on the impacts of responsible tourism on local livelihoods. Simpson's research demonstrates that in areas of high population and extreme poverty, isolated tourism enterprises have only a limited impact on prevailing livelihoods, and that tourism should be considered as one element of an integrated local economic development approach. A destination approach with greater economies of scale is critical. The work also highlights how case studies are generally cross-sectional research, while longitudinal studies can demonstrate how the impacts of tourism enterprises (and modifications to their operating and institutional structures) can adjust the level of impacts and also local perceptions of benefits. A comparison of Murray's research undertaken in 2004 and 2005 with earlier studies at Rocktail Bay Lodge (Poultney and Spenceley, 2001) and more recent analyses of its sister enterprise, Rocktail Beach Lodge (Spenceley, 2008d), illustrate how tourism operators learn and adapt their management systems over time. Recognizing where initiatives with local communities have failed, and adapting to re-think partnership arrangements is fundamental to change within the tourism sector, and the evolution of approaches Responsible tourism approaches need to address revising and improving the performance of existing operations, and not only focusing on establishing new ones.

Concluding the responsible nature-based tourism section, Piers Relly evaluates the local economic impacts of nature-based tourism lodges in Madikwe Game Reserve in South Africa. Relly demonstrates that by taking a destination approach, substantial and tangible benefits can be derived by local people. In 2007 investment by the private and public sector in Madikwe was estimated at around US$93 million from 20 commercial lodges and 14 corporate lodges. The 20 commercial lodges provide capacity for visitors in 412 beds. These enterprises have resulted in the employment of 773 people: 74.5 per cent of whom live locally and earn 48.4 per cent of the total cash remuneration (an estimated US$3.3 million per year). However, Relly found that there has been little transformation from unskilled to skilled labour among local people, indicating limited opportunities for training and advancement. One of the two community-owned commercial lodges in the reserve has been estimated to currently generate an average annual income of $371 per household, for the 600-household Lekgophung community. This is substantial, given that the lodge only has 16 beds. Considering all of the establishments, Relly estimates that the 1850 households in the area had an average income of $225 per month in 2003 to $373 in 2007: reflecting a 65 per cent increase in nominal terms. Building from this solid baseline information, Relly promotes the need for further work at the household level to investigate multiplier effects and non-labour lodge expenditure. This type of study is vitally important in demonstrating tangibly the type of local economic benefits that can be provided by nature-based tourism destinations, and that can be used to track changes in impacts over time as more responsible practices are implemented.

This section of the book demonstrates that responsible nature-based tourism can have substantial positive impacts in both the local economy and biodiversity conservation, but that the level of those impacts depends on a number of critical factors. For example, to enhance local economic development, nature-based tourism needs to include meaningful equity and ownership of businesses by local people; skills development so that residents in destinations can be employed in managerial, rather than menial positions; it requires transparency of decision making and equitable distribution of tourism benefits to ensure good relationships and reduce conflict; and it is important to adopt a destination approach in order to achieve economies of scale in areas where poverty is widespread. The chapters also show clearly the importance of monitoring, verifying and reporting the economic, environmental and social indicators to demonstrate progress in responsible tourism. Without tangible and comparable information, it is not possible to track whether tourism is actually more responsible than a 'business as usual' approach.

Part 3: Community-based tourism

The community-based tourism section of the book opens with a review of the impacts of 215 accommodation enterprises in Botswana, Lesotho, Mauritius, Madagascar, Malawi, Mozambique, Namibia, South Africa, Swaziland, Tanzania, Zambia and Zimbabwe by Anna Spenceley. A systematic survey of community-based tourism enterprises (CBTEs) reveals that although there are some success stories, the majority struggle to survive with problems of accessibility in remote locations, limited market access, poor promotion, low motivation and constrained communication. Apparently interventions by third parties (e.g. NGOs, donor agencies, etc.) have not promoted business plans or market-led approaches of the CBTEs, because the intermediaries were primarily focused on capacity building and empowerment of the poor rather than commercial viability. Despite operating from a difficult basis, the CBTEs demonstrate tangible benefits to local people, including the employment of 2504 people and access to finance, community infrastructure, education and product development. Local procurement totalled nearly US$1 million per annum on products such as craft, food, décor, building materials and services including entertainment, guiding, catering and construction. Most of the enterprises consider that they practise sustainable tourism, with many having policies and commitments on conservation and local benefits. However, until CBTEs adopt a business, many will continue to struggle and frustrate the intended beneficiaries, who have not been empowered to recognize their failings and adapt to improve, or to move on and pursue alternative livelihood options. The review highlights the importance of systematic and comparable studies in drawing out recommendations for tourism and development interventions (e.g. Blangy, 2008; Jones, 2008; and in Chapter 8 by Suich, and Chapter 15 by Dixey). Using a modified version of the UNWTO/RETOSA questionnaire, Jones (2008) found a different emphasis of training needs to Spenceley among 27 CBTEs in Latin America, with an emphasis on English language (93 per cent of CBTEs) and general business management and accounting (89 per cent), with training in staff and operational development, internet and marketing, and guide training rated as at least 'necessary' by at least 70 per cent of businesses. Her work shows that the scope of comparative studies is also valuable in demonstrating differences between destinations.

In Tanzania, Fred Nelson's analysis shows that pioneering tour operators have recognized the socioeconomic pressures on both wildlife and the land use system of pastoralists. This awareness has led to the development of agreements with village councils (as elected representatives of the pastoralist communities) that are mutually beneficial. Communities receive annual rents and bed-night payments from tour operators operating non-consumptive wildlife tourism, and pastoralists continue to graze their livestock on concession areas on a seasonal basis. However, the viability of the joint-ventures is threatened by central government's allocation of the lands as tourist hunting concessions – which appears to be a continual source of conflict between the parties. Despite this, the level of community-based tourism investments have risen, particularly where there is strong local governance and accountability, with open and transparent decision-making processes. There have also been conservation benefits, with seasonal livestock grazing practices enforced by village by-laws. However, Nelson warns of major challenges in Tanzania, including that tourism revenues are often captured by elites in village governments, rather than benefiting entire communities. Also, government policy has provided in-principle support for community-based tourism, but legal and administrative actions undermine it (e.g. by granting hunting companies exclusive access to village lands, even if non-consumptive photographic tourism is taking place there). Nelson argues that if communities can secure commercial tourism agreements that recognize their jurisdiction over village lands, and create economic benefits, this can support their influence with government to maintain their resources and be more secure. Security of resources – whether land or wildlife – is vital in developing stable tenure systems for community-based tourism. Nelson's work therefore supports the findings of Rylance and Massyn in this volume.

With a survey of CBTEs in Zambia, Louise Dixey demonstrates that community-based tourism can be a useful development tool, if products learn from their experiences and are market-oriented. Dixey found that only 9 of the 25 CBTEs evaluated had sufficient information on their income to compare their level of donor investment, visitor numbers, gross revenue and net income. Similarly to problems identified earlier by Spenceley, enterprises in Zambia were constrained in the level of business and tourism skills, accessibility because of remote locations, and poor communication for bookings. There were also problems where donor-funded infrastructure had not created assets that were owned by community institutions; where there was poor accountability for community income; and land use conflicts where hunting and non-consumptive wildlife tourism were operated in the same area (similarly to Nelson's findings in Tanzania). She reports that some community members felt abandoned by NGOs, and were unable to manage failing businesses, and sought assistance from private sector partners. Key determinants of success were linkages to tourism companies, proximity to main tourism routes, competitive advantage, financial management, visitor handling and community motivation. Dixey concludes that community-based tourism has to be market related with regard to consumer demand, if it is to be viable and benefit the poor in the long term. Governments can also provide an enabling environment, by acting as a facilitator in the tourism industry.

This section concludes with an analysis of community-based natural resource management (CBNRM) and conservancies in Namibia, where Jon Barnes demonstrates the impacts of community-based tourism at both a local and national level. He poses important questions regarding whether CBNRM can generate sustainable and viable returns outweighing the costs, and if the extensive donor investment in this sector over the past 16 years has been justified. His cost–benefit analyses of five conservancies (Torra, ≠Khoadi //Hôas, Nyae Nyae, Mayuni and Salambala) indicated that the communities derive positive net returns from their investments in tourism related CBRNM, particularly in arid and semi-arid areas. In addition, Barnes reports that donor and government grants significantly enhanced the returns that communities obtained (although some would be viable without grants). The five conservancies demonstrate that they are economically efficient and contribute positively to national economic well-being. For example, the economic internal rate of return of the conservancies over 16 years was 14.91 per cent, with an economic net present value over this period (with an 8 per cent discount rate) of US$7.8 million. His chapter is critically important, because it provides the first evidence that community-based tourism in Namibia is economically viable. Here Barnes has built on a great deal of previous work by himself, and by many other resource economists in Namibia. Over the years a rich array of case studies quantifying impacts of wildlife management and tourism have been undertaken (see www.met.gov.na/pub_all.htm). This is highly important work that should continue, so that the lessons inform both policy, industry and communities.

The practitioners contributing to this section have effectively shaken the premise that community-based tourism enterprises are always a useful development tool in poor, rural areas. The authors demonstrate that although CBTEs can provide greater economic benefits than agriculture in some areas, it is imperative that they are planned and operated as commercial entities. There is little value in establishing a CBTE which tourists do not know about (because of poor promotion); cannot reach (because of poor infrastructure); where the establishment is product-rather than demand-led (because no market research was done); where a low level of service is given (because of poor training); and which does not make a profit (because expectations remain unrealized, and third parties have to subsidize the operations in the long term). It is clear that the concept of community-based tourism should be reconfigured, to take a market-led approach that concentrates on small business development and maximizing linkages between tourism and communities through the supply chain, rather than stressing collective ownership and management. Where donors and NGOs work with the poor to establish small tourism businesses, they have a responsibility to provide an enabling framework for partnerships with tourism professionals, to ensure a realistic and commercial approach is adopted. Policy makers also have a key role to play, by providing a consistent enabling policy framework that empowers communities to capitalize on their natural environment and heritage in a sustainable way.

Implications for responsible tourism

This book has, I believe, provided a wealth of critical issues for conservation and development that should be considered in the future adaptation of existing enterprises, and when planning new tourism destinations and operations. In answer to the question 'Can responsible tourism be used for conservation and development?' the response is a resounding 'Yes', with a caveat: whether it does or not depends on a multitude of factors relating to policy framework, governance, planning, operation and also market demand. The practitioners who have contributed to this tome have used empirical evidence and a suite of analytical approaches to demonstrate that responsible tourism is taking place in southern Africa – but that there is much work to be done by government, civil society, the tourism industry, local communities and academia to make the positive results more consistent and less fragmented.

Building on the Cape Town Declaration on Responsible Tourism (Cape Town, 2002), the Kerala Declaration resulting from the Second Conference on Responsible Tourism in Destinations contains recommendations for responsible tourism that are highly relevant to the chapters and critiques presented in this book, and serves as a useful list of actions to take forward. Among a suite of other considerations, the Declaration states (Kerala, 2008):

- Planning control, highways, environmental management, police and a host of other government agencies at the national and local government level need to be encouraged to play their role in managing tourism. All relevant departments in national and local government need to exercise their responsibility for ensuring the formulation and implementation of regulations.
- Tourism has to contribute to socioeconomic development by supporting the conservation of natural and cultural heritage.

- Encourage local government scrutiny of joint ventures, cooperatives and public–private sector partnerships; it may be appropriate for local government to assist communities in maintaining some control over the forms of tourism development in their area.
- Partnerships need to be based on transparency, mutual respect and shared risk taking, ensuring clarity about roles and expectations.
- Through their supply chain tourism businesses can increase their linkages to the local economy and to economically poor producers.
- In considering proposals for community-based tourism development, there needs to be more focus on business planning and administration, consumer orientated product development, quality, cooperation with the commercial sector, communication, sales channels, marketing and the management of the interaction between tourists and local people.
- Care needs to be taken to avoid regulation causing corruption or excluding small businesses and communities.
- Robust and transparent financial management systems are needed to empower the community to ensure that earnings are distributed equitably within the community.

Practitioners have presented evidence from across southern Africa, and systematically addressed whether tourism can be used as a development tool for biodiversity conservation and poverty alleviation. Although the contributors have tended to largely concentrate their efforts on local economic development issues, the implications of responsible tourism for conservation have also been addressed. The majority of the contributors have taken a critical and objective stance in their analyses, and seem to support the actions recommended in the Kerala Declaration. This book has, after all, been compiled in an attempt to disseminate more of the lessons practitioners have learned in southern Africa, as presented by the people working in the field. It is hoped that their ability to communicate their understanding of tourism's impacts will assist governments, development agencies and the private sector in promoting tourism in a more responsible manner, and in the words of the Cape Town Declaration, for them 'to take responsibility for achieving sustainable tourism, and to create better places for people to live in and for people to visit' (Cape Town, 2002).

Notes

1   Friday, 1 July 2005, 1 Botswana Pula = 0.18370 US Dollar

References

Ali, S. H. (ed) (2007) '*Peace Parks: Conservation and Conflict Resolution*', MIT press, Cambridge, MA and London

Ashley, C. and Jones, B. (2001) 'Joint ventures between communities and tourism investors: Experience in Southern Africa', *International Journal of Tourism Research*, vol 3, no 5, 407–423

Ashley, C. and Mitchell, J. (2008) 'Doing the right thing approximately not the wrong thing precisely: Challenges of monitoring impacts of pro-poor interventions in tourism value chains', *ODI Working Paper 291*, Overseas Development Institute, SNV and International Finance Corporation

Blangy, S. (2008) 'Indigenous guidebook on line, Web based survey and Google map results', Carleton University, Canada, available at www.aboriginal-ecotourism.org

Boonzaier, E. (1996a) 'Negotiating the development of tourism in the Richtersveld, South Africa', in Price, M. F. (ed) *People and Tourism in Fragile Environments*, John Wiley and Sons Ltd, New York, 123–137

Boonzaier, E. (1996b) 'Local responses to conservation in the Richtersveld National Park, South Africa', *Biodiversity and Conservation*, vol 5, no 3, 307–314

BSP (Biodiversity Support Program) (1999) 'Study on the development of transboundary natural resource management areas in southern Africa: Highlights and findings', Biodiversity Support Program, World Wide Fund for Nature, Washington DC

Bushell, R. and Eagles, P. (eds) (2007) *Tourism and Protected Areas: Benefits Beyond Boundaries*, CABI, Wallingford and Cambridge, MA

Cape Town (2002) The Cape Town Declaration of Responsible Tourism in Destinations, August 2002

De la Harpe, D., Fearnhead, P., Hughes, G., Davies, R., Spenceley, A., Barnes, J., Cooper, J. and Child, B. (2004) 'Does 'commercialization' of protected areas threaten their conservation goals?' in Child, B. (ed) *Parks in Transition: Biodiversity, Rural Development and the Bottom Line*, Earthscan, London, Sterling VA, pp217

Goodwin, H. and Francis, J. (2003) 'Ethical and responsible tourism: Consumer trends in the UK', *Journal of Vacation Marketing*, vol 9, no 3, 271–284

Gujadhur, T. (2001) 'Joint venture options for communities and safari operators in Botswana', CBNRM Support Programme Occasional Paper No. 6

ITC UNCTAD (2005) 'Conducting an opportunity study on community-based tourism: Guidelines', International Trade Centre /UNCTAD/WTO (INT/W2/11), Geneva

Jones, H. M. (2008) 'Community-based tourism enterprise in Latin America: Triple bottom line outcomes of 27 projects', ElperWood International, May 2008, available at www.eplerwood.com/publications.php

Kerala (2008) Kerala declaration on Responsible Tourism in Destinations, available from www.icrtindia.org/kd.htm on 27 March 2008

Massyn, P. (2008) 'Madikwe community lodges', paper presented at the African Safari Lodges Practitioners Workshop, The Grace Hotel Rosebank, South Africa, 19–21 May 2008, available at www.asl-foundation.org/news.php?id=241&catid=

Mahony, K. and van Zyl, J. (2001) 'Practical strategies for pro-poor tourism. Case studies of Makuleke and Manyeleti tourism initiatives', PPT Working paper No. 2, Overseas Development Agency/Centre for Responsible Tourism/International Institute for Environment and Development, London, April 2001

MINTEL (2001) *Ethical Tourism*. © International Group Limited, October 2001

Mitchell, J. and Faal, J. (2007) 'Holiday package tourism and the poor in the Gambia', *Development Southern Africa*, vol 24, no 3, 445–464

Müller, H. R. and Landes, A. (2000), Tourismus und umweltverhalten. Befragung zum eeiseverhalten', Forschungsinstitut für Freizeit und Tourismus (FIF), Hans Imholz-Stiftung, Switzerland Travel Writers & Tourism Journalists Club Zürich (STW), Bern März 2000.

Poultney, C. and Spenceley, A. (2001) 'Practical strategies for pro-poor tourism, Wilderness Safaris South Africa: Rocktail Bay and Ndumu Lodge', Pro-Poor Tourism Working Paper No. 1, Overseas Development Agency/Centre for Responsible Tourism/International Institute for Environment and Development, London, April 2001

Ramutsindela, M. (2007) *Transfrontier Conservation in Africa: At the Confluence of Capital, Politics and Nature*, CABI, Wallingford and Cambridge, MA

Reid, H. (2001) 'Contractual national parks and the Makuleke community', *Human ecology*, vol 29, no 2, 135–155

Robins, S., and van der Wall, K. (2008) 'Model tribes and iconic conservationists? The Makuleke restitution case in Kruger National Park', *Development and Change*, vol 39, no 1, 53–57

Sandwith, T., Shine, C., Hamilton, L. and Sheppard, D. (2001) 'Transboundary protected areas for peace and co-operation', *Best Practices Protected Area Guidelines Series No. 7*, IUCN and Cardiff University, available at www.peaceparks2007.org/resources.php

Spenceley, A. (2006) 'Tourism in the Great Limpopo Transfrontier Park', *Development Southern Africa*, vol 23, no 5, 649–669

Spenceley, A. (2008a) 'Requirements for sustainable nature-based tourism in transfrontier conservation areas: A southern African Delphi consultation', *Tourism Geographies*, vol 10, no 3, 285–311

Spenceley, A. (2008b) 'Phinda Private Game Reserve, South Africa', Paper presented at the African Safari Lodges Practitioners Workshop, The Grace Hotel Rosebank, South Africa, 19–21 May, available at www.asl-foundation.org/news.php?id=241&catid=

Spenceley, A. (2008c) 'Torra Conservancy, Namibia', Paper presented at the African Safari Lodges Practitioners Workshop, The Grace Hotel Rosebank, South Africa, 19–21 May, available at www.asl-foundation.org/news.php?id=241&catid=

Spenceley, A. (2008d) 'Rocktail Beach Lodge, South Africa', Paper presented at the African Safari Lodges Practitioners Workshop, The Grace Hotel Rosebank, South Africa, 19–21 May, available at www.asl-foundation.org/news.php?id=241&catid=

Spenceley, A. and Rozga, Z. (2007) 'IFC tourism training network: Market research report', Report to the Global Business School Network, International Finance Corporation, Washington DC

Spenceley, A. Dzingirai, P. and Tangawamira, Z. (2008) 'Economic impacts of transfrontier conservation areas: Tourism in the Greater Limpopo transfrontier conservation area', Report to IUCN Southern Africa Sustainable Use Specialist Group and the University of the Witwatersrand, 4 April

Tearfund (2001) 'Guide to tourism: Don't forget your ethics!' 6 August 2001, available at http://tilz.tearfund.org/webdocs/Website/Campaigning/Policy%20and%20research/Poli cy%20-%20Tourism%20putting%20ethics%20into%20practice%20policy% 20report.pdf

Tearfund (2002) 'Worlds apart: A call to responsible global tourism', January, available at www.icrtourism.org/Publications/WorldsApart.pdf

Index

SCAT

'Carl Hiaasen is a supremely entertaining writer whose novels also bear a timely message . . . all the Hiaasen trademarks are there: wit, particularly in the vituperative repartee . . . an abiding belief in the power of the individual to alter things, and an instinct for ingenious plotting that never lets him down.'
Nicholas Tucker, *Independent*

'Scat, by veteran crime heavyweight Carl Hiaasen is a great choice for the eco-aware . . . Hiaasen manages to tackle big themes such as conservation and the Iraq war without being patronising.' *Big Issue Scotland*

'The third punchy, funny, eco-mystery from Hiaasen focuses on the endangered Florida panther and the strange fate of Nick, Marta and Smoke's terrifying biology teacher, released into the wilds of the black vine swamp. The plot is as thick as the vines' *The Bookseller*

'Carl Hiaasen definitely has a knack for adventure. Every story he creates always has some crazy plot that makes you think as well as laugh! . . . Hiaasen poses the problem of destroying the environment for monetary gain and how it affects the ecosystem in a hilarious manner. He also throws in some other great themes to think about: not judging people by their history/the way they look, believing in yourself and never giving up, learning to live with what you've got, and working as a team.

'Wow! This is a brilliant fast paced adventure which even the most reluctant reader will be unable to put down. Equally suitable for boys or girls it is both humorous and thought provoking. With serious issues like the emotional impact of the Iraq war on the families involved and the impact on the environment when man becomes too greedy.' *Waterstones.com*

'fast paced environmental thriller . . . fun, often surprising, with lots of very eccentric teachers and pretty smart kids. You will also learn a lot about biology and panthers along the way. Carl Hiaasen knows his Florida and the Everglades really well and any reader 10 and up will really thrill to this topical adventure.'
Hackwriters.com

'Totally topical, *Scat* is a brilliant, fast-moving eco-aware thriller set in the swamps of Florida . . . Behind the great adventure are serious messages and warnings about the despoliation of a very special area.'
Lovereading4kids.com

'As ever with Hiaasen, rambunctious humour and twisted French-farce plotting make the book a joy to read, and there's the usual undercurrent of scathing indignation against moden civilisation's stupidities.' *Financial Times*

'*Scat* is a funny and furiously fast-moving novel populated by engaging characters and fuelled by a strong sense of moral outrage.' *Guardian*

'this is full of intrigue and plotlines cleverly entwined to give plenty of food for thought . . . an exciting, unputdownable read.' *Primary Times*